MEAN STREETS

AMERICAN CROSSROADS

Edited by Earl Lewis, George Lipsitz, Peggy Pascoe, George Sánchez, and Dana Takagi

MEAN STREETS

Chicago Youths and the Everyday
Struggle for Empowerment in the
Multiracial City, 1908–1969

Andrew J. Diamond

UNIVERSITY OF CALIFORNIA PRESS Berkeley Los Angeles London

University of California Press, one of the most
distinguished university presses in the United States,
enriches lives around the world by advancing
scholarship in the humanities, social sciences, and
natural sciences. Its activities are supported by the
UC Press Foundation and by philanthropic contributions from individuals and institutions. For more
information, visit www.ucpress.edu.

University of California Press
Berkeley and Los Angeles, California

University of California Press, Ltd.
London, England

© 2009 by The Regents of the University of California

Library of Congress Cataloging-in-Publication Data

Diamond, Andrew J.
    Mean streets : Chicago youths and the everyday
struggle for empowerment in the multiracial city,
1908–1969 / Andrew Diamond.
        p.   cm. — (American crossroads ; 27)
    Includes bibliographical references and index.
    ISBN 978-0-520-25723-8 (cloth : alk. paper) —
ISBN 978-0-520-25747-4 (pbk. : alk. paper)
    1. Juvenile delinquency—Illinois—Chicago—
History—20th century.   2. Gangs—Illinois—
Chicago—History—20th century.   3. Immigrants—
Illinois—Chicago—History—20th century.   4. Social
integration—Illinois—Chicago—History—20th
century.   5. Group identity—Illinois—Chicago.
I. Title.

HV9106.C4D53   2009
364.3609773'1109041—dc22   2008041622

Manufactured in the United States of America

18   17   16   15   14   13   12   11   10   09
10   9   8   7   6   5   4   3   2   1

This book is printed on Natures Book, which contains
30% post-consumer waste and meets the minimum
requirements of ANSI/NISO Z39.48–1992 (R 1997)
(*Permanence of Paper*).

Contents

Illustrations

Abbreviations

CAFSNCC	Chicago Area Friends of SNCC
CAP	Chicago Area Project
CCCO	Coordinating Council of Community Organizations
CCHR	Chicago Commission on Human Relations (originally MCHR; name changed to CCHR in 1947)
CCRR	Chicago Commission on Race Relations
CFM	Chicago Freedom Movement
CHA	Chicago Housing Authority
CIO	Congress of Industrial Organizations
CORE	Congress of Racial Equality
CUCA	Coalition for United Community Action
CYC	Chicago Youth Centers
CYDP	Chicago Youth Development Program
GIU	Gang Intelligence Unit
HTRYP	Hard-to-Reach-Youth Project
IJR	Institute for Juvenile Research
MCHR	Mayor's Commission on Human Relations (originally MCRR; name changed to MCHR in 1945)

MCRR   Mayor's Committee on Race Relations

OEO   Office of Economic Opportunity

OSC   Organization for Southwest Chicago

RAM   Revolutionary Action Movement

SCLC   Southern Christian Leadership Conference

SNCC   Student Nonviolent Coordinating Committee

TWO   Temporary Woodlawn Organization

WSO   West Side Organization

Acknowledgments

Mean Streets began many years ago in Ann Arbor, Michigan, moved on to Chicago, and, quite unexpectedly, ended up in Paris, France. I am deeply indebted to many friends and colleagues who provided advice, encouragement, friendship, diversion, and countless other forms of support at every leg of the journey. The project would never have even begun were it not for two people in particular—my brother, David Diamond, who, after my frustrating first semester at Michigan, convinced me to unpack my bags and give graduate school another year; and my advisor, Terrence McDonald, who was kind enough to take on a confused Latin Americanist looking to move his work north. Terry was an excellent mentor throughout my long years of doctoral work, dispensing timely advice and wisdom about the historical profession that helped me to complete a dissertation that looked something like a book manuscript. I was fortunate enough to have other mentors as well during the early years of the project. Earl Lewis and Timothy Gilfoyle both demonstrated great generosity by taking time out of their busy schedules to offer guidance to an aspiring scholar. They read and commented on early chapters, enabling me to get the project moving in the right direction.

Ann Arbor was a great starting point because of the friendship of people like Christopher Schmidt-Nowarra, John McKiernan-Gonzalez,

Greg Shaya, Alexis Stokes, Chris Ogilvie, Steve Soper, Susan Rosenbaum, Niels Hooper, Riyad Koya, and Elizabeth Horodowich. Kathleen Canning and Susan Juster gave me support and encouragement during a difficult period, and a seminar with Robin Kelley sparked my early interest in history from below. Once in Chicago, James Grossman, Dominic Pacyga, and Tim Gilfoyle helped me find my bearings, and Gabriela Arredondo, Eric Goldstein, Ramón Gutiérrez, and David Roediger offered some useful suggestions during those early years. Some lovely friends in Chicago made my life there engaging and unpredictable. Ed Koziboski, Kathy Flynn, Dan Kiss, Lyle Rowen, Roshen Hendrickson, Friese Undine, Jayson Harsin, and Meagan Zimbeck provided ample opportunities for refuge from the archives and the office. Special thanks go to the public defenders Ed and Dan, whose insider perspectives on criminal justice and machine politics in Chicago energized my ideas and renewed my sense of purpose.

As fate would have it, *Mean Streets* would come to fruition far from the Windy City, in the City of Light. As luck would have it, I would find myself surrounded by a community of talented and committed American historians in Paris who helped me to refine my ideas and keep up the energy to finish the job. My work has definitely benefited from numerous seminars, conversations, lunches, aperitifs, and dinners with the likes of Pap Ndiaye, Romain Huret, Jean-Christian Vinel, Paul Schor, Nathalie Caron, Denis Lacorne, Pauline Peretz, Jim Cohen, Catherine Collomp, Isabelle Richet, Catherine Pouzoulet, Donna Kesselman, Yann Philippe, and Justine Faure. Special mention goes to Jonathan Magidoff, a dear friend and fellow traveler, who gave me critical feedback on several parts of the manuscript. I am also grateful for the support, cheer, and encouragement I have received from colleagues and staff at the Université de Lille 3— Charles de Gaulle. Richard Davis, Thomas Dutoit, Philippe Vervaecke, Olivier Esteves, Vanessa Alayrac, Emmanuelle LeTexier, and Mathieu Duplay have been ideal colleagues; and the support staff at the UFR (Unité de Formation et de Recherche) Angellier—Odile Thieffry, Muriel Perrin, Francine Lafrance, and Christine Lesaffre—made my life so much less difficult than it could have been during the book's final stages. It also seems in order to acknowledge some other friends in Paris who kept me well fed, well amused, and thus ready to head to the library in the morning—Jeanne Lazarus, Ninon Vinsonneau, Georges Debrégeas, Judith Roze, Philippe Quintin, Gustavo Guerrero, Laurence Ficht, Heidi Knoerzer, and Pierre Sillard. Finally, a very special thanks to the Michelets and Rollands, who opened their homes to me from the start.

Completing this book in Paris would have been much more difficult had it not been for some timely contributions from colleagues overseas. I am particularly indebted to Matthew Countryman, Victoria Wolcott, Thomas Guglielmo, Dionne Danns, Joseph Lipari, John Hagedorn, and Thomas Sugrue, all of whom shared their work and their ideas with me at critical times, and to Phillip Tawanchaya, who was always willing to carry boxes of books on his frequent trips between Chicago and Paris. Thanks also to George Sanchez, James Barrett, and Thomas Guglielmo for their excellent comments on the manuscript, and to Niels Hooper at the University of California Press for believing in the book from the beginning.

My research for this book depended on the patient assistance of several archivists: Mary Ann Bamberger of Special Collections at the University of Illinois and the late Archie Motley and the rest of the staff at the Chicago History Museum (formerly Chicago Historical Society) deserve special mention. I will never forget the many nights I closed up the Chicago Historical Society with Archie, talking about a range of topics from the pennant race to city politics. I am also indebted to archivist Nancy Webster, who helped me navigate my way through the Red Squad files.

Financial support from a number of institutions was indispensable to this project. The History Department and the Rackham School of Graduate Studies at the University of Michigan offered me generous funding throughout the research stage of this project in the forms of travel, research, and block grants. A Dissertation Award from the Harry Frank Guggenheim Foundation, a Rackham Predoctoral Fellowship, and a King V. Hostick Award from the Illinois State Historical Society enabled me to devote several years to the writing of the book. Finally, the Centre d'Études en Civilisations, Langues et Lettres Étrangères (CECILLE, E. A. 4074) at the Université de Lille 3–Charles de Gaulle helped finance some of the book's production costs.

Finally, I would like to express my deep gratitude to my parents for instilling me with a love of knowledge and an appreciation for the fight for social justice at an early age. They and the rest of my family have offered me their unconditional support throughout the long journey here. Most of all, however, I wish to thank my wife. Caroline, whose contribution to this book and to my life can hardly be conveyed in words, let alone in a few sentences. She has stood by me through thick and thin and has never stopped inspiring me to do things I never imagined possible before she first spoke to me that fateful day in Chicago. I dedicate this book to her as a small token of my appreciation for all she has given to me over the last glorious decade we have shared.

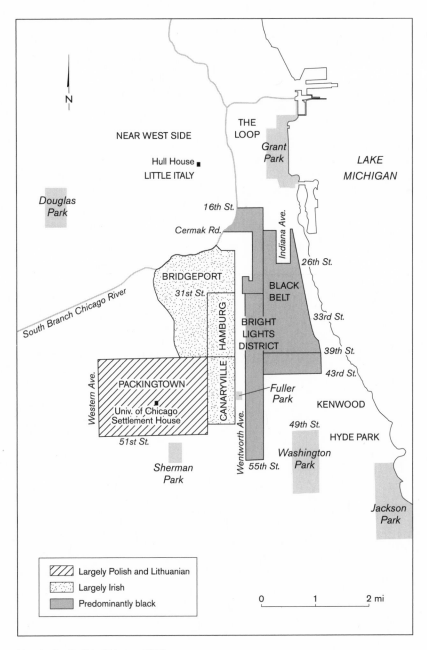

Map 1. South Side Chicago, 1919

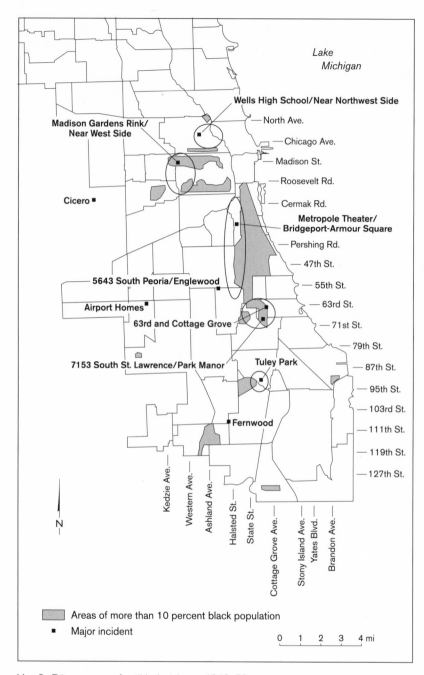

Lake
Michigan

Wells High School/Near Northwest Side

— North Ave.

Madison Gardens Rink/
Near West Side

— Chicago Ave.

— Madison St.

— Roosevelt Rd.

Cicero ■

— Cermak Rd.

Metropole Theater/
Bridgeport-Armour Square

— Pershing Rd.

— 47th St.

5643 South Peoria/Englewood

— 55th St.

Airport Homes■

— 63rd St.

63rd and Cottage Grove

— 71st St.

— 79th St.

7153 South St. Lawrence/Park Manor

Tuley Park

— 87th St.

— 95th St.

— 103rd St.

■Fernwood

— 111th St.

— 119th St.

— 127th St.

Kedzie Ave.—
Western Ave.—
Ashland Ave.—
Halsted St.—
State St.—
Cottage Grove Ave.—
Stony Island Ave.—
Yates Blvd.—
Brandon Ave.—

N

▨ Areas of more than 10 percent black population

■ Major incident

0   1   2   3   4 mi

Map 2. Primary areas of antiblack violence, 1946–52

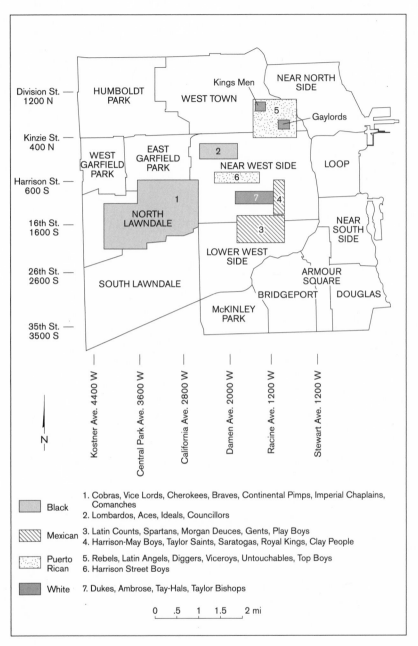

Map 3. West Side gangland, 1960. Source: List of Street Gangs, Detached Workers Program, Young Men's Christian Association, Welfare Council Papers, Box 424, Folder 6, Chicago History Museum.

Introduction

Bringing Youths into the Frame

On Wednesday, November 9, 1949, around 10:30 P.M., Chicago police responded to a call from the South Side Englewood area claiming that an angry mob had gathered in front of a two-flat apartment building at 5643 South Peoria Street and was threatening to burn the place down. Arriving at the scene and questioning several of the sixty people assembled at the front steps of the two-story brick building, police learned that several people of color had been spotted entering the premises, and rumors were circulating through the all-white neighborhood that a real estate transaction was in the works. Turning to the building's owner, Aaron Bindman, who had come outside to find out what was going on, the officers discovered that a party of sixteen men and women, including nine African Americans, had been dining together in the apartment. This meeting, however, had nothing to do with real estate; it was a gathering of members of Local 208 of the Warehouse Distributors Union. This information seemed to mollify the crowd, and after bringing the building owners and some of the mob's self-proclaimed leaders to the station for questioning, the police managed to disperse the remaining protesters.[1]

The next several days witnessed a less orderly state of affairs. On Thursday afternoon a crowd assembled once again in the same area, growing to more than two hundred by eight o'clock. The talk circulating

1

through this group was more aggressive, with shouts of "Burn the house!" "Lynch 'em!" "Get the sheenies!" "Communists!" and "Dirty kikes!" filling the crisp night air. Bindman was a Jew, and this was Visitation Parish, where Monsignor Daniel Byrnes had already been busy mobilizing his largely Irish Catholic congregation to oppose the attempts of blacks to buy property in the area. Despite the presence of twenty police officers, rocks smashed through windows, and the crowd pushed menacingly forward against the police cordon protecting the building. Friday and Saturday saw more of the same. On Friday night police made some twenty arrests, but a great many of those taken in were counterprotesters from the University of Chicago. On Saturday night, however, the command went out to officers on the scene to take a stronger stand against neighborhood instigators in order to quell the four-day-long campaign. By early Sunday morning, twenty-nine locals had been booked for disorderly conduct. Whether due to this clampdown, the arrival of inclement weather, or the realization by rioters of the futility of venting their rage at an empty building, what became known as the Peoria Street riot came to an end on November 13.[2]

Relatively few people outside the Englewood vicinity heard much about the events that transpired there between November 9 and 13. In an effort to avoid violence in the neighborhoods surrounding Chicago's swelling Black Belt—the massive area of solidly black neighborhoods covering a huge swath of the city's West and South Sides—Mayor Martin Kennelly had prevailed on the editors of Chicago's dailies to bury such stories. Yet the existence and meaning of this and similar incidents have more recently attracted the attention of scholars examining various aspects of the histories of race relations and urban politics. Indeed, events like those recorded at 5643 South Peoria Street have generally come to make sense in three interrelated narratives that occupy central places in the project of historicizing the twentieth-century American city.

The first of these emerged out of the pathbreaking work of Arnold Hirsch in the mid-1980s on what he referred to as "the making of the second ghetto" in postwar Chicago. Building on Hirsch's analysis of how grassroots mobilization of the type witnessed at 5643 South Peoria interacted with planning goals, political strategies, and institutional interests to reinforce the segregation of black Chicagoans in the postwar decades, a number of urban historians have contributed new perspectives to the development of a racial order that some have referred to as "American apartheid."[3] The second of these narratives has largely branched out of the first but has focused more specifically on the changing political landscape that accompanied the making of the second ghetto. Challenging long-standing notions that the Democratic Party sustained some semblance of the "New Deal order" that formed in the 1930s until urban race riots and black nationalist ideology fractured it along racial lines in 1968, scholars working on the political implications of the second-ghetto story have taken the actions of whites at South Peoria Street as evidence that the origins of the Great Society backlash date all the way back to the 1940s and are to be found at the urban grass roots—in middling neighborhoods much like Englewood.[4] Finally, a third narrative has emerged alongside these other two, which seeks to link the circumstances of South Peoria Street in 1949 to broader shifts in ethnic and racial consciousness and, more specifically, to the development and meaning of white identity. For many scholars attempting to answer questions such as how ethnics "became white" and why working-class whites so vehemently opposed the racial integration of their neighborhoods, what transpired on South Peoria reveals the centrality of whiteness in the minds of working-class European Americans.[5]

The interpretive and methodological concerns shared by these three historiographical strands are not hard to see. On the broadest level, they each reflect the intellectual shift ushered in by the "new" social movements of the late 1960s and the tendency of modern social theory in the late 1970s to place issues of identity and culture at the center of our understanding of politics and, more generally, of power and agency. More specifically, they reflect the move within this larger shift to place racial and ethnic consciousness at the core of our understanding of identity.[6] From a methodological standpoint, this project of investigating the formation of racial and ethnic identities and examining their role in the public sphere implies incorporating the social with the political; that is, it involves explaining the link between how these identities were inscribed in the texture of neighborhood life or played out in the "practice of everyday life"—in the words of Michel de Certeau—and how they became the bases for political thought and action.[7] In this book I intend to contribute to this line of inquiry by revealing a facet of the interconnected stories of racial consciousness and mobilization that scholars working on these issues have largely overlooked.

Viewing the Peoria Street riot through a different lens, it is possible to observe yet another key phenomenon in operation. What every eyewitness on record with the Chicago Commission on Human Relations (CCHR) found worthy of mention was the overwhelming presence of youths in the crowd. In fact, while scholars who have subsequently examined what transpired in Englewood have emphasized the dominant Irish Catholic profile of the crowd, references to the youthfulness of the actors outnumber those indicating their ethnoreligious character by seven to one.[8] "Older men and women" are spoken of but once in the CCHR's riot report, and then only to say that they were mostly "on the edge of the area." Further confirming these impressions are the arrest data from Saturday night (November 12), when the police stopped taking in victims and counterdemonstrators from outside the neighborhood. Of the twenty-nine locals arrested, all were male and only one did not fall between the ages of seventeen and twenty-five.[9]

As I will demonstrate, this high level of youth participation in collective racial action was more the rule than the exception. From the key involvement of the Irish athletic clubs in the race riot of 1919, to an epidemic of racial violence in 1946 that city officials dubbed "juvenile terrorism," to another wave of racial aggression in 1957 that the editors of Chicago's biggest black newspaper identified once again as "juvenile terrorism," to the marked participation of teenagers in white supremacist demonstrations against civil rights marches on the Southwest Side in the mid-1960s, teens and young adults stood at the vanguard of grassroots mobilizations in white working-class Chicago, playing leading roles in articulating community identities, defending neighborhood boundaries, and, ultimately, making the first and second ghettos.

Following in the footsteps of Arnold Hirsch's fine research on the housing riots that struck metropolitan Chicago from 1946 to 1957, I began this study as an attempt to bring a more nuanced perspective to the structural, cultural, and emotional conditions underlying such intense displays of hate and fear. More specifically, I wanted to reexamine the story of the second ghetto while keeping in mind the insights of scholars such as John Hartigan Jr., who have pointed to the need to more carefully examine the "disparate and unstable interpretations of racial matters that people develop in the course of their daily lives" by paying closer attention to "the local settings in which racial identities are actually articulated, reproduced, and contested."[10] Although Hirsch's analysis was pioneering in its meticulous ground-level approach, its binary conception of Chicago's racial system obscured certain aspects that were far from peripheral to the story of racial and ethnic formation and action in twentieth-century Chicago.[11] How did Chicago's large populations of Puerto Ricans and Mexicans fit into the story? What should we make of the increasing participation of Mexicans in antiblack violence throughout the 1950s? How should we interpret the racial hostility of European Americans toward Mexicans at the very same moment when Mexicans were joining European Americans in apparent struggles to defend their whiteness? How was the formation of Puerto Rican and Mexican enclaves during the 1950s and 1960s related to the making of the second ghetto?

Taking on the burden of seeing racial identities through a finer lens also enables a more detailed view of how such identities gave rise to collective forms of racial action. On examining the body of evidence excavated by Hirsch, I was struck by the number of times eyewitnesses signaled the youthfulness of the actors involved in antiblack demonstrations—by the number of instances that the terms *hoodlums, teenagers, boys, youths, young men, groups of youths,* and *gangs* appeared in their accounts. Then, moving the lens back from the riots to allow the flow of everyday life in neighborhoods resisting racial integration to fit into the frame, I found that youths—and quite often young men in their mid-teens and early twenties—played essential roles in constructing and maintaining cultures of racial hostility at the boundaries of their communities before and after the major outbreaks of group violence that made the papers. Youth subcultures stretching between schools, street corners, and, perhaps most important, public and commercial recreation spaces were central settings within which urban residents constructed, negotiated, defended, and reified racial and ethnic identities between the 1910s and 1960s.[12] If Chicago authorities considered the affair at 5643 South Peoria Street concluded by Sunday morning, it by no means indicates that African Americans were then free to settle in or even walk through this Englewood neighborhood. Why they were not had a great deal to do with the existence in its streets of a predominantly male youth gang subculture predicated on defending the neighborhood against racial invasion.

This was hardly the first time groups of young men had come together for such purposes. Indeed, throughout the early decades of the twentieth century as well, street gangs exerted a formidable presence at the boundaries between different racial and ethnic communities. While the well-established circumstances of the 1919 race riot have left the impression that members of Irish American athletic clubs were the principal practitioners of ruthless methods of maintaining barriers between themselves and African Americans in their midst, a closer look reveals that young men from a range of ethnic groups were quick to follow their example. Yet male youth groups operated not only along the color line but also along interfaces between different European American groups— between, for example, communities of Irish and Poles, Poles and Italians, Swedes and Italians, Jews and Poles. Prior to the 1940s, when the massive migration of southern blacks and the recession of the European-born generation from public life facilitated broad identification with a universal form of white identity, intense competition between European groups for limited resources at work and in their neighborhoods played out very visibly on the terrain of male youth subcultures. It was here, in some sense, that many Chicagoans came to understand their status within Chicago's racial system and where they acted to defend that status or challenge the forces imposing it upon them.[13]

Numerous circumstances explain why youths, and particularly young men, came to occupy this role. To begin with, crossing into other parts of the city to get to and from school, passing hours on street corners, and most important, hanging out in leisure spaces that often lay precariously between the neighborhoods of different communities, youths had the greatest access to racially mixed city spaces.[14] Their presence in interracial spaces, however, was not merely a matter of circumstance. Rather, youths were drawn to such areas as a means of negotiating problems they faced as they came of age, some of which related to uncertainties surrounding group identities and others of which had more to do with feelings associated with the predicaments of class, gender, and sexuality. As we will see, these facets of group identity were often impossible to disentangle out on the streets. Racially charged acts of aggression against racial and ethnic others were captivating homosocial rituals for working-class young men because they offered resolutions to two forms of anxiety—those surrounding the initiation into manhood and those arising from racial instabilities.

The appeal of racial and ethnic violence, however, was not all that accounted for the presence of youths in racially mixed areas of the city. As scholars of popular music and dance have well documented, white youths were invested in black cultural forms throughout most of the twentieth century: from the early jazz years of the 1920s, to the swing craze of the 1930s and early 1940s, to the birth of rock 'n' roll in the mid-1950s, to the emergence of soul and funk in the 1960s and 1970s, and up through the ascendance of rap, hip-hop, and R&B over the past few decades. Yet unlike the post-1960s era, which witnessed the dramatic spatial separation of working-class and middle-class whites from the urban black population, in prior decades cities like Chicago offered a range of venues— schools, parks, beaches, city streets, vice and commercial areas—where the white fascination with black styles and cultural forms could be explored and indulged firsthand.[15]

While historians are well acquainted with the story of the black-and-tans—the racially mixed nightclubs that sprang up in many northern cities during Prohibition—they have largely underappreciated the extent to which white working-class commercial leisure in the urban North continued to be organized around the transgression of racial boundaries between the 1910s and the 1960s. As historian Kevin Mumford has argued, white young men increasingly passed their leisure time in interracial commercial leisure and vice districts—what he refers to as "interzones"—in cities like Chicago and New York during the interwar years.[16] Such districts were alluring, not only because they offered interracial vice experiences, but also because the general atmosphere infused the more legitimate—that is to say, exclusively white—dance hall venues within their environs with an added sense of excitement and danger. For working-class young men residing in neighborhoods along Chicago's color line, these districts continued to constitute regular leisure destinations through the 1950s.

Why such areas would also prove to be fertile ground for incidents of racial aggression will be a question of great interest to us here. Indeed, examining both emotional poles of the interracial encounter—that of attraction and desire and that of repulsion and fear—is necessary for moving toward a richer understanding of race and racism in the twentieth-century American city. Drawing on the insights of W. E. B. DuBois, Frantz Fanon, Michel de Certeau, and Henri Lefebvre, historian Thomas C. Holt has called for studies aimed at uncovering how race came to be embedded within the practices and spaces of everyday life—"how racial selves . . . were made in the social environments of theatrical and street performances."[17] In this study I do precisely that, arguing that youth subcultures were central domains within which performances of racial and ethnic formation were staged, and that male youth gangs and peer groups were principal players in such dramas.

Still other circumstances, however, explain why white youths found themselves propelled into racial and ethnic confrontations—dynamics whose impact opens another window onto the intertwined histories of race, youth, and community politics in postwar urban America. The violent actions perpetrated by white groups elicited reactions by those perceived as being on the other side of the color line, or somewhere along it. Between the 1910s and the 1960s, the predominant groups in Chicago with the most reason to view themselves as racialized, and thus at odds with mainstream conceptions of Americanness and whiteness, were African Americans, Mexicans, and Puerto Ricans. Among these groups, beginning most notably in the 1940s, experiences of grassroots discrimination in spaces of public leisure, work, and school increasingly provoked tactics of resistance and protest, and, once again, these dynamics were most visible on the terrain of youth subcultures. The militant posture struck by young black and Mexican zoot-suiters in the 1940s—the widely recognized actors in the race riots that broke out in several American cities during the Second World War—was born out of the climate of everyday racial hostility created by their young white peers. As we will see, the will to fight back against such aggressions grew progressively stronger among young men and women after this time, giving rise by the late 1950s to fighting-gang subcultures within which blacks, Mexicans, Puerto Ricans, Italians, and various other groupings of European Americans mobilized in increasingly larger numbers to defend their turfs and their senses of honor—two notions that were deeply entangled with their group identities. In this book I show that these fighting-gang subcultures served as conduits into the political sphere for an increasing number of the youths on both sides of the color line—not because of the activities of formal political organizations to radicalize them, as we have previously assumed, but rather because they served to magnify racial injustices in the field of everyday life, as well as to articulate and reify ethnic and racial bonds that constituted powerful bases for grassroots mobilization.[18]

In fulfilling these roles, youth subcultures functioned in ways that transcended their own boundaries and contributed greatly to shaping the histories of the larger communities encompassing them. In its findings on the 1919 race riot, for example, the Chicago Commission on Race Relations argued that the actions of Irish athletic clubs were absolutely critical to the riot's origins. Researchers examining the race riots that ripped through Los Angeles, Detroit, and Harlem in 1943—events that changed the complexion of American race relations—have made similar observations regarding the involvement of young Chicano and black zoot-suiters, white youth gangs, and mobs of young servicemen.[19] Furthermore, without the dogged participation of youth gangs in creating and sustaining cultures of daily racial hostility in Chicago from the 1940s through the 1960s, the making of the second ghetto would have been a somewhat different story. On the other side of the color line, moreover, youths played leading roles in struggles against racial aggression on the streets and in public leisure spaces beginning in the 1940s, and in so doing infused a sense of militancy and an appreciation of the value of direct action into African American and Puerto Rican communities.[20] Youths of color and the street gangs they joined were vital participants in the wave of civil rights activism that swept through Chicago in the 1960s, joining massive school boycotts in 1963 and 1964, filling the militant ranks of local direct-action organizations like ACT and the Student Nonviolent Coordinating Committee, marching with Martin Luther King into vicious ambushes on the lily-white Southwest Side, challenging police harassment and taking to the streets in violent rebellion on numerous occasions, and eventually building a range of student organizations whose struggle for control of black high schools had come to define Black Power politics in Chicago by 1968. Historians such as Matthew Countryman and Robert Self have recently drawn attention to misperceptions that have distorted our vision of the rise of Black Power, arguing that rather than "an outside ideological influence" that worked to divide and derail the more effective nonviolent civil rights movement, as the story goes, Black Power consciousness and the tactics that came with it grew out of years of failed integrationist efforts by local activists in cities such as Philadelphia and Oakland.[21] This study contributes another layer to this perspective by examining the micropolitics and emotional preconditions of Black Power's emergence where such ideologies took hold most powerfully—on the terrain of black youth subcultures. This will involve exploring not only the frustrations of young activists and the indignities faced by black students at the hands of white teachers and administrators, but also the brutal campaign of harassment waged by the city's police department against black youths out on the streets. All these circumstances worked together to push black Chicagoans, and particularly the younger generation of them, away from integrationist goals and toward interrelated ideals of racial solidarity and empowerment.

Hence, unlike much of the extant literature on youth subcultures and street gangs, this study illuminates certain facets of the complex and intimate relationship between these structures and the communities surrounding them in working-class Chicago—both their own communities and those of neighboring groups.[22] In particular, I view how events transpiring within youth subcultures played critical roles in articulating group identities and in facilitating the collective will to defend those identities. The capacity of youth subcultures to accomplish such ends was not merely associated with their influence on the consciousness and behavior of the young men and women who inhabited them; it also hinged on their ability to invoke responses in the larger communities surrounding them. Youths and the groups they formed generally managed this in two ways. First, their conspicuous presence in the spaces of daily neighborhood life, and their propensity to defend those spaces from what they perceived as outsiders, provided youth gangs with an uncanny ability to make city blocks into what geographers have referred to as "spaces of representation."[23] While most historians now take for granted the idea that racial and ethnic identities are the products of collective "invention" or "imagination," our notion of how such processes have unfolded on the local level remains schematic at best.[24]

The communal actions against people of color witnessed in Chicago neighborhoods in the 1940s and 1950s depended on the development of communal sensibilities among people of relatively disparate backgrounds and values. In the context of neighborhood life, this occurred less through print media forms than through street performances often staged by youth gangs and peer groups. This was not merely true of the white ethnic communities that waged protracted campaigns against people of color. Even more striking in this sense were the cases of antagonistic relationships that developed between neighboring African Americans, Puerto Ricans, and Mexicans during this same period. For example, in order to fully understand how and why working-class Mexicans and Puerto Ricans in Chicago—groups with obvious religious, linguistic, and cultural affinities—came to see themselves as antagonists in the postwar decades, we must explore how Mexican and Puerto Rican youths differentiated themselves on the streets and enforced this separation through gang violence. Informed by the work of Henri Lefebvre on the dialectic relationship between identity and urban space—a process he refers to as "the production of space"—I view such actions, along with those of their white ethnic peers, as means by which youths contributed powerfully to the construction of communities in working-class Chicago. Throughout the twentieth century, communities were not only "imagined" but also performed in working-class Chicago.[25]

The second way youths played decisive roles in the politics of identity on both sides of the color line involved their ability to both crystallize and organize episodes of grassroots mobilization. This tendency was closely linked to the propensity of youth subcultures to expose sources of power and injustice. As social movement theorist Alberto Melucci has argued, the location of youth culture at the juncture between school and the labor market imbues it with the special capacity to "reflect the tension between the enhancement of life chances and diffuse control, between possibilities for individuation and external definitions of identity."[26] In other words, communities tended to measure their social status and political potential in terms of the opportunities available to their children. This tendency explains why, for example, problems associated with youth leisure and delinquency were so central to discourses about Americanization for immigrants in the interwar period, and why schools would provide focal points for grassroots civil rights mobilization in Chicago's African American neighborhoods from the 1940s through the 1960s. The overdetermined investment of communities in the future of their young has indeed been a somewhat overlooked vector of urban political culture, but even less understood has been the agency of youths in drawing attention to their condition. Even the scholars working on youth subcultures who have noted their remarkable presence in popular discourses about a range of urban problems—their key role in producing "moral panics" that symbolize deeper anxieties surrounding social transformations—have tended to view this process in a top-down manner, failing to see how youths themselves have contributed to the production of such discourses.[27] If the media, for example, tended to sensationalize the Zoot Suit Riots and the wartime delinquency problem in general, the emergence of such discourses nonetheless reflected actual changes on the terrain of youth subcultures: namely, the increasing tendency of white servicemen and youth gangs to cross into interracial leisure areas, and the complementary development of a will among Mexican and African American youths to defend the young women of their communities against such encroachments. Moreover, between 1945 and 1947, just before the high time of the so-called communal housing riots, schools and youth recreation areas constituted key sites for white campaigns against black integration. Far from following directives issued by older community leaders, students in this moment took the initiative in mobilizing collectively to wage school strikes and mob actions against black youths attempting to attend schools and use recreational facilities in formerly all-white neighborhoods. On the other side of the color line, African American youths acted on their own and in ways seldom evidenced in public records to oppose these campaigns by refusing to submit to such forms of intimidation—even at the risk of considerable injury.

This dialectic on the terrain of youth subcultures served to raise awareness of perceived injustices in both black and white communities. For whites, incidents provoked by youths highlighted the perception that they were somewhat powerless to prevent changes they believed would dramatically affect their property values, social status, and general well-being; for blacks, they illuminated the broken promises of American democracy. While a range of factors shaped these sensibilities of injustice, from discourses generated in the mass media to the more local efforts of homeowners' associations, civil rights groups, and other political organizations, the more palpable actions of youth groups served to provide the everyday emotional components—particularly the sense of anger—that students of social movements have argued are necessary for stimulating and sustaining collective mobilization. Youth gangs thus played vital roles in constructing what sociologist William Gamson has referred to as "injustice frames," local maps of meaning that "personalize" injustices and blame others for their existence. Such processes, according to Gamson, are necessary in moving people to act, especially when doing so puts individuals at considerable personal risk.[28] Yet this was not the only way in which youths proved vital to grassroots mobilization in the era of civil rights and white backlash. In addition to sparking broader forms of collective action, youths were able to sustain cultures of local activism by providing what social movement theorists call "networks" and "mobilizing structures."[29] Indeed, prior to the advent of the Chicago Freedom Movement, the coalition of local and national civil rights groups that formed in Chicago in 1964, one would have been hard pressed to find more effective networks for the transmission of information, ideas, and emotions than the informal youth subcultural ones that bridged schools and neighborhood leisure venues, and more potent mobilizing structures than the large fighting gangs of the late 1950s and 1960s, which often possessed the loyalty of hundreds of youths and the potential to mobilize hundreds more with their claim to defending community honor.

While in much of this study I seek to illustrate this involvement of youths in the microdynamics of racial formation and collective action, I am also concerned with the question of why youths, and young men in particular, were so suited to performing such roles. What was it about youth as a life stage that made those within it so prone to such forms of behavior? In examining these questions, it is necessary to keep in mind that, not unlike like race, ethnicity, and masculinity, youth is always a socially constructed and historically contingent social identity. Youths by definition occupy a condition somewhere between the life stages of childhood and adulthood, but how this condition is defined and understood in any particular social setting at any moment depends on the interplay between larger structural conditions, social policies, and ideologies on the one hand and local practices of everyday life that take shape within the contexts of families, peer groups, and state institutions on the other.[30] While age generally holds some relevance in the definition of youth, more important are the markers that lie at the threshold of adulthood—marriage, a family, a home, a stable job, a car—the absence of which can relegate an individual to the condition of youth well past an age that is normally considered to be that of an adult. In the working-class neighborhoods of interwar and postwar Chicago, those people generally understood to be "youths" or "young adults" normally fell between the ages of sixteen and twenty-five, although it was not uncommon for social workers to place individuals as old as thirty in this category.[31]

However, if youth was a socially constructed and continuously shifting category, belonging to this category nonetheless carried with it some very real implications. In addition to their location at the interfaces between different racial and ethnic communities, youths in working-class Chicago occupied very different positions vis-à-vis the state, the labor market, and mass culture. Whether as enrolled students or as dropouts idling on the streets, they had much more regular contact with state power, which passed through the figures of teachers, principals, truant officers, beat cops, juvenile officers, probation officers, social workers, and judges. That incidents of police brutality against youths out on the streets would serve as catalysts for race riots in Chicago and several other cities in the mid-1960s speaks to the explosive potential this proximity to the state held. As job-seekers and laborers, moreover, youths lacking experience and skills were often the first to be laid off and the last hired. Hence, youth unemployment rates throughout much of the period under consideration here often substantially exceeded general unemployment rates. Finally, mass marketing techniques geared toward market segmentation, along with the propensity of youths to use commercial culture for social experimentation and the fashioning of identities, meant that youths would also have a more intense and intimate relationship with mass culture.

In this study I demonstrate that that those touched most deeply by all of these factors were youths between the ages of sixteen and twenty-five. These were the individuals who were particularly prone to occupying the precarious condition between school and work, and therefore between childhood and adulthood. Most of all for young men, whose sense of masculinity depended a great deal on achieving the sense of autonomy and potency associated with establishing a home, holding a regular job, starting a family, and possessing certain valued consumer items, this intermediary condition could be radicalizing in ways that often played out at the boundaries between communities. While juveniles were frequent participants in rituals of racial and ethnic hostility, they were largely emulating the actions of those in their neighborhoods they most admired—young men in their late teens and early twenties. These were the most active members of the crowds, mobs, gangs, and peer groups that mobilized to defend their neighborhoods, their rights, their identities, and their honor in working-class Chicago between the 1910s and the 1960s. Understanding the circumstances of their daily lives and how those circumstances translated into the activities they engaged in also lies at the heart of my analysis.

Chicago from 1908 to 1969 presents a case study that lends well to comparisons with other American metropolitan areas. As did many other northern industrial cities, it received a massive influx of immigrants from eastern and southern Europe and a substantial migration of southern blacks between the 1890s and the 1910s that transformed its social geography and its political culture. While historians have dealt extensively with how the foreign-born and their second-generation children negotiated issues associated with their racialization and Americanization in the interwar urban context, few have focused on the role of youth subcultures as forums within which such processes transpired. Exploring how young working-class ethnics in interwar Chicago learned the meanings of whiteness, blackness, and Americanness in the context of youth subcultures and collectively articulated their own identities according to the lessons they learned will be the burden of chapters 1 and 2.

As it did in many other northern industrial centers, the mobilization for World War II introduced dramatic changes to Chicago's demographic landscape, including, most notably, the rapid growth and ghettoization of its African American population. As mentioned above, many historians have viewed such changes as facilitating corresponding shifts in the American urban racial order—the emergence of a more binary racial system, in which European Americans were unquestionably white, African Americans certainly not, and Latin Americans and Asian Americans somewhere in between.[32] With its existing patchwork of European American and Latin American neighborhoods bordering the Black Belt, which expanded ceaselessly into the 1960s, Chicago constitutes a useful model for understanding this epic "second ghetto" moment in American urban history. Chapters 3 and 4 examine how youth gangs and youth subcultures fit in this story between the 1940s and the mid-1950s, illuminating the key role played by youths in processes of racial identity formation and collective mobilization on both sides of the color line, and exploring the structural, cultural, and emotional conditions that shaped their actions. Focusing on youth subcultures as critical fields of racial and ethnic conflict during this period allows me to bring together two narratives that until now have been largely treated apart: white violence and black response.[33]

Finally, chapters 5 and 6 build on the central elements of earlier chapters by returning to an examination of the role played by youth subcultures both in the articulation of group identities and in the organization of collective actions in defense of those identities from the late 1950s through the late 1960s. However, although such dynamics distinctly resembled those operating in previous decades, the social context had changed dramatically by this time. Distinguishing Chicago from many other northern industrial cities in this era were its rapidly expanding Mexican and Puerto Rican populations, groups whose presence was made all the more impressive by the development of new, vibrant colonies ("spaces of representation") at the edges of the Black Belt on Chicago's West Side— the Mexican Pilsen neighborhood and the Puerto Rican Humboldt Park barrio. The analysis in chapter 5 illuminates the part played by youth gang subcultures in such processes of identity and community formation. In neighborhoods cohabited by these groups, Puerto Rican and Mexican youths were quick to form street gangs whose everyday activities exhibited strong impulses for separation from each other, and especially from neighboring blacks.[34] Along with rising youth unemployment and school dropout rates, the flight of jobs from the city, and urban renewal programs that uprooted entire neighborhoods, the prevalence of such practices contributed to the creation of the more aggressive fighting-gang subcultures that took shape in the late 1950s and early 1960s on Chicago's heterogeneous West Side, where European Americans, Mexican Americans, Puerto Ricans, and African Americans lived in close proximity.

The book will conclude in chapter 6 with a consideration of how these fighting-gang subcultures had a profound but somewhat paradoxical impact on the political culture of working-class Chicago. In one sense, Chicago's racially and ethnically defined fighting gangs mobilized a great many youths to defend their communities, and in the process managed to raise awareness about injustices associated with their position in the city's racial order and political machine system. In black neighborhoods, in particular, the spirit of racial solidarity and direct action championed by local gangs spread to youths throughout the community, gang-affiliated or not, creating a general atmosphere of racial militancy that yielded some impressive demonstrations against the forces of racial discrimination. If civil rights leaders from a range of direct-action organizations sought to channel the raw emotional energy emanating from the youth subcultural milieu to sustain pressure on city authorities in the early and mid-1960s, youths of color had begun taking matters into their own hands by the summer of 1966, at first rising up in violent rebellions against police brutality and then beginning to organize in more structured political ways for the purpose of empowering themselves and their communities. Some of Chicago's most fearsome black gangs were at the vanguard of these transformations, taking advantage of opportunities handed them by the federal government and private foundations to embark on ambitious community development projects that sought to challenge a political machine that had for years refused to address the dramatic racial inequalities in the city's school system and labor market. By 1968 the sensibilities behind such campaigns had spread through the black South and West Sides, spurring the development of powerful Black Power and Latino student movements capable of bringing the school board to the negotiating table. Tragically, however, the same dynamics were also in operation on the other side of the color line, a situation that both balkanized the communities that had the most to gain in challenging the status quo and energized those that had the most to gain in preserving it.

1

The Generation of 1919

So far as I can learn the black people have since history began despised the white people and have always fought them. . . . It wouldn't take much to start another riot, and most of the white people of this district are resolved to make a clean-up this time. . . . If a Negro should say one word back to me or should say a word to a white woman in the park, there is a crowd of young men of the district, mostly ex-service men, who would procure arms and fight shoulder to shoulder with me if trouble should come from the incident.

Chicago police officer Dan Callahan (1920)

If I ventured to state my opinion in regard to the matter, I should say that these gangs have exercised considerably greater influence in forming the character of the boys who compose them than has the church, the school, or any other communal agency outside of the families and the homes in which the members of the gangs are reared.

Robert E. Park (1925)

"THE YOUNG, IDLE, VICIOUS"

The Chicago race riot of 1919 thrust the athletic clubs of Chicago's stockyards district into a nefarious spotlight. "But for them," the twelve-member commission assembled to study the riot concluded, "it is doubtful if the riot would have gone beyond the first clash." After stating that up front, however, the Chicago Commission on Race Relations (CCRR) then approached the riot and the overall problem of race relations in Chicago by exhaustively examining the debilitating conditions of black life and only superficially treating the motivations behind white aggression on the streets. While somewhat counterintuitive from a sociological perspective, since working-class whites had clearly instigated the whole affair, this approach was nonetheless understandable from a political and rhetorical standpoint. Finally given an official platform to pronounce the effects of institutional racism in the areas of education, work, and housing, the civic leaders on the commission, six black Chicagoans among them, were not about to dwell on the origins of white working-class discontent around the stockyards. Implicit in *The Negro in Chicago*, the product of their efforts, is the view that the amelioration of race relations hinged on uplifting the black community as a whole. The commission, therefore, was less concerned with the specific causes of the riot and largely dispensed with such considerations, including its conclusion about the key role of gangs, in an initial chapter that summarized the background and major incidents of the riot. In view of this agenda, the CCRR would have been loath to give the impression that the athletic clubs represented the major cause of the riot. Nevertheless, in its recapitulation of the riot itself and its analysis of racial contacts in the years preceding it—those parts that dealt directly with acts of interracial violence rather than their surrounding context—the CCRR presented a persuasive body of evidence for the central role of youth gangs in a culture of racial violence that for decades had been shaping street-level relations between communities of African Americans and white ethnics in the neighborhoods around the Black Belt. "There had been friction for years," the CCRR stated, "especially along the western boundary of the area in which the Negroes mainly live, and attacks upon Negroes by gangs of young toughs had been particularly frequent in the spring just preceding the riot."[1]

Such racial violence occurred most commonly along the edges of the city's South Side Black Belt, in neighborhoods and parks where blacks and whites commonly encountered one another. The struggle to defend such borderland spaces greatly intensified with the vast increase in the black population and the virtual cessation of new housing construction during the war. Between 1916 and 1919, a half million southern African Americans migrated to northern industrial cities to take advantage of the higher wages created by the wartime production boom. During these years, the black population of Chicago doubled, causing the increasingly overcrowded South Side Black Belt—home to nearly 80 percent of Chicago's existing black population—to expand to the west, east, and south. Most of this growth, however, occurred in 1916 and 1917, before white residents had managed to erect walls of opposition along the Black

Belt's eastern and western borders, forcing its subsequent growth to proceed within the confines of a narrow corridor extending southward. The battle to hold the color line, particularly in the more respectable "native" middle-class neighborhoods like Hyde Park and Kenwood, often involved legal means, such as newspaper publicity, rallies, boycotts, and restrictive covenants—contractual agreements among property owners that forbade the sale or lease of property to "colored persons." When such methods were not enough, bombings and physical attacks were the next recourse. And nobody was more eager to engage in such risky forms of guerrilla warfare than the teenagers and young men who composed the numerous street-corner gangs and social-athletic clubs around the stockyards district. If the more affluent lakefront home owners along the Black Belt's western edge preferred tactics that would allow them to keep their hands clean, the self-styled street toughs patrolling the eastern edge of the Black Belt looked forward to an opportunity to bloody their knuckles. Wentworth Avenue was their line in the sand. Chicagoans commonly referred to it as the "dead line."

Between July 1, 1917, and July 27, 1919—the first day of the riot—gangs of whites in neighborhoods bordering the Black Belt bombed twenty-four black homes and stoned or otherwise vandalized countless others.[2] In early June 1919, the notorious athletic club called the Ragen's Colts, which boasted of possessing two thousand members ready for action, went on a rampage on 54th Street between the Western Indiana and Pennsylvania Railroad tracks, breaking the windows of black homes and knocking out the only streetlight on the corner.[3] That the athletic clubs were seasoned practitioners of such acts quickly became apparent by the third day of the riot, when the Colts descended on the 5000 block of Shields Avenue, where an enclave of nine black families had resided for years on the "wrong" side of Wentworth Avenue, hidden somewhat by the Pennsylvania Railroad embankment. The word on the street was that the Colts wanted to show the Shielders—another Irish gang known for its ability to keep blacks on their side of the color line—how to "run all the niggers out."[4] They championed this cause by shooting into the black homes, bombarding them with rocks, and finally setting them ablaze. Not to be outdone, the Shielders then marched down to Wentworth and Wells Street, one block to the west, smashing windows, breaking down doors, and ransacking the homes of blacks on 47th and 48th Streets.[5]

Such accounts indicate that the harassment of African Americans had become a competitive sport among athletic clubs, and nowhere was this sport engaged in more frequently and more enthusiastically than in the parks, beaches, and playgrounds around the edges of the Black Belt. In the months prior to the riot, groups of young men carried out repeated attacks against blacks in Washington Park. In the middle of June, the level of violence began to escalate when a fight by the boathouse in Washington Park resulted in twenty arrests. This particular conflict arose in the aftermath of an incident in which a black parent struck the white principal at the nearby Dewey School for failing to protect children of color against the assaults of "white boys" who had taken to stoning them as they left school.[6] Eight days later, a squadron of two hundred police officers responded to reports of the beating of blacks by "a small army of white men." In one instance, a white mob, pouring out of a nearby tavern, killed a man in an orgy of violence, shooting, stabbing, and, in a gesture that poignantly bespoke the male sporting culture within which this violence erupted, whacking him on the head with billiard cues.[7] The *Chicago Defender* had no doubts as to the perpetrators of these acts, proclaiming on the front page of its next edition: "Ragans' [*sic*] Colts Start Riot, Gang of Hoodlums Riddle Man's Body with Bullets." Further confirming the accusation, the story included an interview with a local white man who claimed that many of the attackers had recently been to Boys' Court (which handled the cases of youths between the ages of seventeen and twenty-one at that time) on similar charges, but because they were the sons and relatives of police officers at the stockyards station, the judge merely handed down warnings. Both blacks and whites in the district knew all too well that these repeat offenders were the young men of the athletic clubs.[8]

While the tacit or more active complicity of local politicians, police officers, judges, and even school principals in such situations indicates the systemic nature of antiblack aggression in these neighborhoods, these incidents also demonstrate the dynamic role played by athletic clubs and other youth groups in structuring the everyday milieu of racial hostility. As the attacks around the Dewey School reveal, if the athletic clubs spearheaded much of the violence that filled the streets at this time, many other more loosely defined groups of younger boys joined them eagerly in their cause. In fact, the connection to the coffers of a local politician, who usually provided a clubhouse and funding for various social activities, was at times all that separated the typical athletic club from a street gang. After years of field research on Chicago street gangs in this period, the sociologist Frederic Thrasher concluded: "There can be little doubt that most of the 302 so-called athletic clubs listed in this study have first developed as gangs, many of them still retaining their gang characteristics."[9]

Thrasher's colleague John Landesco, also a sociologist, made a similar observation in his study of organized crime in the 1920s, arguing that the processes that brought young men into the services of politicians began "with the child at play in the street."[10] Nowhere else in the city did such views seem more valid than in the South Side Irish neighborhood areas of Bridgeport and New City, just east and northeast of the stockyards, where the young toughs of the athletic clubs and their legions of wannabes filled the streets, saloons, and smoke-filled billiard halls.

When the call to arms came in the sweltering heat of July 27, the young habitués of this milieu responded in a manner so rapid and so concerted as to raise the question of premeditation. While the CCRR, for its part, was largely silent about such possibilities, the author of the only existing monograph on the race riot of 1919 has argued that "these gangs, composed of white teenagers and young men in their twenties, many of the roughest of whom were of Irish descent . . . had been anticipating, even eagerly awaiting, a race riot."[11] This view is based on the development of some very obvious motives for such an onslaught earlier that spring. While keeping blacks on the other side of the color line was an objective generally shared by white residents in borderland neighborhoods, the wild mayoral election of April 1 had added another dimension to the story. After a campaign filled with rancor and race-baiting, the Republican and reputed anti-Catholic candidate William Hale Thompson managed to defeat his Democratic opponent by a slim margin of victory that, according to most press accounts, was made possible only by Thompson's overwhelming support in the black Second Ward. As the Democratic Party rag, the *Chicago Daily Journal.* so bluntly put it in bold front page headlines, "NEGROES ELECT BIG BILL."[12]

However abhorrent "Big Bill" Thompson's anti-Catholic and pro-black sentiments were to the Bridgeport area Irish, his challenge to the patronage resources of Democratic cadres throughout the city could not be tolerated without a fight. And many of these political fixers had the muscle and resources behind them to start one. The numerous Irish athletic clubs that possessed the status and luxury of a warm clubhouse within which to pass the frigid winter nights did so largely at the expense of Democratic political sponsors—aldermen, committeemen, and other municipal officials—who expected something in return. Frank Ragen, for example, was a Democratic Cook County commissioner, and he attached certain strings to the rent he paid each month on the Colts' clubhouse. Such considerations help to explain why the Irish athletic clubs were so ready and willing to perpetrate acts of racial aggression when the time came. The Colts represented perhaps the most notorious organization at the time, and as such they drew the most press coverage, but the testimony of eyewitnesses before the coroner's jury implicated an array of other well-established clubs as combatants and agitators in the 1919 riot: the Lorraine Club, the Our Flag Club, the Sparklers' Club, and the Aylward Club. Several others—the Pine Club, the Hamburgers, the Lotus Club, the Emeralds, the White Club, and the Mayflower—also appeared prominently in the body of riot testimony, prompting police to shut them down for months after the riot.[13]

Overall, the body of eyewitness accounts collected by the CCRR confirmed that the typical members of these organizations—Irish-Catholic, American-born men in their late teens and early twenties—constituted the core of the many mobs that assembled again and again to direct their collective fury against black pedestrians and property. Reviewing such testimony, along with arrest reports from the riot, the CCRR described the mob profile in unequivocally age-specific terms in a passage that is worth quoting at length for the way it reveals the clear predominance of "boys" and young men in the gamut of terrorist actions that characterized the riot:

> Witnesses before the coroner's juries testified to the youth of the participants in mobs. Many of the active assailants of street cars were boys. In the case of the Negro Hardy who was killed on the street car, it was said that the murderers were not over twenty years, and many were nearer sixteen. In the raids on the Ogden Park district the participants were between the ages of fifteen and twenty. The raid just west of Wentworth Avenue, where a number of houses were much damaged, was perpetrated by boys of these ages. The attacking mob on Forty-Third Street near Forrestville Avenue, was led by boys of eighteen to twenty-one. The only two hoodlums caught participating in the outrages in the "Loop," the downtown business district, were seventeen and about twenty-one. Most of those arrested on suspicion in the arson cases were taken before the boys' court.[14]

Ultimately, then, while the coroner's jury registered its skepticism about the view that "race hatred and tendency to race rioting had its birth and was fostered in the numerous social and athletic clubs made up of young men and scattered throughout the city," it settled on a position that contained similar implications. "Hoodlums," the jury concluded, "are the nucleus of a mob—the young, idle, vicious, and in many instances degenerate and criminal, impatient of restraint of law, gather together, and when fortified by sufficient numbers, start out on a mission of disorder, law-breaking, destruction, and murder."[15]

It was not until thirteen days after the initial outbreak of rioting on July 27 that the Illinois state militia finally evacuated the riot-torn streets of Chicago. By that time, the epidemic of aggression had passed through at least two distinct phases. The first lasted from Sunday afternoon until Wednesday evening and witnessed the most savage acts of mob brutality. During these days, mobs of whites chased down African Americans to indiscriminately beat and stone them in front of the transfixed gaze of large crowds of onlookers. On the first two days alone, clashes between blacks and whites caused twenty-nine deaths and 368 injuries. Such frenzied activity strongly suggests that the final tolls of deaths, casualties, and property damage would likely have been much higher had a spell of rain and lower temperatures on Wednesday night and Thursday not cooled down the heated battles raging in the streets. From then on, white-on-black violence was much more sporadic and coordinated, with the athletic clubs and their coteries of hangers-on quite visibly engineering most of the raids into black neighborhoods. The agents behind this second phase of rioting fell into the two categories laid out by Charles Tilly to describe the kinds of actors that often make the deployment of collective violence possible: "political entrepreneurs"—that is to say, those who "promote violence . . . by activating boundaries, stories, and relations that have already accumulated histories of violence"—and "violent specialists . . . who control means of inflicting damage on persons and objects."[16] Regardless of the veracity of rumors that whites with blacked-up faces had set fire to a Lithuanian tenement building in an attempt to ignite racial hatred among immigrants who had apparently remained mostly on the sidelines of the conflict, it was clear that the hit-and-run raids in the final days of the riot served somewhat rational ends—whether the preservation of the neighborhood from black invasion or the growth of anti-Republican opposition.[17]

Yet youth gangs and athletic clubs also became "violent specialists" in the 1910s for a range of reasons that had little to do with ward politics, and their investment in the race riot went far beyond their instrumental actions in the riot's final days. In fact, if youth groups seemed to be acting on command by the end of the riot, they also played a leading role in the far more emotional and chaotic first stage of rioting, before anyone had much of a chance to take stock of the possibilities the situation presented. The intensity of the bloodshed that characterized these first four days of the riot cannot be satisfactorily explained away by deferring to theories of mob behavior or to accounts casting the perpetrators of this terror as paramilitary mercenaries manipulated by political

Figure 1. A mob of white youths chases down an African American man during the 1919 race riot. Photo by Jun Fujita, courtesy of the Chicago History Museum, ICHi-31915.

bosses. What is missing from such accounts is revealed, if only impressionistically, by some of the few riot commission photographs documenting the more spontaneous, impassioned forms of racial brutality witnessed in the first few days of rioting. In particular, a series of horrifying action shots capturing a group of youths frantically hunting down and stoning to death at point-blank range a helpless black man points to how much is still not understood about what was occurring on the South Side of Chicago in the summer of 1919.

Historians attempting to decipher the various meanings of such fervent demonstrations of white racial hatred have largely taken approaches that prevented them from adequately contextualizing or conceptualizing the structures of feeling behind these acts. The first line of scholars trying to make sense of the riot located the sources of white racism that ultimately produced it in struggles over municipal politics, labor organizing, and neighborhood boundaries, all of which developed very quickly out of the massive movement of blacks into the city during the war.[18] If these studies have served to dispel the idea that the events of the summer of 1919 were ineluctable by illuminating how Democratic politicians,

Figure 2. Two members of the mob stoning the man to death. Photo by Jun Fujita, courtesy of the Chicago History Museum, ICHi-22430.

antiunion employers, and home-owners' associations fomented racial animosities to advance their own interests, they have left largely unexplored how such animosities could metastasize into a generalized sense of "race war"—an idea that was gaining increasing currency on both sides of the color line in the years leading up the riot. Indeed, generally when historians of this period have dealt with the idea of race war at all, they have done so mostly by examining the ways in which such notions emerged within black communities—in the militant New Negro sensibilities developing among the growing numbers of returning war veterans and young, unmarried male migrants who filled black ghetto neighborhoods across the urban North around 1919.[19] The fact that somewhat similar processes also occurred on the other side of Chicago's color line, within a semiautonomous subculture largely composed of Irish American young men living around the stockyards, has been implicitly acknowledged but hardly taken seriously. Accounting for the eagerness of the Colts to engage in the riots, for example, Landesco argued, "Patriotism for the United States [was] a potent sentiment among the Ragens," explaining further that such feelings stemmed from some five hundred of the gang's members having served in the armed forces during the war.[20]

More recently, historians interested in understanding the structure, power, and meaning of whiteness for a range of different ethnic groups have zeroed in on the 1919 race riot as a test case for their interpretations, the assumption being that a group's degree of faith in its whiteness must have some correspondence to its propensity to riot against blacks. Agreeing, as virtually all observers of the riot have, that the predominantly Irish athletic clubs around the stockyards engaged in a disproportionate share of the rioting, historians pursuing this line of analysis have taken the relative abstention of southern and eastern European groups—Italians, Poles, Lithuanians, Slavs, and Jews—as evidence of their perceptions regarding their own whiteness.[21] In addition to reducing agency to a mere reflex of racial self-awareness, such perspectives are again based on the rather dubious assumption that the activity of gratuitously attacking an unknown person, and thereby risking serious injury or legal repercussions, was something from which it was difficult to abstain. Based on such reasoning, it is logical to conclude that the mostly second- and third-generation Irish youths who were so active in the riot were desperately seeking to reinforce their sense of whiteness—an idea that squarely contradicts recent studies demonstrating that recent European immigrant groups surrounding the Irish in this moment viewed them as "Americanizers" and referred to them as "whites" or "Americans" in contradistinction to themselves.[22] In fact, beyond their eager participation in a culture of racial violence at the boundaries of their neighborhoods, there is little evidence to suggest that the American-born sons of Irish packinghouse workers doubted their whiteness any more than they did their Americanness or their Irishness. Yet if their whiteness per se was not at stake, those who took to the streets around the stockyards and elsewhere in the city were nonetheless articulating a response to profound insecurities that, as the events of the summer of 1919 so strikingly bore out, translated into racial feelings. That most of those who rioted were young, male, and Irish is critical to any understanding of how a race war materialized out of these insecurities. If the 1919 race riot can be said to have had a ground zero, it was, as the CCRR's map of deaths and injuries accompanying its report so clearly reveals, in the space between the eastern fringe of the Irish neighborhoods of Hamburg and Canaryville and the western edge of the Black Belt. It is here that any attempt to understand the origins and meaning of the riot should begin.

     • • •

Walking amid the rowdy throngs of young men in the neighborhoods of Canaryville and Hamburg during the warm spring months leading up to the riot, few streetwise Chicagoans would have been too surprised at the prospect that the eastern boundaries of these areas would soon become racial battlefields. The normalcy of such an idea was due in part to the established tradition of aggression against African Americans that youth gangs from this district had followed since at least the 1890s. However, the Irish athletic clubs here did not earn their nasty reputation for attacks on blacks alone; Jews, Poles, and Italians were also targets. Decades before the World War I migration of southern African Americans, a massive immigration wave from southern and eastern Europe had transformed the social geography of the stockyards area—commonly referred to as the "Back of the Yards"—and much of the city. From the 1890s to the 1910s, Italians, Poles, Russian Jews, Slovaks, Lithuanians, Croatians, Greeks, and others flooded into Chicago's rapidly expanding industrial labor market. Between 1900 and 1910, the foreign-born population of Chicago increased more than 33 percent to a total of 783,340. By 1920, nearly 30 percent of the city's residents (808,560) were foreign-born, while only about 25 percent (642,871) fell into the census category of "native white of native parentage."[23] The largest group of all, with well over a million, was the second-generation children of immigrants. In Bridgeport, where first- and second-generation Irish and Germans had shared a quasi-urban area amid cabbage patches, marshes, and the foul-smelling Bubbly Creek from the 1870s through the 1890s, the effects of this immigration were dramatic. Large numbers of Poles, Lithuanians, Slovaks, and Croats poured into the district after the turn of the century, and the older Irish and German families moved southward to the more enviable environs of Englewood. The Poles quickly became the largest group in the Back of the Yards area, a position symbolized by the new church steeples that sprang skyward out of their congested neighborhoods. By 1920, Poles dominated the area to the west of the stockyards known as Packingtown, making up two-thirds of the foreign-born population in the two census tracts adjacent to the stockyards.[24] These newcomers—the so-called new immigrants from southern and eastern Europe—were hardly welcomed by the largely native-born Irish and Germans who composed the "butcher aristocracy" of the packinghouses and were the longtime residents of Bridgeport and the Back of the Yards. Ethnic fault lines opened up on the killing floors as well as within the packinghouse workers' unions, where divisions of skill and ethnicity weakened workers' efforts to gain a greater degree of control over their work routines and their lives. Outside the packinghouses and stockyards, young men played out these antagonisms in the streets. As longtime Chicago journalist Mike Royko once described it: "Go that way, past the viaduct, and wops will jump you, or chase you into Jew town. Go the other way, beyond the park, and the Polacks would stomp on you. Cross those streetcar tracks, and the Micks will shower you with Irish confetti from the brickyards. And who can tell what the niggers might do?"[25]

By the summer of 1919 the question of "what the niggers might do" had become the source of heated conversation in the stockyards area, overshadowing lingering tensions with the "Wops," Jews, and "Polacks." Within the milieu of the Irish social and athletic clubs of Canaryville and Hamburg, moreover, such expressions were coming to seem more and more like preludes for a race war. The reasons for this went far beyond the new influence wielded by blacks in city politics. Historian William Tuttle's meticulous analysis of the Chicago race riot of 1919 suggests that the rising level of antiblack violence by Irish athletic clubs also corresponded to the increasing will of African American youths to fight back— and, in particular, to fight back against the Irish. As one former resident recalled, black youths hurled rocks and yelled back "Mick" when faced with shouts of "Nigger!" The *Chicago Defender,* whose circulation was exploding with the new sensibilities of race consciousness and militancy associated with the New Negro rhetoric of Marcus Garvey, Cyril Briggs, and W. E. B. DuBois, went out of its way to point out the Irish identity of racist police officers.[26]

Such conditions help explain why, as African Americans poured into the South Side Black Belt and into the stockyards workforce, what might be considered the city's first "super gang" developed out of two coalitions of Irish youth groups that had been fighting it out around these neighborhoods since the first years of the twentieth century. The Dukies and the Shielders, along with the Ragen's Colts and some of the other larger athletic clubs, had for years been engaging in street brawls with one another while uniting on occasion to confront threats posed by outsiders, especially blacks. The Dukies and the Shielders, in particular, claimed affiliates from a long stretch of city blocks, from well north of Hamburg around 22nd Street all the way down to 59th Street—far past the southern boundary of Canaryville. By 1919 the occasions that united these gangs were becoming more and more frequent, and residents in the area began referring to them as a kind of unified entity known as "the Mickies."[27] In the months preceding the riot, the antiblack intimidation carried out by this group was so persistent and the sense of Irish pride motivating it so marked that, as the historian James Grossman has noted, "many blacks mistakenly assumed that all the white gangs were Irish."[28] Although the territory encompassed by the Mickies overlapped with turf that the Ragen's Colts claimed to control, the extent to which the Colts made common cause with the Mickies before the riot is hard to know.

The Colts, it should be remembered, had designs on "running" an enormous area of the city that included the southern part of Canaryville but which also stretched far eastward to the area around Washington Park—a territory split in two by the narrow strip of Black Belt between Wentworth and State that extended, daggerlike, from 43rd to 55th Street. As several black witnesses claimed to have heard a Colt tell a black man on the first night of the riot, "Remember, it's the Ragen Colts you're dealing with. We have two thousand members between Halsted and Cottage Grove and 43rd and 63d streets. We intend to run this district. Look out."[29]

The grand ambitions of the Colts aside, that a sense of common purpose and shared community came to develop among the thousands of youths somehow affiliated with "the Mickies" was hardly self-evident. Canaryville and Hamburg were, in fact, separate neighborhoods with somewhat distinct and at times even rival identities. While each was home to families of longtime packinghouse workers and industrial laborers, Hamburg, which extended from 31st to 39th Street between Halsted Avenue and the Penn Central Railroad tracks, had a leg up over its southern rival, which, with its western edge along Halsted between 39th and 49th Street, offered precious little separation from the smoke and odor of the stockyards. Canaryville was, moreover, too close to the increasingly overcrowded Packingtown sector to the west of the stockyards, with its decrepit two-story, wood-frame tenements packed with the Polish and Lithuanian immigrants whom Irish Bridgeport's experienced meat cutters and butcher workmen commonly accused of undercutting their wages. Such conditions had produced a street subculture that took teenagers and turned them into career criminals—the "Canaryville School of Gunmen," as it was sometimes called.[30]

While Hamburg was nothing if not hard-boiled and working-class, it was more akin to the Bridgeport that produced three mayors and numerous other political, civic, and business leaders out of the generation of 1919. One of these was Hamburg's own favorite son, the future "Boss" of Chicago, Richard J. Daley, who used the strict guidance provided by the Our Lady of Nativity Parish School and then the commercial orientation of nearby De La Salle High School to help him ascend the ranks of the city's political machine to the mayor's office.[31] Yet when not in the classroom or at his summer job in the stockyards, the young Richard Daley passed his time in another world—as a member of the Hamburg Athletic Club, an organization which, as Mike Royko opined, "never had the Colts' reputation for criminality, but [was] handy with a brick."[32] Members of the Colts generally had less to lose, a situation that translated on the streets into an increased willingness to take great risks for the sake of gaining or maintaining a reputation. Yet as Daley's story reveals, both the Hamburgers and the Colts served more utilitarian roles. These organizations developed, in some sense, as the muscle for neighborhood bosses and as such represented quasi-legitimate opportunity structures. In 1914, for example, the president of the Hamburg Club, Tommy Doyle, used the club's leverage to unseat an alderman who had held the position for over twenty years. Four years later, Doyle won a seat on the state legislature, and another Hamburg president, Joe McDonough, took over as alderman. For his part, Daley became the club's president in 1924 and held the post for fifteen years while climbing the ranks of the Democratic Party machine.

Canaryville, on the other hand, was much less capable of producing this kind of political clout and cultural capital, even if the Colts still managed to grab their share of patronage. What Canaryville lacked in political resources, however, it made up for with criminal ones. Questioned by the CCRR about this particular neighborhood in the riot aftermath, the state's attorney of Cook County claimed that "more bank robbers, payroll bandits, automobile bandits, highwaymen, and strong-arm crooks come from this particular district than from any other that has come to his notice during his seven years as chief prosecuting official."[33] Canaryville was the breeding ground for some of the city's most notorious beer-running gangsters—people like "Moss" Enright, "Sonny" Dunn, Eugene Geary, and the Gentleman brothers—who drew much of their manpower from the pool of ready labor provided by the athletic clubs. The Chicago Crime Commission well understood this vital link between the crime syndicates and the gangs of Canaryville, reporting in 1920: "It is in this district that 'athletic clubs' and other organizations of young toughs and gangsters flourish, and where disreputable poolrooms, hoodlum-infested saloons and other criminal hang-outs are plentiful."[34]

Criminal enterprises and machine politics thus yielded some very significant returns for young men in Canaryville and Hamburg, but there was not nearly enough to keep everyone happy, and most of the generation coming of age in these neighborhoods in 1919 were more proletarian than slick. Those who ran with the athletic clubs and other aspiring street gangs of both of these neighborhoods were predominantly the sons of packinghouse workers and factory laborers, and the world they made on the streets was intimately linked to the affairs of the enormous meat-processing machine next door. Examining this world in the 1920s, Landesco concluded that "the sons of Irish laborers in the packing houses and stockyards" joined gangs like the Ragen's Colts because "Americanization made them averse to the plodding, seasonal, heavy and odoriferous labor of their parents, beset with the competition of wave upon wave of immigrants who poured into the area and bid for the jobs at lesser wages."[35] In reality, it was perhaps as much Taylorism as Americanism that made the Irish youths of these neighborhoods unwilling to cast their lots in the stockyards and killing floors. As James Barrett has compellingly shown, the advent of mass production methods in the meatpacking industry of the early twentieth century transformed both the experience of packinghouse work and the workforce that engaged in it. As packers sought to keep up with increasing demand, they quickened the pace of work, maintained closer supervision, and introduced division of labor and continuous-flow production methods.[36] Upton Sinclair described a packinghouse floor just after the turn of the century this way: "Looking down this room, one saw . . . a line of dangling hogs a hundred yards in length; and for every yard there was a man, working as if a demon were after him.[37] Such was the nature of the work available to unskilled youths seeking their first jobs in the 1910s, and by no means were these circumstances confined to the meatpacking industry. Moreover, by this time a job handling hogs in a room like the one Sinclair depicted would have meant working side-by-side with Poles, Lithuanians, or members of a host of other new immigrant groups whose status in urban society was clearly inferior to that of the Irish.

What all this suggests is that the Irish youths coming of age around the stockyards district in the first few decades of the twentieth century occupied a niche that resisted incorporation into the Fordist order then being swiftly established. Their unwillingness to fill the degraded jobs now available in the increasingly rationalized mass production workplaces of the city ultimately stemmed from their understanding that other options were open to them. This was a large part of the "Americanization" that sociologists like Landesco noted in them, and it was something that sharply distinguished them from their immigrant neighbors and potential co-workers, who had little choice in the matter of their employment in tedious, dangerous, low-wage labor.

Yet for many working-class Irish youths, this perception of choice was something of an illusion. In fact, the Irish youths of the generation of 1919 were not so far removed from the American Protective Association's "No Irish Need Apply" campaign of the first decade of the twentieth century; they were now facing four more years under a mayor considered by many to be anti-Catholic, and the Ragen's Colts would soon be turning their attention to another enemy—the Ku Klux Klan, which by the end of 1921 had capitalized on a mounting wave of anti-Catholic, nativist sentiment to launch an aggressive recruiting campaign in Chicago and other northern industrial cities. Institutions like Daley's alma mater De La Salle High School were beginning to show the Irish sons of packinghouse workers the way to the white-collar world, but those enrolled in such schools were still a rather select group. If Irish Bridgeport was then in the process of producing an illustrious cohort of political and business leaders, few growing up in Canaryville and Hamburg were aware of it; a local beat cop's description of the neighborhood as "one tough hole" was closer to the truth.[38] The Colts, for example, knew intimately the nativist-tinged sense of outrage that middle-class reform organizations cast their way.

All these conditions shaped the subculture of social and athletic clubs that existed in these neighborhoods in the late 1910s and early 1920s. For one thing, the forms of discrimination the Irish faced, as well as the sense of being pushed out of their neighborhoods and workplaces by social inferiors, meant that despite neighborhood and club rivalries, broader solidarities came to be forged out of sentiments of both Irishness and Americanness. The intense feelings of "patriotism for the United States" Landesco remarked upon were evidence of a strategy of empowerment deployed in the face of such conditions and that he felt obliged to specify the nature of their patriotism—this was, after all, a critical moment for Irish nationalist thought—indicated that such feelings mingled with sentiments of ethnic pride. Yet beyond such processes of group identification, the forms and rituals structuring this world reflected two other interrelated facets of the everyday struggle for empowerment Irish American youths waged in these years. The first was the attempt to develop structures of opportunity, whether through criminal or political means (which were at times hard to tell apart). The second was the effort to create a system of individual valorization that would order these structures of opportunity and provide symbolic forms of compensation when they failed to provide material ones.

The culture of physical combat that defined the athletic club milieu of Hamburg and Canaryville in the first two decades of the twentieth century grew largely out of this latter strategy of empowerment. As in nearly all male-dominated fighting gang cultures that have been studied by historians and sociologists before and after this particular conjuncture, claims to powerful manhood and the sense of honor or status it bestowed constituted the stakes of the street brawls in this area. "[A group's] status as a gang among gangs, as well as in the neighborhood and the community," Frederic Thrasher observed after surveying more than 1,300 Chicago gangs, "must . . . be maintained, usually through its prowess in a fight."[39] No other neighborhood area personified this idea more than the blocks of Hamburg and Canaryville, where demonstrations of "prowess in a fight" had been integral to the street culture since at least the 1880s. According to one resident, youths from these communities "thirsted for a fight," and Saturday night turf battles between "Canaryvillains" and "Hamburg lads" often produced "broken noses and black eyes that were . . . too numerous to count."[40] Such accounts, in spite of their residues of nostalgia, warn against dismissing the street violence rampant among youths in neighborhoods around the stockyards as frivolous. In a period when handguns were rarely used in such street fights, the not infrequent fatalities that occurred came the hard way— from skull fractures and stab wounds. That gangs arriving at designated fights expected to see their enemies holding clubs, bats, blackjacks, and knives that they were not afraid to use suggests that the drive for manly prowess was anything but trivial—rather, it was something worth risking one's life for.

All this suggests that the underlying conditions for the murderous violence unleashed in the 1919 race riot developed several years before the mass migration of blacks between 1916 and 1919. Before race became the problem it did for white young men around the stockyards, the intertwined predicaments of class and masculinity were what pushed Irish-Catholic young men into deadly confrontations—often with each other— in these neighborhoods. Why race would become the prevailing reason for the troubles these youths faced in the summer of 1919 seems all too easily explained by the changes wrought by the massive racial migration and the accompanying struggle over political resources between blacks and whites on the South Side. Yet there was more than this to the outbreak of race war on the South Side of Chicago. Often overlooked as a dimension of the intense racial violence greeting blacks when they arrived up North during World War I is the problem of masculinity for segments of the white working-class in this era. Hence, before white working-class youths became fixated on "what the niggers might do," they were preoccupied with the problem of manliness in their daily lives. This was not just reflected by the culture of physical combat they created on the streets; the quest for manly honor was, on one level or another, at the moral center of the movies they saw, the books and magazines they read, and the sporting culture they were part of—both as spectators and participants.

By the late 1910s and early 1920s, silent movies, in particular, had become a near-obsession with working-class youths. Of the more than one hundred Chicago youths Thrasher interviewed about their leisure pursuits, all claimed to attend three movies a week and some 30 percent went every day. As for their preferred genre, pictures of the "wild west" type topped the list of nearly half of the youths, with the next most popular category being other kinds of thrillers and action films involving "fighting, shooting, adventure, racing, war, or some kind of 'rough stuff.'" Some three-quarters of the youths surveyed, in other words, preferred to see films that were, on a very fundamental level, predicated on depicting fantasies of manly bravado. This penchant for the manly action film genre was further reflected in the results of a film star survey distributed among teens in several Chicago public schools around this time. The overwhelming choice for favorite actor, with nearly three times as many votes as the runner-up, was the cowboy film icon Tom Mix. Behind Mix was the other prominent cowboy film hero of the day, William S. Hart.[41]

Hart and Mix emerged as exemplars of manliness at a time when the modes of hegemonic masculinity prevailing in the urban United States were undergoing a dramatic process of transformation. Between the 1890s and the 1910s, urbanization; bureaucratization; the waning of small-scale, competitive capitalism; the growing importance of consumer culture; and the increasingly assertive presence of women in the spheres of work, politics, and leisure posed serious challenges to the Victorian ideal of manly self-restraint.[42] In this context, the frontier life depicted by silent westerns offered an antidote to the emasculating conditions of modern urban life. By the early 1920s, Hart much more than Mix was the pioneering star of a genre that depicted the two dominant notions of masculinity then in circulation—one oriented around more traditional Victorian ideals of self-restraint and respectability and the other based on emerging notions of physical strength and aggressiveness. While the perceived dangers posed by this latter form called for corrective doses of Christian morality and the social gospel to appease censors and attract a broad middle-class audience, with titles like *His Hour of Manhood* (1914), *The Roughneck* (1915), and *Breed of Men* (1919), these films left little doubt as to the brand of manly fantasies they were designed to transmit.[43]

That such fantasies were apparently in great demand among working-class Chicago youths during the 1910s and 1920s is a matter that has generally eluded the attention of historians. Those who have investigated the shifting modalities of manhood between the 1890s and 1920s have done so almost exclusively from the vantage point of white, urban middle-class men—those seemingly most susceptible to the appeal of new ideals of physical male potency. Behind such thinking is the implicit assumption that working-class men in this same period engaged in the kinds of activities that middle-class men lacked—namely, employment in manual labor and participation in sporting leisure forms—and therefore did not face the same kinds of challenges to their sense of manhood. Historians of gender relations have thus characterized the turn-of-the-century cult of the "strenuous life," "masculinity crisis," or "unusual obsession with manhood"—as they have variously termed it—as a largely middle-class phenomenon. Working-class masculinity, by contrast, has largely appeared in the historiography as unproblematic and the working class itself as the natural repository of male virility.[44]

The apparent investment of working-class Chicago youths in the visions of manhood offered by B-Westerns in this period warns against such reductive accounts. Not unlike their middle-class peers, working-class youths in Chicago looked to such forms during the 1910s and 1920s as they attempted to act like men. And, as they did for middle-class men, the cultural resources available to working-class men as they engaged in this process drew heavily upon racial narratives and languages. Race was more than just a subtext, for example, in the stories silent westerns told about masculinity. Indeed, Indians, Mexicans, and swarthy-complexioned bandits were the stock characters of silent B-Westerns that racialized the filmic frontier and the narratives that unraveled within it in the 1910s and 1920s. While some film scholars have described a kind of soft, "noble savage" moment of Indian and Mexican representation in the early years of the silent western, movies like *Captured by Mexicans* (1914), *Birth of a Nation* (1915), and *The Aryan* (1916) heralded a new trend of hard racial stereotyping in B-Westerns.[45] In *The Aryan*, starring William S. Hart, the protagonist and eventual hero starts out as the leader of a town called Devil's Hole, which is inhabited by "fierce men, outlaws, murderers and thieves, most of them half-breeds or Mexicans." The conversion of Hart's character from bad man to hero comes when he prevents the town's "half-breed greasers and Indian cut-throats" from raping a white woman.[46] Opening just months after D. W. Griffith's Civil War epic, *Birth of a Nation*, *The Aryan* evidenced the western's incorporation of the theme that had made *Birth of a Nation* into a national blockbuster: the demonstration of heroic white manhood in vanquishing nonwhite predators bent on violating white women. If at times the rape nightmare scenario fell out of the picture, the forces arrayed against the white hero in countless B-westerns, whether about the Alamo, the Mexican-American War, or a simple family trying to survive on the frontier, were commonly nonwhite. By the mid-1910s such race war narratives had entered the popular American imaginary, and they had done so hand-in-hand with the new modalities of strenuous masculinity.

Nor was such ideological groundwork limited to B-westerns. Similar ideas were to be found in even more explicit forms in some of the most popular literature of the moment. *Tarzan of the Apes,* which ran serially in at least eight major metropolitan newspapers in 1914 and which appears at the top of Thrasher's list of "the books most frequently mentioned by gang boys in institutions," turned on analogous narrative devices.[47] Tarzan, whose awesome manly power results from the combination of his Anglo-Saxon blood with his primal upbringing among a family of apes in the jungle, commonly refers to himself as "THE KILLER OF BEASTS AND MANY BLACK MEN," some of whom meet their end while attempting to carry attractive white women off into the jungle.[48]

Tarzan's racial components were not incidental to its popular appeal. It was no matter of coincidence that the same year that *Tarzan of the Apes* was running in newspapers across the country, these same papers were detailing the scandalous misdeeds of the first black heavyweight boxing champion, Jack Johnson, and the nationwide search for the "Great White Hope" that could restore the supremacy of the white race by defeating him in the ring. Denied a shot at the title by longtime champion Jim Jeffries, who refused to fight against a black man until his retirement, Johnson pummeled Tommy Burns for the heavyweight crown in 1908. Johnson's victory sparked keen interest—and, in some cases, near hysteria—by white working-class and middle-class men.[49] Social Darwinism had already taken hold among proponents of laissez-faire individualism, and its ideas of "natural selection," "survival of the fittest," and "the struggle for existence" were beginning to filter into debates about the nation's role in international affairs and about the problems its exploding population of immigrants posed to its future. In this context, heavyweight prizefighting emerged as the center stage and laboratory where biological fitness was put to the test in the most graphic and seemingly indisputable of ways. Boxing spectators always identified fighters—whether Irish, English, Polish, Jewish, Italian, black, or other—by the racial and ethnic groups they hailed from. In short, boxing was where the intellectual currents of social Darwinism and popular common sense met.

A black heavyweight champion was thus a serious concern; one who made of show of pounding white challengers senseless was a national emergency. Making matters worse was the fact that this particular black champion made no secret of his relations with white women, including the high-priced prostitutes at Chicago's famed Everleigh Club, at a time when antimiscegenation laws forbade interracial marriages in most states. The *New York Times* captured the state of anxiety surrounding Jack Johnson's reign when, prior to his bout against former champion Jim Jeffries, it editorialized: "Even those who have an absurdly exaggerated horror of prizefighting as a 'brutal' sport should gently warm in their sensitive minds a little hope that the white man may not lose, while the rest of us will wait in open anxiety the news that he has licked the— well, since it must be in print, let us say the negro, even though it is not the first word that comes to the tongue's tip."[50]

After Jeffries became the next Great White Hope to be trounced by Johnson, angry mobs of whites took to the streets and attacked African Americans in a number of major cities. In Chicago, where Johnson opened a racially mixed nightclub called the Café de Champion at 41 West 31st Street, thousands of whites gathered at the corner of Clark Street and Montrose Boulevard on the North Side and used a black dummy to hang Johnson in effigy. A sign pinned to the dummy's chest read: "THIS IS WHAT WE WILL DO TO JACK JOHNSON."[51] Shortly after, city authorities shut down the Café de Champion by first ordering Johnson to stop all music and entertainment and then by refusing to renew the club's liquor license. In the end, however, it took federal authorities to contain the threat that Jack Johnson posed to the racial order. Charged under the Mann Act for transporting a prostitute—his former lover Belle Schreiber of the Everleigh Club—across state lines, Johnson was convicted in federal court and sentenced to one year in prison.[52] He fled to Paris and did not return until 1920, in the meantime losing the heavyweight championship to white challenger Jess Willard in Havana in 1915.

The rise and fall of Jack Johnson was truly a mass phenomenon; as Al-Tony Gilmore has claimed, it "sparked the first nationwide conflict between blacks and whites."[53] However, in view of Johnson's ties to Chicago as well as the tumultuous racial politics then gripping the city, the search for the Great White Hope was bound to have special significance for young working-class Chicagoans—particularly those in neighborhoods like Canaryville and Hamburg, which lay just across the color line from Johnson's Café de Champion. These youths were fully aware, for example, that shortly after Johnson's defeat in Cuba in 1915, their nemesis Big Bill Thompson had brought the house down in Bronzeville's Pekin Theater when he praised Johnson as a great fighter and "a good man" in his final campaign speech.[54] To be sure, working-class young men in these neighborhoods poured over the details of the Jack Johnson story in the sports pages of the city's dailies, as well as in a number of popular boxing magazines, such as the popular *National Police Gazette*, which they passed among themselves on street corners and in clubhouses, bars, and poolrooms. Indicative of the tone of the coverage they read was the journalist Herbert Swope's epic description of the Johnson-Willard fight in the *Chicago Tribune:* "Never in the history of the ring was there such a wild, hysterical, shrieking, enthusiastic crowd [as] the 20,000 men and women who begged Willard to wipe out the stigma that they and hundreds of thousands of others, especially in the south, believe rested on the white race through the negro holding the championship."[55]

In fact, the interest of these youths in heavyweight boxing was not particular to the Johnson affair. People referred to the athletic clubs of working-class Chicago as such because of their intense engagement in a sporting culture organized around their participation in and spectatorship of sports like football, baseball, and boxing. Of all these activities, boxing, because of the raw physicality of its style of competition and the minimal resources required to conduct a match, was most central to this sporting culture. "Boxing," Thrasher wrote, "represent[ed] the nearest approach to fighting that has social sanction and which can be carried on in a very limited space within the gang's own hang-out. . . . Almost every gang has its pugs, and a flattened nose, a cauliflower ear, or an otherwise battered 'phizz' . . . are marks of distinction."[56] Indeed, prizefighting became a key element of the expanding "popular culture of bachelorhood" in the early twentieth century, when the sensationalist rag the *National Police Gazette* declared itself the "Greatest Sporting Weekly in the World" and began devoting most of its pages to a range of sports, boxing the most prominent among them.[57]

In neighborhoods like Canaryville and Hamburg, the sport held special meaning for working-class youths, who actually knew the sting of punches thrown in pugilist contests. Here athletic clubs boasted of the famed prizefighters among their members. According to one settlement worker in the stockyards district, for example, the Ragen's Colts made it well known that they could count on the skills of a locally renowned prizefighter nicknamed "Diamond Dick."[58] "Boxers and wrestlers,"

William Tuttle claims, "represented the Colts in citywide competition, and the cups and trophies which lined the shelves of the clubhouse testified to their success."[59] However, young men in such clubs also boxed more informally and more commonly in the context of activities sponsored by neighborhood institutions. Reformers in the settlement house movement, which sought to bring youths off street corners and under the watchful supervision of social workers in the 1910s and 1920s, well understood the need to offer boxing as a primary activity.[60]

Despite such efforts, organized boxing could not adequately provide many of the elements that street fighting readily supplied: the esprit de corps that came from fighting together as a unit, the adrenaline rush of real danger, and, perhaps most important, the sense of group identification and pride that came from successfully combating neighboring groups. While this last aspect was at times present in neighborhoods in which two or more white ethnic groups struggled for settlement house resources, most settlement workers observed the color line in the activities they organized and attempted to mollify, rather than incite, inter-ethnic divisions. Out on the streets, however, the will among working-class youths to play out such divisions in theaters of street combat was irrepressible in the 1910s and 1920s, and as the Jack Johnson phenomenon suggests, this will was both a cause and an effect of the normalization of the idea of race war. It would nonetheless be erroneous to attribute such tendencies to the rise of Jack Johnson. If Johnson helped transform the idea of race war, at least momentarily, into a binary notion, the presence of race war discourse in American urban culture predated Johnson's defeat of Burns. As Michel Foucault has argued in the case of Europe, a new form of "biological racism," characterized by "the postevolutionist theme of the struggle for existence," had established itself by the end of the nineteenth century.[61] In the United States, such trends appeared most strikingly in public declarations justifying a range of imperial interventions around the turn of the century, including the Spanish-American War, the annexation of the Hawaiian and Philippine Islands, and participation in the suppression of the Chinese Boxer Rebellion, and then reappeared in debates surrounding citizenship and immigration in the mid-1910s and early 1920s.[62] Yet in working-class quarters, the power and meaning of social Darwinism—and ultimately of the idea of race war—came less from such discourses than from popular cultural forms like prizefighting and the local subcultures that formed in their image.

Structured to a great extent by the activities of street fighting, boxing, and other competitive sports, the Irish athletic club subculture in the stockyards area was permeated with such ideas in the years leading up to the 1919 race riot, and in this it was no exception. As Stephen Riess has argued, "Jewish, Italian, and Polish youth highly esteemed the ability to fight: it was a sign of manliness and was a useful skill because of the frequency of interethnic gang fights at public parks and playgrounds and other border areas separating rival groups."[63] The membership of some of these gangs, like the Miller brothers' gang in the Jewish Douglas Park area, consisted of a significant number of amateur boxers. On one occasion that lived on in the lore of this neighborhood for years, the boxers in this gang led a marauding group of youths, shouting "Wallop the Polack!" into the nearby Polish district to seek revenge on a group of Polish youths who had attacked Jews around Douglas Park.[64] However, if youths from southern and eastern European backgrounds found themselves deeply invested in racially and ethnically charged rituals of street combat and sports competition, the Irish relationship to such forms was rather unique. Irish prizefighters, after all, dominated boxing from its origins in the 1870s through the 1920s. The absolute supremacy of Irish boxers was such that southern and eastern European fighters often assumed Irish-sounding names in the ring—a practice that was no doubt emulated on playgrounds throughout the urban North.[65]

All of these conditions rendered the idea of race war thinkable among working-class youths in Canaryville and Hamburg. This is not to say that they envisioned an apocalyptic fight to the finish actually taking place in the streets. The notion of race war was rather something more of a "structure of feeling," in the words of Raymond Williams, a way of making sense of everyday experiences that the forms of street combat and boxing rendered visible. This structure of feeling bore a close relationship with, but was hardly identical to, the intellectual currents surrounding social Darwinist thought in the 1910s and early 1920s, and a national mobilization for war abroad, which sharply questioned immigrant loyalty and fitness for citizenship. Indeed, the key roles played by eugenicist thinkers like Madison Grant and Harry Laughlin in the immigration policy debates of this moment and the immigration restriction legislation they helped define reveal the clarity of Foucault's observation that the state was by this time functioning principally in the "biopower mode"—as "protector of the integrity, the superiority, and the purity of the race."[66] Yet the appearance of this centralized "state racism" in the United States, did not, as Foucault claims in the case of Europe, mean the disappearance of ideas of race struggle or race war. Such ideas continued to circulate within the field of popular culture as a whole, and especially within the sporting bachelor subcultures of such working-class neighborhoods as Canaryville and Hamburg. In such areas, boxing and its shadow form, street fighting, became central elements of youth subcultures in part because they provided something similar to what Clifford Geertz has argued the cockfight offered to the Balinese—"a metasocial commentary upon the whole matter of assorting human beings into fixed hierarchical ranks and then organizing the major part of collective existence around that assortment."[67] The kind of commentaries these activities offered, in the context of Jack Johnson's reign, the mayoral election of 1919, and the invasion of the neighborhoods and workplaces around the stockyards by new immigrants and African Americans, not only left the whole practice of assorting and ranking unquestioned, but also cast the Irish athletic clubs as the Custer-like defenders of the community and the race in a war that they were in the midst of losing. The sense of fighting a losing war was another structure of feeling that circulated through much of Irish Bridgeport and Canaryville in the 1910s and 1920s. Its existence can be detected in the extensive coverage given at the outbreak of the riot to Fifth Ward alderman Joseph McDonough's claim that blacks "possessed enough ammunition . . . to last for years of guerrilla warfare," and especially his anguished declaration: "For God's sake, arm. They are coming; we cannot hold them."[68] That McDonough was a former president of the Hamburgers reveals the extent to which such sentiments emerged out of the Irish athletic club milieu, where clashes between Irish youths and the racial and ethnic others around them constituted so many rehearsals for race war.

CROSSING THE DEAD LINE

The many reports of racial violence perpetrated not only by the athletic clubs but also by less distinguishable groups of young white ethnic men and teenage boys in the recreational spaces around the stockyards at this time indicate that such acts emerged out of tangible organizational bases and distinct patterns of behavior—what might be thought of as the architecture of a male youth gang subculture. This world was not merely organized by politicians and racketeers who marshaled the energies of working-class ethnic youths for their own ends, although such patrons no doubt played an important role by providing gangs with a sense of legitimacy, as well as a safe haven for their activities. Young men created their own subcultures: matrices of behavior, language, and style that gave, in the words of Stuart Hall, "expressive form to their social and material life-experience."[69] While historians have been reluctant to extend the term *youth subculture* back past the postwar period it has generally served to describe, the world of the Irish youth gangs of the 1910s and early 1920s conformed to the primary characteristics of youth subcultures laid out by Stuart Hall and Tony Jefferson, most notably in its somewhat "tight" coherence around "particular activities, focal concerns and territorial spaces," and its separation—spatially, emotionally, and intellectually—from both its parent culture (working-class, Irish-Catholic) and the dominant culture (white, middle-class).[70] Essential to this sense of separation in both cases, and thus crucial to the subcultural nature of the world of working-class youth gangs in general, was the youthful age range of its core participants. The young men of these groups were in the midst of a set of years in the typical life trajectory of men of their means and circumstances when they would find themselves at odds with the generation before them and more vulnerable to needs and uncertainties that so often sought resolution in acts of aggression.

There was thus more to the uprising of young Irish American men in 1919 than what first met the eyes of contemporary observers, and more recently, historians. As much as the product of political manipulations or a community-wide effort to preserve the neighborhood, the wave of antiblack violence culminating in the race riot of 1919 represented a youth subcultural response which laid bare a generational fault line that began to widen as the sons and daughters of first- and second-generation Irish laborers came of age in the midst of labor unrest, racial and ethnic migration, and the general sense of community decline such changes evoked. The male youth subculture emerging at this juncture articulated in its ritualistic antiblack violence the community-wide anger and desperation associated with falling wages, falling property values, and the fallen image of the neighborhood. However, this milieu and the locus of its anxieties existed in a physical and imagined space apart from the community as envisaged by those of previous generations who had developed the area into a parish so as to preserve their Irish Catholic heritage. In view of the kinds of activities that occupied the Irish athletic clubs around Bridgeport, Canaryville, and the Back of the Yards in the 1910s and 1920s, their members were, at the least, highly ambivalent about Archbishop James E. Quigley's efforts as head of the Chicago diocese between 1903 and 1915 to create a system of parishes in which each was "of such a size that the pastor can know personally every man, woman, and child in it."[71]

The reports of University of Chicago settlement workers employed in this area in the early 1920s, for example, illuminate a troubled relationship between the athletic gangs and older neighborhood residents. After interviewing the parents of a Colt who had recently been arrested in connection with a series of sexual gang assaults in December 1924, a settlement worker noted the deep shame and frustration they expressed about their son's involvement with the group. The father, described by the caseworker as "unmistakably Irish," spoke of his struggle to keep his son away from the club, despite the fact that "he loved the place so much that he could not wait to come home [from his job at a pipe-fitting firm] to change his clothes before going there." Claiming to have lived in the neighborhood for forty years, he also spoke of the humiliation he felt when passing friends on the street. The teen's mother, for her part, feared that this situation would force the family to move, something she did not want to do because of the "good school facilities [parochial]" and the "very good church [Catholic]."[72] Considering the Colts were one of many such clubs, and that this one group's membership alone approached two thousand, such stories were not uncommon.

As this interview reveals, the close-knit network of older residents within which circulated shame-inducing stories of the local athletic clubs in the neighborhood existed in tension with the world of clubhouses and gang hangouts. After speaking to a number of older inhabitants of the area, for example, a settlement worker concluded that the Ragen's Colts was "a rough and impertinent crowd" and "very unpopular in their own neighborhood."[73] This notoriety of the Irish athletic clubs greatly increased following the 1919 race riot, when many residents of the Bridgeport, Canaryville, and Back of the Yards areas claimed that extensive newspaper reportage of the horrible misdeeds of these organizations had tainted the image of their neighborhoods. For the Back of the Yards area in particular, which, for many Chicagoans living outside this part of the city, encompassed Canaryville as well, the situation was even more dramatic. The vaguely defined territory of the city that came to be known as the Back of the Yards became more and more associated with the Ragen's Colts, beer running, and gangland murders in the early 1920s. In fact, the name of the Colts became so poisonous that by 1922—around the time police made numerous raids on the Ragen Athletic Club at 52nd and Halsted in connection with its suspected involvement in beer-running murders—their old patron Frank Ragen announced he was severing ties with the club.[74] The following year, the papers were painting the Colts as bad boys once again after police arrested four of its members for shooting at police officers patrolling Green Street.[75] The infamy such news coverage brought to the area prompted a number of club members to send a sharp riposte to the *Tribune:* "We belong to the boys' club back o' the yards, and protest against lumping us all as bad boys and gangsters who mob policemen." "Green Street is not back of the yards," they added, "and Ragen's Colts are not back of the yards."[76]

Despite this apparent falling out with elements of their surrounding communities, athletic clubs like the Colts nonetheless practiced rituals of racial violence that, in certain moments, signified a defense of the overall community. If some of the members of these outfits were active participants in Prohibition-era beer-running enterprises, they should not be dismissed as mercenaries unwilling to waste their time on affairs that offered them little material gain. Throughout the early 1920s, for instance, when groups like the Colts and the Hamburgers continued to patrol neighborhood borders against black trespassers, they also expended a great deal of energy combating the forces of anti-Catholicism, especially the Ku Klux Klan. In September 1921, for example, the Colts rallied a crowd of some three thousand people from the stockyards district to watch them hang "a white-sheeted Klansman" in effigy.[77] The following January, they broke up a lecture that was to be given by a "spreader of Anti-Papist propaganda."[78] In addition to anti-Catholics and African Americans, moreover, the Colts engaged in persistent warfare against the expanding Polish gangs in the Back of the Yards area in the mid-1920s—most notably, the Murderers and the Wigwams. Explaining why the Colts "waged war" against these groups, two residents of the area told settlement workers that "the neighborhood is changing," referring to the establishment of the "new Polish church"—St. John of God.[79]

However, if such acts seemed to articulate a sense of communalism based on the fiery defense of ethnic identity and neighborhood status, the Irish communities that needed defending were becoming less and less palpable in the 1920s. To begin with, increasing Irish social mobility meant that the old working-class Irish parishes around the stockyards, such as fifteen-thousand-member Visitation Parish, were losing parishioners to the expanding parishes of the outlying middle-class neighborhoods of Englewood and Auburn-Gresham.[80] This not only had the effect of considerably weakening the link between group identity and locality for the remaining Irish youths around the stockyards, but on a more practical level, it depleted the reservoir of new recruits for clubs whose vitality and honor depended on being able to flex their muscles on the streets. A compelling sign of these changes was the somewhat surprising acceptance of a number of second-generation Russian Jews—

traditionally the object of anti-Semitic hatred in Irish Chicago—into the ranks of the Colts in the early 1920s.[81] While one resident at the time explained this state of affairs by claiming that the recent "trouble with the K.K.K." had brought Jews and Catholics "closer together," the need for new muscle and the hatred shared by Irish and Jews for the increasingly aggressive Polish youth groups around the stockyards are probably more accurate explanations.[82] To be sure, consorting with Jews was not nearly the worst of the offenses committed by the young men of the athletic clubs in the eyes of older residents of their communities. This was the Jazz Age, and many of the beer wars that enlisted the talents of good old South Side Irish boys were fought for control of supply lines that extended across the dead line and into the "Bright Lights area" around 35th and State—a district where young white pleasure-seekers sought to mingle among the sights, sounds, and people of the Black Belt. By the mid-1920s, amid recurrent beer-running murders and a sensationalized scandal involving the arrest of eight Ragen's Colts—two Jews among them—for a series of sexual assaults, it was becoming clear to many around the stockyards that the sober, austere vision of parish social life held by many clergymen had fallen out of step with the sporting lifestyle of the generation of 1919. That Reverend Timothy O'Shea sought to boldly revitalize Visitation Parish in 1925 by turning its basement into a recreation center and its auditorium into a gymnasium was a sure sign of the times.[83]

It is no matter of coincidence that in the years immediately after the riot, business boomed for both the controversial black-and-tan cabarets, which provided spaces for interracial flirting, dancing, and prostitution, and the syndicates that supplied them with their liquor. This was an enterprise carried out with the labor of young men in their late teens and early twenties—the age range riot witnesses consistently referred to when identifying the attackers of African Americans. Moreover, the complicity of these men in the rapid expansion of the South Side vice district in the 1920s involved more than financial gain. White ethnic youths living across the dead line were also clients in the bustling establishments filling this district, referred to as "the Stroll," where crowds circulated around the clock, where stores never closed, and where, recalled the poet Langston Hughes, "midnight was like day."[84] So intimate was the relationship between the typical rioter of the young, white working-class sporting set around the stockyards and the 35th Street Bright Lights district across the dead line that in his first report on the outbreak of race rioting, the journalist Carl Sandburg found it important to note that "the cabarets and clubs, however, did business up to the limit of 1 o'clock in the morning." "Dreamland, 3518 South State Street; the DeLuxe, upstairs at 3503 South State Street; the Entertainers at 209 East 35th Street, and the Old Elite at 3030 South State all had bright lights and big crowds," he specified.[85] These cabarets, known not only for their brassy black jazz orchestras but also for opportunities for interracial prostitution, were popular venues for white working-class youths residing across the dead line. Investigating Dreamland in 1923, for example, the Juvenile Protective Association (JPA) reported that female prostitutes of both races sat at tables and solicited clients as they walked by.[86] While such hip venues also attracted a more upscale, middle-class crowd, that many of these clients were working-class young men was indicated by another JPA report some years later describing patrons of the "factory-working type . . . [that] have the urge to move to the strains of music."[87]

Such evidence reveals that by viewing the athletic clubs as fringe elements of the community, scholars have largely overlooked the vital link between youth subcultures and racial violence. They have, for the most part, presented a one-dimensional view of the young men in these groups. Rather than youths negotiating their way through the pursuits and demands of everyday life, they appear in the historiography as pawns, mercenaries, or saboteurs of class bonds. A "thick" perspective on riots and racial violence in general has eluded the interpretive gaze of scholars who have generally considered acts of collective racial violence as "communal" expressions of housing and labor conflicts. Seen from a different perspective, the racial violence of youth gangs and athletic clubs, prior to the more mediated and choreographed scenes of the riot, appears as a subcultural response par excellence. The youths running with the Irish athletic clubs were somewhat typical members of their communities, but they circulated within a subculture that invested them in the bodies of racial others in ways that older residents were not. If, as we have already seen, they represented community-wide sentiments and national cultural currents in their efforts to patrol neighborhood boundaries and exclude racial undesirables, their intimacy with the street violence such activities called for set them apart from the rest of the community. Their closer relationship to the playground of interracial sexual leisure that lay across the dead line had similar implications. In fact, this dual experience of racial hatred and racial desire was integral to the Irish youth subcultures that formed along the dead line—a condition that sheds new light on the interpretation of racial violence initially put forward by the black press in the aftermath of the riot, and then quoted in the report of the CCRR, that "the so-called 'intermingling of races' in the cabarets of the South Side [was] a fruitful source of riots."[88]

As Dick Hebdige asserted was the case for the working-class youth subcultures that emerged in postwar Britain, the world of Chicago's Irish athletic clubs of the 1910s and early 1920s made possible "responses" or "solutions" to the problems posed by the increasing presence of people of color and scorned ethnic groups.[89] The dilemmas Irish youths in these clubs faced as a consequence of increasing labor competition and neighborhood transition resembled those encountered by working-class youths in London's East End during the postwar decades. Like many East Enders, the Back of the Yards Irish felt the sting of being left behind as friends and neighbors moved on to more respectable middle-class environs, defined as such, in part, because of their very separation from the blacks and immigrants moving into the old neighborhoods. Writer James T. Farrell, who grew up in a South Side Irish neighborhood during this era, poignantly evokes such conditions in his novel *The Young Manhood of Studs Lonigan*. In this segment of a trilogy that details the life of the fictional working-class Irish American Studs Lonigan, Farrell portrays a gang of second-generation teenagers from an Irish neighborhood in the Washington Park area dealing with the emotional fallout from seeing friends and neighbors leave the parish as blacks and other ethnic groups begin settling there. Hence, running throughout Farrell's rendering of the spiritual conditions of what he referred to as a "lower middle-class, Irish-American, Catholic environment" is an ambivalent longing for escape that coexists uneasily with feelings of attachment to the old neighborhood.[90]

Like working-class East End youths in postwar Britain, Irish American youths in interwar Chicago devised ways to "symbolically" or "magically" resolve these dilemmas—physical aggression being the most prominent. Yet such rituals were fraught with ambiguities, revealing a subconscious dimension underlying the sport of antiblack violence. To begin with, one must not underestimate the significance of the 1919 riot erupting, in part, because of the mixing of black and white bathers at the Twenty-ninth Street Beach, an incident that followed a distinct pattern of interracial skirmishes in public spaces—parks, schools, beaches, and streets—where black and white ethnic youths frequently crossed paths. "It was no new thing," the CCRR wrote, "for youthful white and Negro groups to come to violence. For years . . . there had been clashes over baseball grounds, swimming-pools in the parks, the right to walk on certain streets, etc." This pattern of conflict indicates that the youths involved at times shared such public spaces, however tenuous and tense this cohabitation may have been. It is further suggestive that while differing versions of the incident at the Twenty-ninth Street Beach emerged as the fighting raged on, one account portrayed the initial skirmish as the outgrowth of a quarrel among black and white gamblers. The veracity of this story remains in question, but that it endured and circulated reveals that such interracial activities were not uncommon on a beach so close to the edge of the Black Belt. This was, after all, the closest beach to the solidly white Irish neighborhood of Hamburg, whose residents would have had to cross through black neighborhoods to get there.[91]

To be sure, the pattern of racial violence in recreational spaces near the boundaries between black and white neighborhoods reflected deep feelings of racial fear and hatred, but such a pattern could develop only within a context of relatively regular interracial contact. In interwar Chicago, repeated racial conflict in parks and beaches reveals that the rules of use and access were by no means clearly defined or uniformly followed. Drawing on information gleaned from interviews of park workers and police officers, the CCRR examined the conduct of race relations in such spaces in *The Negro in Chicago*. Explaining the violence occurring in these recreational areas, many observers pointed their fingers at the athletic clubs. "These clubs, which have only about one athlete on their roster," stated the director of Fuller Park, "are so situated that the Negroes have to pass them going to and from the park." "Those are the boys," he added, "numerous in every park neighborhood, who are keeping the colored people out of the parks." Whereas some park supervisors reported that these "boys" could at times exhibit a spirit of grudging cooperation on the baseball diamond, the situation was quite different in places charged with interracial sexual tensions. Hence, park officials cited public showers, swimming pools, and bathing areas as highly contested spaces and thus flashpoints for violence. Commenting on the situation at South Side beaches near the riot areas, for example, the CCRR noted: "At Thirty-eighth Street Beach the prejudice is such as to prevent any Negro from bathing there, although it is as near the center of the main Negro area as the Twenty-sixth Street Beach, to which Negroes are expected to confine themselves." Elaborating on how white beachgoers enforced this confinement, a black playground director at the Thirty-eighth Street Beach told the CCRR, "They rock you if you go in."[92]

Such conditions suggest that the subcultural meaning of collective racial violence may have rested more in the conflicted allure of the interracial encounter than in the separation that the violence was intended to bring about. The incidents of aggression along the lakefront, quite often instigated by groups of young, white, bare-chested men in the summer heat, combined an urge to display masculine prowess and an ambivalent fascination with people of color. Thus, a police officer stationed at the Twenty-ninth Street Beach in the aftermath of the riot informed the CCRR: "Gangs of young men come from as far away as Halsted Street . . . ready to fight at the slightest opportunity." "Fights," he stated, "usually occur because of some remark made by one group about a girl in another group." The CCRR also reported that many fights in Washington Park started when blacks "showed fight" against "gangs of white boys from sixteen to twenty years of age [who] frequently annoyed Negro couples on the benches of this park." These observations shed light on the vague but compelling statement by the CCRR that so-called sex problems were, along with real estate concerns, the most commonly cited "causes of neighborhood antagonism" regarding the presence of blacks in parks.[93] Attesting to the overall atmosphere of racial unease that surrounded sites where black bodies were either on close display or in actual physical contact with white ones, moreover, is the set of CCRR interviews dealing with racial contacts on public transportation. As several of the respondents reveal, an accidental jostling together of bodies or a dispute over a seat on a streetcar could escalate rapidly from mild annoyance to open hostility. When the bodies involved belonged to a black man and a white woman, the situation was usually volatile. Less frequently the source of outward conflict but nonetheless common, the CCRR interviews further reveal, were advances made by white men toward black women on crowded streetcars and buses.[94] Farrell's vivid account of the troubled voyeuristic gaze of Studs Lonigan and his crew as they encountered black girls suggests that such behavior was not uncommon among working-class Irish youths. In one scene, for example, Studs is tormented by his desire for a "fleshy, light-brown Negress" and considers propositioning her on the street, but in the end he tells himself that "he was pretty lousy getting so het up over a dark-skinned wench."[95]

Such evidence illuminates the complex mixture of fear and desire in the antiblack violence practiced by youths around the Back of the Yards. That youths were coming in groups from neighborhoods several blocks away to engage in such activities, and that their hostility so often flared into overt aggression in situations involving a sexual dimension, indicates that collective racial violence could represent far more than a defensive, communal response to black invasion. As historians of working-class leisure in the late nineteenth- and early twentieth-century city have argued, young working-class ethnics forged their own "networks" and "youth cultures" in order to participate in the rapidly burgeoning world of commercialized leisure and to experiment with changing conceptions of gender, sexuality, and ethnicity.[96] However, they have been largely silent about the role of such working-class youth cultures in mediating the racial encounter during the years surrounding the First Great Migration to the urban North. This omission is partly due to a tendency to underestimate the extent of interracial mixing that transpired on the terrains of working-class youth subcultures. As David Nasaw has argued, the rise of commercial amusements in the first two decades of the twentieth-century was a process that involved both the exclusion of African Americans and their parodic representation on stage for white audiences. Yet in emphasizing the class, ethnic, and gender inclusiveness of this new "world of 'public' amusements," Nasaw tends to present a monolithic vision of commercial culture during this era—a view that many historians have since reproduced.[97] George Chauncey's work on gay male subcultures in New York City has demonstrated that it is more useful to think of the world of public leisure in this era as divided into a "series of distinct but overlapping subcultures centered in the poolrooms and saloons where many workingmen spent their time [and] in the cellar clubrooms and streets where gangs of boys and young men were a ubiquitous presence." More specifically, Chauncey has claimed that these subcultures came together to form a larger "bachelor subculture" between the mid-nineteenth and mid-twentieth centuries, a period when some 40 percent of all men over the age of fifteen were unmarried.[98]

In Chicago, one of the most dynamic of these subcultural spheres took shape around the black-and-tan cabarets, dance halls, and brothels that sprang up in and around the black Bright Lights district around 35th and State in the late 1910s and 1920s.[99] By the late 1910s, dance hall culture had moved to the center of the world of working-class urban youths, whose urge to mimic black dance forms and shake their bodies to the sounds of genuine black jazz made the dance hall a whipping boy for middle-class reformers.[100] Before long, this urge had created another kind of dance venue offering a more visceral means for its satisfaction—the black-and-tan. While the black-and-tans were relatively few in number and their clientele could be somewhat upscale, their presence added an element of mystery and transgression into the atmosphere of the dance halls in their vicinity. This helps to explain why an increasing number of white working-class youths in Chicago were by the late 1910s leaving their neighborhoods to go to the more exciting commercial dance halls in and around the Black Belt vice district. While these establishments were most often strictly segregated, their surrounding context held untold possibilities of racial interactions, including those offered by the rapidly expanding black sex industry.[101]

Thus, the black-and-tan controversy, which became a darling of yellow journalism in a number of northern cities in the late 1910s and early 1920s, drew upon racial anxieties related not only to the expansion of the black population, but also to growing concerns over the changing social habits of white working-class youths. After the advent of Prohibition with the passage of the Volstead Act in 1919, sites of interracial mixing began to proliferate in black vice districts—speakeasies for young adults and dance halls specializing in the illicit sale of liquor and black sexuality for the younger set. Chicago was considered by many at this time to be the city most prone to such interracial socializing.[102] Such circumstances fueled the vice investigations of the 1910s and 1920s, which scrutinized the link between vice and juvenile delinquency, revealing that gang youths were both regular patrons and business associates of speakeasies, dance halls, and cabarets.

Although many scholars have focused on the use of such nightspots by middle-class youths out "slumming," press coverage of the issue was often quite specific about the links between the young men of the Back of the Yards and the interracial cabarets just across Wentworth Avenue. Describing the clientele of the famed Pekin Cafe, for example, a *Daily News* columnist noted, "Seven young men—they looked like back o' the Yards—came with two women, one heavy footed, the other laughing hysterically."[103] The fictional Studs Lonigan and his gang, moreover, are no strangers to either the black "can house" (brothel) or the black-and-tan described here: "The dance floor at the Sunrise Cafe on Thirty-fifth Street quickly crowded, and it became like a revolving wheel of lust, the dancers swaying and turning, every corner and floor edge filled with dancers who move sidewise, inch by inch, socking their bellies together in quick rhythm and increasing frenzy. The fellows watched. Their faces went tight with hostility every time a white girl went by with a Negro. . . . Slug said what the hell he was going to dance too. He left, and soon he was socking with a black girl."[104]

For working-class Irish youths, trips to the Black Belt "can houses," cabarets, and dance halls often served functions similar to the ritualistic beatings of black youths in the parks, beaches, and streets. Farrell himself was well attuned to the feelings of aggression underlying such activities. The above scene at the Sunrise Cafe, for example, concludes with one of the characters storming out of the place in a state of homicidal rage: "As he walked towards the exit, he noticed the snottily suspicious glances he got from niggers, and Christ, how he'd have loved to have gotten a couple of them out on Fifty-eighth Street. . . . The doorman told him to come again. Yes, he thought, he'd like to come with a machine gun."[105] These feelings at times found expression in the darkest of male homosocial rituals—the "gang shag," or "line-up." While the frequency of sexual assaults on African American women by white gangs is difficult to determine because of the large number that went unreported and un-recorded, Thrasher observed that the "gang shag" was "in vogue among older adolescent gangs" in certain districts and that, according to social workers he interviewed, this activity often targeted black women.[106]

The Irish youths of the athletic clubs thus circulated in a milieu that resembled the youthful "male sporting culture" that Timothy Gilfoyle describes as characterizing New York's vice districts between the 1820s and the 1910s. As Gilfoyle argues, public tolerance for middle-class par-ticipation in this subculture, which "promoted male sexual aggressive-ness and promiscuity," began to wane with the municipal reform cru-sades of the early twentieth century.[107] However, the rise of public amusements during this same moment also had the effect of bringing more and more working-class young men on to the increasingly convergent terrains of vice and commercial leisure. Other factors, however, conspired to thrust the Irish athletic clubs and street gangs of neighborhoods like Canaryville and Bridgeport toward the center of this world. Notable in this sense was the marked tendency of Irish men to marry late—a trend that worked to produce an Irish bachelor subculture organized around all-male athletic clubs and gangs with members ranging from the early teens to the late twenties.[108]

Hence, when the new opportunities created by Prohibition arose in 1919, the syndicates had a standing army of recruits to run beer to Black Belt speakeasies and to fight in the Beer Wars waged for stakes in this lu-crative bootlegging business. Indeed, a young male subculture was al-ready firmly in place on the Irish South Side when African Americans be-gan settling en masse across the dead line during the First World War, and it would have continued to exist for years to come regardless of the racial demographics of the area. Yet the growing presence of African Americans and the parallel emergence of the Bright Lights vice and en-tertainment district just across Wentworth Avenue were nonetheless events that transformed the internal dynamics of this world. In addition to posing profound threats to the meaning of Irish identity in Chicago— a problem the whole community faced—the dangerous proximity of blacks reshaped how Irish American youths would handle issues associated with their masculinity and their sexuality. By 1919, these youths found themselves invested in the dark world across the dead line in ways their parents may not have fully understood.

As David Roediger has shown in his work on Irish immigrants in mid-nineteenth-century America, this was not the first time that Irish men had made this kind of a psychological investment. According to Roediger, the fear among Irish immigrants of being associated with the black race—of being nonwhite—combined with an attraction to the sensual and preindustrial aspects of black culture in these years to produce both demonstrations of collective racial violence and avid participation in racially transgressive forms of entertainment, such as minstrel shows.[109] The minstrel show, in fact, occupied an important place in Irish bachelor subculture into the late nineteenth century, when its parodic forms and sensibilities migrated into the newly emerging vaudeville theater routines.[110] Although both minstrelsy and vaudeville had moved to the margins of mass culture by the 1920s, the structures of feeling underlying their appeal—the fears and desires surrounding black bodies—continued to migrate into other forms of commercial leisure.[111] In its mixture of racial aggression and desire, the Irish male youth subculture that formed around the parks, poolrooms, taverns, dance halls, brothels, and black-and-tans in the 1910s and 1920s followed in this tradition. "Socking with a black girl" in a black-and-tan or paying a visit to a black "can house" were rituals that allowed the transgression of racial boundaries, thereby reifying them. The young participants in these activities were, for the most part, no longer recent immigrants in danger of being taken for blacks, and their relationship to a preindustrial past was indeed distant, but they exhibited a similar need to negotiate the nearness of African Americans within a subculture of their own making. Crossing the dead line was desirable to young men from the stockyards area—and from other neighborhoods whose racial boundaries were perceived to be in jeopardy—because it was an activity that offered possible solutions to this nearness.

Therefore, while the young Irish American men of the Back of the Yards area may have constituted the vanguard of what might be thought of as a community defense, they envisioned a lifestyle that opposed not only what the community around them was becoming but also what it had been. Such circumstances call for a reevaluation of the meaning of antiblack violence for communities of white ethnics in twentieth-century Chicago. Expressions of racial hatred, whether in words or deeds, remain as footprints on the terrain of racial and ethnic relations in urban

America. Yet in considering such prescient historical questions as how immigrants come to understand and act upon notions of whiteness, blackness, and ethnic and national identities, scholars have too often assumed that those leaving the footprints were cohesive groups, moving communally through space and time.[112] This is not to say that racial, ethnic, and national solidarities did not at times define and mobilize large segments of communities. However, even in moments of concerted local action, when expressions of community identity surfaced overtly in public life, the meaning of identities—racial and ethnic—could vary significantly along lines of age, generation, and gender.

It is therefore misleading to view youth groups as the appendages of the larger community and their actions as the reactionary reflexes of ethnic solidarity. The athletic clubs and youth gangs in the Back of the Yards and other such neighborhoods belonged to a subculture that had its own boundaries, its own rituals and codes of behavior, and its own history, even if this history shared much with that of the surrounding Irish community. The proliferation of well-organized athletic clubs and their increasing militancy in the years leading up to and following the 1919 riot had much to do with local politicians working to maintain their power in the face of disintegrating bases. "The ward 'heeler,'" as Thrasher colorfully put it, "often corrals a gang like a beeman does his swarm in the hive he has prepared for it . . . and every gang boy in the hive is expected to gather honey on election day."[113] However, what occurred within the world of youth gangs between election days had more to do with the experiences of young men on the job, in school, at home, and in the many different spaces where they spent their leisure time. Looking into the more hidden narratives of this world, one finds that youths had their own ways of handling the problems their families and the rest of the community faced.

LEARNING TO HATE IN POLISH PACKINGTOWN

When Frederic Thrasher asserted that "the gang touches in a vital way almost every problem in the life of the community," he probably had in mind the case of the Irish athletic clubs of the Back of the Yards. That this type of athletic club served as his model one can infer from the litany of problems he pinned on gangs in general: "Delinquencies among its members all the way from truancy to serious crimes, disturbances of the peace from street brawls to race riots, and close alliance with beer running, labor slugging, and corrupt politics—all are attributed to the gang."[114] This was not unlike the reformist line on street gangs in the 1910s and 1920s. Yet Thrasher's perspective was far broader than this, for his research showed that even if most youth gangs aspired to be athletic clubs, the actual number of such well-connected gangs (about one-quarter) was relatively small compared with his overall count. Rather than merely focusing on the role of gangs in popular reform issues of the day—vice, alcohol consumption, political corruption—Thrasher's view on the gang stemmed from its power to influence the behavior of so many of the urban youths he observed, and in so doing, to shape everyday urban life. Thrasher did not believe (as many have since) that gangs were the principal cause of delinquency. Like other adherents to the Chicago School of sociology, he highlighted the effects of social conditions in the "poverty belt": in particular, the state of "social disorganization" and the concomitant loss of moral guidelines resulting from the transition from old world villages to urban slums. "The gang," he wrote, "may be regarded as an interstitial element in the framework of society, and gangland as an interstitial region in the layout of the city." The term *interstitial,* which he described as "probably the most significant concept of the study," referred to an "ecological" condition; the interstitial regions existed between industry and the "better residential districts" and between "immigrant or racial colonies."[115] Yet gangland and the gang were interstitial in ways that were difficult for Thrasher to see in the mid-1920s.

As gangs continued to spring up in the Polish, Italian, Jewish, and other immigrant neighborhoods, which until the beginning of the war received a constant influx of new immigrants, such groups played increasingly important roles in the dramas of the immigrant experience: in private struggles within families, in the adaptation of young ethnics to American values and institutions, and in the politics and business of everyday life in the slums. Thrasher's data revealed that 1920s gangland consisted predominantly of second-generation ethnics whose foreign-born parents arrived between the 1880s and the 1910s. According to his survey, gangs of "foreign extraction" made up more than 87 percent of the total count, a figure that is not surprising considering that children of foreign extraction represented over 70 percent of the population of males from ten to twenty-four years of age in 1920. Also pointing to the generational specificity of gangland was Thrasher's discovery that "most" of the members of the 396 gangs he recorded as "dominantly or solidly of a single nationality group" were children of at least one foreign-born parent, with only "a few of the members of these gangs" being foreign-born themselves.[116]

The making of this interwar gang demographic involved a convergence of macroeconomic and political forces. The industrialization of northern U.S. cities and their emergence as nodes of global capitalism in the late nineteenth and early twentieth centuries required a gargantuan input of human labor. Pulled by rising wages and pushed by unfavorable social conditions in their homelands, waves of largely rural peoples from eastern and southern Europe and the southern United States poured into the congeries of tenement houses and shacks that sprang up around the mills and factories of industrial America. In Chicago, this flow of capital and people brought about nothing short of a sweeping transformation of the city's working class from the bottom up. By the 1920s an array of new immigrant groups filled the ranks of Chicago's unskilled and semiskilled workforce. A 1924 study of lower-echelon workers in twelve Chicago manufacturing firms showed that 60 percent of the "fully employed" were foreign-born, with Poles and Italians the most numerous—at 30 and 16 percent, respectively. Nearly 20 percent of the unskilled and semiskilled workers were African Americans, many of whom, considering the 148 percent increase in the African American population between 1910 and 1920, were likely to have been recent migrants from the South.[117] Thrasher's data on the racial and ethnic composition of gangs mirrors these shifts. Of the 529 gangs he recorded as being of a single race or nationality, Polish and Italian groups were the two most numerous, accounting for 16.8 and 11.3 percent of the total. Next were the Irish (8.5 percent), whom Thrasher referred to as the "aristocracy of gangland," followed closely by African Americans, who accounted for 7.2 percent of Chicago's gangs. Therefore, in relatively proportionate numbers, new immigrants joined the ranks of semiskilled industrial labor as their children entered the ranks of Chicago's street gangs and social-athletic clubs.[118]

Not surprisingly in this interwar era of "one hundred percent Americanism," social Darwinism, and immigrant restrictionism, the gang—because of its obvious connections to the saloon, the machine, and the mob—was a central target of those seeking to disparage or temper the influence of immigration on urban America. In the 1910s and 1920s, the interrelated problems of gangs and juvenile delinquency often occupied center stage in discourses about the state of the urban poor, a position these issues have held in underclass policy debates in many moments since. To an emerging settlement house movement, ethnic youths represented the face of things to come and thus the central objective of Americanization strategies.[119] To the alliances of reformers and government agencies that drove crusades against alcohol consumption, vice, organized

crime, and political corruption, gangs were vital components of such scur-
rilous rackets. To Chicago sociologists, youth gangs were all this and
more. As Robert Park wrote in 1925, "these gangs have exercised a considerably greater influence in forming the character of the boys who compose them than has the church, the school, or any other community
agency outside of the families and homes in which the members of the
gangs are reared."[120]

Indeed, street gangs were significant actors in the everyday life of neighboring communities of Poles and Irish in the Back of the Yards in the
1920s, but the roles of these gangs in public life differed according to di-
vergences between the situations of immigrant Poles and the more assimilated Irish. The Polish youths that filled the alleys, street corners, and
front stoops of Packingtown in the 1920s belonged to a seminal generation of Polish Americans: the sons and daughters of immigrants—many
of them American-born—who had entered the United States between the
1890s and the 1910s. The behavior of their gangs and more informal
cliques grew out of their specific experiences in the streets and in family
life, which departed from those of the more assimilated American-born
Irish youths belonging to the notorious athletic clubs of Hamburg and
Canaryville. Far from being agents of political and business influence,
many of the male Polish gangs of this moment were, for the most part,
defensive groups, engaged in negotiating a course between the more traditional values of family and parish and the lessons of Americanization
on the streets. However, although different in some respects, Polish youth
gangs nonetheless resembled the notorious athletic clubs in others. While
they often detested the Irish toughs who roughed them up and called them
"Polacks," Polish youths also saw reason to emulate the actions of the
"aristocracy of gangland." For the Poles and other new immigrant groups
around the Back of the Yards and elsewhere in the city, the Irish athletic
clubs of the 1910s and 1920s were, as James Barrett and David Roediger have argued, "Americanizers," and their hostile actions against both
blacks and new ethnic groups served as vivid demonstrations of the meaning and power of whiteness and Americanness on the city streets.[121]

While historians have acknowledged the importance of the numerous
processes embedded in the texture of everyday life that instructed immigrants on how to conduct themselves in American urban society, the
project of describing how and where Americanization transpired has only
recently begun to move beyond the workplace. As James Barrett reminds
us, writing such histories in the context of the early twentieth-century
American city requires taking into account how more assimilated Amer-

ican-born ethnics "explained American society" to recent immigrants.[122] While perhaps one of the most shadowy domains for historians to document, the informal spaces of everyday life—street corners, taverns, parks, social clubs, dance halls, movie theaters—constituted powerful sites for the transmission and negotiation of American values for first- and second-generation ethnics. Unlike settlement house activities, juvenile court proceedings, and public school classes, these spaces were where ethnics could lower their defenses to some extent. Whereas they often found the lessons passed on to them by settlement workers and teachers as moralizing, overly pedantic, and generally not useful for coping with the realities they faced on the streets, what they learned in their encounters with more assimilated youths in the flow of everyday life slipped rather unnoticeably into their consciousness—the raw material of common sense. Youth subcultures encompassing neighborhood areas and commercial leisure sites throughout the city thus played key roles in the story of Americanization for young ethnics. If, as Lizabeth Cohen demonstrates, young ethnics chose to "encounter mass culture" in the context of ethnic peer groups, the experiences of these groups on the terrain of commercial leisure frequently involved run-ins—peaceful or otherwise—with other ethnic peer groups. In the crucible of race and nationalism that was urban American society in the 1910s and 1920s, such intergroup encounters taught first- and second-generation ethnic youths powerful lessons about the meaning of their ethnic identities—where they stood in a complicated and continuously shifting racial-ethnic hierarchy that placed African Americans at the bottom, Mexicans just above them, and those who passed for native white Americans—for the most part, the American-born generations of Irish, Anglo, German, and Scandinavian descent—at the top.

Perhaps most important, racializing anti-immigrant feelings transmitted from old to new ethnic groups strongly contributed to the spatial arrangement of race and ethnicity within the working-class districts of Chicago. Of course, forces of ethnocultural cohesion—linguistic, religious, dietary affinities—also accounted for the ethnic enclaves that developed in the low-income neighborhoods of the city, which functioned as ports of entry for immigrants and support systems for newcomers facing language barriers and a host of other difficulties. However, a climate of anti-immigrant hostility, directed principally at the ethnic groups most highly represented in the recent migration wave from eastern and southern Europe, also played an important role in the segregation of new ethnic groups. As Stanley Lieberson's demographic research on Chicago and several other American cities has shown, these new immigrant groups were also highly segregated by 1920.[123] Hence, territorial issues were indeed important determinants of gang conflicts among white ethnics, but because of the understood connection between neighborhood space and ethnic identity, territorial issues were simultaneously ethnic and racial ones. Moreover, indexes of segregation reveal only one dimension of the picture. A key manifestation of this patterning of race and ethnicity in the 1910s and 1920s was the frequent proximity of new immigrant enclaves to less desirable industrial zones and, perhaps most important, to black neighborhoods.

By the 1920s, for example, a vast majority of Chicago's immigrant and second-generation Polish youths came of age in areas of concentrated Polish settlement within such zones—namely, in Packingtown and the neighborhoods in the shadows of the steel mills of South Chicago, an area in the far southeast part of the city.[124] The conditions of social maturation in such neighborhoods gave rise to some fundamental conflicts in the lives of these second-generation youths, which served to further solidify the borders around the ethnic youth subcultures developing in interwar Chicago. Ethnic and racial attitudes were at the core of these contradictions, and the collective struggle to resolve them drove the formation and actions of youth gangs. While one might say the same about the Irish athletic clubs, a markedly different set of problems was in operation in the case of the Polish gangs in their midst. Irish youths may have loathed the idea of blacks moving into their area and taking jobs where their fathers had worked for years—events that in their minds signaled the decline of the community and a certain degradation of their status—but the proximity of African Americans did not shake their sense of group identity the way it did for the children of Polish immigrants, who also had challenges to their Americanness to contend with. Indeed, if wartime nationalism, prohibitionism, the rise of the Ku Klux Klan, and the social Darwinist–infused discourses regarding immigrant restrictionism posed threats to the status of the much more assimilated English-speaking Irish, the stakes were all the higher for the thick-accented "greenhorn" Poles in the 1910s and 1920s. And while the Irish—through the Catholic Church, labor unions, the Democratic Party, and the urban machine— did at times help to assimilate Poles and other immigrant groups, what happened out on the streets was often another matter altogether.

Here, in neighborhoods like Packingtown, perhaps the most significant challenge to Poles' self-image was the street-level hostility coming from their Irish neighbors. One of the most thoroughly explored aspects of James T. Farrell's upbringing in working-class Irish Chicago in his Studs Lonigan trilogy is the incessant enmity between many Irish youths and the eastern European groups moving into their neighborhoods. How all of these groups—Hungarians (referred to as "Hunkies"), Poles, and Jews, among others—lined up in racial contradistinction to the Irish can be glimpsed in an exchange between the now-adult Studs and his wife-to-be, Catherine, in the third book of Farrell's trilogy, *Judgment Day:*

> "We won't be able to come swimming here, though, this summer," he said, pointing at the low gray pavilion of rough-edged stone which housed the Jackson Park beach. "It's become the hunkies' community center here now. I came here one day last summer, and I tell you I didn't think there were as many hunkies and polacks in the world as I saw here."
>
> "Yes, isn't it too bad? And there was trouble here last summer with niggers trying to go swimming along here. Ugh. Think of it, going with niggers," she said shuddering.
>
> "Seventy-third-Street beach is much better, but every year you see more noisy Jews there. Pretty soon there won't be a beach in Chicago left for a white man."[125]

Such attitudes operated on the streets to infuse racial uncertainties into neighborhoods where English was a second language. That many of these lower-income communities found themselves adjacent to expanding African American neighborhoods only heightened their sense of racial insecurity—their feeling of falling somewhere between white and black. As Farrell's account suggests, the Polish were not alone in their situation. Nor were Irish youth gangs the only ones to impose such conditions on new ethnics settling in their neighborhoods. Italians in Chicago faced a similar state of affairs in the 1910s and 1920s, when observers of two Italian neighborhoods in different parts of the city noted the hostile treatment directed at them by young Swedes. Examining intergroup relations in the North Side "Little Hell" community, Harry Zorbaugh remarked that "gang fights on playground and street" between blacks and Sicilians "re-enacted scenes of a generation ago when the Sicilian was forcing out the Swede," a conclusion no doubt stemming from so many of his informants mentioning problems with Italians in the same breath that they described the migration of blacks into their community.[126] As one resident explained, "The coming of the Italians has, of course, caused the Swedish and the Irish to move north. . . . Now the Negroes are pushing in among the Italians."[127] Circumstances like these also prevailed in another Italian neighborhood in the Calumet district at the far end of southeast Chicago, where, one sociology student observed,

"The nationality problem of the gangs in the district is one of nationality prejudice. The Italian boys in the area are resentful towards the Swedes and vice versa. . . . The Swedes regard the 'wops' as they call them, as sneaky and vicious, and they are continually fighting with one another."[128] Owing to financial exigencies associated with their relatively tenuous position in the labor market, Italians all over the city often found themselves living in low-rent neighborhoods, which, not surprisingly, were very frequently adjacent to African American and Mexican areas. This was also especially the case for Mexicans, who, as a result, came to occupy a position in the labor and housing markets below the lowest of European Americans. A situation that arose between Italians and Mexicans at Hull House on the Near West Side indicates how high the stakes of residential proximity to blacks had become by the early 1920s. Recounting the attempts by Italians in the neighborhood to have Mexicans barred from activities at the settlement house, Jane Addams claimed that the problem stemmed from the fact that the Mexicans "mingled freely with the negroes" and "were people of color."[129]

It was in such ways that race and Americanness came to be almost inseparable notions in the minds of immigrants and their American-born children in this moment. What Thrasher could not see in an era long before scholars began to historicize the instability of the racial category of whiteness was that the primary ethnic groups of gangland were also racially interstitial and that so many of their "territorial" conflicts were in many ways struggles to negotiate and define their place within the racial hierarchy. It did not occur to the Chicago School that many of the gang conflicts they observed were actually the everyday vicissitudes of a process of Americanization at the grass roots.[130] In the case of Packingtown, there is no more compelling example of this than the story of a Polish gang called the Murderers, which patrolled an area to the south of the stockyards and to the west of the district inhabited by the Ragen's Colts and several other Irish athletic clubs. University of Chicago settlement workers claimed that this gang of around thirty Polish young men was "especially active" in the race riots of 1919. Shortly after this, the gang attempted to publicize its reputation by posting placards all over the neighborhood that read, "The Murderers, 10,000 Strong, 48th & Ada."[131] Reports that its members "used to 'get' the 'niggers' as they came from the stockyards at Forty-seventh and Racine" and boasted of killing blacks during the riots reveal that the youths in this gang, much like their Irish peers, perceived their reputation as hinging on their ability to do violence to blacks who crossed into their territory.[132] However, this clear imitation of the Irish athletic clubs does not mean that such gangs felt any kind of solidarity with Irish youths in the district, nor does it mean that the actions against blacks held quite the same meaning for Polish youths. In fact, the primary rival of the Murderers was a nearby Irish gang named the Aberdeens, whose members, according to one of the Murderers, "was always punching our kids." A similar rivalry also existed between another Polish gang of this vicinity, the Wigwams, and the Ragen's Colts, who on more than one occasion destroyed the Wigwams' clubhouse at 51st and Racine, in the midst of a predominantly Polish block just north of Sherman Park. Apparently, if the Wigwams were unavailable, any Polish gang would serve as an adequate target for the Colts, who, according to Polish residents in the area, would cruise the Polish neighborhood around the park looking for fights.[133]

Polish youths in the Back of the Yards thus perceived the Irish to be both standard-bearers of Americanization and antagonists to their drive to assimilate, which on a very basic level had a lot to do with immunity from street-level harassment. This view was not entirely a youth phenomenon but rather something the whole Polish community in Chicago understood. It surfaced quite visibly during the 1919 race riot, when Polish-language newspapers accused the Irish of trying to blame the riots on the Polish community, referring to them as the "real enemies."[134] While, as evidenced by the antiblack actions of the Murderers and the Wigwams, such sensibilities hardly brought about more peaceable relations between Poles and blacks after the riot, this increasing Polish antagonism toward blacks hardly paved the way for a rapprochement between the Poles and the Irish in the Back of the Yards area. In March 1922, for example, a Polish newspaper editorial denouncing the establishment of St. Patrick's Day as a city holiday characterized the nativist voice of the Irish in city hall as such: "Away with foreigners! We, are the only one-hundred-percent Americans, who have the right to enjoy special privileges!"[135] These were sentiments that, in the minds of Polish youths, explained their harassment by Irish gangs. While it is true that all gangs in the city were susceptible to attacks, only in the cases of certain gangs did these attacks have racial implications. For the Polish community of the Back of the Yards, it was most expedient to attribute what was a much larger problem to the actions of the Irish, from city hall to the athletic club. As in matters of city government, the Irish hold on political power also shaped the affairs of gangland. For example, in explaining the vulnerability of the Wigwams to raids by the Ragen's Colts, a University of Chicago settlement worker mentioned that this gang "had no political backing and had trouble in paying their rent."[136]

However, as in the case of the Irish, it is a mistake to assume that common perceptions of threats to the community necessarily led to a communal response. For a community dominated by people of foreign extraction, as the Polish community of Packingtown was, the momentous events of 1919 constituted a vivid demonstration of what it meant to be racially stigmatized. While there is evidence that some Polish leaders advised abstention from antiblack actions during the riot, and that some Poles in the labor movement may have even countered such activities by celebrating interracial worker solidarity, the thirty or so youths in the Murderers reveal that a part of the community may have been more inclined to choose racial violence as a strategy of empowerment. Moreover, that the young men of this gang did not represent an extremist or fringe element is suggested by evidence from another story that began to develop around the time of the riot—the tense relationship between Poles and Mexican newcomers to the Back of the Yards. Describing relations between these groups in the mid-1920s, a student of Ernest Burgess stated: "Without any reason other than that he was Mexican, the Polish young men when they saw a Mexican on the street would pounce upon him and beat him up." These actions, the student concluded from her interviews with residents of the area around Ashland and 45th, grew out of a general feeling among Poles of superiority "to the dark-skinned Mexicans who have had to live in very poorly furnished one-room shacks and therefore have standards of living which appear lower to the Poles than their own." The primary focus of this researcher's study, however, is the interactions of youths in the streets, schools, parks, and movie theaters, thus presenting a conflict resembling the pattern of street-level racial hostility established by the Irish athletic clubs. Her scattered evidence of the feelings of older residents reflected a somewhat different situation. Commenting on Polish attitudes toward Mexicans, for example, a University of Chicago settlement caseworker reported: "Some of the older Polish men thought it was wrong to beat the Mexicans and favored allowing them the rights of the street, but these wiser heads were unable to do anything." Kind words also came from an older Polish woman, the leader of a group of mothers that met at the settlement, who told the interviewer that she liked Mexicans, calling them "nice housekeepers and good neighbors."[137]

Such responses contrasted with the tendency of Polish youths to stone

Mexicans and chase them out of local parks. Indeed, as Gabriela Arredondo's research on Polish-Mexican tensions in interwar Chicago has demonstrated, many conflicts between Polish and Mexican young men grew out of "intergroup heterosocial interactions" in youth leisure spaces—pool halls, dance halls, and taverns. Because of the scarcity of Mexican young women in such spaces, single Mexican men were prone to pursuing relations with Polish women, a situation that both threatened the masculinity of Polish men and led to the spread of gossip surrounding the idea that Polish girls were "wild."[138] Such predicaments shaped the development of Polish youth gangs bent on policing the sexual boundaries of the community and reaffirming their manliness through rituals of violence directed at Mexicans. This was not just the case around the Back of the Yards. According to residents of the Polish "Bush" community, gangs in this neighborhood as well "caused the Latins much trouble" around this same time, breaking up picnics, sending menacing letters to Mexican families, and attacking Mexican youths. Explaining such actions, one resident later recalled, "the animosity against the Mexicans started in the Bush area, when single Mexican men dated the Polish girls."[139]

Much like the pattern of Irish violence against blacks in this neighborhood, racial attacks by Polish youths against both blacks and Mexicans took shape within a youth gang subculture that formed at the racial boundaries of the community and along a generational fault line within it. However, there were vital differences between Irish and Polish gang subcultures. The Irish faced little danger of falling from the ranks of whiteness, even if they were touched by feelings of degradation stemming from their increasing inability to distinguish themselves from the foreigners taking over their community. For the second-generation Polish youths of Packingtown, many of whose parents clung to the Polish language and the lifeways of Polonia, the generational fault line within their community was much wider, a situation that raised the stakes of maintaining the boundaries between the Poles and neighboring nonwhite groups. Unlike the Irish, the Poles lived amid ethnic and racial uncertainty, a condition captured colorfully by a young Mexican living in the Back of the Yards in this period, who stated quite bluntly: "I detest the Poles . . . they know nothing—nada, nada, nada. . . . The Poles always pretend they are Americans; they are ashamed to say that they are Poles. They say they are Germans or Americans."[140]

2

Between School and Work
in the Interwar Years

They came to a concession where three Negroes were perched
in cages; for ten cents anyone could hurl a baseball at them. If
the ball struck the proper mark the Negro was automatically
dumped into a tub of water beneath the perch.

Nelson Algren

Of course, there is always the chance of getting one to twenty
years, but what the hell, a guy's got to get dough somehow.

Blake, a South Chicago gang member

THE NEW GENERATION, COMMERCIAL LEISURE, AND RACE LEARNING

In 1935, a youth worker assigned to a gang of teens in a Polish immigrant neighborhood around South Chicago's hulking steel mills overheard
the following complaints and found them worth recording: "I've got to
get some money somehow; now I ain't in school and ain't working, it
ain't like it was when I was in school. Then I had lunch money to use for
shows and things like that, but now I ain't got nothing, and I need a new
pair of white shoes; a guy's got to get new clothes now and then! Somehow I gotta raise three bucks; that's what a new pair of white shoes cost.
I don't want to ask my mother, 'cause now's a bad time."[1] While perhaps a somewhat strange concern in the midst of the Great Depression,
when wage reductions and production cutbacks left blue-collar Chicagoans with shallow pockets, a number of youth worker reports like this
one reveal that the severe economic circumstances of the 1930s altered
but hardly transformed patterns of daily life in working-class Chicago.
This was a period that shook the very foundations of the social order,

giving rise to an industrial labor movement that struggled triumphantly to secure new rights for workers and a government that redefined the role of the state in ensuring the welfare of the destitute, disabled, and otherwise disadvantaged. Yet for this youth, a nineteen-year-old member of a predominantly Polish gang called the Houston Herrings, all of this was somewhat inconsequential next to a new pair of white shoes to show off in the dance halls.

The precarious position between school and work expressed by this youth was symptomatic of a broader rupture in the capitalist social order—a crisis that revealed itself most clearly in the failed capacity of the Fordist system to guide the next generation of working-class citizens into the kinds of "productive" roles their parents filled. By the 1920s, even before the economic downturn of the 1930s, this malady was already becoming apparent on the terrain of working-class youth subcultures. Some of its more obvious manifestations were high youth unemployment figures, high truancy rates, and staggering numbers of felony convictions in the working-class districts. Out of work, out of school, and perhaps just out of the correctional system: such were the circumstances in which children of immigrant laborers often found themselves in the interwar years. If the subcultures they formed in the face of such predicaments bore a close relationship to experiences they shared at work and at school, working-class youth subcultures and the youth groups operating within them cohered most recognizably in the spatiotemporal juncture between these spheres. For second-generation ethnic youths in particular, the core of Chicago's younger generation and of its emerging class of unskilled wage laborers in the interwar period, youth subcultures articulated feelings of alienation from school and a sense of dissatisfaction with the tedious, low-paying jobs that appeared to offer the only viable alternative to dependence on parents. Institutional and grassroots forms of ethnic discrimination, as will be explored further, figured prominently in the development of such sentiments. At work, this meant that teenage Poles, Italians, Mexicans, and other new ethnics would find it more difficult to advance into higher-paid, skilled positions. At school, cultural and linguistic differences would retard their progress and reaffirm their suspicions that high school was little more than a needless delay to their entrance into the labor force.

But while structural conditions related to political economy and the deficiencies of the educational system could be somewhat immovable parameters that determined the options youths had and the choices they made, this Polish gang youth's feelings about a new pair of white shoes, including his trepidation about asking his mother for a handout, suggest there is more to understanding the world of adolescent youth gangs in the 1920s and 1930s. This young man's consumerist dilemma was the sort that many youths of the time put forward as a reason for leaving school and taking a regular job, and one cited by social workers engaged with the problem of juvenile delinquency—no doubt influenced by the cinematic images of the extravagant Capone-like gangster filling the giant screen around this time—to account for elevated crime rates. Another common factor behind decisions about school and work, however, involved quite a different set of feelings. Time and time again teenagers told those willing to listen that they would leave school as soon as legally possible in order to contribute their share to the family income. For many of them, enjoying the world of commercial recreation and lending some support to the family were integral parts of a single but multifaceted issue: the need to attain a status of manhood that hinged on their wage-earning ability.

Yet these drives were, in reality, often contradictory, for they tended to pit the demands and values of families against the very different desires and needs of individual youths passing through a life stage marked by uncertainty and experimentation. As the cases of the Irish athletic clubs and Polish gangs examined in chapter 1 indicate, working-class young men in interwar Chicago engaged in semiautonomous youth subcultures that formed in a complicated tension with their surrounding parent cultures. If some of the activities of these subcultures reaffirmed the values of the larger communities, others needed to be kept at some distance from the eyes of parents and other sources of community authority. Whereas Polish and other new ethnic youths appeared to lag behind the Irish in creating their own well-defined subcultural spaces at the time of the 1919 race riot, the encounter of immigrant and second-generation youths with the world of urban commercial leisure helped close the gap between them and the more Americanized Irish as the interwar years wore on. A great deal of the allure of this world for these adolescents and young men involved its production of images, languages, and narratives that helped them make sense of the desires, fears, and anxieties surrounding sexuality and gender in the transitional moment between childhood and adulthood. Yet in interwar Chicago, where the children of new immigrants constituted such a large portion of this generation, this world also offered solutions to problems involving ethnic and racial self-understandings—solutions often standing in stark contrast to those being put forward by parents and ethnoreligious voices of authority.

Such conflicts made leisure in interwar Chicago a terrain of struggle within the families and communities of second-generation ethnics. The elusive pair of white shoes, for example, was a prop from the dance hall scene—a milieu that garnered not only the disapproval of middle-class reformers but also the disdain of immigrant parents and religious leaders, all of whom mobilized to keep the young of their communities out of the large downtown venues by furnishing neighborhood dance events held under the auspices of churches, settlement houses, and ethnic associations. Moreover, even if a mother did not oppose involvement in this world on moral grounds, there was always the matter of money. For working-class young men coming of age in interwar Chicago, participation in gangs and other peer groups reflected the widely shared need to navigate a course through such predicaments.

• • •

Free of some of the burdens of labor that kept their parents in the home and at work, and less restrained by the bonds of parental supervision that sought to restrict the daughters of immigrants to the domestic sphere, the sons of immigrant laborers eagerly formed gangs and clubs to participate in working-class youth subcultures that pervaded neighborhood and commercial spaces. Although young women felt similar urges for autonomy and experimentation, the patriarchal family structure and the will of parents to thwart those urges in their daughters kept this a predominantly male world in the 1920s and 1930s. Parents managed this, in part, by demanding a high percentage (if not all) of the wages earned by working daughters. In her work on the spending habits of young men and women in the interwar city, Susan Porter Benson finds that working-class daughters were more generally prone to relinquishing their wages "all to mother" in this period, a situation that defined them as dependents.[2] That Frederic Thrasher's exhaustively researched study contains not a single mention of female gangs suggests that such practices did indeed yield strong results.[3]

For young men, on the other hand, the encounter with commercial culture constituted a raison d'être for youth gangs in the working-class neighborhoods of interwar Chicago.[4] Typical, for example, was the comment made by an observer of youths in a Polish enclave of Chicago in the late 1920s: "The first ventures of the individual into the commercialized resorts are usually in company with members of his gang who go off some evening hour for foray and adventure."[5] This is not to say that the peer groups of more middle-class suburban settings did not serve similar purposes. In her work on middle-class youth networks of the 1920s, Paula Fass argues that "the rhythm of commercialism and the constant attention to nuances of style and repeated replacement were a necessary part of peer integration and cohesion." Fraternities and other social clubs, she finds, became forums for experimentation with new personal styles and standards of social and sexual behavior—an expression of generational conflict comparable to that of working-class peer groups. But Fass also states that bourgeois peer networks in the 1920s "rang with the cadences of corporate enterprise" and ultimately tended to reproduce the values of the middle-class adult world.[6] In essence, the organizations of middle-class youth culture mainly functioned within a somewhat bounded educational sphere, in a secure spatiotemporal domain defined as a training ground for adult life. This was a dramatic departure from working-class ethnic gangs, which, as we will explore further, quite often fashioned an oppositional posture to school as well as work. This distinction between middle-class and working-class youth groups, moreover, had a spatial dimension as well. Working-class youth gangs—defined in the most historically flexible terms as formal or casual organizations of teenage boys and young men—tended to occupy a more central position in public life, often locating their headquarters on high-profile street corners and in storefronts on heavily trafficked blocks. Indeed, the visibility of these youth gangs was essential to the roles they would play in community politics and in the ethnic identification of neighborhood space. Unlike the peer groups of middle-class society, working-class gangs came into some very real conflicts with their own communities, the state, and the communities of neighboring groups.

While the black gang tradition was much less established in the interwar years, black youth groups as well began to crystallize around such shared experiences in the interwar period. If institutional education seemed futile for white ethnics, a good many of whom attended smaller parochial schools, it was an even more frustrating experience for blacks, who were often packed into overcrowded classes conducted by white teachers and administrators infected by a belief in the racial inferiority of their students. Not surprisingly, such conditions led to far higher grade retardation rates among African Americans, a state of affairs that damaged self-esteem and doomed many black youths to academic failure.[7] Moreover, in addition to banding together for the purpose of defending themselves and their neighbors from the harassment of white gangs, African American youths resembled their adversaries in their propensity to organize around commercial leisure pursuits. The dance hall craze of the 1920s and 1930s, for example, spread throughout working-class communities on both sides of the color line. In Bronzeville, a neighborhood in the heart of Chicago's Black Belt, sociologists St. Clair Drake and Horace Cayton found that middle-class youths formed "social clubs" to "meet their recreational needs," which largely consisted of hosting dances, while lower-class teens preferred to "cut rugs in the 'jive-joints,' or when they had some spending money, to 'tog down' and go to the cheaper dance halls."[8]

Yet while dance halls, cabarets, brothels, pool halls, and movie theaters were popular destinations for both white and black gangs in the 1920s and 1930s, African American youths possessed quite a different relationship to the world of commercial leisure and to mass culture in general. First, spectatorial leisure forms of this period—especially cinema— generally excluded black characters, except in degrading, sinister, and comical roles. Blacks would thus take from their viewings very different impressions than would the white ethnics who were the target audience of such cultural production. Second, except for some cabarets, dance halls, and brothels, whose inclusion of black women and men (as musicians and sometimes as patrons) was part of their attraction, commercial leisure venues in this period were almost always racially segregated.[9] This does not mean, however, that interracial contacts did not play a central part in the development of youth groups on both sides of the color line. As we saw in chapter 1, a great deal of leisure activity for the younger set took place within "interzones" located inside the borders of black neighborhoods. Largely created by a vigorous but racially selective campaign of vice enforcement in the 1910s, these interracial vice districts sprang up in the interstitial areas of the city, precisely where, as Thrasher discovered, gangs were most commonly found. Gang worker reports of the 1930s noted that venues in such areas were regular destinations for white street gangs. Yet the presence of black male peer groups in these districts is harder to ascertain. Although we know that young African American men worked within the formal and informal economies of Black Belt nightlife and that some black men were counted as patrons of cabarets, brothels, and speakeasies that served both races, most black youth groups socialized apart from this scene.[10]

One key reason for this practice was financial. Relegated to the lowest positions in the labor market of interwar Chicago, African Americans were generally less able to afford the costs of Chicago nightlife. This was the period of the "rent party," when private homes and tenement apartments became the sites for hot jazz, dancing, and partying into the morning hours, with small contributions made by guests going toward next month's rent. That poolrooms served as the regular hangouts for many black youths probably had something to do with their lack of admission fees. But if difficult economic conditions made the development of these alternative leisure spaces practical, the noxious influence of white racism on the streets made them preferable. It is not hard to imagine that young black men would have been averse to sharing the dance floor with the likes of the Ragen's Colts, and establishments that served such a clientele would have done their best to discourage groups of young black men from entering, for fear of a brawl. Thus, while black youth subcultures adopted and created their own versions of the dress styles, dances, and sounds of popular culture, they did so largely in contexts of their own making. Separation from their parents and adult society in general was of course on their minds, but the impulse behind this drive for autonomy had a somewhat different meaning in black communities pushed together by forms of racism that were much more pervasive and potent than those faced by immigrants and their children. While an increasing number of black youths in interwar Chicago were the children of rural southern migrants, who faced challenges in their adaptation to urban society not unlike those of second-generation Europeans and Mexicans, the unique quality of their racial identity made their encounters with both mass culture and their parent culture dramatically different from those of white ethnic youths.[11] The timing of the black migration to Chicago, moreover, meant that the kinds of demographic pressures that made new ethnic youth subcultures so viable in the interwar era would not have a substantial impact upon black communities until the 1940s. For these reasons, the story of black gang formation is best dealt with on its own terms, and in relation to the forms of racism that shaped the conditions of youth for African Americans. This will be taken up at length in chapter 3.

For the American-born children of immigrants from southern and central Europe, however, a very different set of demographic circumstances made the late 1920s and 1930s a golden age for street-corner gangs. Researchers on immigration and generational dynamics in the first half of the twentieth century have described the years between 1910 and 1925 as a second-generation "echo boom" of the fifteen years of mass immigration between 1900 and 1915.[12] By the early 1930s, the manifestations of such conditions were hard to overlook. In 1935, a University of Chicago sociology student ventured into the tenement district of the Lower North Side to examine the behavior of "boys" living there. Touring the vibrant streets of the Italian "Little Sicily" neighborhood (otherwise known as "Little Hell"), this student came across numerous packs of young men huddled together on street corners or crowded into storefront clubhouses. According to this researcher, twenty "clubs," with a combined membership of 966, had hangouts within an area just six by nine blocks, and this count included only the ones considered as "the more important organized groups in the neighborhood."[13] A few of these were social groups of older men, but the overall club scene belonged mostly to younger men in their late teens and early twenties. The center of their world was Seward Park, a small patch of green in the midst of crowded city streets. It was here that the activities of these organizations became most visible: the dice throwing, the baseball games, and the dances and parties, which, according to some witnesses, quite often turned into brawls. But if clubs in this neighborhood were not hard to miss, they were, according to this observer, not at all easy to categorize: "Some of them are organized purely for political purposes, others for sports and athletics entirely. Still others are organized, as one member puts it, 'So we can stick together and so we can have some place to spend our night.' It is hard to classify these groups because even the clubs organized for sports alone take an active interest in politics whenever election time approaches."[14]

Their resistance to classification notwithstanding, youth gangs were prominent features of the landscape of Chicago street life in the interwar years, filling the streets and parks of nearly every working-class neighborhood. The dense concentration of gangs witnessed on the Lower North Side was common to nearly all of Chicago's working-class districts. Thrasher's "empire of gangland," which included 1,313 gangs and an estimated twenty-five thousand members—figures he called "conservative"—did not include even close to the entire geographic area of the city.[15] The poorest immigrant areas contributed more than their share, and it was in this period that many of these districts took on ignominious reputations for the activities of local gangs, particularly certain high-profile syndicate-style outfits. One community worker in the Italian section of the ward known as the "Bloody Nineteenth" on the Near West Side, for example, found that residents complained of the "unfavorable publicity brought to their area through such organizations as the infamous '42' gang and similar delinquent groups."[16] According to Anthony Sorrentino, a resident and activist in this particular neighborhood, "boys' gangs" in this area numbered approximately seventy-five.[17] However, this count did not include the many Jewish gangs that roamed Maxwell Street and the blocks just southeast of Little Italy, the existence of which helps to explain why this subsection of the Near West Side had come to be known as "Jew Town." In addition, historian Dominic Pacyga's research on Polish Chicago reveals that Poles were no less wary of perceptions of their neighborhoods as gang-ridden. "Observers," he finds, "identified Polish neighborhoods with gang activities."[18] African American gangs, for their part, had nowhere near the kind of symbolic importance they would take on in the postwar era, but by the 1930s they had become well-recognized components of the burgeoning Black Belt nightlife. Some gangs in these environs catered to the white folks who came to revel in the cabarets, peddling dope and offering to escort the more timorous to alley hot spots. Outside of the Black Belt, however, African American gangs took on a more defensive posture. On the Near Northwest Side, for instance, Thrasher noted the presence of large groups of black youths, "marooned among hostile gangs of whites," who referred to them collectively as the "Coons from Lake Street."[19]

The emergence of these vibrant interwar youth subcultures revealed a growing generation gap associated with the increasingly powerful flow of American values into the spheres of all working-class ethnic youths— a phenomenon that precipitated generational conflicts over the terms and stakes of education, work, and leisure. New modes of consumption bore a great deal of the responsibility for these generational cleavages. The native-born generations succeeding the massive waves of new immigrants arriving in the early twentieth century came of age during the momentous growth of the culture industries in the 1920s and 1930s, which, by distributing cheap forms of commercial entertainment throughout working-class neighborhoods, brought about dramatic shifts in patterns of leisure. By 1929, Chicago possessed enough theater seats for one-half of the population to attend a movie in the course of a day, and members of the city's laboring class were among the most avid moviegoers. Studies conducted at the end of the decade revealed that wage-earning families spent a greater percentage of their income on movies than did salaried clerks and professionals.[20]

Observations of the dance hall scene told a similar story. While commercial dance halls had become popular destinations by the 1910s, the dance hall scene exploded in the 1920s, with a range of different venues catering to the varying demands of working-class youths—from the risqué black-and-tans of the Stroll neighborhood, to the opulent ballrooms located downtown and around the White City amusement area at 63rd and Cottage Grove, to the North and West Side dance halls that employed black musicians but remained strictly white otherwise, to the smaller taxi-dance halls scattered throughout the city that offered female dance partners on a pay-as-you-dance basis. And, unlike movie theaters, whose audiences could cut across a broad age range, the younger set clearly dominated the dance hall world. Describing the scene at a popular Chicago ballroom in 1926, a reporter for *Variety* claimed there was "not a mature person to be found on the . . . dance floor."[21]

One of the most universally discussed topics among sociologists and youth workers was what lay behind the pressing urge of teenagers and young adults to participate in the dance hall scene. Among the various conclusions they drew, three ideas seemed to predominate regardless of the youths' ethnic background: first, this drive was a primary reason for the formation of gangs and other peer groups; second, the participation of young working-class ethnics in gangs and in commercial leisure was enmeshed in broader processes of Americanization; and third, such activities tended to create a kind of generational divide that sharply contrasted the "old world" ways of immigrant parents with the modern ones of their American-born (or American-raised) children. Examples of this last idea abounded in the late 1920s and early 1930s. Observing the dance hall milieu of a working-class Polish neighborhood on the Northwest Side, for example, a University of Chicago graduate student in sociology wrote: "Which is the culture of these people, that of black bread [and] goat's cheese, or white bread and packer's sausage? Is it of high leather boots or of low shoes and spats? Novels of Polish life or the Hearst dailies? Is it of the Polish Hop or of the Charleston? With their many marks of modernity, how do the young people bear the deeper brands of their parents' ancestry? In this inner life of the dancers' community all of these conflicts lie below the surface of their little urbanites."[22]

Trying to make sense of his experiences with youths living in the Near West Side Italian community, a settlement worker at the Garibaldi Institute drew some strikingly similar conclusions: "Since they have not assimilated American customs and institutions, these parents are unable to cope with the new problems of the modern world. A resulting conflict occurs between them and their children. These young folks—the second generation—gain their knowledge and sophistication in the American way of life. This sets up two worlds—that of the parents and that of the adolescent."[23]

Finally, way down near the southern border of the city, in the Mexican community of South Chicago, yet another sociology student described the situation of youths in analogous terms, although, because of the community's recent development, its first Chicago-born generation was just reaching adolescence in the mid-1930s. "It is in this small group, destined to increase rapidly in the next few years," he claimed, "that a sharp conflict is beginning to occur with the colony and the traditions and values which the Mexican-born generation seeks to uphold." "It is in the children who belong to this category," he further elaborated, "that there is a distaste for things Mexican, as shown by dislike of attending colony social affairs, a resentment toward their parents for their inability to use English fluently, and other small things which symbolize to them the Mexican background from which they strive to detach themselves."[24]

While such views were fashionable among sociologists in the interwar years, owing to the tremendous influence of William I. Thomas and Florence Znaniecki's "social disorganization" theory, which described how the disintegration of traditional forms of family and community authority affected Polish communities in urban America, they also reflected the increasing prevalence of everyday tug-of-wars between immigrants and their children over access to the world of commercial amusements.[25] Beginning in the early 1920s, with the explosion of Jazz Age nightlife in the Black Belt and downtown areas of Chicago, the dance hall scene, in particular, became a central site of such dramas. For many youths, however, the first phase of their struggle to dance in the latest ways took place not in the commercial ballrooms and cabarets downtown, but at dance events held in their own neighborhoods—in church or settlement house facilities or in halls rented out by local clubs and other ethnic associations. Limited by parental restrictions, minimal spending money, and fears of venturing into unfamiliar parts of the city, young ethnics took their own steps to join the scene, forming social and athletic clubs in order to hold their own dances. Faced with the threat of affairs that might lack the proper supervision, parents and settlement workers mobilized to provide their own adequately chaperoned alternatives. In the Polish Northwest Side neighborhood referred to earlier, for example, the local settlement house sponsored dances every Friday night, a hard-won concession, since Friday night was, according to youths in the neighborhood, "a church night," or at least a night during which "you are sort of supposed to stay at home with your family and be quiet." But according to one observer of these affairs, things often got out of hand when youths resisted the settlement's "Puritan-American standards," and, on at least one occasion, chaperones ended up sending the crowd home well before the last dance.[26] Such occurrences, moreover, were hardly restricted to this particular neighborhood. The historian Thomas Philpott characterizes settlement dances throughout working-class Chicago during the

1920s as "a duel of standards between the young people and the social workers."[27]

While such conflicts seemed to adhere to the "two worlds" explanations being described by sociologists at the time, a closer examination of the provocations that gave rise to them reveals another facet of what was at stake in the will of youths to dance as they wished. On the surface, most of the controversy surrounding the comportment of young dancers stemmed from the collective efforts of youths to make dances into opportunities for sexual contacts. This meant not only pairing off in dark corners but also using the latest dance steps to "shimmy," "shake it," and "rub it up." Obviously this was not the first moment in which parents and religious authorities sought to contain the sexual energies of the younger set, yet what distinguished the Jazz Age episode of this long-standing battle was the key role played by black cultural forms in the expression of youthful desires. Indeed, few could overlook that popular dances like the shimmy, the toddle, and the Charleston, as well as the hot syncopated sounds that animated them, were emerging out the Black Belt.

Such associations were surely on the minds of the editors of the Polish-language daily *Dziennik Zjednoczenia*, when in 1921 they published an editorial warning their readers that "indecent dances, such as the 'shimmy,' are creeping into our dance halls," and asking young Poles to "distinguish between true and false Americanization."[28] Yet the outcry against physically expressive dances like the shimmy was also due to young Poles' attraction to these fads from the other side of the color line. Working-class youths, especially during the peak years of the Jazz Age, actively resisted attempts to police the racial boundaries of dance halls and deracialize their dance experiences. In what one historian has described as an "ongoing grassroots dance movement," they made the ballrooms that employed the hottest black jazz orchestras into the hippest spots and devised their own rituals to enhance the racially transgressive nature of their dance hall experiences. Perhaps the most compelling example of this was the tendency of youths to spontaneously turn up at dance halls dressed as "sheiks" and "shebas"—racially ambiguous characters taken from the popular 1921 film *The Sheik,* in which the swarthy-complexioned Rudolph Valentino plays a suave Arabian sheik who kidnaps a white British socialite named Lady Diana Mayo. More than a passing fad, the use of the sheik as reference point for Chicago dance hall denizens was so pervasive that as late as 1925 a reporter for *Variety* referred to the crowd at the White City Casino ballroom as "a sheik and sheikess element." This venue, not surprisingly, had a reputation for the hot rhythms laid down by its all-black dance bands.[29]

The central importance of black expressive forms to the sexual experimentation of young ethnics in Chicago provides a clue to one of the principal ways that commercial leisure served as a site where second-generation youths made sense of their place within American society and its racial system. As the editors of *Dziennik Zjednoczenia* clearly revealed when they decried the shimmy as "false Americanization," this situation was not at all lost on either young or old in Polonia. Whereas historians have focused a great deal on the Americanizing roles played by reformers, agents of the state, and more assimilated "host" groups, they have underestimated the extent to which immigrant and second-generation ethnics sought out ways to Americanize themselves. The commercial dance hall scene was appealing to young ethnics, in part, because it provided the matériel for understanding the American racial system and, in part, because it offered the means for challenging their positions within it. Its capacity to do these things hinged on the experiences of racial mixing, conflict, and identification it made possible.

Yet that any of these processes of racial learning and identification were even necessary was due to the uncertainty that the children of new immigrants felt regarding where they stood in a racial hierarchy that generally placed northern and western Europeans at the top and African Americans at rock bottom. Many of the second-generation ethnics who crowded the dance floors in interwar Chicago were, in some sense, "racially inbetween." As Thomas Guglielmo has persuasively argued in his recent study of Italians in Chicago, this did not mean that their whiteness per se was in question—a contention that would, by implication, also apply to most other new immigrants, since Italians faced harsher and more publicized forms of discrimination than other groups did in this era.[30] Indeed, when push came to shove, Italians, Poles, Jews, and most other southern and eastern Europeans knew on which side of the color line they belonged. It is important, however, not to take this line of argument too far. That Italians and other new immigrant groups were viewed as "white" by the state—by courts, census takers, and naturalization laws, for example—might have meant little to second-generation ethnics facing grassroots forms of discrimination at school, at work, and out on the streets. That is to say, if they felt themselves securely white, they also understood that they were not white in the same way that the Irish or Germans were. Recalling the uphill climb he faced as a young man applying for a job at Sears around the time of the Great Depression, for instance, Chicago Italian Leonard Giuliano was quick to point out that "unless you were Irish, hell, you didn't stand a chance." "Jews and Italians," he added, "didn't stand a chance."[31]

These circumstances contributed to making new ethnic youths in this moment into what Victor Turner has referred to as liminal personae. "Liminal entities," in Turner's thinking, "are neither here nor there; they are betwixt and between the positions assigned and arrayed by law, custom, convention, and ceremonial." In Turner's paradigm of social life as a "type of dialectical process" alternating between "structure" and "*communitas*," young ethnics tended to occupy the latter state, one counterposed to "society as a structured, differentiated, and often hierarchical system of politico-legal-economic positions with many types of evaluation, separating men in terms of 'more' or 'less.'"[32] Therefore, whether they were sizing themselves up as Americans, as ethnics, as men, and perhaps even as whites, new immigrant and second-generation youths in interwar Chicago invariably found themselves somewhere "betwixt and between." As we will explore further, the very common state of being in between school and work during these years accentuated this liminal condition. The in-between racial status of young ethnics in particular was no more clearly expressed than in the oft-told anecdote circulating in Polish neighborhoods during this period of the young Pole who claimed he was Irish in order to impress a girl he met downtown. A youth worker recorded a version of this story he heard shared among gang members in the South Chicago Bush neighborhood: "I told her I was Irish, that my name was Frank Murphy. I look sorta Irish, don't I? Why I'm even afraid to hang around the corner. She's got a car, you know, and she might be driving around here and see me and find out that I live in this Pollack neighborhood."[33]

A nearly identical story of a Polish youth nicknamed "Cosmoline" for his habit of passing himself off at dances as the de-ethnicized "Fred Taylor" also appears in a 1932 study on the assimilation of second-generation immigrants on the Near Northwest Side.[34] If this kind of tale was somewhat folkloric in Polish communities, moreover, it was hardly unique to Polonia. The sociologist who recounted the story of Cosmoline also noted similar behavior among Italian youths, who, according to a study conducted on the Near North Side, were acutely conscious of their appearance as "greaseballs" outside of the neighborhood.[35] This sense of racial uncertainty among Polish and Italian youths in working-class districts underpinned their participation in a practice referred to by this researcher as the "dance hall bluff," a routine involving the dissembling of ethnic and class identities in the context of dance hall courtship.[36] Although the physical characteristics of Mexican youths prevented them from engaging in such deceptions, dance halls nonetheless provided opportunities to court and win the affections of European American girls, an achievement that offered a means to establish a certain status among their peers and distance themselves from African American men, whose access to such girls was sharply restricted.[37]

Such rituals suggest why commercial dance halls, and commercial leisure in general, so captivated youth ethnics in interwar Chicago. There were, first of all, some very practical reasons why youths wanted to get out of their neighborhoods and mix with a more diverse and unfamiliar crowd. A Near West Side Italian social club member explained: "No use monkeying around with Italian babes—you know, you have to get serious and you can't monkey around much because some [of] them know your family and all that kind of thing."[38] Aside from such tactical considerations, however, a more symbolic dimension underlay the will of new ethnic youths to venture downtown or into other neighborhoods to socialize in commercial leisure venues and to pursue sexual relations in interracial contexts. The presence of racial others in and around clubs, bars, theaters, and dance halls marked them as what Turner refers to as "liminoid spaces"—domains set apart from the productive and normative worlds of work, school, family, and the ethnic community. That many popular dance halls were located within or near interracial sex districts heightened the experience of liminality. Several, for example, were part of the "underworld life of West Madison Street," described in Clifford Shaw's *The Jack-Roller*, where youths like Shaw's subject, Stanley, associated the "lure of the underworld" with the possibilities of interracial contact in the context of sexual commercial exchange.[39] In such spaces, youths felt themselves more or less free to engage in symbolic actions that were not permissible in much of their everyday lives.[40]

The presence of racial others in symbolic form or in the flesh offered possibilities for comprehending and symbolically resolving uncertainties surrounding racial identities. In his work on Italians in Harlem, Robert Orsi, borrowing from Paul Ricouer, argues that "ethnicity takes shape along the borders between groups" and that "the self achieves identity and meaning through the detour to the other."[41] Dance halls throughout the city offered precisely such detours. In addition to the grand ballrooms, where youths from neighborhoods throughout the city came together on the dance floor, smaller taxi-dance halls constituted social spaces that allowed patrons to explore their racial self-understandings. Although the dancers for hire in these places were usually white ethnics, and although blacks were denied entry, the crowd was nonetheless thoroughly mixed. Paul Cressey's work on these establishments demonstrates that much of their excitement had to do with the interracial crowd they attracted. In the taxi-dance halls, according to Cressey, European ethnics "rubbed elbows" with Mexican, Filipino, and Chinese patrons, men whose racial ambiguity could taint the integrity of the dancers who served them.[42] If youths viewed such patrons as racially undesirable, however, they nonetheless appeared to enjoy the experience of socializing among them. A 1932 study of the leisure habits of Polish and Italian youths on the Near Northwest Side, for example, found that some two-thirds of those surveyed chose to pay the relatively high fees required by such establishments.[43]

Youths paid these fees in part because the somewhat anonymous taxi-dancers offered a level of access to their bodies that girls from the neighborhood would not, but the elaborate rituals and codes of conduct that youths established within such spaces suggest that more than this was at stake in their involvement in these venues. Cressey, for example, noted a "special vocabulary" among taxi-dance hall patrons, which, in addition to describing a range of sexual forms of behavior, conveyed in detail the codes of racial conduct operating in these spaces: Filipinos were "niggers"; white women who dated or danced with them were "nigger lovers"; and those who did not were "staying white."[44] Moreover, observers of the taxi-dance hall scene noted numerous conflicts erupting between Filipinos and Poles or Italians. At times brawls broke out as a result of competition over certain dancers, but on other occasions gangs of young white ethnics appeared to pick fights with Filipinos for reasons that had little direct relationship with the activity on the dance floor. Describing one incident in which a gang of young Poles waited outside a taxi-dance hall to ambush four Filipinos and then chased them down despite the Filipino youths' attempts to appease them, a Polish gang member boasted: "Them Filipinos hang around those places a lot and our gang sure does beat hell out of 'em."[45] Such rituals thus transformed taxi-dance halls into forums where young, mainly second-generation ethnics and immigrants could, via "detours to others," develop visions of themselves as white ethnics not vulnerable to the same forms of degradation suffered by nonwhite groups.

A similar motivation lay beneath the participation of working-class ethnic youths in another domain of commercial leisure that became increasingly popular in the 1930s—the sex industry, which by the middle of the decade was overwhelmingly dominated by black female sex workers. During this time, rising demand for the services of black prostitutes in white neighborhoods and a political economy that forced African American women into desperate subsistence strategies resulted in the spread of interracial streetwalking prostitution across the color line. According to one park director around the Near North Italian area, "It [was] not unusual for a man to walk the four blocks from Division St. to Chicago Ave., and be 'propositioned' by three or four Negro women."[46] Another resident in the same area complained that not a day went by in which he was not solicited by a black streetwalker.[47] A somewhat analogous situation prevailed on the largely Italian Near West Side, where settlement workers complained of a "certain well-known district" that they described as "a veritable den of vice and cheap commercialized recreation . . . [where] boys take pleasure in 'rolling drunks' and relieving them of their cash, in breaking into cheap movie houses and frequenting taverns."[48] In South Chicago's Bush neighborhood as well, youth outreach worker Stephen Bubacz, related similar habits among three different Polish gangs who made frequent excursions to a brothel named Jack Diamond's in a nearby black and Mexican neighborhood known as the Strand.[49] Here, according to one youth, "you could get a black girl for twenty-five cents."[50]

Suggestively, such activities show up in the records not as aberrant, but as recurrent or, in a sense, normal; they appear to merit documentation but not outrage or recrimination. However, even though these activities seemed unexceptional to observers—in part because the selective policing of prostitution in the 1920s had produced a predominantly black sex workforce in Chicago, making the interracial nature of vice a fait accompli—the interracialism of these forms of sexual experimentation was, nevertheless, not a matter to be passed over or taken as self-evident by the young men engaging in them; rather, it was central to their meaning—a well-utilized source of humor, disgust, fascination, and perhaps most important, group solidarity. Of the many comments made by young men on the subject recorded by youth workers, none is more emblematic than the warning issued by one member of the South Chicago Mackinaws gang to another: "Keep away from the Strand, Casey or those nigger whores will get you and jazz you to death."[51]

And if youths were not going all the way with prostitutes in the 1930s, they were increasingly opting for the vicarious experiences offered by striptease performers in burlesque shows. Burlesque, according to one student of this entertainment form, enjoyed a certain renaissance in the 1930s, when African American strippers entered the industry in force for the first time. Chicago was arguably the capital of burlesque in the mid-1930s, and young men in their late teens and early twenties filled the audiences of some of its most celebrated theaters.[52] The fictional Studs Lonigan and his crew were habitués of strip shows, indicating that the practice was not uncommon among South Side Irish youths, and youth worker reports from the Bush and the Italian Near West Side suggest that Poles and Italians in these areas were no strangers to them either.[53] Even the less assimilated Mexican youths of South Chicago made a habit of attending burlesque theaters. As one Mexican teen freely admitted when asked if he and a friend went to the famed Rialto Theater downtown, "Sure we go and not only Malesio and I but a lot of us." "Sometimes we ditch school and go out there," he reported.[54] As for what they saw at this particular theater, an insider view is provided by Nelson Algren's 1935 novel *Somebody in Boots,* which characterizes the Rialto as offering "white and colored burlesque" to a racially mixed clientele. Moreover, according to Algren's rendering, every Saturday night was "Win a Lucky Garter Night," when several lucky ticket holders in the audience could go on stage and remove a garter from one of the white dancers (the black "choristers" had this night off). Describing this scene, Algren adds the vital detail that the manager "always saw to it that on Saturday night no Negro in the audience ever got hold of one of his 'lucky' tickets."[55]

Such tales from the Depression-era world of sexual commercial leisure indicate the importance of black or other nonwhite bodies in processes of race learning, ethnic identification, and youth subcultural formation, as well as the vital role played by commercial leisure in making these black bodies available to white ethnic youths. Yet racial mixing in such spaces hardly fostered racial accommodation elsewhere—far from it. Perhaps even more powerful than the lesson of segregation in movie theaters and dance halls were the lessons imparted in spaces where blacks and whites mixed—either symbolically or in the flesh. In these spaces, whites paid to satisfy their curiosity about the mysteries surrounding the sexualities of other racial groups, but they also paid for the opportunity to symbolically master all that was perceived as dangerous about these same racial others. In the strip show, brothel, and black-and-tan cabaret, white ethnics paid to be transformed into empowered consumers served by disempowered racial others—even if this just meant having the chance to touch a garter that was reserved for white hands only. Such dynamics explain why, in describing the "swell service" at a downtown brothel, a South Chicago gang member made sure to report: "They got a nigger maid to take your things, they don't charge you nothin' for towels, either, altho' you're expected to leave a tip."[56]

While young women, on the other hand, were very seldom seen in such settings as anything but workers, by the mid-1930s they were increasingly entering more acceptable spaces of commercial recreation, and they were doing so in ways that linked them to expressive forms coming from the other side of the color line. The emergence of a swing subculture around 1935, which made devoted jitterbugs out of so many urban teenagers, was perhaps the clearest articulation of this shift. A phenomenon that brought teeming hordes of young men and women into ballrooms and dance halls to shake their bodies to the driving, rhythmic sounds of both black and white jazz orchestras, swing emerged in a moment when the possibilities of cultural transmission across racial lines had increased considerably. With the advent of the jukebox and the growth of the radio industry in the 1930s, whites listened to black performers more than ever before. Moreover, wide press coverage of the most recent fads in the world of swing highlighted the idea that the new dance steps white youths sought to emulate originated in the famed ballrooms of black neighborhoods, like the Savoy in Harlem. Of course, this was also a detail that was not often overlooked by the many outraged editorialists and reporters who expressed their protests with terms like "primitive," "immoral," and "evil."[57]

Nevertheless, black and white jitterbugs seldom shared the dance floor in Chicago's venues. Yet as the summer of 1938 wound down and the start of the school year approached, the thriving Chicago swing subculture produced an event that would have been hard to imagine ten years before it and ten years after it. On the night of August 24, some one hundred thousand young swing enthusiasts packed into Soldier Field for the Swing Jamboree, a free dance festival featuring twenty well-known orchestras and three dance stages. Remarkable even for this time, the collection of bands and the audience assembled to see them were thoroughly interracial, and, according to reports, black and white dancers jostled on the floors without incident.[58] The audience, however, was also quite heterosocial, and the presence of a large number of women in this kind of setting suggests that the world of commercial recreation also held a great allure for young second-generation ethnic women. In addition, while the reportage of the Swing Jamboree seemed to indicate that many of the female participants came accompanied by a male companion, other evidence from the early years of swing indicates that some may have come to the event in the company of other female friends only.

By the mid-1930s, a number of social workers in Chicago began to turn their attention to the growing number of girls hanging out in the streets, settlement houses, and commercial leisure venues of their neighborhoods. While girls clubs were far less numerous than male groups during these years, they developed for somewhat similar reasons. A 1935 report from the Italian Near West Side mentioned three girls clubs—the Chippewettes, the Farquerettes, and the Vernonettes (the last two taking their name from neighborhood streets)—that had formed within the last few years "to give dances." Since, as the report also stated, female participation in mixed clubs was generally unacceptable because of "parents' suspicions," these clubs likely represented a negotiated compromise that allowed girls access to the terrain of heterosocial leisure. Parents no doubt preferred club dances in the neighborhood, even if given by the youths themselves, to the commercial dance hall scene downtown. Indeed, the list of "well-known" orchestra leaders that were hired at club dances on the Italian Near West Side indicates quite clearly that the dance hall scene here retained a strong Italian flavor: Lousi Di Fonso, Tony Spranzo, Joe Quentieri, and "Sheik" Beasucci.[59]

Evidence from other parts of the city, however, tells a somewhat different story. The handful of sixteen- to twenty-year-old girls who formed a group called My Pals in the South Chicago Bush neighborhood appeared to be nearly as attracted to the leisure scene in the nearby black and Mexican neighborhood as were their male counterparts in the Houston Herrings, Mackinaws, and Burley Lions. According to the reports of their youth worker, Dorothy Benson, these girls smoked cigarettes, loaded up on booze, swore in Polish, and saw Westerns at the local Gayety Theater, a set of habits which led her to conclude: "I believe that the girls live for excitement—the thrill of doing something that has risk attached to it, wild-west stuff, outlaws, etc." One of their favorite ways to attain what she referred to as a "sense of bravado at their breaking of usually recognized social procedure" was "to go chasing around Mexican taverns," an activity that some of the girls did "most of the time." Their regular spot was Manick's Tavern at 89th and Greenbay Avenue, which was located "right in the heart of the Mexican and colored district" and which catered to a mixed clientele.[60] While a relatively small minority of girls in the area may have been habitués of such taverns, these forms of behavior were hardly relegated to a demimonde that concealed them from the rest of the community. As Gabriela Arredondo's work on this neighborhood has shown, the problem of Polish girls dating Mexican men was a hot item of conversation in both communities.[61]

Some of the same dynamics behind the male fascination for whore-houses in the Strand shaped the allure of the "Mexican and colored district" for the members of My Pals. As Chicago Area Project fieldworkers noted about both male and female youths in the Bush, many teens were "ashamed of the fact that they [were] Polaks" and "hated the 'bush' and the stigma attached to living there."[62] And while such feelings of racial insecurity were bound to be more pronounced in a neighborhood as insular and isolated as the Bush, the Polish girls of this neighborhood were not alone in being touched by such sentiments. According to another youth worker in the Girls Department of the Chicago Commons Association, Italian girls on the Near Northwest Side at times displayed considerable animosity toward their Polish peers, at times demanding staff members to "Get those Poloks out of here."[63] Nor, as the previously mentioned "greaseball" complex in Little Sicily suggests, were Italian girls immune to such feelings. Thus, like their male peers, young ethnic women may have been attracted to dance halls and other venues of commercial leisure in part because they offered opportunities for empowerment in the face of racial predicaments. If Mexican youths used relations with Polish girls as status markers in South Chicago, it is likely that the Polish girls choosing to date them were quite aware that they served this role, and that the racially oriented admiration directed at them was part of their attraction to Mexican men. Such treatment differed greatly from that shown to them by their male peers in the Bush, where youth workers described groups of young Poles shouting obscenities at Polish girls passing by.[64] According to a youth worker in contact with the members of My Pals, such behavior led the girls to conclude that "anyone who isn't from the 'Bush' is different in their moral sense than those who are."[65]

Yet if working-class girls in Chicago's ethnic neighborhoods were susceptible to similar needs and desires as their male peers, they faced quite a different set of conditions as they attempted to fulfill them. Until the late 1930s, many parents' efforts to restrict girls' access to unsupervised, mixed-gender social settings—especially those of commercial venues—tended to forestall the girls' collective involvement in milieus of interracial leisure. The development and commercial viability of the taxi-dance hall was, in itself, a testimony to the strong limitations imposed on the behavior of most young women during this period. Such constraints forced dance hall entrepreneurs to hire female dancers, who, in addition to their very presence on the dance floor, could use their bodies in ways that were not acceptable for most young women. The girls of My Pals demonstrate that such control was hardly complete. But even within this group the risqué behavior of the boldest participants elicited some signs of disapproval from the others, as evidenced in the remark of one member: "Yeah, she's going around with a Mexican. I think that's terrible, don't you?"[66] Moreover, if such peer pressure was not enough of an influence, the mother of the girl in question here suggested what might lie in store for young women who have been "hanging around . . . in Taverns with Mexicans" when she told the gang's supervisor, "I wish the police would take her in again. I'd sign the papers and tell them to lock her up for a year."[67]

In most cases, though, less extreme measures were brought to bear on the leisure habits of young ethnic women in working-class Chicago. Immigrant and second-generation parents normally managed to restrict their daughters merely by demanding a large part of their wages for the family. Beginning in the mid-1930s, however, the burning desire of many girls to participate in the dance hall scene increasingly pushed them to find means to work around such obstacles. One study of the leisure habits of teenagers on the Near Northwest Side, for example, described girls walking to and from work several times each week to save their carfare money for admission to dances. Yet in many cases the only dances they could afford were those given at the local settlement house, and, despite the struggles of youths to bring new dance forms into this milieu, the closely supervised settlement dance lacked the transgressive qualities of the scenes inside the big ballrooms and taxi-dance halls.[68] In predominantly southern Italian communities of Chicago, moreover, even the idea of allowing teenage girls to attend a settlement dance was almost unthinkable. Among the findings noted by one sociology student from a 1937 survey of 143 Italian families in Chicago was that "a large number of the mothers . . . never let the girls go to parties at which boys were present unless they knew just who the boys were and knew their families."[69] The resilience of such customs played an important part in making white working-class youth subcultures and the leisure terrains where they formed predominantly male domains in the interwar years. Yet by the end of the 1930s, the forces that had brought this about were markedly waning as a result of the decline of new immigration and the increasing dominance of the American-born generation. For example, the same survey that had revealed the persistence of Italian social customs restricting the freedom of young women also found much weaker observance of such traditions among American-born parents. "Some of the girls," the author reported, "said they had not been kept so strictly because they either had younger aunts or older sisters who knew American ways and would tell the mother that it was perfectly all right for the girls in America to go to parties with boys even though no other member of the family was present."[70]

Such views speak to the need to understand the proliferation of youth gangs in this era as a manifestation of a widening generational divide between immigrants and their second-generation children. Writing in this same moment, Karl Mannheim described the social importance of what he referred to as the "generation unit"—a concept that viewed the generation not as biological construct, but rather as a grouping of individuals with common life experiences, ideas, and forms of action. In fact, Mannheim argued that "generation units" took shape most visibly on the terrain of "youth culture," and that they realized their potentialities most fully in moments of accelerated social and cultural change, when disruptions in the process of cultural transmission created a generation gap that led to the emergence of a new "generation style."[71] The desperate urge for dance hall gear voiced by the Polish youth at the beginning of this chapter suggests that Mannheim's thinking holds a great deal of validity for working-class Chicago in the 1920s and 1930s, when some two-thirds of the city's population consisted of immigrants and their second-generation children. It was not that prior generations had not been tempted by commercial amusements, but rather, with the advent of motion pictures and radio, the rapid expansion of the advertising industry, and the advance of mass production technologies, consumption took on a more pervasive presence in working-class communities. That it did so, however, was not merely due to technological breakthroughs in its distribution. The generations of ethnic youths who neared adulthood throughout the 1920s and 1930s faced a set of predicaments—in the streets, in the labor market, and in school—that both heightened the appeal of commercial culture and restructured patterns of everyday life so as to allow greater access to it.

Hence, if, as John Bodnar has argued, "cultures of everyday life"— located "between the microscopic forces of daily life, often centering around ethnic communal and kinship ties, and the macroscopic world of economic change and urban growth"—mediated the experiences of American immigrants between 1830 and 1930, these cultures began to fracture along generational lines in the last few decades of this time frame.[72] Easily recognizable youth subcultures emerged out of these cleavages because such "micro- and macroscopic forces" produced a unique set of problems and contradictions for the new generation of ethnics—problems the existing cultures of everyday life could no longer adequately resolve.

These forces and the problems they created had not only a generational-specificity, but also an age- and, in some ways, a gender-specificity. That is to say, while broad structural changes forced widespread shifts in the practices of daily life throughout the social fabric of working-class Chicago, native-born ethnic young men in the throes of maturation were particularly exposed to the elements of change. First, the younger urban generation of the interwar period possessed a keen perception of the conflict between ethnic traditions and the values of Americanization. Second, this same group faced conditions in the labor market, in the streets, in the world of commercial culture, and in public institutions like school that made both their identities as ethnics and the paths into adulthood that their parents had followed problematic. In response, young ethnics developed an alternative sphere that retained some forms of communal life while embracing the new American values they picked up in the course of everyday life.

ENCOUNTERING AND COUNTERING SCHOOL

One of the most significant shifts in the structure of working-class adolescence in interwar Chicago came neither from labor market conditions nor from the explosion of the mass culture industries, but rather from a series of legislative measures sponsored by a coalition of Progressive reformers, organized labor leaders, and business owners. Between 1893 and 1902 this alliance of interests, led by Florence Kelley and Jane Addams, pressured the state legislature of Illinois to pass a set of more comprehensive child labor and compulsory education laws that sought to move teenagers between fourteen and sixteen out of the workplace and into the classroom.[73] While these laws managed to raise the minimum working and dropout ages, as well as lengthening the school year, enforcement problems delayed their effect somewhat. This had been a thorny issue since the advent of such regulations. In 1890, for example, the superintendent of compulsory education reported that while the department had investigated 17,400 cases of truancy in the previous school year, their handling involved "not a single instance of interference with parental authority, no prosecution or persecution."[74] With this in mind, Kelley and her committee of child savers fought for more effective means of compulsion through the court system, an objective realized in the Compulsory Education Act of 1897. Declaring the new posture of vigilance a year later, the Chicago Board of Education reserved for itself "the power to arrest all these little beggars, loafers and vagabonds that infest our city, take them off the streets and place them in schools where they are compelled to learn moral principles."[75] To accomplish this, the city employed a unit of 15 truant officers, a number that would grow steadily to 53 in 1914, 88 in 1924, and 131 in 1936.[76] With this enforcement arm in place, the state was now prepared to take a much more active role in regulating the lives of Chicago's working-class adolescents, and through them their families and communities.

The new focus on truancy policing corresponded to another important change in the state's handling of wayward youths: the creation of a juvenile court system in 1899 to bring a more rehabilitative approach to the problem of delinquency.[77] Judges in the juvenile court system pursued this goal over the next few decades by demonstrating an increasing propensity to recommend probation for youths brought into court, with institutionalization as a second but hardly neglected recourse. In the matter of truancy, however, they were not at all reluctant to commit habitual offenders to parental school. In the years 1910–11 and 1912–13, for example, out of 1,203 truancy cases taken to juvenile court, judges committed 934 youths to such institutions. The composite figures for the years 1921–22 and 1923–24 reveal that the rate of commitment had fallen somewhat but that the juvenile bench still preferred this disposition to probation, institutionalizing 973 of the 1,836 truants brought before it.[78] The important point here is that the threat of retribution for truants was a credible one, and a legion of truant officers made this well understood in working-class Chicago. Hence, out of the child-saving framework developed in the final years of the nineteenth century emerged a powerful apparatus of juvenile policing and control that had a vital role in transforming the nature of adolescence in working-class Chicago in the interwar period. In the 1920s and 1930s, truant officers blanketed the city, investigating hundreds of pool halls, theaters, and many other popular youth hangouts, and paying hundreds of thousands of visits to the homes of absent students. References to truant officers appear frequently in the gang worker reports of this period—signs of both the close relationship between the state and working-class youths, and that between youth gangs and the school experience.

This intensification of compulsory education enforcement led to a dramatic rise in school enrollment rates among both immigrants and the native-born children of foreign or mixed parentage between 1910 and 1930.[79] For the fourteen- and fifteen-year-old cohort, the one most affected by the change in the minimum dropout age from fifteen to sixteen, the percentage of second-generation ethnics enrolled rose from 66.3 to

94.4; for immigrant youths in this same age range, the rate increased from 54.9 to 94.3 percent. The sixteen- and seventeen-year-old cohort showed similar gains over the same period, with the enrollment rate of second-generation ethnics rising from 22.6 to 54.7 percent, and the percentage for foreign-born youths increasing even more precipitously from 12.9 to 50.4.[80] More and more youths were thus passing their weekdays in school, whether public or parochial, a change that would have a tremendous impact on the structure of everyday life throughout working-class Chicago. Yet the way youths came to educational institutions—whether by choice, persuasion, coercion, or default—tended to shape their responses to them, including their involvement in street gangs that formed in opposition to the world of school. For many families headed by foreign-born unskilled or semiskilled workers in interwar Chicago, the shortage of promising work opportunities for unskilled teenagers and the coercive efforts of the state combined to keep many working-class youths in the classroom.[81]

What reformers and officers working for the bureau of compulsory education knew from experience was that in these neighborhoods of low-wage industrial workers the battle over school attendance had to target parents as much as their children. This helps explain why prosecutions of parents in municipal court would parallel the rise of those against youths in the juvenile division. The technical name for the offense was "indifference," but the role parents played in truancy was frequently much more active than this term implies, even to the extent of falsifying their children's birth certificates to free them from school requirements a year or two early.[82] As historians of immigration have found, wages from youth labor were vital to the livelihood of the family and probably contributed a great deal to the substantial rise in home-ownership in the 1910s and 1920s. Yet whereas a segment of immigrant families benefiting from a longer period of residence in the city managed to procure mortgages and acquire their homes, the many other families that were unable to reach this goal by the 1930s continued to depend on the labor of their children to supplement the overall household income.[83] Moreover, many immigrants raising children in the 1920s and 1930s had come of age in a time when very few made it past the sixth grade; by 1910, for instance, only 10 percent of Italians, Poles, and Slovaks—three of largest foreign-born groups in Chicago—stayed in school past this point.[84] Understandably, then, adoption of the idea of children remaining in school during years that had traditionally been spent at work was grudging at best in neighborhoods where parents were predominantly foreign-born. The result was a catch-22 situation that placed students between the demands of their families and the requirements of the state. Youth gangs and the subcultures they inhabited formed in part out of this and other such struggles: out of the need for collective negotiation of the interrelated problems encountered in the spheres of work, school, and family life.

To fully understand how youth subcultures related to the complex interplay between the demands of families, the requirements of the state, and the conditions of the labor market, it is necessary to look beneath enrollment figures at the observations of those engaged with the youth problem at the grassroots level. Since the growing recognition of such problems in the fields of sociology and social work paralleled a fashion in the same circles for recording the voices of adolescents themselves, historians have been left with some rich documentation of the shadowy domains of family life and youth consciousness. These trends came together most definitively in the early 1930s, when University of Chicago sociologist Clifford Shaw formed the quasi-public Chicago Area Project (CAP) to bring this grassroots approach to the delinquency problems of three working-class neighborhoods. The centerpiece of this experiment was a blue-collar Polish neighborhood around Russell Square known to locals as the Bush. In 1932, Shaw assigned the task of working with and observing the many delinquent gangs in this far South Side steelworker neighborhood to a charismatic young activist named Saul Alinsky, who along with other indigenous "curbstone counselors" recruited by CAP, spent the next several years attempting to steer youths back to school.

Having pioneered the autobiographical "life history" method of examining the roots of delinquent behavior in his work with the Institute for Juvenile Research, Shaw required CAP's counselors to keep detailed diaries.[85] The records they produced provide a layered perspective on both the factors that determined school attendance, and more interesting, how the vicissitudes of school and work in the 1930s laid the foundations for an alternative youth subculture that existed in a complex opposition to the values of older, foreign-born Bush residents. While CAP confined its outreach efforts to South Chicago's Polish community, interviews conducted by another scholar working in the area reveal that families in a neighboring Mexican enclave were beginning to experience similar generational tensions over the terms of work, school, and leisure. These two groups possessed divergent histories in South Chicago and quite distinct modes of communal life, but Mexican and Polish youths responded in comparable ways to challenges they faced in school and at work. Taken together, their stories illuminate the common circumstances that shaped ethnically bounded working-class youth subcultures in the 1930s; to be second-generation and between boyhood and manhood were conditions that transcended ethnic lines.

However, like the Polish and Irish youths around the stockyards, the Polish and Mexican young men around the steel mills were largely unaware of all they shared. Even more than in most other working-class districts, geographic, cultural, and historical factors combined to drive a wedge between these groups. Census figures from 1930 and 1940 indicate quite clearly that a relatively small number of Mexicans and Poles in South Chicago resided on the same blocks. Foreign-born Polish residents, for example, were most scarce within the tracts containing the heart of the Mexican colony, which formed in the 1920s along Harbor and Greenbay Avenues between 87th and 92nd Streets (tracts 670 and 671), even though this low-rent district should have been attractive to newcomers with modest means. On the other hand, while Mexicans made up 11 percent of the overall population of the community area in 1930, they were virtually nonexistent in the most concentrated Polish section of the area (tracts 663 through 666).[86] This pattern of settlement came about, in part, because Mexicans sought out residences in blocks where their neighbors spoke their language and where they could procure ethnic staples like fresh tortillas, beans, and chorizo. But the unwillingness of Polish landlords to rent to Mexicans at fair market prices and a general tenor of anti-Mexican hostility in the streets and in the mills largely prevented the colony from branching out during the 1920s and 1930s.[87]

The most tangible causes of this antagonism arose out of the initial circumstances of Mexican migration to this part of the city. Brought to South Chicago by Illinois Steel and housed in dormitories within the mill gates to serve as strikebreakers during the failed strike of 1923, the Mexican population grew steadily in the late 1920s until the layoffs of the early 1930s.[88] Loathed by Polish steelworkers for their role as strikebreakers and effectively priced out of housing in many parts of the district, the Mexican settlement developed in the least desirable residential area near the steel mills. By 1928, Mexicans had already established a visible presence in the Greenbay Avenue district by opening thirty-three businesses—pool halls, taverns, barbershops, groceries, and other small family ventures. Yet amid this burgeoning community were other elements that would further stigmatize it in the eyes of Poles, even as Mexican participation in the Steel Workers Organizing Committee in the 1930s began to heal the wounds of the previous decade. Also consigned to this neighborhood was the only small enclave of black laborers in the vicinity—numbering some seven hundred in 1934. And not surprisingly, it was here that a small vice district of brothels, poolrooms, and gambling resorts quickly sprang up to serve the needs of steelworkers.[89]

In view of the casual way that Polish gang youths spoke of the "can houses" in this area—especially the famed Jack Diamond's at 89th and Strand—it is clear that many Bush youths were familiar with this part of town.[90] Nonetheless, if Polish youths ventured down to the Greenbay district for kicks, they certainly would have been reluctant to admit to being part of this scene to their families. This situation was analogous to that of the Irish black-and-tan denizens of the Back of the Yards in the period of the riot. Like the Irish of Canaryville, the Polish community of the Bush envisioned itself as a distinct territorial parish unified by the objective of preserving ethnoreligious lifeways.[91] And like Irish youths in Canaryville, a strong emotional investment in their community and its ethnic identity gave Polish youths from the Bush a heightened sense that the Mexicans and blacks they encountered in the Strand were their antagonists. In some sense, the Bush was even more fiercely defended than Hamburg or Canaryville. Whereas the Irish clearly recognized the declension of their parish in the rapid loss of its parishioners in the 1910s and 1920s, the elder Poles of the Bush probably had little idea that their own parish, St. Michael's, was heading down the same road. The Bush, after all, seemed as tightly knit as a community could be. Roughly three-quarters of its residents were Polish, and nearly 80 percent of the population of Russell Square belonged to St. Michael's Church. It was equally impressive that twice as many of its children under age sixteen attended Catholic parochial schools as public grammar schools, even in the midst of the Depression, when the costs of doing so required a substantial sacrifice.[92] Examining the feelings of Bush residents toward their parish school in 1935, one scholar concluded from his interviews that "the public school does not exist for them," a sensibility he found poignantly demonstrated in their tendency to call the local public school a "Jewish school" despite the scarcity of Jews in this area.[93] It is not hard to deduce from these sentiments that St. Michael's did not exactly embrace its Mexican neighbors—a situation that forced Mexicans to hastily establish their own church, Our Lady of Guadalupe, in an old wood-frame building in 1924.[94] The Mexican colony, however, was not drawn to the church with even close to the same intensity that the Poles of Russell Square were, and both the overall congregation and school enrollment at Our Lady of Guadalupe remained small during the 1930s. The overwhelming majority of Mexican youths attended public schools.

And yet despite all that separated them—including vastly divergent educational contexts, different positions in the labor market and racial hierarchy, and distinct ethnic traditions—Polish and Mexican youths articulated concerns that were surprisingly alike. This was partly a result of the new apparatus of compulsory education, which placed adolescents of both groups between the demands of the state—embodied by the truant officer—and the needs of their families. While gang observers in both communities reported the rare case of a father promising to reward his son with a new suit for consistent attendance, most parents were far less concerned about the problem of truancy.[95] Issued a warning about a two-dollar fine for not attending school, one member of the Houston Herrings claimed: "I showed it to the Old Lady, and she said I didn't have to go!" Moreover, a youth in another Russell Square gang told a CAP worker, "I'm not as old as the records, my mother told me she gave my age one year older when I started school."[96] Considering the devotional strength of St. Michael's parishioners, it is likely that just as many parents in the Bush saw to it that their children made it to school, but that St. Michael's offered instruction only to boys through age fifteen is indicative of the point at which the community drew the line between school and work (and between childhood and adulthood).

In the neighboring Mexican community, parental resistance to mandatory schooling may have been even more adamant. First, considering the small percentage of youths receiving religious instruction at Our Lady of Guadalupe and the apparent lack of concern about second-generation youths losing their native language, Mexican parents saw little reason to sacrifice family income for an education that seemed of limited utility within the South Chicago employment market. Second, with a generally lower household income level and a higher unemployment rate than their Polish neighbors, Mexican families depended even more on the supplemental income of their children for subsistence.[97] This explains the turnabout of one Mexican father after a truant officer caught his seventeen-year-old son, Donaldo, repeatedly skipping school. At first, Donaldo's father scolded him, but when this legal threat no longer presented itself, his outlook changed. "Since he has been in high school," a sociologist who interviewed him stated, "his parents have condoned his nonattendance because he has often used the time to earn a little money."[98] This was a common situation in a community, where, according to this observer, "when boys reach their teens they are expected to obtain a job."[99]

The objections of Donaldo's father were less about his son's truancy than about his use of time away from school. That he could still be a truant at his age was due to his inability to obtain a work certificate—a legal condition for youths leaving school at the age of sixteen. It was in such ways that rising unemployment in the 1930s interacted with the antitruancy campaign to produce a rapid increase in school attendance. With a political economy dominated by the sharply contracting steel industry, South Chicago was probably as difficult a place as any in which to find a job and get a work certificate. However, according to one observer of an Italian neighborhood on the Near Northwest Side, poor labor market conditions and the extended reach of youth services were also largely responsible for "a marked change in high school attendance" among Italian adolescents. "Many families too," she concluded, "preferred to have the children in school than loafing at home since it was impossible to get employment."[100]

While the unemployment situation reached a crisis during the 1930s, prospects may not have been much better for teens and young adults attempting to enter the workforce in the 1920s. While many conceive of the 1920s as a decade of prosperity, the real wages of Chicago's industrial workers increased only minimally if at all between 1923 and 1929. Leila Houghteling's 1924 study of Chicago workers demonstrated that unemployment rates in the main manufacturing sectors remained high throughout the 1920s. In addition, even among the fully employed unskilled and semiskilled workers interviewed by Houghteling, more than half were laid off at some point during the year, most for a period of at least a month.[101] One indication of how these labor market conditions affected younger workers between the ages of seventeen and twenty-one can be found in a survey of Boys' Court offenders from 1923 and 1924, which listed 37 percent of those appearing in this court as unemployed.[102] These numbers, however, pale in comparison to the figures from 1931, when the unemployment rates of Chicago's semiskilled and unskilled workers reached 36.6 and 57.2 percent, respectively.[103]

Mexican youths faced even higher barriers to regular employment. Describing the status of Mexicans in packinghouse and railroad work in the 1920s, one study concluded: "When any of these industries reduces labor, it is the Mexican who suffers most. They are the last to arrive and the first to be laid off." Such suffering was not uncommon in the 1920s. Two employment agencies on Halsted Street that specialized in placing Mexicans were forced to close their doors in the winter of 1928, a time when recently arrived immigrants most often found themselves, according to one observer, "unemployed except at the best season of employment."[104] Yet European American youths were hardly untouched by such conditions. Chronicling the Little Italy community of Chicago's Near

West Side in 1928, resident Giovanni Schiavo noted large groups of single Italian young men in the streets around Hull House, 80 percent of whom he estimated to be unemployed.[105] A similar predicament characterized the Italian enclave of the Near Northwest Side, where, according to an anthropologist studying the area, "unemployment was felt . . . long before the depression was felt generally."[106]

As in working-class Mexican and Polish communities, the prevailing expectation in Italian Chicago was that teenage boys were to be gainfully employed and turning over most of their earnings to their families. The failure to fulfill such expectations created potent conditions for social change and cultural innovation in the lives of working-class ethnic youths throughout Chicago. Under such circumstances, the combined effect of a tight labor market and a vigorous antitruancy campaign was thus to establish another stage somewhere between childhood and the laboring role of adulthood. This stage not only existed in time but also had a spatial dimension. Required attendance at school in many cases pulled youths out of their ethnic enclaves and away from their parents for several hours each day. In interwar Chicago, the nearest public school was often located a substantial distance from home, and even for those going to the parish school down the street, the daily routine forced youths to occupy an age-defined space that offered countless opportunities to develop forms of age-based solidarity. In the case of parochial schools, this solidarity often involved resistance to ethnoreligious education, a phenomenon that once again highlights the generational cleavages characterizing ethnic communities in interwar Chicago. Yet whether public or parochial, school experiences served as catalysts for the collective questioning of timeworn values of work, kinship, and communal life and, ultimately, for the invention of new identities.

Ethnic parochial schools responded to the same forces that were filling public school classrooms in interwar Chicago. Constituting a substantial part of the growth in school enrollment between 1910 and 1930, these schools represented, on one level, communal responses to the state regulation of adolescence. That a set of discrete ethnic Catholic schools rather than a Catholic school system would prevail in this era involved a number of factors: the territorially minded conceptions of parishes existing in most ethnic enclaves, the widespread distrust among religious leaders in the neighborhoods of centralized bureaucratic authority, and the often inhospitable reception shown to southern and eastern European groups by the well-established Irish and German congregations.[107] However, the impulse to fortify parish boundaries took shape not only out of interethnic friction but also out of generational conflicts within different ethnic communities over the terms of Americanization. These struggles had been an important part of the immigrant story since the dawn of industrialization, but their scale and scope changed dramatically in the interwar period as a result of the profound demographic shift entailed by the massive wave of immigration in the first two decades of the twentieth century and the rise of the second generation on its heels.

Such circumstances meant that just when the flow of new immigration was slowing considerably from previous decades, a large segment of the second-generation boom was coming of age—a situation that gave rise to discourses about the "new generation," "the fate of the race," and the dangers of "American ways." Polish and Italian newspapers were some of the more assertive ones in reminding their readers how the adoption of "American ways" threatened the moral and intellectual development of the new generation of ethnics, and thereby the future viability of the ethnic community. Faced with the erosion of their foreign-language readership, the editorial voices of the ethnic press frequently served as mouthpieces for conservative nationalist organizations and religious interests. The Polish press, in particular, displayed an unwavering commitment to the cause of ethnoreligious preservation, running editorials with such titles as "Let's Treasure Our National Wealth," "How to Get Our Children to Read Polish Books," "Polish Youth Succumb to Melting Pot," and "Send Your Children to Poland for a Vacation."[108]

In many new immigrant neighborhoods, sentiments like these translated into efforts to utilize the parish school as a bulwark against the over-Americanization of the younger generation. The Polish vision of the parochial school, though, was far more extreme than that of Italian parishes, which, because of the greater reluctance of Italians to join congregations, placed a much greater emphasis on serving the Americanizing needs of their parishioners. In 1930, thirteen times as many Poles attended parochial schools, although Poles only outnumbered Italians in Chicago by two to one.[109] Italian churches thus had to tone down their appeals to reluctant Italian communicants. Nevertheless, Italian religious leaders pressed the language of cultural nationalism into service to encourage parochial school enrollment. For example, a 1925 bulletin from St. Philip's, the parish serving the Near North Side's Little Sicily neighborhood, told parents: "It is the school where your children learn that there does exist in this world a land called Italy, mother of every present civilization and center of Christianity. It is the school where they will learn not to be ashamed of being known as Italians, offspring of saints and heroes. It is the school where they will learn to speak the language of Dante, the sweet and beautiful language."[110] The school's head Italian instructor was even more elemental in her invocation, beginning her appeal with the phrase, "Italian blood runs in their veins . . . "[111] Declarations like these, furthermore, did not fall on deaf ears in a working-class district that had served as a port of entry for so many Italian immigrants in previous decades. Between 1920 and 1940, St. Philip's School grew from 160 to 610 students, becoming the largest Italian parochial school in Chicago.[112] Yet St. Philip's was exceptional, for Italian parochial school enrollment in Chicago lagged far behind that of the Poles, Irish, and Germans in this same period.

As the Italian case demonstrates, issues of cultural nationalism could be divisive, with some immigrant and second-generation parents taking a greater interest in seeing that their children equipped themselves with the skills and knowledge to advance in American society. The presence of such concerns among Italians in the 1920s and 1930s made their parishes what Stephen J. Shaw referred to as "way-stations of ethnicity and Americanization." Yet that the foreign-born and their American-born children composed such a large part of the demographic profile of working-class Chicago ensured that backward-looking ideals would persist and debates over the costs and benefits of assimilation would occupy a central place in the political cultures of ethnic neighborhoods in the interwar period. Moreover, the fragmentation of many ethnic enclaves by the forces of invasion and flight, coupled with the degradation of new ethnic groups in the mass media, only heightened the tone in which nationalist and religious interests depicted the stakes of Americanization.[113] Commenting in the mid-1930s on the problems he faced as the spiritual leader of St. Philip's, Father Luigi Giambastiani revealed how this convergence of generational change and community breakdown framed the worldview of those on the side of cultural nationalism and tempered Americanism: "The old Sicilians will die off," he claimed, "and the younger generation will come back to the Church when they see other people going to church and think it is the thing to do. There are many negroes in the neighborhood now."[114] Like the ethnic papers, many churches thus felt they were literally fighting for their lives as they sought to retain their base of support.[115] At times they could outpace their bases in their demands for fealty, but proponents of ethnocultural preservation also touched on some secular anxieties that gripped many immigrant and some second-generation parents, and they did so in overlapping languages of ethnic pride, racial fear, and youth estrangement.[116]

In some communities this latter concern was all too real, as parents witnessed the impending loss of their native tongue in their second-generation children and its replacement by a language that many immigrants could barely speak. In the early 1930s a Polish scholar studying the Bush viewed this as a serious problem. One longtime resident explained why: "It is this way . . . when 23 years ago, I came here, I went to a shop to work, where, to tell you the truth, I didn't hear a word of English. There were only Poles and we talked Polish. . . . So, I am here for so many years and cannot speak English. This lack of English comes from this, that every one of us who came here thought of earning some money and returning back to the old country."[117] Finding this to be a common set of circumstances for immigrant laborers raising children in the Bush in the 1920s and 1930s, this scholar viewed the fading of the Polish language as a fundamental challenge to family relations and the primary reason why parents sent their children to St. Michael's. "Teaching them the native language," he claimed, "saves them for the family, because with the loss of the Polish language they would be lost for their parents who speak only Polish."[118] While the insularity of the Bush may have made it an extreme case, this kind of language barrier was common, to some extent or another, to nearly every working-class ethnic community in interwar Chicago. The gravity of this situation was such that Thomas and Znaniecki would predict that second-generation Poles attending public schools instead of parish ones would become "completely estranged from their parents."[119]

The Catholic school movement of the 1920s and 1930s was therefore, in large part, a product of these drives for ethnic pride and community preservation. Not surprisingly, the appeals to the primordial— to true heritage and blood—entailed by such a project created a set of institutions that intersected with processes of ethnic and racial identification already under way in the context of youth subcultures. As John McGreevy has shown in his analysis of Catholicism in urban America, the formation of territorial parishes throughout the working-class districts of Chicago in the early twentieth century had profound implications for the subsequent history of race relations. What has been left largely unexamined in his account and others before it, however, is the specific impact of the parochial school movement—the organization of large numbers of adolescents into educational institutions defined by religion and ethnicity—on this history of intergroup conflict.[120] If McGreevy's work informs us that parishes "strengthened individuals while occasionally becoming rallying points for bigotry" and lends some support to the conclusion that these functions were at times codependent (that one might replace *while* in this last phrase with *by*), one of the principal ways parishes managed this was through their educational role.[121] Most of the older parishioners had contact with church once weekly, if that much, but parochial students spent several hours each day in its environs. In the case of St. Philip's, this was time in an institution presided over by a spiritual leader, who, in a letter to the Chicago Housing Authority protesting the presence of blacks in the Francis Cabrini Homes project in 1942, wrote that "the Negroes might be uplifted, but the whites by the very laws of environment will be lowered."[122] For Giambastiani, moreover, African Americans were the most threatening but not the only group whose entrance spelled the destruction of the Italian community. Interviewed many years earlier, in 1928, he stated: "Since the war there has been a great change and it is no longer an Italian community for there are so many nationalities who live here and so many Negroes."[123] This was a viewpoint echoed by younger members of the community as well. A thirteen-year-old boy interviewed around this time was more specific about other dark-skinned outsiders that had motivated his family's departure from the area. "There are some Italians west of the river leaving the North Side with the rest of the old Italians down there," he claimed. "The reason all are leaving is because there is too much shooting, and it isn't as nice as it was when our parents first went there, for today Mexicans and colored people have filled up the old Italian streets."[124]

Giambastiani may have been one of the more outspoken of parish leaders on such issues, but he was certainly not alone in his convictions of intolerance. That the city's Irish priests played a similar role in leading campaigns of racial exclusion is suggested by James Farrell's portrayal of the Irish reaction to the settlement of blacks in St. Patrick's parish, where residents speak admiringly of another pastor's ability to mobilize resistance against invasion.[125] Years later, in the 1940s, members of Visitation Parish, one of the remaining Irish strongholds in the area south of the stockyards, lauded their pastor, Daniel Byrnes, for leading the resistance to black settlement.[126] Indeed, while it is important to remember the efforts of Catholic organizations such as the Catholic Interracial Council in battling citywide against racial intolerance, parish leaders at times worked to coordinate racial hostility into concerted action in order to prevent the breakup of their congregations; and as Giambastiani's acerbic comments reveal, they were often waging a losing battle—a battle often depicted as falling on the shoulders of the American generation.

Between 1900 and 1930, the overall Catholic elementary school enrollment grew from 49,638 to 145,116, and that of secondary schools increased from 3,640 to 15,663. By 1940, Catholic primary schools accounted for nearly 30 percent of the Chicago total.[127] As for the handling of the racial encounter during this enrollment boom, Archbishop Mundelein laid down a policy in 1917 that maintained segregation and set a tone of intolerance in parish schools over the coming decades. His solution to the racial conundrum was to grant black Catholics their own parish, St. Monica's, and to deny them any claim to full membership in any other parish in the city. This meant, among other things, that they could not send their children to a parochial school other than St. Monica's, which rapidly filled its seats and had to turn away three hundred students by 1922.[128] Neither the Catholic Church nor its underlings in the parishes, however, invented the racial feelings that pervaded their congregations. It is more accurate to think of both levels of the church hierarchy as responding to and directing processes of racial formation that unfolded at work and in the streets. The reality was that financially able residents were moving to outlying middle-class areas and suburbs, a fact reflected in the growth of parishes in these parts of the Chicago metropolitan area during the 1920s and 1930s.[129] Their motivations for leaving the old neighborhood were indeed colored by worries over racial invasion, but these often had more to do with economic self-interest and status concerns than perceptions of the dissolution of the parish per se. The parents of the Italian youth quoted above, for example, had moved in order to purchase a three-story apartment building in a more stable area to the north of Little Sicily. Nonetheless, one should not underestimate the influence of the Catholic school movement of the 1920s and 1930s on the subsequent history of race relations. Even if we leave aside the very difficult issue of the transmission of racial intolerance in the classroom, the mere presence of all-white parochial schools put additional brakes on the integration of not only African Americans but also Mexicans.

Yet if the parochial school experience of the 1930s tended to reinforce lines of demarcation between neighboring ethnic and racial communities, it also exposed the widening generational fissures within white ethnic communities. No less integral to the texture of youth subcultures forming in areas like the Bush in these years were forms of solidarity organized around the struggle to resist the imposition of ethnoreligious values. In the context of the parochial schools, where ethnoreligious values were often reinforced with the lash of a whip or the rap of a stick, such forms of solidarity slipped easily into postures of resistance. Speaking of the sisters at St. Michael's, for instance, a Polish teenager in a group calling themselves the Red Wings, told a gang worker that "now-a-days they don't fuck around trying to slap your face, they just get the God-dam whip, and LACE you!"[130] Such treatment evoked equally violent responses from Polish gang youths in the Bush when asked about their feelings toward school. Barney, a member of a gang named the Burley Lions, stated it most succinctly: "I don't care, I don't want to go to St. Michael's! I hate the Living Ghost! If they want to take me to Parental School, they can, that's all, I'm not afraid."[131] That this was the prevailing view among the many gang youths of the Bush put on record by CAP intervention workers demonstrates the existence of what Paul Willis calls a "counter-school culture"—"a zone of the informal . . . where the incursive demands of the formal are denied."[132] The vitality of this culture of the "informal" within the "formal" structure of St. Michael's is evidenced by the frequency with which school officials there were forced to expel students for absenteeism and disciplinary problems. Even in a time when school authorities would have been reluctant to take this course of action, it was so commonplace that one CAP investigator in the Bush claimed, "So long as a family can afford the costs of the parochial school or the children avoid being expelled, they are sent to parochial school."[133] In Giambastiani's Near North Side neighborhood as well, schools—both parochial and public—provided focal points for the development of oppositional youth subcultures. As one observer noted of the situation in the mid-1930s: "The school situation is more serious than most teachers or principals are willing to admit. Numerous visits to all the schools in the area, parochial as well as public, showed them to have poor discipline. The children pretty much do as they wish. At one school the older boys from a saloon hang-out across the corner were walking up and down the halls and making wisecracks to the women teachers. . . . At another school it took several days to seed out the non-pupils who were attending classes 'just for the fun of it.'"[134] Suggestive of the anticlerical thrust these counterschool cultures could take, youths assaulted a priest in this area after he testified against some teens accused of committing thefts on parish grounds.[135]

The formation of these counterschool cultures, however, involved more than merely lashes taken at the hands of the sisters. Labor market conditions, family pressures, and difficulties in school also contributed to feelings of resentment over required school attendance. As discussed earlier, most seventeen-year-olds in such working-class neighborhoods as the Bush or Little Sicily had great difficulty finding uses for parochial or public education in their efforts to procure decent work in the Chicago labor market of the 1930s. Among the mainly Polish members of the Houston Herrings in 1935, the general outlook on the possibilities of a high school education was grim. As one sixteen-year-old member so bluntly put it: "What the Hell good is a diploma? They give you a piece of paper, but it won't give you no job! You think you're pretty big when they first give it to you, but you learn quick enough it doesn't mean nothin'! I got one, but it ain't worth nothin'. I can't even wipe my ass on it—it's too stiff!'"[136]

Indeed, of the many youths in this gang and in the Red Wings who described their views on school, only one mentioned plans to try to graduate from high school; in fact, most were unequivocal about their intention to quit at the age of sixteen and work in the mills.[137] Saul Alinsky understood this antischool sensibility to be so fundamental an element of the world of Bush youth that he persuaded his gang to rename themselves the University Juniors and to impose fines on members for cutting school.[138] For neighboring South Chicago Mexicans, who faced the added burden of racial discrimination in the mills and at school, the idea of a university education was too remote to even dream about. The Mexican youths of the Lions Club, for example, came from families dependent on the severely contracted labor market of the local steel mills. Typifying their situation was the case of club member Donaldo's father, who had worked as a laborer in the steel mills since 1919 but because of frequent layoffs had to go on relief in 1931, 1932, and 1935. The strain this pattern of erratic employment placed on the whole family throughout Donaldo's childhood shaped his vision of his time at school as "filling the gap until he can obtain a job."[139] That this was a common set of circumstances is suggested by the case of another youth of the same neighborhood, an eighteen-year-old named Albino, who arrived in South Chicago in 1923 at the age of three. Albino's father had worked for Illinois Steel for several years but lost his job during the Depression, forcing him to join the ranks of the Works Progress Administration at a greatly reduced monthly salary. The effects of this event on Albino's feelings about school, according to the same interviewer, were decisive: "Albino wanted to graduate from high school before going to work but at the same time he said that he owed it to his father to look for a job and help support the family."[140]

Economic pressures such as these worked their way through the family structure and into the consciousness of Polish and Mexican adolescents coming of age in this period. A high percentage of school-age youths in this era represented the first generation of their families to attend American schools; in the midst of the Depression, neither they nor their parents had reason to believe that a high school education was anything more than a restriction on their wage-earning capacity. That some like Albino did see value in a diploma is remarkable, suggesting the strength of emerging notions of citizenship among first- and second-generation ethnics raised in the United States in this period. Albino, for example, proudly stated, "I am going to stay here until I die. . . . United States is my country and I am for it."[141] For other Mexican adolescents, however, the experience of watching their fathers lose their jobs in the mills eroded their faith in the school system and galvanized their understanding of the racial injustices they faced. No doubt reflecting on the years in which his father had been laid off from Illinois Steel, another member of the Lions, Ramon, told an interviewer: "What the hell good is high school. I know a kid that went through Bowen [a public high school in the area], and now he is working at the mills. No Mexican has a good job at the mills."[142]

Hence, if Mexicans and Poles inhabited a similar political economy that shaped comparable views on their distinct school experiences, Ramon's remark suggests that additional circumstances in the 1930s would come to inform how Mexicans understood the problems they faced and the subcultures they formed in response to this understanding. Attending public school brought Mexicans face-to-face with both institutional and grassroots forms of racism, an encounter that informed their awareness of the meaning of their own identity. Such experiences produced the bitter feelings that Donaldo, Albino, and Ramon expressed about the racial prejudice of those they all referred to as "whites." Moreover, for Mexican adolescents whose parents spoke little or no English at home, linguistic problems compounded the challenges school posed. A common result was that many Mexicans were placed in classes with students several years younger. As in the case of Ramon, who was still in grade school at age seventeen, difficulties in these situations could easily lead to truancy, which in turn could further retard progress.[143] This cycle was not infrequent among European Americans as well, but like the many Polish boys in the Bush who attended St. Michael's, European ethnics often benefited from attending smaller parochial schools in their younger years. Moreover, one should not overlook how even slight gradations of skin color and foreignness operated within the racial schema of interwar Chicago. From the outset of their settlement, Mexicans had a harder time finding affordable housing in white neighborhoods, which pushed them closer to African Americans in many parts of the city. Mexicans in South

Chicago, for instance, lived amid the only pocket of African Americans in the area, a spatial arrangement that further reinforced their nonwhite racial status among white students at Bowen High School.[144]

Unlike their Polish neighbors, the Mexican community had inhabited the area only since the early 1920s, and because of this, had only just started to see its first American-born generation reach early adulthood. As a result, the kinds of generational issues that had surfaced in communities of Poles and Italians had only just begun to be felt in Mexican Chicago. Without these generational cleavages, which crystallized so powerfully for Poles within the repressive setting of the parochial school, Mexican youth subcultures were only just beginning to form in the 1930s.[145] These factors militated against the development of Mexican counterschool cultures of the kind that emerged at St. Michael's. Nonetheless, for Mexicans, as well as for Poles and other new ethnic groups, schooling served as a catalyst for collective processes of ethnic self-reflection that constituted, on one level or another, the workings of Americanization from below. "The relations of the gang to the school," observed a student writing on the South Chicago Mexican community, "are generally those of defiance, avoidance, and conflict. Yet, at the same time, the school is also one locale for the formation and growth of gangs."[146] Even for the Polish adolescents of St. Michael's, immersed in the ethnoreligious world of Polonia, resistance to the values and rules of the life it prescribed entailed the invocation of an alternative vision constructed out of elements outside of the parish walls: elements that were inescapably American. And in each case, school provided a very important locus for the formation of youth groups—the infrastructure of ethnic formation and Americanization. These groups functioned much like the ones Paul Willis viewed as structuring the English counterschool cultures, which, he claimed, "coalesce and further link up with neighborhood groups, forming a network for passing on of distinctive kinds of knowledge and perspectives that progressively place school at a tangent to the overall experience of being a working class teenager in an industrial city."[147] In the American interwar context, however, school focused attention as much on ethnic and racial difference as class inequality.

YOUTH CULTURE, THE GANGSTER, AND WORK IN THE 1930s

Counterschool cultures reflected not only discontent over the conditions of school, but also a larger critique—a denaturalization, in a sense—of the interlocking ideologies of labor and kinship that had guided the previous generation. As mentioned earlier, notions of work in early-twentieth-century immigrant communities hinged on the supreme value placed on supporting the family economy. If Mexican youths tended to reaffirm their investment in this idea in the testimonies recorded by a student of the South Chicago community in the 1930s, such sentiments do not show up nearly as prominently in accounts of the somewhat more assimilated Polish youths in the Bush. While one fifteen-year-old Russell Square youth nicknamed Doc told his gang worker of his intention to quit St. Michael's in order to help his parents, most of his peers expressed more individualistic motives for leaving school and entering the workforce. For example, speaking to a CAP worker about the difficulties he had encountered in trying to hold a steady job in the two years since leaving school, a Houston Herring member defined his employment problem in the following terms: "When you're workin', you got plenty of money, and even if you do have to work hard during the week, you can raise plenty of Hell on week-ends."[148] In a similar vein, another Herring nicknamed Gaga was fortunate enough to have had work but quit his job because, as he told the same CAP worker, "I hadda go to sleep too soon every night; I was always missin' somethin' I wanted to do! Whenever the guys was goin' to do somethin' I wanted to do . . . I was always goin' to sleep!"[149]

The youth subculture of the Bush and many other neighborhoods witnessing the coming of age of a large contingent of second-generation ethnics was, on a very basic level, structured around the imperative of "raising plenty of hell." In the context of youth subcultures in interwar Chicago, this drive depended on access to commercial leisure, and thus to readily available sources of spending money. In the new age of commercial recreation, sociability now came at a cost like never before. While young ethnics were not pulled blindly and inexorably into this expanding market of commercial leisure offerings, neighborhood-based events and activities sponsored by churches, ethnic associations, and settlement houses were clearly falling out of favor with the younger set by the end of the 1920s. Perhaps no other popular commercial venue embodied the new pay-as-you-go quality of youth leisure than the taxi-dance hall, where men paid a dime for each dance they shared with young women employed by the house. Observing such establishments in the late 1920s, the sociologist Paul G. Cressey wrote: "It is a mercenary and silent world—this world of the taxi-dance hall. Feminine society is for sale, and at a neat price. Dances are very short; seldom do they last more than ninety seconds. At ten cents for each ninety seconds of dancing, a full evening would total the man a tidy sum."[150]

Such perspectives help explain why youth workers in the 1930s would blame the thwarted need to participate in commercial leisure as the primary factor in the high crime rates they observed among gang youths. Clifford Shaw and Henry McKay's statistical analyses of juvenile delinquency in the 1920s and 1930s corroborated such an interpretation, revealing that throughout the poorer working-class areas of Chicago most juvenile offenses (as high as 70 percent between 1917 and 1923) involved some form of theft. Furthermore, that a great majority of these acts involved more than one perpetrator indicated their gang or peer group orientation.[151]

Lacking funds, adolescents in the Bush and other working-class neighborhoods turned to collective strategies of garnering what they felt they needed for consumer gratification. Theft, however, was more than merely a means to a consumerist end; as students of delinquent subcultures have repeatedly found, criminal activities of all kinds have fed the need for demonstrations of courage, fearlessness, or bravado, and as such have served as rites of passage in these masculine worlds. Yet the frequency of references to desires associated with commercial pursuits in interviews of working-class youths from this era suggests that consumption, in itself, had come to play a more significant role in the expression of masculinity.[152] As Cressesy's view of the taxi-dance hall suggests, commercial culture—whether that of the taxi-dance halls, downtown palaces, black-and-tan cabarets, or the celluloid world of darkened movie theaters—offered something that neighborhood institutions administered by religious leaders and moralizing settlement workers could not. He referred to it as "feminine society," but his account of the many violent scuffles that broke out between groups of young men over claims to taxi-dancers indicates that the fees paid out for such amusements may have been just as much about masculine society.[153]

The great value of what the world of commercial leisure had to offer to young ethnics can be glimpsed in the tedious activities they engaged in to gain access to it. There was little glory, for instance, in the practice of "junking," which basically meant taking anything that was not nailed down to pawn off for pocket money, but in the 1920s and 1930s it became a principal venture of many youth gangs. As one CAP worker observed of a youth under his supervision: "He had gone junking, but as ten hours work only netted about one dollar on the average, he didn't think it worthwhile; he wanted a regular job. He said he got so God-damn tired just hangin' around the corner doin' nothin', particularly as he never had any money."[154] If junking did not pay off, many gangs took to the more aggressive and risky practice of "jackrolling," the common expression for the strong-armed robbery of drunks and old men, and a practice that Clifford Shaw highlighted in his famous study of juvenile delinquency, *The Jack-Roller.* While junking and jackrolling were mon-etary pursuits that increased in frequency during periods of high unem-ployment, observers noted that youth gangs did not usually engage in these activities as a means of subsistence. Rather, the involvement of gangs in these and other more petty forms of crime usually had more to do with making enough money to "raise plenty of hell." Gang crime no doubt served as a basic source of income for some, and in the case of a hand-ful of syndicate gangs, may have even provided a real alternative to low-wage work, but for the majority of youths it was largely associated with an irrepressible urge to participate in commercial leisure activities. In South Chicago, for instance, Mexican youths learned from their Polish neighbors the practice of hijacking goods from the backs of produce trucks stopped at railroad crossings, but the fruits of their efforts were quickly sold "in order to get money for the picture show, cigarettes, or a dance."[155] If all else failed, gangs took to perhaps their most common pursuit—"just hangin' around the corner doin' nothin'."

"Doin' nothing" was, in actuality, a euphemism for a range of activ-ities that have characterized youth subcultures from the interwar era to the present. Its forms have been the basis of a street-corner world that most students of gangs and youth culture have presented as developing in relation to the progressive diminution of the manly occupations of in-dustrial wage labor. That is to say, it was a milieu that attempted to recre-ate the sense of potency and pride that the "shop-floor culture" of the industrial workplace had provided—a set of feelings organized around the ideas that scholars have variously described as "honor" and "re-spect."[156] While no doubt a constructive analytical trail, and one that is useful for understanding the values working-class youths invested in the rituals of their street-corner world, this compensatory theory of street culture at times tends to romanticize the view that youths had of the hard laboring lives many of their fathers led. The drive to partake in the ex-citing world of commercial leisure and style was, as we will explore fur-ther in chapter 3, integrally linked to the problems of maturation for working-class youths in Chicago, and to the multifaceted issues of work-ing-class youth identity in general. And that manhood was problematic in the first place did have a lot to do with the dearth of acceptable employment opportunities in the industrial labor market. Yet the threshold of acceptable work began to change in the interwar era, in part because of the propagation of new ideas and norms by the increasingly obtrusive media industries, but also because the bedrock values that had formerly infused tedious and at times degrading labor with a sense of social utility and dignity were beginning to crumble.

Passing from the everyday culture of young ethnic Americans in this moment were the masculinist ideals—the honor or respect—attached to the role of contributing wages to the family economy. As John Bodnar, Roger Simon, and Michael Weber found in their interviews of Poles and Italians in Pittsburgh, young men in these communities possessed strong feelings about the obligations they had to support their families—the fulfillment of which connoted a sense of self-worth.[157] Yet while scholars of both Polish and Italian communities have emphasized the resiliency of such family ties in the transition to life in American urban society in the first three decades of the twentieth century, Susan Porter Benson's findings on youth spending habits during the Depression suggest that second-generation youths were challenging the notion of the family economy in this period of economic strain.[158] Since young women faced comparatively limited work opportunities and stricter parental supervision of their activities outside the home, young men led the way in questioning their responsibilities to the family. Hence, Porter Benson's research on Depression-era families reveals that "substantial numbers of sons— and virtually no daughters—were portrayed as shirkers." "Sons, as a group," she concludes, "seemed less able to balance their own consumer desires and their own interests in controlling their time and effort with their families' demands for support in a way that convinced other family members that they were doing their best for the family."[159]

While to claim that the children of Chicago industrial workers had already entered "the nonproductive world of childhood" by the 1930s— as one historian has—would be stretching the point, a struggle over the nature of childhood was surely under way in working-class ethnic Chicago.[160] Thus, while observers of Polish and Italian communities in interwar Chicago continued to note the expectation among parents that this role would be fulfilled, no such clarity seemed to exist in the consciousness of their children. As one sociologist noted, "The immigrant family will exact its dividends for its child-raising investment. Opposed to that family draft-on-demand are the youths' own longings for automobiles, clothes, dances and theaters."[161] The persistence of this conflict into the 1930s, when pressures of the family economy were at their height, played a significant role in structuring the youth subcultures that formed in opposition to the family, school, and work. Commenting on the delinquent habits of Polish gang youths under his supervision, a CAP worker explained: "In many, if not the majority of cases of boys who have repeatedly stolen the families are either too poor to afford spending money for their children or else the parents do not have the social point of view which causes them to make the necessary arrangements for spending money for their boys."[162]

This shift toward more individualistic modes of thinking among youths did not entail a wholesale abandonment of the family; traditional values of kinship were more stubborn than that, and their persistence infused an anxious ambivalence into acts that flouted them—an ambivalence that could at times give youth subcultures an aggressive and even somewhat nihilistic edge. Nonetheless, in an era when real wages for most workers did not rise significantly and consumption spending did, something had to give way. Probing further into the desire for white shoes that began this chapter reveals that such changes had profound emotional consequences. Hardly facilitated by any rise in household income, the purchase of this item would have entailed cutting into an already tight budget, a fact that indeed weighed upon the youth's mind as he explained that his mother was a maid in a hotel who earned a meager $7.50 a week—"only enough to feed us, and pay rent," according to the youth.[163] Moreover, this youth was entirely aware that his intention to buy these shoes, and his idleness in general, represented a kind of resistance to what was expected of him by both his mother and the state. Referring to the aid that the county provided his family, for instance, he defiantly stated: "That ain't nothin' either, and I s'pose that lady who sends it to us will be around to see why I'm not working, or not in school. But the Hell with her! I'll tell her to keep her God-damned check!"[164]

That two women—the mother and the county aid worker—were the targets of this belligerence is telling. A similar temperament marked reactions to the sisters at St. Michael's and to the female teachers at the public and parochial schools of the Near North Side, where youths roamed the halls "making wisecracks to the women teachers." "Goodbye, sweetheart, I'll be back sometime," was reportedly one reply that typified the attitude toward female authority figures.[165] These were expressions of the widespread turn away from traditional ideals of work and the modalities of masculinity linked to them. The loss of these ideals created a deeply gendered sense of powerlessness, making nothing more threatening than the face of female power. While economic conditions during the 1930s limited access to the traditional paths of maturation through gainful employment for youths in their late teens, working-class ethnic youths themselves were also agents in the erosion of traditional values of work. It was not that youths absolutely could not find employment, but that what they could find was unsuitable in their eyes. Thus, when a CAP worker looked through gang reports in the mid-1930s to find excerpts to place under the heading "Attitudes toward Work," he found the following exchange emblematic of the overall situation:

> "Aw, I quit that last Saturday!" he explained. "I'm not gonna work all day like a son-of-a-bitch for three dollars a week. . . ."
> "It ain't worth the trouble," replied Harry. "Any guy's a chump to work all week for three dollars even; you'd never catch me doin' it!"[166]

Such posturing was integral to male sociability within youth subcultures whose values began to eclipse traditions that had held sway for previous generations.

A kind of antiwork ethic thus found increasing expression in the social world of working-class male youths existing in the space between school and work. Even if a great number of Polish and Mexican youths in South Chicago continued to look almost instinctively toward a future in the mills, they did so with more individualistic and often consumer-oriented goals in mind. For example, it was just after his third paycheck from Carnegie-Illinois Steel that Juan I., a nineteen-year-old Mexican gang member, placed a down payment on a new Ford, despite the heavy debt this purchase saddled him with. Outweighing the financial risks was the consideration voiced by a fellow gang member: "From that day on Juan became quite an important person around the neighborhood."[167] Even Albino, who expressed a strong sense of responsibility for supporting his family, claimed he had left school and taken a job as a track worker partly out of his desire to have "clothes I need, and . . . a little spending money."[168] Perhaps most compelling, however, was the response of a Polish youth in a Bush gang called the Mackinaws to the question of what he wanted to do with his life. "I don't know and I don't care, and anyway I'm too young to be thinking about that," he stated. "I've got to get my share of liquor and girls before I get old, so why should I worry about work."[169]

The nickname this youth took—Dillinger—exposes a vital source of this antiwork sensibility. Bush youths were avid moviegoers, even to the extent that they would risk expulsion from St. Michael's in order to make it to a matinee.[170] But Dillinger was a name that one could also hear bandied about on corners south of 87th Street. Ramon, one of the more fearless members of the Lions Club, spoke frequently of his intention to outperform the career of this notorious outlaw. "Dillinger wasn't so bad," he claimed. "He only stole from the rich people and the guy he killed was only a cop."[171] This idea of John Dillinger as a kind of class bandit was not entirely of Ramon's making; it was a subtext of much of the media coverage of the events leading up to Dillinger's demise in 1935.[172] Yet the appeal this notion held for this youth had a lot to do with his year spent watching his steelworker father live off public relief, an experience that contributed to an antiwork sensibility not unlike that displayed by his Polish neighbors. "The one thing no son of a bitch is going to kill me with," he told an interviewer, "is hard work. I just wasn't born for labor." Furthermore, Ramon took Dillinger's image to heart. Rather than trying to break into the industrial workforce, he attempted to get by rolling drunks and selling stolen goods to a Polish "fence"— operations that landed him in court on more than one occasion.[173] A portion of the profits from this venture, one must assume, he earmarked for movies, as the Lions passed many of their evenings (several a week, according to one member) in the darkness of the local theaters, where Dillinger's story played out for them in the newsreels preceding the feature attractions.

On many nights these news clips faded almost imperceptibly into the gangster stories that filled the giant screen in the 1930s. In fact, the fascination with John Dillinger and the cinematic gangster figure was so immense in the early 1930s that Will Hays, the head of the Motion Picture Producers and Distributors of America, called for a moratorium on gangster films in 1935. Whether Edward G. Robinson's Little Caesar, James Cagney's Tom Powers, or Paul Muni's Scarface, the gangster was often a figure from the old ethnic neighborhood who managed to attain the dream of social mobility without the years of drudgery put in by the fathers of many of the young ethnics that filled the audiences of these films.[174] This was one reason their stories were provocative fantasies for working-class ethnic youths between work and school. In the form of the gangster, honor and respect came with the ability to drive expensive cars, wear fine suits, and gain access to the more extravagant venues of urban nightlife. It was not merely his homicidal tendencies and crude treatment of women that stirred censorship campaigns among middle-class reformers; it was also his blatant mockery of the cherished Protestant work ethic in the midst of a catastrophic economic crisis. Social status within the world of the gangster hinged not on the ability to produce but to spend—a lesson youths took outside the theater.[175] The self-styled Dillinger, Ramon, displayed precisely this kind of behavior. "When Ramon has money," his youth worker observed, "he is a liberal spender and uses it to establish himself with other persons: his friends, adults, and girls. . . . He considers it an honor to loan them money."[176]

Such evidence reveals why the meteoric rise of the 1930s filmic gangster was, as Jonathan Munby has recently argued, "a post-Crash phenomenon." Framed by the stark economic circumstances of the 1930s, the gangster embodied the problem of ethnic exclusion from the ranks of the American middle class. Speaking in the heavily accented vernacular of the immigrant slums and making his money subverting regulations against the sale of liquor, the gangster was one of the first truly mainstream mass cultural figures that represented the young men of the ethnic working class.[177] His story began with the obligatory moral disclaimer and ended with an inexorable fall, but as the body of gang worker transcripts from the 1930s vividly reveals, many adolescents seemed more captivated by all that came between.[178] The box office smash *Public Enemy* (1931), for instance, pits the gangster protagonist Tommy Powers against his hard-working, morally upright brother. Mike Powers embodies everything the gangster ethos rejects: he attends night school, works diligently in an arduous job, and to make his purpose in the film even more salient, enlists to fight in World War I. All this Tommy views dismissively; according to him, Mike is merely "learning how to be poor." Of course the grim demise of Tommy—his alienation from his family, his ignoble shooting on the street in the midst of a driving storm, and his bed-ridden recantation—leaves little doubt about whose path is the "right" one.

Yet how much this kind of resolution penetrated the minds of working-class young men, dispelling the glory of the rise to success that preceded it, is a more complicated matter. At least outwardly, the youths of the Bush seemed more interested in the rise than the fall. They found nothing more degrading than being reduced to "a chump" by working the poorly paid, menial jobs available in their neighborhood, and they articulated these sentiments in ways that echoed the streetwise and sarcastic voice of gangster figures like Tommy Powers. For example, when prodded by a CAP worker to show appreciation for his new job delivering papers, a member of the Burley Lions known as Fat facetiously told him, "Sure, I'm a big shot now."[179] Thus, regardless of the intended moral of the gangster narrative, working-class youths viewed the gangster as an image of empowerment and affected his persona as a means of handling the profound sense of powerlessness inherent in the condition between school and work. It was his vernacular and his sensibilities that inflected the words of Bush adolescents facing the demoralization of underemployment in the 1930s, as in these complaints of a Houston Herring after failing to get a job in the mills: "If you ain't got no pull, it's no use! You gotta have a drag these days to get anywhere."[180] The gangster, if nothing else, had "drag."

Part of the power of the cinematic gangster for working-class ethnics lay in the reflection of real-life characters living in the very ethnic neighborhoods in which these movies played. Capone's organization and the 42 Gang on the Near West Side, the Black Hand outfit of the Near North Side, the Ragen's Colts and many other Irish athletic clubs around the stockyards—these were but some of the crime syndicates that were hard to miss on the streets of interwar Chicago. If not somehow affiliated with these organizations, youths growing up in their locales would probably have known, either directly or indirectly, someone who was. Places like the Palermo Club, within which Robinson's Little Caesar begins his criminal career, would have been very familiar to many Chicago youths. But even more important, while most working-class adolescents were not involved with full-blown crime syndicates, many belonged to gangs that did sporadically engage in petty and more serious forms of crime. In the Back of the Yards and the Near West Side—two community areas notorious for syndicate activity—Clifford Shaw found that more than one in four males between the ages of seventeen and twenty-one faced arraignment in Boys' Court on felony charges from 1924 to 1926: staggering rates of criminalization by almost any standard.[181] Viewed together with the high truancy and delinquency rates characterizing these areas, it is not hard to see why the ethnic outlaw had a sympathetic audience in these environs. Moreover, young ethnics commonly ventured into the same kinds of cabarets and clubs that provided both the settings for gangster films and the business enterprises for syndicates in the world outside the screen. A Houston Herring, for example, spoke admiringly of the bustle down at a nearby house of prostitution: "I was down there one night, and they was so full, they was closin' the doors, an' not lettin' nobody else in; they musta bin more than fifty guys in there."[182]

Such real-life experiences made working-class youths in Chicago into a kind of privileged audience set apart from the older generation—a situation that the genre incorporated into its narratives. Scarface's turn to a life of crime, for example, sharply contradicts the ethnoreligious values of his mother, who, like Mike Powers, refuses to take gifts from the hands of the gangster. This kind of conflict is further played out in *Scarface* in a scene that portrays the reaction of an Italian civic figure—uttered in a thick, parodic accent—to the bad publicity that press coverage of organized crime activities is bringing to the Italian people. Here again, the gangster film did not invent, but rather recast, what was a common occurrence in Italian Chicago. Throughout the 1920s and 1930s, the Italian-language press in Chicago railed against what its editors perceived as anti-Italian sensationalism by the mainstream newspapers in their reportage of crime. In 1925, an editorial of the *Bulletin Italo-American National Union* exclaimed, "Crime has no nationality!" Similar rallying cries were heard again and again in succeeding years, as in 1928, when the same source complained, "We fail to see the names of O'Donnell and Saltis in heavy type."[183] The editors of such papers were also vigilant about what they viewed as "offensive" representations of Italians on the big screen.[184] These were the very same voices that urged American-born Italians to learn the language and culture of the motherland. "It is only in such a way, and on that basis," one Italian-language publication argued, "that the Americanization of the younger generation can be accomplished."[185] A similar mix of editorial content characterized the Polish-language press as well. While Poles had nowhere near the same preoccupation with their media representation, Polish publications did consistently remind readers that the ways (or rather, waywardness) of the new generation debased the image of the community. And the most immediate threat at hand often involved juvenile delinquency and crime in Polonia. One editorial, entitled "For the Benefit of Our Youth," for example, expressed concern that "the Chicago Police bulletins are publishing a vast number of crimes committed by our Polish-American youth." The purpose of this piece was to stir up support for the Polish Welfare Association "to extend care for the straying Polish youth in Chicago."[186] Once again, the proliferation of such sentiments in this era revealed growing fissures between immigrant parents and their native-born children. For the older, foreign-born segments of ethnic communities, the result was a conflicted *mentalité* that left them with one eye on the forces of ethnic prejudice that sought to exclude them from mobility and the other on a native-born generation they believed to be in danger of overassimilation. For the younger, native-born generation, forces of discrimination also informed their response to Americanization, but in the context of youth subcultures, the middle ground between ethnicity and assimilation proved problematic.

Hence, the gangster movie and the street gang each arose like heat from the friction between the values of the ethnic community and the ideals of mainstream American culture in an age of rising expectations and diminishing opportunities. It was something of a cruel twist of fate that the film and advertising industries would grow to such massive proportions in a time when their products became so hard to possess for the working class. Despite his inability to assimilate into middle-class society ("go legit," as Little Caesar put it) or avoid a tragic end, the ethnic gangster nonetheless presented an answer to this dilemma. More specifically, the gangster offered a solution to problems of masculinity that arose out of the experiences of the new generation in the domains of school and work. After all, youths were more concerned about their immediate situation than the more abstract notion of future mobility. Logically, then, the gangster's antithesis was the low-wage worker that so many working-class ethnics felt themselves so powerless to avoid becoming in the 1920s and 1930s. As the gangster character in *Playing Around* (1933) replies to his date when questioned about the high cost of their show tickets, "Say, who do you think you're out with—a soda jerker?" Yet the gangster film perhaps had as much to do with the creation of the problem as it did with the solution. Gangster movies, as David Ruth has argued, were powerful vehicles for promoting the values of the "new consumer society."[187] These values were not easily incorporated into existing ethnocultural frameworks—a predicament such movies poignantly depicted. However, the cinematic trope of the kingpin being snubbed in his attempt to help out the family was a utopic, inverted reflection of the more common real-life scenario of the young ethnic struggling with his family to retain a larger part of his wages to support his consumption habits.

Students of gangster films have focused largely on their dialogic aspects—in the sense of their expression of conflicts between working-class ethnics and middle-class society—and in so doing have implicitly attributed the invention of the gangster image to the culture industries themselves. This view tends to look past the more organic origins of many of the principal elements of the genre. With the penetration of mass cultural forms into the deepest ethnic enclaves by the 1920s, a synergistic relationship between young ethnics and commercial culture developed. However much young ethnics engaged in commercial leisure within the mediated context of their own ethnic neighborhoods, the essence of the mass cultural experience for so many ambiguous Americans was about fashioning an American identity, even if it was unavoidably a hyphen-ated one. The symbols of mass culture provided the most available means for fulfilling this need, which grew intense in the minds of second-gen-eration youths throughout the interwar period. This was a message that the film industry delivered to this audience with a whole constellation of images—sheiks, gangsters, shebas, flappers—that celebrated consump-tion and the use of style by characters who frequently embodied the racial ambiguities of the many new ethnics in the audience. In a sense, Valen-tino's Sheik was really the forerunner of the gangster. Like the gangster, the Sheik placed a taste for high style and savoir faire within the body of the working-class ethnic. However, these images were not merely the constructs of writers and producers, hammered out and sold to the blindly consuming masses; they drew their inspiration from the vibrant youth subcultures of the time and in the process managed to reshape them.

The ethnic gangster films of the early 1930s thus spoke to a genera-tion of working-class youths suspended between childhood and man-hood, and between the ethnic past and the American future. The incor-poration of the ethnic gangster style and ethos into the subcultures of young ethnics, however, was also part of a larger strategy to recreate new forms of honor and status to replace the ones that structural and cultural shifts had caused to slip from everyday life into the cracks of history. If young ethnics of the 1930s took to the filmic gangster, it was because he was of their world. Yet this connection was not always comforting. While openly seeking to dispel the idea that the lifeway of the gangster could lead to anything other than downfall, the ethnic gangster films of the in-terwar years nonetheless reaffirmed to the new ethnic *Lumpenproletariat* what they were already beginning to suspect: that respectability in Amer-ica was to be found outside the old neighborhood.

In the years to come, the ethnic implications of this idea would be-come harder to digest for a segment of the white working class that found itself trapped by financial circumstances in what remained of old neigh-borhoods, as they watched more and more friends and relatives depart for the more leafy suburbs and outlying urban areas. Indeed, one can trace the end of the old-style ethnic gangster in the industry moratorium that followed the Dillinger controversy of 1935. Yet other, larger forces were at work. By the beginning of the 1940s, Italians, Poles, and other new ethnics clearly no longer constituted the racial problems they had in what John Higham has referred to as the "Tribal Twenties," when many deemed them unfit for citizenship. The reactionary forces of middle-class

Protestant Americanism were no match for the rise of the American-born generations of new ethnics, who found a home in the resurgent industrial labor movement and in Franklin D. Roosevelt's New Deal order.

Such changes did not, however, eliminate the popular fascination for ethnic gangsters. In 1941, *High Sierra* ushered in a new version of the gangster in Humphrey Bogart's Roy Earle, a noble character hailing from Chicago but without a trace of ethnicity. Earle is the pure embodiment of manliness, without the stylish pretensions of his predecessors, and he is unambiguously white and American—a far cry from the post-Crash ethnic gangsters. Yet that racial concerns still lurked in the consciousness of the audience is revealed by the seemingly gratuitous presence in the narrative of the wide-eyed, slow-witted black servant, Algernon. What I will show in the next chapter is that such characters responded to certain needs in the minds of working-class ethnics. Black jazz was hardly a passing fancy. An interracial world of vice and entertainment continued to serve as a primary destination for groups of young ethnics living in Chicago's working-class districts. Yet as southern African Americans made their way to Chicago to take up work in the bustling war industries of the 1940s, this world would take on quite a different significance. Once again, migration would act as a culturally transformative force in working-class Chicago in the decades to come. Race became a new problem for working-class white ethnics in Chicago: a problem that youth gangs would seek to resolve in their own ways.

3

Hoodlums and Zoot-Suiters
Fear, Youth, and Militancy during Wartime

Well, the only thing that happened in the Second World War
was that we were having trouble with the blacks. . . . Now
they said they fought with us, so we can go live any place we
want to. Do you know what I mean? Well, the white people
didn't go for this at all. Let's face it, who the hell wants to—
would you want to have a black guy living next door to you?
Let's face it. Of course, maybe now, you know, now that
we're older, we don't care . . . but in those days, oh man, if
a black guy came into our neighborhood, he was dead.

West Side Chicago resident

To smash something is the ghetto's chronic need. Most of the
time it is the members of the ghetto who smash each other,
and themselves. But as long as the ghetto walls are standing
there will always come a moment when these outlets do not
work.

James Baldwin

BLACK MIGRATION AND WHITE RESPONSE: THE DANGERS OF YOUTHS AT PLAY

On April 3, 1944, the Committee on Minority Groups of the Chicago
Council of Social Agencies invited representatives from community agencies on the Near Northwest Side to discuss an urgent situation: "Recent
incidents following the moving of Negroes into the community." The most
notable of the group was Lea Taylor, longtime administrator of the area's
Chicago Commons Association and tireless advocate of the settlement
house mission to propagate civic values and racial tolerance. Taylor opened

the session by depicting what she referred to as the "tight knit Italian community" where a number of African American families had recently attempted to rent apartments in "badly deteriorated buildings which had been half empty for many years." "She described the fear and resentment of the neighborhood," the transcript of the proceedings record, "expressed in broken windows and fires." To put an end to such actions, Taylor had petitioned the city for around-the-clock police protection.[1]

Such an account of pitched resistance might give the impression that the number of African American migrants here numbered several thousand. In actuality, it was more along the lines of several hundred, a total that was not even 1 percent of the overall population of the community area; the particular crisis at hand involved reactions to the settlement of blacks in just two buildings. Nor was this a situation of residents living along the color line attempting to stave off its advance. This neighborhood, in fact, lay far away from the densely packed Black Belt ghetto on the South Side of Chicago, the boundaries of which were stretching to the breaking point because of the influx of southern African Americans seeking work in the booming war industries. Whereas many white residents living around the color line could actually see the black ghetto they feared would spread into their communities, the whites on the Near Northwest Side saw the black newcomers occupying only an obscure corner of the area. Nonetheless, the scenario in this setting bore a basic resemblance to the more storied situation around the Black Belt. Those under attack were primarily recent migrants from the rural South, many of whom had obtained jobs in a nearby defense plant. Since the commute from the Black Belt would have cut substantially into their earnings and cost them valuable time, they had sought housing closer to work. It is likely that many of them had little idea of the kind of neighborhood in which they were attempting to settle—that is, until some of their neighbors welcomed them by throwing rocks through their windows and setting their buildings afire. In the years to follow, the glass would continue to shatter, vicious words would be uttered, and the flames of racial hatred would light up the sky on many a night, leaving many homeless and several others dead.

What was transpiring in this relatively small pocket of the city, into which large numbers of Polish and Italian immigrants had flowed decades before, was a manifestation of a larger historical development. Inspired by the promise of relatively high-paying jobs in defense plants and the expectation of a warmer racial climate, hundreds of thousands of African American sharecroppers and agricultural laborers packed up what they could carry and boarded trains for the industrial centers of the northern Midwest. Having begun in the early war years, the pace of this migration gained momentum in the second half of the 1940s. Chicago was one of the central destinations up North, and its black population grew from 277,731 to 492,265—more than a 77 percent increase—between 1940 and 1950.[2] Sociologists St. Claire Drake and Horace Cayton estimated that out of this total, roughly sixty thousand African Americans entered the city from 1940 to 1944.[3] Of those in this initial group, most understandably gravitated toward the Black Belt, where things seemed more familiar and predictable. By 1944, an acute housing shortage gripped the city, particularly within the Black Belt, where one study estimated that 375,000 inhabited an area suited for no more than 110,000.[4] Addressing a meeting of the Dearborn Real Estate Board in July 1943, the chairman of the Chicago Housing Authority, Robert Taylor, cited statistics indicating that the Second and Third Wards—the heart of the city's South Side black ghetto—were more densely populated than the slums of Calcutta.[5]

Such circumstances forced more and more families of color to seek lodgings in some less-than-inviting environs, such as the run-down buildings below Grand Avenue on the Near Northwest Side. A handful of black residents had lived here prior to 1940, but these folks inhabited the blighted and somewhat isolated industrial section in the southeast corner of this community, along the left bank of the Chicago River. In the early 1940s, however, landlords all over the city recognized the opportunity a tight and racially stratified housing market offered them. Black migrant families had few alternatives but to pay a great deal more to secure an apartment, and it did not take long for slumlords on the Near Northwest Side to get in on the action. Looking to exploit the normally low-rent properties below Grand Avenue, they actually began targeting black newcomers by advertising in the *Chicago Defender*. According to Lea Taylor's report in 1944, the owner of one building began charging his new black tenants thirty dollars per month for living spaces that had cost the previous inhabitants only twelve dollars per month.[6] In the face of such housing pressures, racial boundaries laid down in the interwar period began to crumble. One manifestation of this wartime housing shortage, demographically speaking, was the expansion of the interface between black and white residents, which created more city spaces where some form of interracial contact could occur—even if just a fleeting exchange of glances on a crowded street.

The extent to which interracial contact increased around this time has been a matter of some speculation. Observers have used census data to render some different readings of the impact of the black migration of the 1940s on Chicago's social geography. Both city agencies and the first scholars to examine the period found these population changes indicated a reversal of a long-standing trend of intensifying segregation. Between 1940 and 1950 the number of "mixed" census tracts grew sharply from 135 to 204, the percentage of "non-Negroes" living in exclusively "non-Negro" tracts dropped from 91.2 to 84.1, and the number of tracts without a single nonwhite resident fell from 350 to 160. Reconsidering this story of residential change decades later, however, historian Arnold Hirsch arrives at a somewhat different conclusion. As he points out in his study of the postwar housing situation, such trends should be viewed alongside the coincident increase in the proportion of African Americans living in uniformly black tracts from 49.7 percent to 53 percent, a measure that suggests to him that "black isolation was, in actuality, increasing even as the Black Belt grew."[7]

As much as anything, perhaps, these statistical discrepancies demonstrate the difficulty of piecing together fragments of census data to produce an overall portrait of the urban landscape and the everyday experiences it contained. First, residential data take little account of the myriad public spaces around the city—parks, beaches, commercial venues, workplaces, street corners—where people from different areas mixed. Second, census tract lines seldom reflect the boundaries people draw around their own communities. Moreover, statistical analyses covering the entire metropolitan area in the 1940s encompassed a number of peripheral areas, particularly in the far northwestern and southwestern parts of the city, with population densities and housing arrangements more like that of suburbs. At the time, these were sparsely populated, quasi-rural areas, with predominantly single-family dwellings, located far from industry and the downtown business district. Lacking affordable housing and accessible forms of rapid transit, these recently incorporated areas lay largely outside the story of ethnic and racial succession under discussion here. And yet the addition of many exclusively white tracts to the total tends to make some indicators of increasing interracial contact appear less striking.

Limiting the scope to the general environs of the downtown business district and industrial zones of the urban core, where the vast majority of black migrants settled (or might have settled) in the 1940s, one finds quite another context of race relations. Here the changes in the spatial patterning of race were nothing short of dramatic. This was the beginning of a phase of accelerated black migration and white flight that in the span of a few decades transformed a few African American neighborhoods into an immense "second ghetto," spreading westward from the Loop all the way to the city limits, while at the same time doubling the area of the extant Black Belt by extending it eastward to the lake and further southward. There is good reason to point out the rise in the proportion of blacks living in racially uniform tracts—in retrospect, this obviously portended the modus vivendi of the years to come—but for a span of some two decades the massive increase in the overall black population in Chicago would substantially outpace the rather moderate gains in this index of segregation. In other words, regardless of the persistence of the dynamics of segregation, the magnitude of the black migration in the 1940s made the heart of Chicago a far more interracial and racially uncertain environment.

While census numbers are again admittedly inadequate to the task of describing the ground-level experience of this change, they do at least begin to convey the staggering pace of racial succession in the densely packed working-class neighborhoods around the Black Belt and growing West Side ghetto in the 1940s. In the five community areas that would constitute most of the black West Side ghetto by the 1960s, very little of which was solidly "nonwhite" at the end of the 1930s, the African American population climbed from 32,533 to 110,437 between 1940 and 1950. In the eight community areas into which the South Side Black Belt swelled in the same period—those that were not already close to uniformly black when the decade began—the influx of African American inhabitants was even more impressive, raising the overall total from 23,951 to 88,362.[8] Unlike in the 1930s, a substantial amount of the growth of both of these major black residential sectors in the 1940s involved settlement in tracts that had just years earlier been entirely or predominantly white. Figures for the whole city show that of the 227,193 "nonwhites" to arrive in the 1940s, 138,216 of them, or nearly 61 percent, took up residence in tracts classified as less than 30 percent "nonwhite" at the beginning of the decade, while only 44,984—less than 20 percent—settled in areas with a "nonwhite" population of 90 percent or more.[9] The experience of racial transition felt even more turbulent than it might have, particularly in the first half of the 1940s, because the preceding decade had been relatively stable. Although the black population did increase by some 44,000 (almost 19 percent) during the 1930s, the vast majority of migrants settled in already existing black neighborhoods. "The period of the 1930s, consequently," Hirsch writes, "was an era of territorial consolidation for Chicago's blacks."[10] In fact, the severe housing shortage that wartime migrants would encounter originated here, as depression conditions put the brakes on new housing construction, but it was not until the mid-1940s that this problem would attain crisis proportions. Complementing the sense of residential stability prevailing in the 1930s had been the decrease in Mexican migration, which was attributable to the threat of repatriation, and the considerable lessening of European immigration after the passage of restrictive immigration laws in 1921 and 1924.

Rupturing this status quo was the precipitous addition of many tens of thousands of southern black migrants into Chicago's social geography and wartime labor market, and with them powerful new sensibilities about the rights owed them. Indeed, such population shifts throughout much of the urban north had by the mid-1940s forced open a discursive space within which the state of race relations would be questioned and racial attitudes reshaped. Several factors contributed to this change: powerful protest campaigns such as A. Philip Randolph's 1941 March on Washington movement for racial equality in the defense industries and the Double-V campaign for victory over fascism abroad *and* at home; the increasing legal and political activities of black institutions like the NAACP and the Urban League; and the growing role of African American newspapers such as the *Chicago Defender* and the *Pittsburgh Courier* in raising awareness about housing problems, school overcrowding, and law enforcement injustices. However, the events that decisively thrust the problem of race relations on to the national stage for working-class whites and blacks alike were the more explosive expressions of wartime racial turmoil at the grass roots—the widely publicized race riots that broke out in Los Angeles, Detroit, and New York in the summer of 1943.

Somewhat surprisingly, Chicago, which arguably witnessed the most tumultuous and eventful history of race relations in the decade following the end of the Second World War, was spared any such spectacular conflagration of racial violence during the war. However, there were numerous sparks. On May 13, 1943, for instance, two white police officers fatally shot a sixteen-year-old African American boy several times in the back after he had allegedly hurled rocks at them. The youth, Elmo Vasser, was a student with no prior record of criminal activities, a detail that further belied the outlandish claim that a stone-throwing adolescent justified the use of lethal force. If that was not enough, shortly after the incident the *Defender* reported that the boy's father had received a note threatening the same fate for him if he did not "keep his mouth shut" and move from his Morgan Park neighborhood. Days later, hundreds of angry citizens gathered to seek redress for Vasser's slaying, but the community ended up heeding the Reverend Archibald Carey's plea to "guard against any resort to violence."[11] This was not the first time that year that residents had rallied against police brutality targeting black youths. In February, a police officer patrolling the hallways of Morgan Park High School had viciously clubbed a sixteen-year-old black student, who, according to several eyewitness testimonies and the decision of a juvenile court judge, had done nothing to provoke such treatment.[12]

Had such incidents occurred some months later, in the wake of the June riots in Los Angeles and Detroit, black Chicago may very well have erupted into violent rebellion. Nonetheless, while Chicago did not itself witness its own wartime race riot, the startling events elsewhere had a noticeable local impact. Days after the violence in Detroit, for example, a settlement house official addressing an emergency meeting of the Chicago Council of Social Agencies warned against "too much public discussion" of the recent events and claimed that coverage of the riots by the citywide press and the community papers had caused what he referred to as "a reorganization of prejudice and fear." Many believed that Chicago had a racial crisis on its hands, and the mayor hastily moved to establish a high-level commission to monitor racial flare-ups and recommend strategies for keeping the peace. The situation appeared so grave, in fact, that community leaders in several racially mixed neighborhoods urged their aldermen to make provisions for first aid stations and safety shelters.[13]

This sense of impending disaster, moreover, was not limited to community workers and city officials. The disturbing news from Detroit seemed to have a palpable effect on ordinary Chicagoans as well, especially working-class youths residing in and around interracial neighborhoods. Just hours after the stories of race warfare in the Motor City had hit the streets of Chicago, police responded to a call from one such area of Hyde Park, where a mob of white youths armed with shovels, pick handles, and other weapons had taken to the streets in search of African Americans. The youths claimed to be seeking retaliation against a group of black teens that had allegedly threatened them on their way to the beach.[14] Three days later, the well-connected black community leader and sociologist Horace Cayton observed that African Americans were "arming" themselves in case of rioting, and two social workers in Mexican areas reported that Mexican adolescents were discussing the riots and "waiting" for something to happen. Another community worker, a representative of the Hyde Park Neighborhood House, remarked on the "changing attitude of white boys," noting that several of those he was in contact with had taken to carrying large knives around the streets and "expressing themselves as preparing for fights against Negroes."[15]

Such responses stemmed in part from the dramatic, even anarchic way the Chicago press had depicted the situation in Detroit. To begin with, as news of the violence spread, Detroit officials could offer no explanation for its origins, other than a vague report of an interracial incident in a crowded recreation area on Belle Isle, a park situated on a patch of land in the middle of the Detroit River. The absence of a sense of causality contributed to the perception that what was being witnessed was the outbreak of race war, pure and simple: "a frenzy of homicidal mania, without rhyme or reason," according to one writer for the *Detroit Free Press*.[16] This was the conclusion drawn by many Chicagoans upon reading in their own city's leading paper the quotes of riot victims, white and black, expressing shock at having been attacked by mobs for no apparent reason other than the color of their skin. Further adding to the apprehension was the lack of clarity regarding which race had acted as provocateur. The following description was typical of press coverage of the riot: "Groups of Negroes and of whites milled about on street corners in a wide section bordering the northeastern side of downtown Detroit and hurled bricks and stones at passing automobiles bearing members of the opposite race."[17] Such treatment left in tact the perception that the aggression might have been initiated by members of Detroit's African American community, perhaps even in an organized fashion, an idea that had much deeper implications for racial attitudes in Chicago than if the riot were merely another case of white aggression and black response.[18]

In the end, however, the bomb planted in Chicago in the summer of 1943 never blew, even if its ticking continued to be heard in the city for months, if not years. It is difficult to know for sure how much these spectacular expressions of race war touched ordinary Chicagoans. Much easier to detect is the vigorous institutional response that followed the riots—documented in the activities of the Mayor's Committee on Race Relations (MCRR) and the numerous meetings of community workers and local political leaders. The reconnaissance reports aired by community representatives in the aftermath of the Los Angeles and Detroit riots in June suggest that these events had a particular resonance in working-class youth subcultures in Chicago. Indeed, the very fact that such meetings focused at times single-mindedly on youth behavior indicates how much observers took for granted the notion that the dreaded large-scale racial disturbance to come would begin in a space where youths congregated and mixed. This was a prevailing assumption in 1944, for example, in the first Mayor's Conference on Race Relations, which fixed its eyes on the kinds of leisure spots that brought crowds of black and white youths together. "Public parks, bathing beaches, sports events, dance halls, bowling alleys, street car transfer points" rounded out the list Chicago Urban League president A. L. Foster highlighted in his presentation to the MCRR. These were the settings, according to Foster, which were most susceptible to "the problem created by roving bands of white and colored boys."[19]

Several sources underlay this nightmare vision of "roving bands" of reckless youths. First and foremost, a more generalized perception of youth crisis emerged at the beginning of the war mobilization. Even before the chaos in Los Angeles and Detroit, a barrage of news items announced the rise of juvenile delinquency rates as a result of the overseas deployment of fathers and the entrance of mothers into the burgeoning wartime labor force, thus putting the nation's youth at risk.[20] Observers cited such circumstances, for example, to explain the disconcerting phenomenon of "Victory Girls"—young women who, out of some apparently misguided sense of patriotism, engaged freely in sexual relations with soldiers, raising fears of both deteriorating moral standards and an epidemic of venereal disease. Youth leisure, in particular, was coming under increased scrutiny by the spring of 1943. Literally hours before news of the riots in Los Angeles broke, Dean William F. Clarke of the DePaul University Law School proposed to a meeting of the Chicago Academy of Criminology a "nation-wide curfew to keep young people off the streets, out of the late dances, movies, and gangs for the duration of the war," an idea that the *Chicago Tribune* duly reported under the heading "Curfew Urged by Dean in War on Delinquency."[21] Eight days later, under the bold-faced words "Moral Crackup of War Perils Chicago Homes," the *Tribune* ran an article describing the "alarming" increases in both crime and delinquency rates, claiming that divorce and delinquency were "breaking up Chicago homes far faster than battle front casualties."[22] The ideological groundwork laid down by such reportage worked to initially obscure the racial dynamics of the Los Angeles riots, referred to as the "Zoot Suit Riots," despite the fact that the first days of rioting witnessed mobs of white servicemen chasing down, beating, and publicly disrobing Mexican and African American youths clad in the flamboyant zoot suits—the uniform of young, hip denizens of the urban nightlife consisting of an oversized, knee-length coat and baggy trousers. Indeed, much of the media coverage indicated that the riot was caused not by racial tensions but by unruly youths: the kind of "teenaged thugs," "zoot suit rowdies," "young gangsters," or "juvenile hoodlums"—as the press referred to them—who chose to dress themselves in clothing that flaunted textile rationing regulations and offended home-front sensibilities of sacrifice and loyalty.[23]

Yet what people like A. L. Foster and others engaged in riot prevention knew very well was that race and youth were vital and inseparable factors in outbreaks of racial violence. The idea of a wartime delinquency crisis no doubt informed Foster's menacing invocation of "gangs of boys riding the surface or elevated lines far into the morning hours," but Foster understood the circumstances which, to some extent or other, had sparked each of the 1943 riots—circumstances he knew prevailed in his own city as well.[24] In each of the riots that summer, leisure areas and other public spaces where large numbers of black and white youths crossed paths turned into flash points for collective racial violence. In Los Angeles, for example, most eyewitness accounts traced the start of the riots to disputes arising from white servicemen attempting to pick up Mexican girls in a downtown "Skid row district" where African American, Mexican, and white youths mixed. Similar situations preceded the riot in Detroit, where white youths and black zoot-suiters clashed repeatedly on youth leisure terrains around the city. The first outbreak of violence, for example, occurred outside a dance at a Catholic high school.[25] Then, just five days before the riot, a mob of servicemen and high school students battled a group of about fifty black teenagers, many of them outfitted in the highly controversial zoot suit, in an East Detroit amusement park. The riotous culmination of this pattern of interracial youth violence came the following Sunday in a crowded and racially mixed park on Belle Isle. Sparking the disorder that hot June day, according to many accounts, was a dispute between black and white youths over a craps game. As the riot raged on, the most intense action transpired around Detroit's Woodward Avenue nightlife strip, where white gangs assaulted blacks leaving all-night cinemas and pulled passengers out of cars to beat them.[26] Finally, even the Harlem riot, which, on the surface appeared to have more to do with police-community relations, had something of a causal link to the world of youth subcultures. A major precipitating factor of this eruption of black anger, according to many observers, was Mayor LaGuardia's decision to close the Savoy Ballroom, a nationally known dance venue reputed for racial mixing on the floor. This helps to explain why groups of zoot-suited black hipsters were so visible in the crowds of rioters that took to the Harlem streets.[27]

Although Foster's nightmare vision never came to pass, his warnings about the threat posed by gangs of youths nonetheless proved portentous. In the spring of 1944, as resistance to black settlement increased in several Chicago neighborhoods, the term *hoodlum* became almost synonymous in the black press with the white rock throwers, arsonists, and thugs—often running in "gangs"—who appeared to be leading the charge against racial integration. The *Defender* also occasionally applied this expression to black criminal gangs preying on their own communities, although not nearly as regularly. In any case, *hoodlum* tended to mean male and young. The age range it encompassed, much like that which characterized the membership of gangs and other such groups that hung out on the streets, seemed to stretch from the midteens through the early twenties. Its appeal as a buzzword in this moment reflected the increasing activism of such elements in the business of protecting the neighbor*hood* against racial invasion. Thus, it was a "gang of hoodlums" who in May 1944 threw rocks at praying congregants through the door of a black church in the Bridgeport area.[28] The one "youth" apprehended in this incident, it is easy to imagine, likely frequented the same social settings as—and perhaps even knew quite personally—the teenagers whom witnesses saw days later fleeing the scenes of two fires in the same neighborhood, including the "boy, about 15" running from a blaze that took the lives of two black children.[29] These youths belonged to the same "vicious anti-Negro ring," as one reporter put it, operating in this neighborhood during these years.[30] Also indicative of the key role played by working-class youths in generating wartime resistance to racial integration was the round of hate strikes carried out by students in several Chicago high schools. In September 1945, thousands of students at four different Chicago high schools walked out of classes to protest small increases in African American enrollment. At Calumet High School, way down in the southernmost sector of the city, some seventeen hundred white students staged a three-day walkout over the presence of twenty-nine black classmates.[31] Such actions paralleled an increase in acts of racial terrorism perpetrated by youths in several neighborhoods throughout the city around this time. About a month after the strikes, for example, arson again struck blacks residing around the Bridgeport area. After one such attack left a black grocery store owner in critical condition, blacks in the neighborhood were quick to identify the young perpetrators of the acts, telling reporters and police that "clashes between white and colored gangs" had been common in the area.[32]

Such evidence pointing to the centrality of working-class youth subcultures in the story of wartime race relations in Chicago and other major U.S. cities has gone largely unexplained. Generally, the tendency of youths to occupy leading roles—to be in the middle of things—during moments of heightened social insecurity has been dealt with by students of youth culture as predominantly a discursive phenomenon. For example, both Stanley Cohen's explanation of the "moral panic" that erupted in response to the violent clashes of Mods and Rockers in 1960s Great Britain and Stuart Hall's discussion of Great Britain's racially charged "mugging crisis" in the early 1970s emphasize the capacity of the media, the state, and civic institutions to articulate social concerns on the site of deviant or criminal youth subcultures. Each of these studies views the emergence of youth subcultures as signaling social instabilities—cracks in the postwar hegemonic order that the ideological project of the crisis or panic sets out to mend. More recently, Charles Acland has brought such perspectives into the U.S. context by arguing that youth or youthful deviance has served as one of the most consistent focal points for the constitution of threats to social order in twentieth-century America.[33]

This centering of youth culture is indeed a useful analytical move for understanding American political culture from the 1940s through the 1960s. National youth crises recurred continuously during this period: the wartime delinquency scare, as we will soon see, would give way to another delinquency panic in the 1950s focused on the effects of film and television, followed in the 1960s by the reaction to the dual specter of campus countercultures and revolutionary ghetto youths. If not cracks in the hegemonic order, these discourses revealed widespread anxieties surrounding certain profound social and cultural changes. However, understanding why youth crisis or youth deviance have been principal modalities through which people understand and live such experiences of social flux is not something students of youth culture have attempted to explain. They seldom ask what it is about the idea of youth that makes it such a resilient and symbolically pivotal metaphor for conveying broader forms of social crisis and change? Social movement theorist Alberto Melucci provides a possible answer to this question by focusing on the ability of youths themselves to engage in what he refers to as "conflictual action." The reason they so commonly play this part, according to Melucci, stems from the condition of ambiguity and uncertainty they experience in the transitional state between childhood and adulthood.[34]

Although this explanation emerges from a broader discussion concerning the question of why youths have so often been vanguard actors in mass-based social movements in the postwar United States and Europe, it is also helpful for understanding why they were principal actors in the very different context of collective racial violence in wartime America. Despite the intense social investment in the idea of youth during the war years, a phenomenon that predates this moment, the key role of youths in the unfolding drama of race relations was not merely a matter of representation. Rather, youths were central "conflictual actors" in the 1940s as a result of their location within the urban racial geography and their motives for being where they were. The prominence of the skid row setting in the media representation of the Los Angeles riots was not incidental; it reflected two interrelated trends shaping the context of race relations in Chicago and several other American cities receiving substantial migrations of blacks in the early twentieth century. The first was the increasing level of interracial exchange in commercial sex districts and other leisure spaces beginning around the mid-1930s, a phenomenon reflected by the emergence of interracial sex districts on the borders of working-class neighborhoods, the popularity of burlesque, and the concomitant spread of black streetwalking prostitution across the color line; the second was the increasing presence of white male youth groups in such areas of interracial sexual leisure.

As we have seen, Chicago had its own youthful interracial cruising areas like the one in downtown Los Angeles, where, according to some accounts, the first round of violence had occurred after Chicano youths took offense to the attempts of white sailors to have sexual relations with Mexican girls. These areas were, in most cases, located in and around black neighborhoods, where groups of young white males would go to pursue illicit thrills—prostitution, gambling, acts of petty thievery, and sometimes strong-armed robbery. While Bronzeville's Bright Lights district remained the largest of such areas during the war years, conditions associated with the wartime migration of southern blacks began to discourage white visitors. In addition to deteriorating housing and living conditions in the increasingly overpopulated Black Belt, the emergence of militant sensibilities related to the Double-V campaign, the race riots, and the return of black veterans made the Black Belt a much less hospitable place for white pedestrians and race tourists. As will be explored further, the war years witnessed the emergence of numerous black youth gangs and increasing attacks on whites who ventured across the color line. Partly as a result of such changes, North Side vice areas began to proliferate and expand. Perhaps the most significant of these surrounded the bustling intersection of Clark and Division on the Near North Side, within easy reach of the sizable Italian and Polish neighborhoods of the

Near North and Near Northwest Sides. Characterizing this corner of the city in a travel guide, two longtime Chicago crime beat journalists listed the following: "Gambling houses, neighborhood gangsters, Negroes, Poles and prostitutes."[35] Indeed, some of the main attractions here were nightclubs repackaging the Black Belt experience—in the form of risqué performances by black burlesque dancers—in these more friendly environs. The Parody Swing Club on North Clark Street, for example, boasted that its Bronzeville Revue put on the "Hottest Show in Town," while Club Marathon just down the street advertised four shows nightly featuring "Exotic Dancers" and "Blues Singers." The minstrel-like cartoon rendering of the dancers in this latter club's ads left little doubt as to the color of the performers it employed.[36]

Such evidence suggests that even in the midst of widespread resistance to racial integration, an ambiguous fascination with black bodies and a desire for racial mixing prevailed among many white young men. Although this was not a phenomenon restricted to the terrain of youth subcultures, the world of youth leisure offered unparalleled possibilities for the production and indulgence of such forms of fascination and desire. As we have already seen, young men were a target audience for a range of commercial amusements oriented around experimentation with black sexuality—burlesque shows, brothels, streetwalking prostitution, and dance halls. Yet such commercial activities represented only one form of interracial encounter experienced by working-class youths in Chicago in this moment. Perhaps much more important, as A. L. Foster well understood, were all of the casual contacts that occurred in everyday life— contacts made possible by youths' frequent location in settings like schools, parks, street corners, and even settlement houses. For example, it came to the attention of community workers just days after the Detroit riot that some two to three hundred black teens had been crossing into a predominantly Italian neighborhood on the Near West Side to attend dances at the Hull House. Even though such events were racially segregated, white youths in the area were not out of the picture. Recounting one such affair, a former Hull House representative described how Italian and Mexican youths would gather in the streets to "watch very closely" as the black dancers filed into the building.[37]

Racial mixing of this scale and nature would have been hard to imagine outside of youth leisure spaces. This was due in part to the very different relationship working-class youths—a good many of them second- and third-generation ethnics—possessed with the world of commercial leisure, and leisure in general. As we saw in chapter 2, the condition of being suspended between work and school, childhood and adulthood, American and ethnic meant that youths had much more routine access to the domain of leisure and were more prone to taking play seriously. As the 1943 riots suggest, leisure emerged as a central field of social conflict in the wartime city, a change that made youths into principal actors in the various struggles unfolding there. Why youths became such explosive actors in the drama of race relations, however, also hinged on the psychological investment they had for years made in the bodies of racial others. When, in the midst of racial crisis on the Near North and Near Northwest Sides of Chicago in 1944, a group of Near North Side youths blackened their faces for a minstrel show fund-raiser at the Near Northwest Side's Chicago Commons settlement, they were following decades of intimate relations between popular youth amusement and black expressive forms.[38]

While we know very little about this show, if it was indeed true to the minstrel tradition, then several of its skits no doubt turned on sexual innuendos and references to the supposed excessive, abnormal nature of black sexuality.[39] Perhaps most suggestive of the psychological investment youths made in black bodies during the 1930s and 1940s was the frequency with which they associated blacks with the interrelated notions of pathological sexuality and bodily filth. Once again, youths were hardly the only members of communities to express the dangers associated with the presence of racial others in sexual terms. For example, the same year the Chicago Commons hosted the minstrel show for the North Side Boy's Club, Lea Taylor remarked that residents concerned with the problem of racial invasion had made numerous references to the well-known commercial sex district to their east. "Do we want Grand Avenue to be like Division and Clark?" they repeatedly asked.[40] Moreover, years before, in the 1930s, when the North Side Improvement Association spoke of the "Negro problem" in the area of Clark and Division, residents generally understood this to mean the increasing number of black prostitutes on the streets.[41] Yet in the context of youth sociability, where predicaments of gender, sexuality, and race were almost constantly in play, racial others tended to be more deeply inscribed in the languages, rituals, exchanges, and routines of everyday life. Suggestive in this sense is the work of the historian Thomas Guglielmo, who has found that Italian girls and boys on the Near West and Near North Sides bantered frequently about blacks and Mexicans in their midst in the 1930s and 1940s, and that such banter quite often had sexual connotations. According to one Near West Side social worker, girls in the neighborhood would playfully insult each other by invoking the idea of familial or sexual relations with Mexicans and African Americans. Upon seeing a group of Mexicans on the street, for example, one would joke to another, "There goes your cousin"; when a carload of blacks passed, the taunt was "There's your boyfriend."[42] Another youth worker on the Near Northwest Side was somewhat taken aback by the barrage of racial epithets thrown at him by a group of boys at the Chicago Commons when he attempted to feel them out about their views toward blacks and Jews in January 1942. Taking breaks from their almost continuous back-and-forth about girls, the youths reflexively blurted out declarations like "niggers smell," "ninety percent . . . are syphilitic," and "Negroes should keep their place which is shining shoes and cleaning toilets."[43]

While the perpetrators of arson and physical attacks against African Americans seldom left clues about their motives, there are compelling indications that ideas surrounding the dangers of black sexuality provided the groundwork for violent and collective youth action in neighborhoods facing the threat of racial invasion in wartime Chicago. Such was the case in a particularly brutal incident that took place in the Near North Side Italian neighborhood of "Little Hell" in August 1941. Just blocks from the burgeoning nightlife district around Clark and Division, from which streetwalking prostitutes poured into its streets, Little Hell was one of the first communities in Chicago to feel itself seriously threatened by the increasing presence of African Americans in the early 1940s. Even in the 1930s, well before migration pressures began heating things up, the area around Little Hell was known to be unsafe for blacks. Looking back on the situation in the 1930s, one former resident remarked that "discrimination was fierce."[44] As blacks continued to settle in the area west of Larrabee Street in 1940 and 1941, a more marked pattern of racial conflict developed in spaces of youth leisure that were prone to racial mixing. In the summer of 1941, a group of youths calling themselves the "Black Hand Gang" began congregating on the corner of Sedgwick and Division Streets, where they carried out raids on black youths attempting to walk to nearby park facilities. Such activities remained almost entirely contained within this youth milieu; in the gang fights that resulted from such challenges, the *Defender* reported, "*even* the older whites and Negro people . . . are sometimes victimized." On August 8, 1941, a group of youths revealed the kinds of fears that motivated such strategies of empowerment when they pushed twenty-two-year-old African American Hershel McKnight into a car, took him to a nearby vacant lot, and shot him five times at point-blank range. McKnight's miraculous recovery from this assault allowed authorities to learn that the four youths who so viciously attacked him were incensed about his apparent amorous pursuit of a local white girl, Miss Valentia Vitto, who, according to other eyewitnesses, had recently rejected the advances of several white youths in the neighborhood.[45]

Such fears were powerful in neighborhoods like Little Hell, which lay close to racialized sex districts that tainted their status and threatened their property values. Yet such conditions were by no means necessary prerequisites for the emergence of these fears. Indeed, by the end of the war it was clear that perceptions regarding dangerous black sexuality had become entrenched in working-class youth subcultures throughout the city. Telling in this sense was the extent to which rape rumors and comments about predatory black sexuality circulated around a series of 1945 hate strikes carried out by white students protesting against small increases in black enrollment. In one school, for example, the visit of two police officers looking for an escaped juvenile delinquent led to wild rumors that two black students had raped a white girl. Moreover, strikers across Chicago told reporters repeatedly that blacks were "dirty" and "all look alike." Some female students interviewed claimed, "We girls are afraid to go anywhere alone."[46]

Such expressions provide a glimpse into the microdynamics of a much broader transformation in the history of racial and ethnic relations in the United States. Highlighting the intensified grassroots mobilization around racial concerns on both sides of the color line in the early 1940s, historians have argued that these years witnessed a major shift in the American racial order. They have viewed the war mobilization—both at home and abroad—as a watershed moment in the development of a binary racial system based on color, within which European Americans would see themselves and be seen by others as essentially white.[47] The interwar experiences of young European Americans in school, at work, in the neighborhoods, and in the domain of commercial leisure not only allowed them to negotiate racial anxieties but also led them toward a greater awareness of their own whiteness.[48] The war years greatly accelerated this process, and perhaps, on some level, even completed it. Thus revealed in the 1945 school strikes and the wartime wave of antiblack resistance was the new ease with which whites of different ethnic origins would take to the streets under the banner of whiteness.

Yet the white response to black migration in wartime Chicago also demonstrates a less understood facet of this story of white identity formation. The pervasive role that black sexuality played in the white imaginary and in white racial action warns against viewing the more universal sense of white identity emerging in this moment as the logical and inevitable product of black migration and ethnic generational succession. Slavoj Žižek's description of the function of the racial or ethnic other in the production of national identification offers a useful insight as to what else was transpiring as white youths were firing bullets into Hershel McKnight's body and striking over rumors of black rapists. Žižek points out that nationalistic sentiments and the racial and ethnic feelings associated with them are more than the result of the discourses that refer to them: what gives them their "substance" is the Lacanian idea of *enjoyment*. As Žižek argues, "What really bothers us about the 'other' is the peculiar way it organizes its enjoyment: precisely the surplus, the 'excess' that pertains to it—the smell of their food, their 'noisy' songs and dances, their strange manners, their attitude to work."[49] Such an analysis points instructively to the centrality of leisure in processes of ethnic and racial formation from the 1920s through the 1940s and, by implication, to the key role played by youth subcultures in organizing, mediating, and shaping these dynamics. Enjoyment in the very provocative form of black sexuality emerged very clearly in wartime Chicago as the substance of white fear, and, ultimately, white identity, and nowhere else but in the milieu of working-class youth subcultures along the color line were such fears so potent and so visible.

ZOOT-SUITERS AND CATS: BLACK YOUTH SUBCULTURES AND RACIAL MILITANCY

In the summer of 1943, as Chicagoans exchanged views on what the chaos in Detroit meant to them, the term *race problem* seemed everywhere. Yet this idea was Janus-faced. If it was for whites a construct that would inform white resentment about a range of political and social issues, it was becoming for African Americans both a festering sore of resentment and a rallying point for racial solidarity and political mobilization. Both facets of the "race problem" were on the table, for example, when social workers and community leaders met days after the convulsions in Detroit to discuss how to keep the peace. As Horace Cayton listened to the recommendations of his mostly white colleagues, including one who called for an effort to persuade city newspapers to stop referring to "the race problem" and emphasize instead the "war effort" and "civic pride," he was perhaps struck by their blindness to how such discussions came across to folks on the other side of the color line. When his turn came to speak, Cayton began by demanding that those around him and in the city at large begin to see the situation they were referring to as a "white problem" rather than a "race problem." Then he stressed the need for a "token payment" to be made to blacks in Chicago, a gesture that demonstrated the white community's "recognition" of the "real, underlying, and fundamental reasons" for the disturbances at hand: "bad housing, unfair employment practices, and the lack of recreational and educational facilities in Negro communities."[50] Cayton's demands that day reflected the emergence of emboldened structures of racial consciousness in black urban communities, which developed in part because of a series of very effective campaigns for wartime racial justice initiated by national black institutions and popularized by the black press. Randolph's March on Washington movement, the *Pittsburgh Courier's* Double-V campaign, the NAACP's efforts to defend black voting rights in federal courts, the formation of the direct-action Congress of Racial Equality (CORE), and the *Chicago Defender's* vigilant reportage of injustices faced by black soldiers and war workers alike made the first years of the war momentous ones for the idea of a black movement for racial equality.

In addition to such institutional factors, the first years of the war witnessed a groundswell of black assertiveness at the grassroots level, particularly in ghetto neighborhoods overcrowded with migrants facing discrimination on the job and in neighborhood life. It was in the urban North, where the sting of racism was all the more jolting as it was less expected, that this new sensibility came to be most powerfully articulated—in the riots in Detroit and Harlem. Recalling his experiences as a young man living in New Jersey in 1942 and working in defense plants, James Baldwin claimed it was the year he "first contracted some dread, chronic disease, the unfailing symptom of which [was] a kind of blind fever, a pounding in the skull and fire in the bowels." Baldwin explained that this "disease," which he also referred to as a "rage in [the] blood" of all blacks, was a condition he picked up facing racial indignities at "bars, bowling alleys, diners, places to live."[51] His affliction eventually caused him to put his life on the line in order to take a forceful stand against a restaurant that refused to serve him—the kind of act that was occurring with much greater frequency in the months leading up to and following the riots in the summer of 1943. The increase in such acts and the feelings underlying them explains the widespread circulation in white Chicago of rumors that blacks in Chicago were plotting so-called Bumper Clubs and Push 'Em Days in order to carry out concerted attacks against whites on public transportation and in other common areas throughout the city. Though Chicago newspaper reporters and community workers repeatedly searched in vain for evidence of such conspiracies, these rumors were, in some sense, not entirely baseless.[52] If such visions lurked menacingly within the white imaginary during the war years, they were not conjured out of thin air; rather, African Americans forced them into the white mind when they began defying the rules of racial conduct. While historians have demonstrated how such forms of consciousness took hold throughout black communities during this period, most have overlooked the key role played by black youth subcultures in developing, structuring, and propagating militant sensibilities concerning racial injustices and the ways to challenge them. Indeed, when whites imagined "Bumper Clubs" and "Push 'Em Days," the black hands shoving them generally belonged to young males—the black youths they increasingly saw grouped together on street corners, buses, and trolleys and in schools and parks.

A number of explanations exist for why black youth subcultures came to play this role during the war years. Like their white peers across the color line, black young men were prone to be in the process of negotiating the precarious liminal stage between adolescence and adulthood, boyhood and manhood, school and work. This was a condition that pushed them very often out onto the streets and into venues of commercial leisure— frequently in the company of their male peers—in pursuit of adventure, honor, manhood, and respect. Moreover, while Chicago's black community at this time did not exhibit the kinds of deep generational cleavages that formed in white ethnic communities wrestling with the trials of Americanization, African American youths in Chicago nonetheless embodied a distinct outlook developing from their specific generational circumstances that tended to instill them with an edgier sense of frustration with the northern racial system. A good many youths coming of age in Chicago in the 1940s were, as James Baldwin described it, "part of that generation which had never seen the landscape of what Negroes sometimes call the Old Country."[53] The Chicago-born generation stood largely outside an old South frame of reference and thus possessed none of the coping mechanisms that grew out of it. They adhered, in some sense, to anthropologist John Ogbu's conception of "involuntary minorities," who, having no former homeland with which to compare their situation, tend to view the discrimination against them in starker terms and thereby develop "oppositional identities." Moreover, if the southern-born youths who mixed with them in the streets had more of a southern frame of reference, their "homeland" hardly seemed the kind that "voluntary minorities" use to construct compensatory alternative identities.[54] They had arrived in the North with great expectations, and everywhere they heard comparisons with the "Jim Crow South" bandied about to express all that was wrong with race relations in Chicago. Indeed, contemporary observers and historians have commented on rising tensions between southern- and northern-born blacks in cities like Chicago during the heavy migration years of the 1940s—tensions which also had a great deal to do with class. Yet few have sufficiently appreciated the extent to which black discourses about crime, excessive partying, and the general immorality of migrant culture also took shape at the interface of two different generations within the black community.

The controversy within the black community surrounding the proliferation of zoot-suiters in the streets offers a prime example of such generational dynamics. The zoot suit phenomenon exploded in the summer of 1943 after the news media placed young black men wearing these outlandish outfits at the center of the riots in Los Angeles, Detroit, and Harlem. Moreover, while the Los Angeles affair appeared mostly a situation of white vigilantism, the source of the uprising in Detroit (somewhat ambiguously) and in Harlem (unmistakably) was black—black, young, and, in a remarkable number of cases, zoot-suited or otherwise hip. While wearing a zoot suit had already become something of an act of resistance by March 1942, when their sale was forbidden as part of the War Production Board's rationing regulations, the press representation of zoot-suited black and Mexican youngsters as the provocateurs in the disorders of Los Angeles, Detroit, and Harlem more than one year later greatly increased their subversive cachet on both sides of the color line.

The response was immediate in many black communities. Although most of the violence in Los Angeles targeted Mexican youths, the *Chicago Defender* understood right away how such events threatened blacks Chicagoans:

> Zoot suits today have become synonymous with bad conduct, loud talking, violence, and crime. Zoot suits no more represent the Negro than watermelon, dice, switch blades or muggings. The wave of violence against zoot suiters on the West Coast has a lesson for our community. Unjustified as the attacks are, they still strike home the immediate need for drastic action to curb the unbridled minority of our race that is giving us a bad name. They show that zoot suits are a community, rather than an individual affair. So put the zoot suits in moth balls, fellows—at least for the duration.[55]

Such expressions of black middle-class opposition to what many black civic leaders viewed as an urban youth subculture dominated by excessive thrill-seeking have led historian Robin Kelley to conclude that the zoot suit represented "a rejection of both black petit bourgeois re-

spectability and American patriotism."[56] However, aside from its articulation of class tensions, Kelley's analysis of the role of this zoot suit subculture in the political consciousness and radicalization of Malcolm X
(whose autobiography later disavowed his participation in this milieu)
points to how experiences in this world shaped an oppositional racial
consciousness among black youths.[57]

While the middle-class voice of the *Chicago Defender* wanted its readers to see this subculture as a product of the "unbridled minority . . . giving us a bad name," it was perhaps more accurate to see the zoot suit as
more of a "community affair." Indeed, if a teenage Malcolm Little was
perhaps not yet poised enough to articulate the political meaning of this
world and its flamboyant symbol, other black intellectuals and leaders
were captivated and even inspired by what Ralph Ellison referred to as
the "riddle" posed by the potentially "profound political meaning" of
the zoot suit.[58] Horace Cayton, for example, had a very different outlook on the zoot-suiter than that of the *Defender*'s editorial board, telling
city officials that "the Negro zoot-suiter is very tough, occasionally even
dangerous." "He is the result of the depression," Cayton explained, "an
American and not a Negro liability."[59]

Using a theoretical framework drawn from the work of the anthropologist James C. Scott, Robin Kelley has argued for the centrality of
what Scott terms "infrapolitics" in understanding the emergence of grassroots black militancy during the postwar era of civil rights activism. Kelley demonstrates how often hard-to-see "daily confrontations, evasive
actions, and stifled thoughts . . . inform[ed] organized political movements" in this period, highlighting, in particular, the role of black youth
subcultures as the soil from which these actions and sensibilities grew.
"Infrapolitics," according to Kelley, constituted a "hidden transcript"
whose existence was essential to black political mobilization.[60] This transcript took shape in a number of different sites of everyday life that are
not normally associated with political consciousness and struggle—parks,
street corners, buses and subway cars, and a range of commercial leisure
venues; it sometimes involved somewhat direct challenges to the white
racial order—spontaneous and overt acts of civil disobedience—and
other times much more subconscious ones, such as participation in leisure
activities that expressed a sense of liberation from the repressive work
regime faced by many working-class blacks.

This analytical framework is particularly instructive for understanding the development and function of black gang subcultures in wartime
Chicago. Indeed, as Frederic Thrasher observed in the early 1920s, the

defense against white youth aggression had been a central dynamic in the formation of black male youth groups in the years following the First Great Migration. This was no less true decades later, in the 1940s, but around the time of the 1943 race riots, more and more observers began remarking on a more offensive posture on the part of black youth gangs. Longtime crime beat journalists Jack Lait and Lee Mortimer, for example, described numerous black youth gangs roaming the streets of the Bronzeville neighborhood between 39th and 41st Streets, several of which, they reported, numbered some two hundred teenage members. Generally presenting an unapologetically racist and sensationalist view of the situation, Lait and Mortimer's claim that these gangs "frequently invade[d] white neighborhoods to pillage, rob, rape, and beat up people of any race for the sheer pleasure of it" needs to be used very carefully.[61] We should be skeptical, for example, about the "frequency" of such raids as well as the idea that color played no role in the selection of their victims. Lait and Mortimer would certainly have been averse to injecting some rationalizing sense of racial solidarity or protest to their story of black youth crime. Yet even within their very own account, one finds evidence of an alternative explanation for black-on-white violence: as Lait and Mortimer write later in their book on the Chicago underworld, "white strangers" crossing into Bronzeville "were met with . . . hot hatred."[62]

Moreover, despite its yellow journalist tendencies, Lait and Mortimer's depiction of black gang attacks against white residents was by no means groundless. A series of interviews with black civic leaders and residents on the South Side conducted by the Chicago Crime Commission around the end of the war confirmed certain aspects of their account. For example, the executive secretary of the YMCA branch on 38th and Wabash, O. O. Morris, spoke at length about "the resentment of the negroes to whites in their district," recounting the story of his light-skinned son who, upon getting off the street car at State Street and 38th, was nearly beaten up by "a gang of colored boys" demanding to know what he was doing in the neighborhood. Morris also claimed that "gangs of negro boys" often attacked Western Union bike messengers and that black youths displayed considerable "resentment" toward white police officers attempting to make arrests in the neighborhood.[63] Moreover, Benjamin B. Church, the director of the South Side Boys Club, mentioned several "incidents" of interracial youth violence along Wentworth Avenue between 35th and 55th Streets that he believed were "strongly indicative of the general tenor" of black residents in the area. According to Church, these incidents, which arose out of the desire of blacks to move westward beyond Wentworth Avenue, were "forerunners of more serious clashes to come."[64]

Thus, numerous observers in black Chicago were noting the emergence of new forms of assertive behavior and of militant sensibilities in the 1940s. While these structures of feeling were also taking hold of the larger working-class black community, they seemed particularly accentuated in the milieu of black youth subcultures. First, if Lait and Mortimer's nightmarish depiction of mobs of marauding black teens was heavy-handed, the demographics of the wartime migration and the accompanying process of ghettoization had, in fact, filled the streets of black neighborhoods with teenagers and adolescents by the mid-1940s, and many of these youths had begun to organize into gangs. Ruth Coleman, a community activist and resident of the Ida B. Wells housing project, reported "numerous gangs of young boys" in the area around 47th Street, taking such names as the Thins, the Black Shirts, and the Crusaders, and many other South Side residents spoke of the activities of "bottle gangs," the name given in black neighborhoods to groups of youths who passed their nights drinking wine and beer on street corners.[65] Yet in addition to their sheer presence on the streets, as well as their exhibition of behavior that appeared to challenge middle-class values of thrift and respectability, black youth groups came to embody and to propagate new sensibilities of racial mobilization in more direct and conscious ways.

As mentioned earlier, if wearing a zoot suit became a gesture of rebellion after the imposition of rationing restrictions in March 1942, it became a much more direct statement after the riots of the summer of 1943. This explains the considerable presence of zoot-suiters among the most active black rioters in both Detroit and Harlem. Indeed, the historian Dominic Capeci confirms the view that a "so called 'zoot-effect'" was a dynamic in the riot, finding expressions of both collective rebellion and fatalistic thrill-seeking in the interviews of young male rioters he surveys.[66] In Chicago, despite the notorious implication of the zoot suit in the recent riots and its obvious flaunting of wartime restrictions, black youths remained determined to strut their stuff in these flamboyant outfits. Not even two months after the incident in Harlem, a nearly half-page ad in the *Defender* told jitterbugs to "wear your zoot suit" to the "Zoot Suit Dance" at the Parkway Ballroom on 45th and South Parkway Avenue, where a prize would be given to the "zootiest."[67] In the wake of the riots, the will of black youths to continue wearing these outfits served to rekindle a sense of collective struggle against racial injustice. Nor were zoot-suiters the only youths to inscribe a statement of protest on their bodies. The *Pittsburgh Courier*'s Double-V campaign spurred the spread of a Double-V hairstyle among many young African American women, who expressed their opposition to racism at home by weaving their hair into a v-shape.[68]

However, the ability of black youth subcultures to organize and articulate racial solidarity and militancy went beyond such symbolic displays. By the end of the war, the new spirit of rebelliousness circulating through the world of working-class black youths had begun motivating more direct challenges to racial discrimination. As Robin Kelley has described in the case of the black working class in Birmingham, Alabama, around the same period, the milieu of black youth leisure served to organize feelings of both racial solidarity and opposition. A compelling example of this was the high incidence of interracial conflicts instigated by groups of young black males going to and leaving parties and dance halls. Observers in Chicago remarked on similar trends; we should recall, for example, A. L. Foster's warning about "the problem created by roving bands of white and colored boys" riding the El trains all night long, as well as Lait and Mortimer's description of black-on-white gang violence at the edges of Bronzeville's lively nightlife district. Moreover, in July 1945, the *Defender* reported the stationing of a special police patrol in the Woodlawn district, at the "busy" intersection of 63rd and Cottage Grove in order to "prevent possible friction among the races and to halt rowdyism among jitterbugs who are said to frequent the Pershing ballroom."[69] In this same neighborhood around this time, moreover, movie theater managers were reporting "rowdyism" during movies, and numerous "disturbances" between white and black patrons.[70]

While the actions and feelings that crystallized in these contexts were at times somewhat inarticulate, arising out of frustrations that could have had more to do with the trials of adolescence and manhood than with racial injustices, at other times they appeared to be aimed directly at discriminatory practices restricting African American youths from using leisure resources. The problems encountered by at least two of the movie theater managers in the Woodlawn district, for example, had a great deal to do with the earlier refusal to allow people of color to enter. In January 1946, the manager of the Tivoli, also located at the intersection of 63rd and Cottage Grove, told the Chicago Crime Commission that he had formerly turned blacks away but that "the pressure exerted by various groups and colored persons attempting to purchase admission" had forced him to change his policy. This situation sheds light on the subsequent "disturbances" and "arguments" between black and white moviegoers. Similar circumstances prevailed at the nearby Ark Theater, 70 percent of whose patronage, according to its manager, came from "colored people mostly of high school age." Not surprisingly, the white manager reported having "considerable trouble" with his predominantly black audiences, most of whom must have resented a management that had previously excluded them.[71]

While activities like these carried out in spaces of youth leisure remained mostly within the domain of "infrapolitics," they could bear a close relationship to forms of activism that appeared in more overtly political contexts. In the winter of 1946, for instance, a number of black organizations, including CORE and several local church congregations, staged a series of picket demonstrations against racially discriminatory practices at the White City roller rink in this same Woodlawn neighborhood.[72] Such actions continued until late that year, when management finally changed hands and a new admission policy was implemented. There are indications, moreover, that the entrance of these and other organizations into the domain of leisure followed upon the more spontaneous actions of youths. In April 1946, for example, the determination of African American youths—both male and female—to break down the racial barriers at the Madison Gardens roller rink on the Near West Side drew the attention of the Chicago Urban League and forced the intervention of the Mayor's Committee on Human Relations. Facing mobs of white youths attempting to forcefully impose their own admission policy, black youths initiated these actions on their own and at the risk of considerable physical harm. One teen was even hospitalized after being shoved into a car and beaten with the butt of a pistol.[73]

Such circumstances indicate that, particularly after 1943, many black youths were becoming attuned to the idea of a collective struggle against racial injustices and that black youth subcultures represented dynamic forces for spreading such ideas throughout the larger working-class community. As in the case of grassroots demonstrations against Jim Crow practices in commercial leisure venues, the role of youth groups could be quite direct. Yet youth subcultures served as vital sources of grassroots mobilization in less direct and less heroic ways as well. Like their counterparts in ethnic and white communities, black youths became conflictual actors that forced themselves to the center of discourses about the state of the community or the race, opening up some significant generational and class cleavages in the process.

As wartime juvenile delinquency discourses began to proliferate in the early war years, black Chicago found itself on the defensive against racial theories seeking to explain elevated crime rates in African American neighborhoods. In December 1942, the *Chicago Defender* ran a series of front-page articles authored by the well-known University of Chicago sociologist Ernest Burgess, the second of which appeared below the headline "Blasts Racial Theory As Cause of Juvenile Crime."[74] Moreover, African Americans were not the only people of color touched by such trends. Just a week before the Los Angeles riot, the Chicago Area Project released a report on Mexican Americans that went out of its way to emphasize how the delinquency of Mexican adolescents followed "the strong pattern . . . already existing in the low-income areas prior to their coming." The report concluded: "All available evidence supports the assumption that delinquency in these areas results from conditions which obtain in the community rather than from any inherent delinquency-producing qualities in the population."[75]

In the black press, in particular, such defenses intermingled with tendencies to exploit the black crime problem and to cast it in class terms. Typical of this was a story published by the *Defender* nearly two years prior to the riots of 1943 comparing the area around 58th Street and South Parkway with the "Wild West." The outlaws responsible for such conditions, according to its author, were "'reefer' gangs and wine mobs" who "fearlessly congregate on the streets." "In the alleys near the corner of fifty-eighth street and Prairie avenue they toss the 'bones' and drink their wine, emerging in a 'mellow' mood but ready for a fight," the article further reported.[76] For the middle-class segment of the *Defender*'s readership, such diatribes against working-class leisure habits no doubt evoked images of the increasing population of recent migrants from the South. Indeed, even if many civic leaders in the black community were quick to dismiss the notion that migrants were mostly responsible for high black crime rates, the idea was nonetheless resilient. After the Zoot Suit Riots, though, the middle-class vision of the "minority of our race that is giving us a bad name" changed its form somewhat. The stylishly outfitted zoot-suiters seemed to have less to do with the idea of the maladjusted migrant.

Thus the zoot suit moment gave rise to a distinctively black variant of the mainstream delinquency panic. In the following years, the black press would give repeated exposure to "teen-age gangs" peddling dope, throwing "reefer parties," committing robberies, and most of all, killing and maiming each other in the most brutal ways. One cannot overstate the role of newspapers like the *Defender* in producing through sensationalistic reportage the perception of a youth crisis in the black community.

Detailing the phenomenon of after-school "reefer parties" in May 1944, for example, the paper described a "rising tide of youth and juvenile waywardness which is responsible for a score or more of hoodlum gangs committing almost every crime on the calendar."[77] All the same, the appearance of such discourses did, in fact, coincide with a set of conditions that could only have engendered the development of delinquent juvenile gangs in black neighborhoods. The most important of these was, of course, the accelerating migration of black families from the South, many of whom came with young children. The next was the housing shortage and the discriminatory real estate practices that forced most black families to take undersized apartments, a situation that necessarily filled the streets of black neighborhoods with adolescents and young adults, particularly during the hot summer months. Further compounding this situation were the city's grossly inadequate school and recreational facilities. By 1943, most black school districts in the Black Belt had implemented a double-shift system, making the detection of truancy next to impossible and disrupting family routines of youth supervision. Finally, there was the matter of discrimination in the workplace, a force that became abundantly clear in the immediate postwar months, when the Illinois State Employment Service reported that Chicago employment service offices had been flooded with job orders which requested "referral of white workers only."[78]

Black youth gang subcultures organized around thrill-seeking and rituals of violence emerged out of these circumstances. While these subcultures fostered feelings of racial solidarity and resistance to racial injustices, such sentiments were more often manifestations than causes of black gang formation in the 1940s. Indeed, while we should be wary of the sensationalizing tendencies of the sources that revealed its existence, an intraracial gang culture predicated on demonstrating masculinity through rituals of leisure and physical violence did, in fact, take shape in black working-class Chicago in the mid-1940s.[79]

Chicago's black press gave this world broad exposure in the spring of 1944 with its coverage of the vicious knife slaying of a fifteen-year-old youth by a teenager known on the streets as "Little Wolf." A police investigation of the incident could find no immediate motive for the murder, aside from a plan by Little Wolf's South Side gang, the Fins, to "beat up anybody" outside a dance sponsored by DuSable High School. Indicative of the intensity of such gang violence on a typical Friday night in the Fifth District was the fact that the police picked up Little Wolf just hours after the murder in connection with another gang fight on Garfield

Boulevard.[80] Following this incident, police confiscated a staggering 264 knives during searches at three South Side high school dances, prompting the formation of an organization of black community leaders for the purpose of assisting the police to halt the "juvenile crime wave" in the black community. The committee's first objective was the passage of a city ordinance prohibiting the sale and possession of "switch-blades," which, according to some black leaders, were sold to juveniles by numerous merchants in the black community.[81]

Many of the purchasers of these products belonged to street gangs with names like the Spiders, Deacons, Counts, Cobras, Cats, Invaders, Vikings, and Vipers. As the predatory connotations of these names intended to convey, one of the primary activities of such groups was engaging in street warfare with rivals. The ardor for such violence, in fact, often pushed youths to extreme and quite creative methods of keeping up in what was an arms race in the Fifth District. A juvenile officer in this area, for example, claimed to have seized crude forms of pipe guns (also known as "zip guns") made of wood, iron pipe, and rubber inner-tubing. Despite the relatively high probability of these homemade pistols backfiring, an occurrence that could cause serious harm or worse to the shooter, youths in this district exhibited an increasing willingness to take their chances with them in the mid-1940s. The meaning of such risk-taking behavior is suggested by an incident investigated by this same juvenile officer that left one youth dead after being struck in the head with a brick. According to the officer, the lethal blow occurred when fifteen youths began hurling bricks and rocks at each other in order to settle a dispute over who among them was strongest.[82]

The emergence of such rituals of masculinity in a milieu dominated by adolescents and young men in their mid- to late teens reveals, once again, their relationship to the condition of arrested maturation faced by youths suspended between work and school. Little Wolf, for example, was a teenager who had left elementary school to roam the streets. The chaotic atmosphere in black high schools that resulted from overcrowded classrooms and double shifts pushed many youths like him out of school. Moreover, even in the nearly full employment conditions of wartime Chicago, systematic discrimination at work meant that young black men would fill only the lowest, most tedious positions. The racial injustices inherent in the everyday experience of black teens, especially those that revealed themselves clearly—as in cases of Jim Crow discrimination in skating rinks and movie theaters and in instances of attacks perpetrated by white gangs along the color line—could give rise to group actions that articulated notions of racial solidarity and collective resistance to white racism. More often, however, such conditions created a need to express individual or group potency through demonstrations of fearlessness and prowess in ritualistic street fights.[83]

While conditions of racial marginalization ultimately shaped this need, it came to be expressed and understood in ways that were most often color-blind. This was particularly true in the racially insulated heart of the black ghetto, where many of the largest and most cohesive gangs formed in the 1940s. There, according to Useni Eugene Perkins's history of black Chicago street gangs, some gangs began to increasingly use physical intimidation to force youths to join and to employ initiation and membership rituals indicating a high level of organized activity.[84] A Chicago Crime Commission informant confirmed that such practices were indeed in operation by the spring of 1945 among the numerous gangs around the Ida B. Wells housing project, located between 37th and 39th Streets along South Parkway (now King Drive) and Cottage Grove Avenue. According to this source, gangs such as the Thins, Black Shirts, and Crusaders, obligated members to take loyalty oaths under "penalty of death" and forced younger boys to "engage in acts of sexual perpetration," perhaps as some form of initiation process.[85]

Fighting and other displays of physical power, however, were not the only means for self-realization on the streets. Interspersed between stories of youth violence in the black press were reports of reefer parties, dope peddlers, bottle gangs, and wine mobs. While such accounts, once again, reflected the class biases of an editorial board that decried the leisure habits of working-class blacks, the appearance of such views in both the black press and among black community leaders reflected a burgeoning youth leisure milieu in black Chicago in the 1940s. The center of this world lay in the famed Bronzeville drag along South Parkway Avenue, between 43rd and 47th Street. In the mid-1940s, this area was filled with businesses catering mostly to a teenage and young adult crowd: dance halls, ballrooms, bowling alleys, skating rinks, movie theaters, taverns, and snack restaurants. Here, on Bronzeville's main strip, according to Chicago Urban League official Frayser T. Lane, "large nocturnal gatherings of persons who are pleasure bent" were responsible for a great deal of the crime witnessed in the black community.[86] In view of the concentration of gangs just north of this area, both around Ida B. Wells and a bit further south, between 41st and 43rd Streets, it is likely that Bronzeville provided the context of many a gang war and many a gang party.[87]

Thus, not unlike the white ethnic gang subcultures of the late 1930s, the black gang subcultures in the 1940s were structured around "raising hell" and "having a good time"—pursuits that also corresponded to the fashioning of masculinity. For youths in the amorphous life stage spanning late adolescence and young adulthood, distinguishing oneself in this domain of leisure often involved some form of sexual exploit. In this sense, the black youth subcultures of the 1940s were hardly different from the white ethnic ones. Male group activities quite frequently revolved around various forms of sexual performance, ranging from catcalls on the street corner—a source of complaints voiced frequently by women residing in neighborhoods around Bronzeville—to gang rapes.[88] One movie theater manager complained of youths committing "acts of perversion" during the screening of "risqué" movies, a situation that had forced him to show only "straight pictures."[89] Moreover, while not a matter of public discourse in the ways that gang fights and dope parties were, youth workers in the black community spoke rather frequently about the problem of sexual delinquencies perpetrated by young men affiliated with gangs.[90] In their meticulous 1945 study of black life in Chicago, *Black Metropolis,* Drake and Cayton referred to the "more prevalent . . . thousands of lower-class young men who were never arrested as delinquents but who skirted the borderline of crime": "These were the 'cats' who, clad in 'zoot-suits,' stood around and 'jived' the women. . . . 'Sexual delinquency' was probably more widespread than petty thievery and violence."[91]

Much more frequently, however, African American youths sought to define their manhood in the more conventional realm of consensual sexual relations. Indeed, the "large nocturnal gatherings" witnessed in Bronzeville during this time were more often than not attended by members of both sexes. The appearance of several rather large and formally organized female gangs in the neighborhoods north of Bronzeville indicate that young women in working-class black Chicago had somewhat greater access to public leisure spaces than did many of their European American peers. The most visible of these was the Deaconettes, the female contingent of the largest black gang of the 1940s—the Deacons. Despite its name, this gang of teenage girls did not consist only of the girlfriends of the Deacons, but rather possessed its own leadership and engaged in its own activities, which included physical battles with other female gangs.[92] That girls like those in the Deaconettes shared in the festivities of black nightlife is suggested by police reports about "reefer parties" attended by both teenage girls and boys.[93] In addition to such backroom affairs, young male and female jitterbugs in black Chicago mixed openly and expressively in the big ballrooms of the South Side. Indeed, the scarcity of taxi-dance halls catering to blacks attested to the more substantial presence of women in its leisure settings.

The role of black youth leisure spaces in structuring sensibilities of racial solidarity and resistance to racial injustices helps to explain why some young women in this milieu would display a precocious activism in defense of their civil rights. It was a group of African American teenage girls, for instance, that sparked a near-riot and a wave of spontaneous protests against the Jim Crow policy at the Madison Gardens skating rink in the spring of 1946. Indicative of the clear sense of purpose that informed their actions, one of the girls, a fifteen-year-old sophomore at McKinley High School, later told a *Defender* reporter that "she and her friends were determined to secure their rights" and that "she was particularly bitter against the police, some of whom had been colored."[94]

Indeed, the tenacity displayed by working-class African American youths, both male and female, in carving out spaces of leisure, despite the forces of white racism and despite the recriminations of middle-class blacks, was an important catalyst in the spread of wartime civil rights consciousness throughout the community. As I mentioned earlier, youth subcultures possess an almost uncanny ability to articulate social crises and to expose the sources of power behind them. Once again, this was not always merely a discursive matter. While the emergence of a black delinquency discourse in the black press in the mid-1940s surely had a great deal to do with the larger wartime delinquency panic, bottle gangs, wine mobs, and violent street gangs were not merely ideological constructs, but highly visible features of everyday life in black Chicago.

The presence of these features, in effect, made juvenile delinquency prevention a focal point for grassroots mobilization during the early 1940s, when numerous citizens joined community campaigns to launch youth programs. In addition to the work of the settlement houses, residents in several black neighborhoods initiated their own efforts to deal with juvenile delinquency. In Englewood, for example, a community that would be one of the key racial battlegrounds in years to come, a large group of black residents worked for several months in the spring of 1943 to build a YMCA outpost for the youths of the neighborhood, a project that received the sponsorship of nearly every church and community organization in the area.[95] Around the same time, the Chicago Area Project was enlisting resident participation in the gang-ridden district between 22nd and 43rd Streets for its South Side Community Committee. Like most CAP organizations, the SSCC sought to develop youth clubs to be supervised by counselors.[96] Hearing about such efforts, several residents in the neighboring Near West Side area contacted CAP to sponsor the formation of a similar organization in their own community. Meeting in a local barbershop and in the homes of various members over several weeks, the group launched what became the West Side Civic Committee in the spring of 1946.[97]

While such organizations frequently adopted CAP's vaguely self-help rhetoric of "community betterment" rather than trumpeting a call for racial struggle, the fight against delinquency in the context of race riots and the Double-V campaign could not help but become a fight against racial injustice. Thus mobilization against delinquency in the mid-1940s went hand-in-hand with grassroots protests against the horrible conditions prevailing in black schools. According to Drake and Cayton, "saving the youth" was a theme persistently taken up by Bronzeville ministers in the late 1930s. "Older people in Bronzeville, like oldsters everywhere," they wrote, "spend a great deal of their time shaking their heads and denouncing the younger generation." Such sentiments could lead to somewhat conservative perspectives. According to Drake and Cayton, much of the blame for the youth problem at hand, particularly from the perspective of both the pulpit and the press of black Chicago, fell largely upon parents who neglected to bring their children to church and to show them proper guidance.[98] Yet by the early 1940s and especially after the summer of 1943, the issue of black delinquency was taking on an increasingly different tone. Paradigmatic of the changes under way was a 1944 letter addressed to the president of the Chicago Board of Education, James B. McCahey, by a South Side community group calling themselves the Parents' Club of Abraham Lincoln Center. Protesting overcrowded classrooms in the area between 22nd and 65th Streets, the leaders of this organization were sure to point out that "this deplorable condition contributes primarily to existing delinquencies." Demonstrating how the delinquency issue could give rise to languages of race and rights that focused attention on the state rather than the moral failings of the community, the authors stated in the next line: "We protest against such racial discrimination and urge the Board of Education to correct this injustice."[99]

4

Angry Young Men
Race, Class, and Masculinity
in the Postwar Years

... but the kids also say that the grown ups are damn mad
and that this time maybe they will get out and fight and not
sit around like they always do. The kids are tough and there
[*sic*] idea of fun is a good fight and they do not know what
the danger is and they don't care—if and when they get a
chance they will start it.

> ACLU informant on the anti-integration campaign
> in a South Side neighborhood, June 9, 1954

"UNRULY BOYS AND YOUTHS": JUVENILE TERRORISM AND COLLECTIVE ACTION

On July 4, 1946, Engelia McCain was awakened in the early hours of
the morning by a loud crash outside her South Side home. This was not
the first time she had been jolted from her sleep by such sounds. Since
taking up residence a little more than a month before in this restrictive
covenant neighborhood of the Englewood area, right on the historic color
line of Wentworth Avenue, McCain had twice seen attempts to set her
property afire. On more than one occasion she had heard the shattering
of glass as rocks flew through her windows. Rushing to the window on
that warm July night, she discovered her worst fears were true. Flames
had already engulfed her garage and were spreading to the second-floor
flat above it. This was but one incident in a wave of attacks against blacks
daring to make their homes on the "wrong" side of the color line. Mc-
Cain was the twenty-ninth victim of such terror in that week alone.[1]

Police were either unwilling or unable to track down the perpetrators of these late-night hit-and-run strikes. McCain, for her part, had a good notion of where to start looking. A "gang of teen-age white youths," she told a reporter for the *Chicago Defender,* had made a habit of loitering around her building in the weeks leading up to the event. She reported this to the police, but her complaints fell on deaf ears. When McCain asked police on the scene about the chances of finding the perpetrators, "the officer," she claimed, "replied that he was afraid someone would knock his head off."[2] Such was the case with a great many of the attacks against black property at the fringes of the South Side Black Belt. About a week before, in the adjacent Park Manor neighborhood, a similar arson attempt struck the home of Grace Hardy, once again under the watch of a police patrol. According to the officer on hand, a "young white boy" ran from the scene immediately after throwing flaming oil-soaked rags on the rear porch. That same week, just a few blocks from the Hardy residence, a "young hoodlum . . . with several other youths" was the first to stone the home of another African American family, initiating a mob action that at its peak involved some two thousand "hate-crazed people," as a reporter for the *Defender* referred to them.[3] Several days later, another incendiary projectile crashed through the window of a black home at 4302 Wells Street, a bit north of the previous incidents, but still along the South Side color line. Once again, there were no eyewitnesses, although the owner did report seeing a white youth hurl a rock through her rear window on a previous occasion.[4]

On July 11, 1946, the Civil Rights Department and the executive director of the Mayor's Commission on Human Relations (MCHR) met with representatives of the state's attorney's office, the fire attorney, and the chief justice of the Municipal Court to discuss how to end this epidemic. They referred to the occasion as a "Conference to Devise Means of Apprehending Juvenile Terrorists." The "juvenile terrorists" the organizers of the meeting had in mind, were, as they referred to them, "the brick and bomb throwers who use these lawless methods to prevent Negroes from living in heretofore white communities."[5] As the earlier episodes reveal, police intransigence combined with the hit-and-run guerrilla-like tactics of youths had allowed for only a small number of convictions. Yet from the handful of successful prosecutions and from the many testimonies of eyewitnesses describing "teenagers," "young hoodlums," or "youths" running from the scene, authorities had little doubt as to the central part played by young men in such crimes. "During 1946," the MCHR thus concluded in its annual report, "participation by juveniles and teen-agers in interracial incidents was marked. . . .

Of the 19 incidents of interracial friction where participants were identified, juveniles or young men were involved in 13."[6] It was no mere coincidence, then, that the "wave of terroristic attacks" in that year began in the last week of June, right around the restless time when classes let out for the summer.

By 1946, the idea that this group was largely responsible for such acts passed as common sense to many. The commission, though, still faced the problem of how to disarm a trend that might eventually ignite into the riot situations it had been trying so hard to avoid. This problem was not only one of detection; it was also one of prosecution. Both "juveniles *and* young men" fell under the jurisdiction of different court systems with much less punitive inclinations. As for the objective of pursuing convictions for youths aged seventeen and under, the commission was up against what it termed as a "trend in the juvenile court . . . very strongly toward reclamation and reformation."[7] Moreover, the commission already perhaps sensed that it would prove no less difficult to make examples out of "young men," by which it meant the eighteen- to twenty-year-olds whose cases were heard in Boys' Court. This was the court that in October 1947 would dismiss the cases of all but one of the 118 defendants arrested in connection with a fury of racial violence directed against a handful of black families in a South Side housing project at the edge of the lily-white Roseland community.

Yet even if the Juvenile and Boys' Courts were more inclined to take a hard line in such cases, there were other practical circumstances that stood in the way. First, unlike other categories of criminals and delinquents, the young perpetrators of such hate crimes were somewhat more likely to be first-time offenders—youths "from good homes and not delinquent in the traditional sense," as MCHR director Thomas Wright described them.[8] At least in incidents that did not inflict serious physical harm to anyone, the clean records of such offenders almost always yielded a sentence that sought to reprimand rather than to punish. Second, all this presupposed that the state could actually furnish a witness, which was not easy to do in view of the nocturnal nature of many of these acts and the reluctance of witnesses to testify, either out of sympathy with the cause of the perpetrators or out of fear of retribution. As for police cooperation, the officer on watch at Engelia McCain's house was perhaps more the norm than the exception. Complaints against members of the Chicago police would pile up in the years to come, alleging intransigence out of sympathy with the mob.[9] In July 1946, the MCHR reported several such cases of police negligence, including an officer who refused to arrest two vandals because he was off duty, an officer asleep at his post, and another who "expressed opposition to guarding residences of Negroes."[10]

With such considerations in mind, the MCHR formulated an approach, hammered out in meetings with police officials, which focused on youth subcultures as the wellsprings of interracial conflicts. The prescriptions it outlined for the challenge ahead seemed well attuned to the idea that groups of young men were crucial components of community infrastructures of racial hatred and violence: "(1) when, in these interracial conflicts, youths were apprehended, the law enforcement officers and the courts obtain all possible information as to their connections with youth groups, in order to break up such gangs; (2) such cases be viewed not as simple altercations between two individuals, or as simple acts of violence committed by individuals, but as premeditated, and with social consequences affecting the peace of the entire community; and (3) these factors be taken into account in the investigation and prosecution of these youthful offenders."[11] To institute these methods, the commissioner of police, at the behest of the MCHR, established a new Juvenile Bureau in the fall of the 1946 to develop a "statistical system" for collecting information on youth groups and their activities. Bringing together the work of juvenile and truant officers, this agency sought to more effectively target not only youth vandalism against black property, but also "the problems of conflict between groups of white and Negro youths."[12]

This discovery of youth gangs as autonomous actors warranting attention on their own account may have involved factors beyond an actual increase in youth participation in interracial conflicts. It is arguable that rather than any substantial change in the behavior of men in this age group, all this represented little more than an administrative awakening to the role of white youth gangs, elicited initially by the wartime delinquency panic and sustained by the establishment of an institutional apparatus—the MCRR—to record such patterns of racial violence. However, there is more reason to believe that the first years after the war did indeed represent a watershed in the story of racial conflict, and in the involvement of youths in its most visible forms. As Thomas Wright, the director of the MCHR, revealed in September 1946, the previous six months had witnessed an all-time high in the number of assaults against black Chicagoans. "The present racial violence," he concluded, "is more serious today than it has ever been." Moreover, Wright also disclosed that for the first time in several years police had reported a resurgence of attacks on African Americans at public beaches.[13] The few of these incidents that made it into MCHR files reveal that groups of young men in the age range highlighted by the commission were largely behind this trend. On June 28, 1946, for example, a crowd of "approximately fifty white youths" attacked twelve black youngsters riding bikes on the path in front of the Twelfth Street Beach. A week later, on July 4, so often an active day for white hatred, five "Italian-American youths" assaulted a black teen at the Oak Street Beach.[14]

Moreover, what was going on at the beaches was merely one manifestation of a larger wave of white youth violence in leisure areas of neighborhoods undergoing racial transition. By the spring of 1946, white youths, sometimes in crowds numbering more than forty or fifty, mobilized regularly against the presence of blacks in roller rinks, parks, libraries, and schoolyards. In April, whites waged a prolonged battle to prevent black teens from skating at the Madison Gardens rink at 2500 West Madison Street, in a racially mixed neighborhood on the Near West Side. Their efforts culminated in a "near-riot" when "35 armed white teenage hoodlums," wielding knives, pistols, and blackjacks, threatened a group of black girls when they tried to enter.[15] This show of intimidation apparently prevented blacks from using the rink until it closed down for the summer. When it reopened in mid-September, white youths again organized to keep African Americans out, gathering at the rink's entrance and attacking blacks trying to enter.[16]

A few days after these incidents, residents of the area near the rink reported to the Chicago Urban League that whites had been harassing black students in and around John Marshall High School to discourage them from returning to Madison Gardens. Inquiries sent to the school principal revealed that black students feared leaving school and were gathering in the halls at the end of each day.[17] Hence, a year after whites had used their schools to organize hate strikes against blacks in their midst, they had apparently begun taking to more violent forms of opposition. On September 26, a mob of between 100 and 150 teenagers from the Burnside School, deep on the South Side, carried out a raid against a black high school football team practicing in Tuley Park. When the players attempted to collect their belongings and leave, the mob proceeded to shower them with rocks.[18] Eight days later, at nearby Calumet High, the site of the largest strike of the previous year, an eighteen-year-old amateur boxer led more than sixty white students in an attack against several African American students that a police squadron managed to stave off just in time.[19]

The details of these last few attacks militate against becoming too fixated on the notion of the gang, the social club, or even the less formal arrangement of the street-corner clique in understanding the dynamics of white racial aggression in this moment. Involving large mobs assembled by word of mouth during the school day, these were the expressions of a much broader racial consensus that would make the spectacle of the mob action, at times numbering in the thousands, more and more familiar in many areas of the city in the late 1940s. Yet while the racial consensus transcended the world of youths, the fact that so many expressions of racial enmity materialized in this milieu is an important aspect of the story of race relations in postwar Chicago.

Why this youth phenomenon has been somewhat overlooked by observers and scholars of the Chicago scene has something to do with the conspicuous absence from the historical record of the 1940s of the kinds of notorious gangs that brought a mythology and color to gangland in the interwar years and then again in the late 1950s and 1960s. While large groups of youths in their teens and early twenties were so often behind racial attacks and while city officials and eyewitnesses frequently referred to them as "gangs," instances in which specific gang or club names show up in the reports are few. This was in part a manifestation of the demographic changes wrought by the war. With the draft sending a large number of young men abroad and the wartime production boom pulling a high proportion of those who remained into well-paying jobs, gangland lost much of the older leadership element that had sustained its most visible manifestations in prior years. Describing such changes on the Italian Near West Side, where storefront clubs had for decades been fixtures throughout the neighborhood, resident and community activist Anthony Sorrentino claimed: "During World War II most of the social and athletic organizations in our community temporarily disappeared, since they were composed predominantly of young men."[20] This was no doubt a common state of affairs in the working-class districts of Chicago. Yet the apparent disappearance of youth gangs was also somewhat a matter of perception. Not only did the war effort take youths off the streets, but it also took those who were paid to monitor them. Sorrentino, for example, mentions losing the only two local youth workers to better-paying jobs in the war industries.[21] Moreover, with child employment more than tripling by as early as 1942, adolescents were spending much less time in the settlements and community centers under the watchful eyes of social workers.[22]

Such conditions changed dramatically with the end of the war, but demobilization brought continued upheaval rather than stability to working-class Chicago. Several factors made the first few years of the Cold War uncertain ones, particularly for working-class residents of American cities. First, while bringing obvious happiness and relief to family members, the mass return of veterans exerted some serious strains on the urban social fabric. With cities like Chicago in the grips of a severe housing crisis, many veterans had difficulty finding a decent place to live. In addition, the end of the wartime production boom meant that securing a good job was no longer going to be easy. In 1946, the national unemployment rate more than doubled, and while still at a low level compared with that of the 1930s, widespread perceptions of a postwar recession allowed few in the workforce to feel secure.[23]

The tumult of demobilization shows up in the precipitous changes in certain social indices. Between 1945 and 1946, for example, the total number of divorces nationwide leapt from 485,000 to 610,000.[24] In the same year, the overall number of nontraffic arrests in Chicago increased more than 15 percent, and the more revealing figure of arrests for disorderly conduct, public intoxication, and vagrancy jumped 20 percent.[25] Such conditions reflected not only occupational and housing concerns but also the effects of post-traumatic stress disorders and other forms of psychological distress associated with the return of soldiers to civilian life. In his research on the families of World War II veterans, for instance, William Tuttle has found that alcoholism was an important factor in many postwar divorces, a fact that sheds light on the dramatic increase in disorderly conduct and public drunkenness offenses.[26]

As for how all this came to touch the world of the young, the juvenile delinquency epidemic that many sociologists and criminologists had been forecasting throughout the war years finally hit in 1945 and 1946. In 1945, delinquency cases shot up a staggering 43 percent from the previous year. The number dropped a bit in 1946, but it nonetheless remained at a historically lofty level, 71.5 percent higher than the figure recorded for 1941.[27] The expansion of the juvenile division of the police force after the war may partly explain such sharp increases, particularly given that truancy constituted more than one-third of the delinquency cases. More than other violations, the number of truancy cases corresponds directly to the number of truancy officers to process them. However, personnel increases cannot wholly account for the magnitude of the escalations in both assault and concealed weapons charges among juveniles. Between 1944 and 1946, juvenile assaults climbed 120 percent and weapons arrests nearly tripled.[28]

Although the link between delinquency and the difficulties faced by returning veterans must remain speculative, Tuttle's claim that in the large body of correspondence he surveyed "the letters that detailed troubled reunions when fathers returned . . . outnumber by four to one those that described happy reunions" is certainly suggestive.[29] Yet perhaps more than in the capacity of troubled fathers, veterans influenced the rise in juvenile violence as older peers and role models within neighborhood youth subcultures. The proliferation of weapons among adolescents in the first years after the war logically bore a close relationship to the homecoming of many young men fresh from battle experience. As Eric Schneider argues in his work on youth gangs in postwar New York, young veterans brought home with them not only the experiences of battle but also souvenirs from the battlefield—guns and knives that would find their way into the hands of youths on the streets.[30] As might be expected, then, weapons charges in Chicago increased most in the age bracket between twenty-one and twenty-five, more than tripling between 1944 and 1946. This age group racked up 231 such arrests in 1946, compared with 130 for all juveniles (under eighteen), 107 for those aged sixteen to twenty, and 170 for adults between twenty-six and thirty[31] Moreover, if young men in their early to mid-twenties were packing lethal weapons more commonly on the streets, they were also engaging in forms of behavior in which they would more likely find use for them. In 1946, police officers picked up a then-historic high of 6,898 men in this age range for disorderly conduct, a kind of catchall category commonly used to charge those involved in public disturbances that did not involve any significant harm to persons or damage to property. This was a 95 percent increase from the number recorded in 1944, far outpacing the more moderate 50 percent rise in the twenty-six to thirty range.[32]

Once again, these were changes that grew out of the uncertainties of the first few postwar years, uncertainties that struck young men on the threshold of maturity in different ways. Yet the uneasiness and anxiety of this moment, for many working-class Chicagoans, would take form and play out within another kind of narrative. Although the war had ended, the migration of southern blacks it had stimulated was still going strong as veterans sought to resume their civilian lives and former war production workers looked for new jobs. The wartime housing crisis was now a peacetime problem, and its thorny racial aspects could no longer hide under the cover of home-front unity. In fact, the return of veterans had quickly transformed it into a tinderbox; the claims of black veterans, invigorated by having risked their lives for their country, would now come up against those of white veterans and their families, who, having had their lives disrupted by the war, were in no mood to make sacrifices for the larger cause of racial justice. In this context, an increasing white constituency of home owners and longtime residents who found themselves in the path of racial succession began focusing, at times almost single-mindedly, on the dark skin of those who sought to be their neighbors.[33]

Thus, along with the many other categories of crime, racially motivated attacks against black persons and their property increased in the initial postwar years. While police departments were decades away from keeping special statistics on hate crimes, the black press and the MCHR covered enough of these incidents between 1946 and 1949 to convey that the terrain of race relations shifted rather dramatically after the war.[34] This became apparent to city officials in August 1947, when police arrested over one hundred residents of the Roseland community in Southwest Chicago, far from the Black Belt, for attacking anyone with dark skin in the area around the Fernwood Homes Housing Project. For three evenings crowds ranging from fifteen hundred to five thousand people protested the placement of black veterans in this Chicago Housing Authority (CHA) project. When a squadron of several hundred police officers effectively cordoned off the apartment buildings, large groups of marauding whites took to attacking African Americans passing by in automobiles and on streetcars, injuring some thirty-five. The Metropolitan Housing and Planning Council referred to these events as "about as bad a situation as any seen since the riots of 1919."[35]

The Fernwood affair paled in comparison to the 1919 race riot in terms of numbers of dead and seriously injured, but it represented what amounted to a paradigm shift in the story of racial conflict. First, and perhaps most significantly, it confirmed that residents of white communities would take to the streets by the thousands to prevent blacks from living in their neighborhoods and that they would not withdraw so readily to the presence of police squadrons. In essence, they would put themselves at considerable risk to accomplish this goal. On at least two occasions after the end of the war but prior to the rioting at Fernwood, white mobs of this size had gathered in violent demonstrations of racial intolerance, but these incidents had been somewhat short-lived and yielded only a handful of arrests. The first of these occurred in December 1946, when between fifteen hundred and three thousand residents of the West Lawn area on the Western fringe of the city tried to prevent blacks from moving into the new Airport Homes Veterans Housing Project. The second such incident took place on July 1, 1947, in the usually racially tense run-up to Independence Day, when a crowd of some two thousand stoned and tossed firecrackers at a black home on the border between the Black Belt and the white Englewood community. The Fernwood Homes demonstrations, however, far surpassed both of these earlier displays in the intensity of the emotions involved and in the duration of their expression.[36]

Second, along with the preceding riots, the Fernwood affair made clear that resistance to black invasion was no longer the business of schoolyard brawls or teens hurling rocks and incendiaries at black homes under the cover of night. As Arnold Hirsch's seminal study shows, the postwar housing riots were in many ways "communal" protests: "ecologically based struggles" to maintain the racial boundaries of the neighborhood waged by a cross-section of the local community. Surveying the evidence of riot participation contained in arrest lists and eyewitness accounts, Hirsch finds that the crowds taking to the streets against African Americans combined "new" and "old" immigrants, men and women, young and old. The list of arrestees from Fernwood, for example, reveals significant levels of participation from several different ethnic groups, including Poles, Italians, and Slavs. Older Anglo, Dutch, and German stock constituted the bedrock of the Roseland community, as they did in many such communities far from the urban core at this time, but newer settlers here seemed just as eager to join the cause. Moreover, while women were hardly represented on arrest lists, several eyewitnesses found their presence on the front lines noteworthy. This was indeed an important change from the interwar and wartime experiences of interracial violence.

This "communal" vision of the series of race riots over housing and neighborhood resources in Chicago between 1946 and 1957 has become a cornerstone of a larger interpretation of the origins of postwar working-class conservatism in urban and suburban America. Viewing such racial mobilization as broadly based and politically strategic, as Hirsch's account suggests, Thomas Sugrue and others have concluded that rather than in the frenetic moment of Black Power, urban rebellion, and the apparent failure of Great Society social programs, the white backlash that would make George Wallace a viable candidate and help lift Richard Nixon to the presidency began here at the urban grass roots way back in the 1940s.[37] Before assuming a place in this historiographical project, however, Hirsch's revelations concerning the "truly communal" nature of the racist mob were directed more toward debunking the prevailing view of the moment, the spin that shamed local leaders and city officials often sought to put on these rabid displays of intolerance—that the mobs of angry whites hurling stones and racist epithets were fringe or "hood-lum" elements rather than the good folks of the community. To this effect, residents and local politicians referred to the mobs as "agitators," "outsiders," and "uncontrollable youths" in their attempts to deflect responsibility. After the Fernwood riot, for example, the *Chicago Defender* decried "the efforts of various agencies to make the violence appear [as] spontaneous outbursts by unruly boys and youths."[38] As we have thus far seen, this was indeed consistent with the official view on the situation prior to the start of all these mass demonstrations. Early in 1947, for example, a newly issued training manual for Chicago Park District employees advised: "As far as possible, a careful check should be kept on the activities of all juvenile gangs, since they are the spearhead for group conflict. . . . Wherever there are found places or hangouts for street-corner gangs, one finds the natural settings for many racial incidents."[39]

While it would be erroneous to view them as marginal or extreme elements of their communities, it would be just as misleading to overlook the fact that young men in their late teens and early twenties were indeed the core actors in the local mobs that assembled for these demonstrations of racial hatred. What Hirsch and others have underestimated is just how much those in this age range initiated and sustained the campaigns against residential integration, a situation that arrest lists hint at but do not fully divulge. This is an impression acquired not only by pro-filing crowds but also by contextualizing the rather exceptional events that these neighborhood race riots were within the more quotidian cultures of everyday racial violence that surrounded them in time and space. Seen from a different angle, the Fernwood arrest list reveals that city officials may not have been too far off the mark in viewing "unruly boys and youths" as playing a leading role, although they should have known better than to categorize their actions as "spontaneous outbursts." What becomes lost in an analysis of the overall arrest list of the Fernwood fiasco, for example, is that on the first few nights of violence, which set the stage for the turnout of some two thousand on the third, nineteen of the twenty-three locals arrested (excluding one person whose age was not noted) were under the age of twenty-five, and eighteen of these were between fifteen and twenty-two. Moreover, even after the demonstration had snowballed, the overall record of arrestees nonetheless reveals that members of the crowd were disproportionately young men and adolescent boys. Out of the 109 people whose ages appear on the arrest lists for this three-day event, sixty-six (or nearly 61 percent) were aged twenty-five or under.[40]

Even more telling than the arrest profile, however, is the compelling eyewitness account turned in by Gail Salisbury, a representative of the MCHR, which stated at the outset: "All of this was due to a group of youngsters from the age of 16 to 20, who, in search of some excitement, found that excitement in the acceptance of directions from a few hot-headed, short-sighted mob organizers, mostly from the neighborhood." Elaborating further on this point, Salisbury highlighted the anticipation of the crowd regarding the arrival of a youth gang from the neighboring community of Pullman and the rush of adrenaline that energized it when these youths actually did appear. It is not possible to ascertain from the report, moreover, whether it was this gang or other groups of local youths who rallied a posse to break away from the larger crowd and stone cars carrying black passengers on Green Street, but according to Salisbury, this group "was nearly all made up of boys from the age of sixteen to twenty." "They were by far," he concluded, "the most reactionary and the most violent of all the people involved in the whole mass."[41] From this detailed account, it thus appears that many of those swelling the ranks of the protesters in Fernwood were more spectators than actors. It is hardly surprising that people in the area would come out to witness such spectacular events in their own backyard. This does not mean that a great many of these people were not sympathetic to and even complicit with the activities of the mob's core actors. It does, however, suggest that were it not for the actions of groups of young men, the whole affair might have taken a very different course.

In Park Manor, a neighborhood just below the southern tip of the Black Belt, adolescents and young men likewise played a pivotal role in a protracted campaign of terrorism to hold off the advance of African Americans into the area between 67th and 71st Streets. In March 1948, for example, a conference on the situation devoted half of its time discussing with the city and park district police "the tensions reflected in the schools and libraries." According to a report on the meeting, "It was pointed out that young people of high school age have been involved in most of the anti-Negro demonstrations."[42] In October 1948, the problems in Park Manor came up again in a meeting of the Committee on Minority Group Relationships. Reporting on the rise in racial gang attacks in Chicago, and in racial violence among youths in leisure areas, Thomas Wright designated Park Manor as an area of "serious tension."[43] Youths, it seems, kept the pressure on African Americans in this part of the city for years on end, but their tactics could only slow the movement of blacks. Thus, on July 25, 1949, the crossing of the 71st Street boundary brought some two thousand incensed residents to the front door of a two-flat building at 7153 South St. Lawrence that had recently been purchased by Roscoe Johnson, a teacher, and his wife, Ethel, a social worker. What ensued came nowhere near the level of intensity of Fernwood, but this disturbance was nonetheless quite serious. A significant part of a crowd that at its peak numbered a few thousand rallied around the flames of burning mattresses and threw stones and other incendiaries at the besieged house until daybreak. In another testimony to police inaction, the *Chicago Defender* reported only eight arrests were made in the several hours that all this was occurring. While a small sample, of these eight only one was not between the ages of seventeen and twenty.[44]

A similar but even more striking picture of collective youth involvement is also suggested by the arrest profile of the next large-scale racial disturbance, this one at 5643 South Peoria Street. While assaults and property damage marked the three nights of rioting here, the style of violence was much more controlled than it was in either the Fernwood or Park Manor disturbances. Police made a handful of arrests on the first few nights, and several of those taken in were either victims or counterprotesters apparently mobilized by the Progressive Party. On the third night, however, the group of thirty-three protesters taken into police custody was composed almost exclusively of young men between the ages of seventeen and twenty-two from the Englewood area.[45] While police records provide few clues on what transpired on the previous nights, the Chicago Commission on Human Relations collected three eyewitness reports on the first evening, each of which singles out young men for special mention. The first referred to a crowd that by 11:30 was "still predominantly teen-age and younger." The second, filed by the acting director of the commission's Department of Information, stated that after each time police tried to clear the area, "the crowds of teenagers would trickle back to the area directly across the street." The last report, by the commission's director of the Department of Civil Rights, pointed to "gangs of teen-agers from around the vicinity" as one of the main elements of the crowd. The report also noted that "groups of young men, 19–25," were among the first to gather at the scene and that "groups or 'gangs' of community youths" were passing through the crowd trying to identify "outsiders" and harassing journalists. Most interesting, in its list of three "conclusions" about the Peoria Street disturbance, the CCHR claimed, "Gangs of young men from other parts of Chicago attracted to the area by anti-racial and anti-religious disturbances were getting to know each other and act as an organized group."[46]

Along with Gail Salisbury's account of the role played by the Pullman gang in Fernwood, this observation suggests two overlapping trends taking shape in white working-class neighborhoods in Chicago experiencing racial transition in the late 1940s. The broader phenomenon was the mass mobilization of white residents behind a sense of shared white identity and the common cause of racial separation. Aside from labor activism, this kind of grassroots collective action had few precedents in the interwar period. Unlike the race riot of 1919, moreover, some of these actions of the 1940s looked a great deal more like semicoherent protests than inchoate outbursts of racist anger. Yet this overarching process of racial identity formation and mobilization relied somewhat on another set of circumstances to push it out of the half-filled meeting rooms of home-owners' associations and civic organizations, out of the local taverns and lunch counters—out of all the casual places where neighbors exchanged words on what should be done to protect the property values, the community, the wife, the children, perhaps even the white race—and boldly into the streets. Many locally oriented institutions—the Fernwood-Bellevue Civic Association in Roseland and the Visitation Parish in the Englewood area around 5643 South Peoria, to name a few—did their part, but it was never clear that these entities had a direct role in actually bringing people out into the streets for the demonstrations that so effectively enabled their communities to see themselves as just this—communities. The overall pattern of antiblack violence from the late 1940s, including both the crowd demonstrations and the many smaller incidents that nonetheless had a powerful impact at the grass roots, indicates that youth groups, whether just neighborhood cliques or more tangibly defined gangs or clubs, were the most vigilant and the most effective entities in consolidating and maintaining struggles for racial separation.

This role in mobilizing collective action was closely associated with the youths' capacity to bring about what Douglas McAdam refers to as "cognitive liberation"—a process through which people "collectively define their situations as unjust and subject to change through group action."[47] This, of course, was a capacity home-owners' groups and parish associations also possessed. Yet as scholars working on the part played by emotions in oppositional political action have suggested, if such cognitive transformations are to spawn risky actions, they usually require some form of emotional jolt—a "hot button" component, as William Gamson refers to it.[48] It was in this sense that the aggressive actions of male youth groups proved vital not only to the mounting of collective resistance to black integration, but ultimately, as we will see in greater detail in chapter 5, to the construction of group identity. Just as emotions—of both anger at perceived injustices and hope for change—are indispensable for bringing about the move to collective action, they are equally so in the formation of "attachments" between individuals and "imagined communities."[49]

Perhaps the most compelling evidence for the centrality of youth groups in mobilizing and sustaining white resistance to racial integration arises from what was in some ways the final large-scale housing protest of the postwar period in the Chicago area. This battle actually occurred not within Chicago, but just outside the western city limits, in the suburb of Cicero. There, during a series of nights in July 1951, thousands rallied outside a twenty-unit brick apartment building within which a single black family sought to reside. While the mobs confined themselves mostly to property damage, the Cicero riots hit newswires all over the world when the town's mayor called in 450 national guards to reinforce its overwhelmed police force. As a result, the Chicago papers were forced to break from their habit of burying such stories. The ensuing reportage further confirmed the trend that representatives of the CCHR had found remarkable in the events at both Fernwood and Park Manor—that groups of young men were crossing into other neighborhoods to answer the calls of racial hatred.

Notwithstanding Hirsch's contention that the absence of arrests from the first few nights of rioting obscures the fact that the violence was initiated mostly by residents of Cicero, the arrest records for the final few nights suggest that once news of the demonstration spread it changed from a territorially based communal action to a much broader rally against integration that pulled in participants from West Side Chicago neighborhoods a considerable distance from the scene at 6139 West 19th Street. Once again the vast majority of those who joined the cause of racial hatred appeared to be young men in their late teens and early twenties.[50] According to the *Tribune*, the first group of arrests made by police consisted of "mostly of young men from outside the town."[51] A detailed list of arrestees for the following night further corroborates this conclusion. Of the sixty-eight males (there were no women listed) taken into custody, forty-five were aged twenty-one or under (fourteen of these were juveniles); only twelve were over the age of twenty-five. The youthful appearance of the crowd was so evident that the leading Chicago-based white supremacist organization, the White Circle League, singled out "the brave youth of Cicero" for praise in a pamphlet it distributed outside a court hearing of arrested rioters.[52]

Figure 3. "The brave youth of Cicero": On July 13, 1951, hundreds of young men gathered outside a Cicero apartment building where a single black family resided. Police dispersed the crowd with tear gas minutes after this photo was taken. Photo by *Chicago Daily News*, courtesy of the Chicago History Museum, DN-N-7049.

As for the residential background of the agitators taken by police that night, all but six of the fifty-four adults (the juveniles were not listed by address) lived outside of Cicero or the neighboring town of Berwyn. More than half (twenty-seven) of the remaining forty-eight on the list came to Cicero that night from neighborhoods on the West Side of Chicago, a great many from the areas to the west of Humboldt and Garfield Park.[53] While these neighborhoods were in the general vicinity of the town border, Cicero was still a bus trip or car ride away for most of the Chicagoans arrested. That the attempt of a single African American to inhabit an apartment in an area some forty or fifty blocks away would mobilize a young man to join the cause of racial hatred and end up in police custody suggests that communal or territorial conceptions fail to explain the dynamics behind this white collective action against housing integration.

Thus, if the Cicero disturbance began as a neighborhood event, it ended up as something very different. Motives and feelings that had little to do with defending the racial sanctity of Cicero were being played out as crowds of between two and three thousand tried to break through cordons of soldiers in fighting gear, risking injury and arrest. As the list of those who actually were arrested indicates, a richer understanding of these motives and feelings requires an exploration into the milieu of young men—into the infrastructure of places, rituals, and styles that together composed a youth subculture that took shape in ambiguous contradistinction to a parent culture centered on conceptions of work and family life. Within this subculture, aggression against those with dark skin was becoming much more than a defensive response.

THE CULTURAL AND STRUCTURAL CONDITIONS OF WHITE RACIAL AGGRESSION

The years following the Second World War ushered in widespread changes in the material conditions and cultural practices of working-class youths in Chicago. With the national unemployment rate doubling in 1946, and then rising another 30 percent in 1949 (to more than triple the 1945 level), and the teenage employment rate dropping from its elevated wartime levels, the street corners, storefront clubs, and park hangouts were filled anew with youths "raising plenty of hell" or "doin' nothing." While the postwar recession many economists predicted never materialized, employers nonetheless braced for it, scrambling for ways to reduce their payrolls. Moreover, as veterans returned to old jobs, those lacking seniority were the first to be laid off to make room for them; along with wage-earning women and African Americans, many teenagers who had first entered the workforce during the war were among the first to go. Although the United States was heading toward a prolonged period of economic expansion that would see per capita income grow a robust 35 percent between 1945 and 1960, working-class Chicagoans had little reason to feel optimistic about the future in the first years after the war. Partly as a result of the rising costs of living faced by the rank and file, this was a moment of intense labor strife. Organized labor waged a strike campaign in the year after V-J Day comparable in magnitude only to the struggles of 1919. Moreover, the results of these efforts were far from heartening for many workers. In the highly publicized General Motors strike, for example, the company endured a 113-day stoppage and nearly $89 million in losses to defeat what amounted to a one-cent wage increase.[54]

This was not the most auspicious moment to be young, inexperienced, and in need of work, a situation that spurred the revitalization of street-corner gangs and clubs. Hence, after watching the ranks of youth organizations on the Near West Side dwindle during the war, Anthony Sorrentino claimed they "mushroomed all over the community" after the war's end, estimating that social and athletic clubs in this part of the city alone claimed a membership of some two thousand young men.[55] And this figure represented only those who were easy to count—the youths affiliated with more formally recognized organizations. Similar circumstances were being noted in other parts of the city as well. In a 1950 meeting of the board of directors of the Chicago Area Project, a youth worker in the West Side community of Lawndale spoke of his experiences the year before with a less distinguishable but nonetheless substantial network of youth groups: what he referred to as the "many boys [who] were part of a large gang which in turn was related to many of the other teenage groups in the community." Working with these youths "in hangouts and street corners," this worker was able to organize "a group of parents and other adults" into the Lawndale Community Committee.[56] The first years after the war were indeed active ones for the Chicago Area Project, which stepped up its efforts to organize residents to implement their own programs for dealing with juvenile delinquency. The appearance of more and more street-corner groups idling away the hours on the streets provided a stimulus for such efforts.

Youth subcultures, however, do not form simply because youths living in the same neighborhood find themselves with more time on their hands. What gives subcultures their visibility—that is to say, what gives them, according to the framework laid out by Stuart Hall and Tony Jefferson, "a distinctive enough shape and structure to make them identifiably different from their 'parent' culture"—is their focus on a set of shared fears, feelings, needs, and desires, as well as the existence of activities, rituals, styles, and languages that articulate these concerns. As these theorists point out, subcultures can vary between more "loosely-defined strands or 'milieux' within the parent culture" and those "which have reasonably tight boundaries, distinctive shapes, which have cohered around particular activities, focal concerns and territorial spaces."[57] Working-class youth subcultures in postwar Chicago, not unlike their interwar predecessors, most often fell somewhere in-between these two types. Even in their most scandalous forms, they still reflected, on some level or another, the values and ideas—racial, class, gender, sexual, and otherwise—of the broader communities surrounding them. They were, in the terms laid out by Raymond Williams, more "alternative" than "oppositional" in nature, though in some ways they were merely reflective of the local cultures surrounding them more than anything else.[58] Generally, Chicago's working-class subcultures tended not to challenge the way things were. If youths within this milieu sought at times to carve out a space safe from the workaday world for social experimentation, they seldom took seriously the idea of escaping the normative trajectory prescribed to them—as the bohemian "Beat" subcultures on the West Coast did. Ultimately, empowerment in the world of working-class Chicago youth subcultures rested on a reaffirmation of the values prevailing in the adult world—in particular, those that circulated around notions of manhood, which, in the context of racial transition, quite often played out in racial forms.

Despite all the resemblances that youth subcultures bore both to mainstream culture and to the local working-class cultures surrounding them, they nevertheless remained visible and distinct in the years following the end of the Second World War. As in the interwar era, the youth subcultures that took form in postwar Chicago in the late 1940s and 1950s depended on a set of converging factors and conditions that touched the generation coming of age in distinct ways, and, as in this earlier period, their emergence would come to find powerful expression in the mass media. The postwar analog to the Depression-era gangster was the thrill-seeking juvenile delinquent running roughshod—often in the company of the gang—over the American social order. The image of the dangerous youth filled the screens of American theaters nationwide beginning in 1955, after the tremendous success of the Academy-Award-winning delinquency-issue films *The Blackboard Jungle* and *Rebel without a Cause* opened the floodgates to a deluge of teen exploitation B-movies. This was the same year that Bill Haley and the Comets' "Rock Around the Clock" shot to the top of the pop charts, and RCA signaled rock 'n' roll's takeover of the popular music industry by signing Elvis Presley. This boost to record sales was not overlooked by Hollywood, which quickly turned out a bevy of formulaic teen pictures that strung flimsy narratives between performances by the hottest rock stars. The dangerous teen would thereafter become hard to imagine without the menacing sounds of rock music droning in the background from some far-off jukebox or transistor radio.

Almost overnight the youth market was reinvented on the terrain of mass culture. This was not the first time that the culture industries had targeted the spending habits of youths, but never before had youth culture become so distinct. The gangster, for instance, was certainly both a poster boy for consumerism and a youth icon, but he appealed to an audience that traversed generations. By contrast, the wild youth films of the 1950s targeted an exclusively teenage audience. Such changes brought about what the film scholar Thomas Doherty has aptly described as "the juvenilization of American movies in the 1950s." But the trend was much larger than this. The aural landscape of mass culture transformed in step with the visual, as the ballooning teenage market for rock 'n' roll revolutionized what Americans understood to be pop music. Historian W. T. Lhamon has gone so far as to claim that in the American mid-1950s "youth culture became largely the main culture; it became the atmosphere of American life."[59]

Whether one subscribes to such a totalizing vision of 1950s youth culture, the precipitous growth in the teen market surely brought about massive shifts in the ways Americans viewed youths and the issues associated with them. As James Gilbert has argued, more than any actual rise in juvenile crime rates, this perception of a dramatic change in the condition of youths, embodied by the new relationship between mass media forms and youth culture, fueled a widespread delinquency panic in the mid-1950s.[60] Culminating this juvenile crime scare were the highly publicized proceedings of the Senate Subcommittee to Investigate Juvenile Delinquency, which, under the leadership of former antimafia crusader Estes Kefauver, spearheaded the charge for censorship in the mass media in order to resolve the apparent youth problem. Importantly, this cognitive move to the ubiquitous mass media as the cause of juvenile crime was also a move away from the traditional locus of such crime in American society: the lower-class urban slums. As James Dean's gripping portrayal of suburban teen Jim Stark in *Rebel without a Cause* demonstrated, delinquency could just as easily strike the bedroom communities of suburban America. If the explosion of the gangster genre in the 1930s represented the urban ethnic demographic of interwar America, the teen movies of the 1950s generally catered to the rapidly expanding middle-class suburban audience. This did not mean that the urban slums would not at times provide the backdrop for teen dramas, nor did it mean that class issues would never again find expression on the big screen. But the gangster was a working-class hero in a way that the dangerous youth would never be.

Yet it is important to remember that the transformation of American popular culture by youth culture was largely a post-1954 phenomenon. While films like *The Wild One* and hit singles like "Sh-boom" provided a glimpse into what was in store as early as 1954, the juvenilization of American movies and the birth of rock 'n' roll did not occur until the latter part of 1955. Moreover, while the Senate subcommittee hearings actually began a few years earlier, they did not make many headlines until 1955, in the midst of the controversy stirred up by rock music and the box office success of *Rebel without a Cause* and *Blackboard Jungle.* Hence, although concerns over the state of the young—ideas of "youth in crisis"—were seeing increased exposure by the late 1940s, the notion of dangerous or wild youths living in an incomprehensible world of their own was still years from full realization. Despite the absence of such popular conceptions and the relative dearth of commodity markers that made youth subcultures easy to spot, working-class youths in Chicago nonetheless continued to negotiate their lives in subcultural contexts of their own making in the late 1940s and early 1950s. While these subcultures more often fit the description of "loosely defined strands or 'milieux' within the parent culture," they still fulfilled the youth subcultural function of attempting to symbolically resolve the contradictions between material conditions and the ideological promises of postwar prosperity. Before the proliferation of ready-made versions of youth rebellion hit the market in the mid-1950s, youth subcultures in working-class Chicago reflected more localized class circumstances—predicaments, we will see, that were becoming more and more entangled with the problem of race. As in the Depression years, the milieu of street-corner groups in the late 1940s to the mid-1950s spanned an age range wide enough to include adolescents in their early teens and young men in their mid-twenties. Those in their late teens and early twenties—the ages dominating the arrest lists from the first night at Fernwood, Park Manor, South Peoria Avenue, and Cicero— were at the center of this world. And while emerging within a different political economy from that of the 1930s, the working-class youth subcultures they formed, especially those located in the older neighborhoods around the urban core, nonetheless bore the imprints of frustration and disillusionment from experiences in a school system and a labor market that seemed to offer few avenues of social mobility.

In instances for which occupational data on antiblack mobs are available, such as the Cicero riot and a later outbreak of collective violence in Calumet Park in 1957, the evidence clearly indicates that those most likely to participate were young men in their late teens and twenties occupying a life stage characterized by school, periodic stretches of unemployment, and employment in a range of unskilled and semiskilled entry-level jobs in the manufacturing and services sectors. In the group of forty-five Cicero arrestees between the ages of seventeen and twenty-nine (83 percent of the total), roughly two-thirds of those apprehended filled such positions in the workforce, while the other third claimed to be unemployed or still in school or offered no response to the question.

Figure 4. A Near Northwest Side youth gang poses for a photo at the Chicago Commons settlement house. Leather jackets and greased hair were prominent stylistic elements of Chicago's white working-class youth subcultures in the mid- to late 1950s. Photographer unknown; photo courtesy of the Chicago History Museum, ICHi-38931.

The jobs that *were* identified break down evenly between those that were clearly unskilled (e.g., "laborer," "clerk," "stock boy," "cashier," "filling station employee") and those that could be classified as semiskilled (e.g., "office employee," "printer," "machinist," "carpenter," "cutter," "welder," "draftsman," "pressman," "die caster," "metallurgist").[61] Almost six years later, a list of forty-four men arrested for disorderly conduct in connection with mob attacks against African Americans in Calumet Park revealed similar elements in the racist crowd. Once again, rioters were overwhelmingly teens and young adults, with only four over the age of twenty-eight (and only six over the age of twenty-five). Total figures for this event compiled by the CCHR show that just 18 of 114 arrested were above the age of thirty.[62] Moreover, twenty-five of the thirty-eight arrestees (about two-thirds) indicated to police that they were currently in school, unemployed, or working low-wage entry-level jobs (eleven claimed to be "laborers" or "clerks").[63]

   This occupational profile was not unexpected for young men between the ages of seventeen and twenty-one, a group that constituted well over half of those arrested in Cicero and Calumet Park combined. Moreover, even if the jobs they held were low paying, some two-thirds of the crowds in these demonstrations were nonetheless gainfully employed. Yet if obtaining some form of steady work was less of a challenge for Chicagoans in the postwar years than it had been in the prewar Depression decade, having an unskilled low-wage job seemed much less respectable in an era when prosperity, mobility, and commodity consumption became synonymous with the American way of life. While a more than 70 percent increase in the consumer price index wiped out the wage gains of the late 1940s, real income did increase 20 percent over the 1950s. This surplus revenue supported the emergence of a range of new consumption habits, all of which could be promoted more effectively than ever before with the penetrating new medium of television. Youths became primary targets of the music, film, fashion, and automobile industries, all of which found in rock 'n' roll a revolutionary means to consolidate and exploit them. Hollywood churned out reels and reels of films—from Academy-Award-winning blockbusters to low-budget B-movies—directed at the youth market throughout the 1950s: juvenile delinquency thrillers like *Rebel without a Cause, The Blackboard Jungle,* and *Teenage Crime Wave;* rock 'n' roll showcase movies like *Rock around the Clock* and *Rock All Night;* hot rod films like *Hot Rod, Hot Rod Girl,* and *Hot Rod Rumble;* and wild teen girl exploitation pictures like *Teenage Tramp, Teenage Rebel,* and *Dragstrip Girl.* Binding all of these films together was an ethos of rebellion against adult authority and middle-class norms in the incessant pursuit of excitement or so-called kicks.[64]

Although this fantasy of nihilist escapism may have appealed to many working-class Chicagoans, it slipped rapidly away with the darkness when the house lights came on. The forms of rebellion celebrated in many teen films were hard to sustain for the youths of working-class Chicago, many of whom would find themselves trying to make do in the lowest tier of the labor market. Even in the late 1940s and early 1950s, prior to the post-1955 youth marketing explosion, those working closely with youths in Chicago commonly commented on the difficulties faced by working-class youths as they sought to acquire the items they coveted. "They are restless and want the material possessions that will give them status in their community," one observer in three Chicago neighborhoods noted. "If these possessions cannot be obtained by legal methods," he concluded, "they can and will be obtained by other means."[65] The most desirable and inaccessible of these possessions was, of course, the automobile. Within the logic of rebellious youth culture, a young man needed "wheels."

By the early 1950s, the car had become the dominant icon of postwar youth culture, a multilayered symbol of mobility, and the most celebrated marker of manhood nationwide. As central as it was to the formulaic narratives of many teen B-movies, it was equally so to the everyday experiences of working-class youths. Reflecting on years of handling cases in Chicago's Boys' Court, municipal judge Jacob M. Braude claimed in 1956 that the automobile was one of the two leading factors in juvenile delinquency. He told the *Chicago Daily News*, "A lot of the trouble that kids get into nowadays is due to the mobility a car gives them."[66] That this need for "mobility," in more than one sense of the word, could often propel youths into the criminal justice system was corroborated by a story recounted by a Near West Side youth worker about the gang of teens he supervised. In 1952 he reported that the gang spent a great deal of its time stealing hubcaps and figuring out ways to finance the purchase of an automobile. Finally, one of the boys managed to buy a used one with the help of his part-time employer, who agreed to guarantee the loan, but it was not long before the gang had its eyes on better things—newer, flashier models that would give them respect on the streets. Not "satisfied" with their car, the boys ended up in court on charges of attempted auto larceny.[67] If the automobile could bestow power upon its owner, the inability to possess the right set of wheels, or any wheels at all, could just as forcefully signify powerlessness or a low social status—a much more common situation in the lower-income districts of Chicago.[68]

In fact, the escalating fear of halted or downward mobility was far more than just a youth problem. Such anxieties gripped entire communities that found themselves anywhere near the edges of the Black Belt or the grounds of a CHA housing project. Regardless of how an individual felt about having black neighbors, a well-understood cycle of white flight and panic-peddling posed an unavoidable threat to home equity, which for many working-class families constituted a large part—if not all—of the family wealth. For renters, the stakes were perhaps not as high, but financial interests only partially explain why residents become attached to their neighborhoods and fervently averse to change. In addition to emotional ties to community and place, there were other more practical factors. For some tenants, especially older ones whose rents lagged behind the going rates as a result of long-standing tenure and close relationships with landlords, the prospect of finding another place to live in the midst of a citywide housing shortage had significant financial implications.[69] Such concerns explain a great deal about why white people reacted so violently to the possibility of racial integration instead of just moving away.

Young men coming of age in such areas, however, faced additional challenges to their present ambitions and longer-range visions of the future, circumstances that help to illuminate why they were "by far the most reactionary and the most violent of all."[70] To begin with, the postwar political economy was considerably more treacherous for youths entering the workforce. While the national unemployment rate reached a short-term peak in 1949, only once climbing above the moderate level of 5 percent until the sharp recession of 1958, this economic indicator belied the labor market conditions for youthful job seekers in Chicago and many other industrial cities.[71] First, youth unemployment rates throughout this period tended to be significantly higher than the overall numbers. In 1950, for instance, the rate for the sixteen- to twenty-year-old group reached 10 percent—almost double the overall rate.[72] Second, despite robust economic growth nationally, the number of production, retail, and wholesale jobs in Chicago proper dropped steadily between 1947 and 1958. Production work, the largest sector of the local economy, saw the sharpest decline, falling nearly 27 percent. At the same time, the population of Chicago rose 12.6 percent while the total number of jobs fell 14.8 percent.[73]

These figures reveal the initial stages of a dual process of decentralization and deindustrialization that would radically transform the political economy of Chicago and other northern U.S. industrial centers in the postwar decades. As a whole, jobs were not so much disappearing as migrating out of the city center to the suburbs and outlying areas. Production jobs in particular, though, were declining all over metropolitan Chicago, and by the late 1950s service work constituted a significantly larger share of the labor market. As for the manufacturing jobs that remained, the advance of technologies of automation in this period increased the pool of unskilled and thus somewhat interchangeable workers on factory floors. Such changes can be detected (if perhaps impressionistically) in the distinct differences between the occupational data from the Cicero demonstration and the Calumet Park riot six years later. Suggestively, whereas the teenage and twenty-something Cicero arrestees named some ten different types of industrial jobs, the Calumet group identified only four. In addition, out of the twelve Calumet youths claming to be employed in some form of production work, eight placed themselves within the amorphous categories of "laborer" or "factory worker."[74]

Historians and sociologists working on postwar youth gangs and street culture in cities throughout the United States have largely agreed that the shift to a service-based economy, along with the concomitant process of deskilling, restructured forms of masculinity for young male laborers. According to this view, young men no longer able to secure the kind of industrial union jobs that had offered the previous generation both a decent wage and the masculine pride of the shop floor began to invest the violent rituals of street life with compensatory ideals of "honor" or "respect."[75] While the interviews of the sons of Polish and Mexican steelworkers presented in chapter 2 suggest that the appeal of shop-floor identity may already have been deteriorating by the mid-1930s, the new service-oriented economy posed substantial challenges to young men looking to attain the established baseline markers of manhood—a family, a home, a car, and the less tangible but nonetheless essential feelings of personal accomplishment, autonomy, and control over the affairs of daily life.

These needs vary somewhat from one generation to the next, and they are certainly felt differently by the middle class than by the children of lifetime wage laborers. Indeed, while postwar youth subcultures, like those of the 1930s, owed some of their vitality and allure to the fact that many youths were reconsidering and sometimes rejecting such norms, rebellion against these expectations nevertheless connotes a kind of engagement with them. While youths coming of age in the postwar era were less pressed than their Depression-era peers to be family providers, masculinity still typically became problematic for them as they entered the liminal period of maturation which was commonly understood to begin soon after the end of high school. The kind of turmoil encountered by those in this life stage is evidenced by the observations of sociologists and youth workers from the first years of demobilization to the late 1950s. Surveying several neighborhood youth agencies in the late 1940s, for instance, a Chicago graduate student in sociology singled out the age group between seventeen and twenty-three as that which posed the most difficult hurdles for their programs:

> Everyone admits that the young adults were a serious problem and the main source of our crime but no one could offer any constructive suggestions on how to meet this problem. Many in this group have been in the military service and now have no desire to continue their schooling or take up in-service training under the G.I. Bill of Rights. They have expended their 53 week readjustment pay at $20.00 per week. Now these young adults are adrift, they can not get jobs they desire and are depending on their families or friends for support. These young adults are the greatest social problem at the present time.[76]

In 1952, the Chicago Commons Association voiced similar concerns when it reported on "the great uncertainties teenage and young adult men face" and their "growing inability to plan carefully for and to stay at work or school."[77] That same year, the Welfare Council of Metropolitan Chicago highlighted the particular ordeals faced by those in this age group. Summarizing the goals and activities of its Youth Services Committee, council officials explained the need to define youth "broadly"— "as older adolescents and young adults." "Chronologically they are those between the ages of 18 and 30," the committee stated. In justifying this surprisingly expansive definition of "youth," it further stated: "The Committee recognized that not all people within this age bracket are youth and that many have achieved adult status in terms of their emotional and social growth, their independence economically from their parents or in terms of their marital status. It was concerned, however, with all those within this age range who have not yet achieved adulthood."[78] In the eyes of this agency, these were the young men who fell so easily into the routines of a "'corner group society' with a philosophy and value system of its own . . . in opposition to the middle class ideals of our society."[79]

These comments described quite saliently the characteristics of the "youthful condition" that Alberto Melucci has more recently outlined in examining the question of collective action within the context of youth culture. For Melucci, the key moment is when "the youthful condition, the phase *par excellence* of transition and suspension, is protracted and stabilized so that it becomes a mass condition which is no longer determined by biological age." This "suspension," he further argues, results from "imbalances between school and the labour market" that prolong the transition into adult roles, thereby imposing a "lived marginality, characterized by unemployment and a lack of any real economic independence." "In complex societies," Melucci concludes, "the condition of the young . . . is marked by this stable precariousness, by this lack of limits, to such an extent that it turns into a void, a hiatus that is known to be bogus and controlled from outside."[80]

This is an apt paradigm with which to think about the downwardly mobile segment of the generation of working-class youths coming of age in Chicago in this moment. Many young men in postwar Chicago—like those of the 1930s cohort—found themselves uneasily "suspended" between school and work. The moment of demobilization witnessed the onset of this crisis for some, but the broader forces of deindustrialization and decentralization made this suspension a prolonged and widespread problem in working-class districts. Hence, by the mid-1950s, despite employment figures that indicated a rebound from the lows of the 1954 recession, Chicago's working-class youths seemed to be faring no better, a situation that facilitated gang and youth subcultural formation. A survey of 172 youth groups undertaken between 1955 and 1959 reveals that close to half of all gang members were not in school, and of this group only 12 to 15 percent were employed full- or part-time. According to the report, "Most, are in unskilled jobs in the service and trade industries."[81]

If working-class youths in postwar Chicago were having trouble catching on in the workforce, moreover, this did not deter them from dropping out of school soon after they reached the legal leaving age of sixteen. A 1957 investigation into the problem revealed that 50 percent of the students entering Chicago high schools dropped out prior to graduation, a rate that substantially outpaced the national dropout average of 40 percent that year. Attesting to the close relationship between this elevated school-leaving rate and the resurgence of street-corner gangs, the study cited a recent Welfare Council survey of some three thousand members of teenage gangs that found 65 percent had left school before graduation. The vast majority of these youths were simply quitting rather than being somehow expelled from the system; only 20 to 25 percent of the dropouts had ever been reprimanded by their schools for behavioral problems. As to how these youths were managing in the labor market, the researchers claimed: "The overwhelming majority of youngsters who drop out of school are unable to find satisfactory employment—or employment at all. . . . The increased demand for more highly skilled workers, created by technological advances and automation indicates that many of these drop-outs will spend the greater part of their adult lives as recipients of public assistance."[82]

As will be shown in chapter 5, these structural changes were significantly more severe for the increasing populations of African Americans and Mexicans, as well as for recently arrived Puerto Ricans, all of whom would be up against the additional factor of employer discrimination as they sought to gain a foothold in an eroding workforce. However, white working-class youths were by no means untouched by such postwar structural shifts.[83] Summarizing data recorded by field-workers throughout much of working-class Chicago between 1955 and 1958, a report by a leading youth outreach organization, the Hard-to-Reach-Youth Project (HTRYP), concluded: "The decrease in the availability of unskilled jobs, the stigma attached to many service jobs; the complicated dissuasions to choice of the kind of work youth want to do . . . all result in the general aspiration to get 'any kind of a job.'" This was an observation the HTRYP applied to all "youth," regardless of race or national origins, although the authors of this particular study did note that "discriminatory employment practices" created additional obstacles for job seekers of color.[84] However, that in 1956 an HTRYP official reported that "almost all" of the thirty-five gang youths he supervised in a "Polish-Catholic area" were attending Continuation School suggests that white skin did not ensure a respectable job for a great many of the working-class youths who gave up on school to enter the labor market in the 1950s.[85] It is therefore important not to lose sight of the adverse conditions faced by young working-class whites lacking the requisite skills for anything but menial services jobs and unskilled factory work. That many were, in fact, negotiating the often arbitrary circumstances of what was an expanding pool of surplus unskilled labor—a situation that, according to an HTRYP study, made young men "very uncertain and frightened"—resulted in a welling up of frustrations that would demand some kind of resolution in another arena.[86] It was on the streets and in the leisure spaces of the community, in the empowering company of peers, that such feelings of powerlessness could most readily be effaced. The controlled and atomizing world of service work held few such possibilities, and while failure here could be passed off to an unjust boss, in the neighborhood it could be avenged actively in a collective struggle against an unequivocal enemy.

"IF YOU EVER DANCE WITH A NIGGER AGAIN, I'LL BREAK EVERY BONE IN YOUR BODY"

That a widespread deficit of respect, honor, and status led to the formation of postwar youth gang subcultures is a view supported by an abundance of the literature on street gangs. While several such studies have examined this process in relation to the changing political economy of postwar cities, few have placed the story of youth subcultural formation within larger postwar narratives of racial transition, racial and ethnic formation, and race relations.[87] Reflecting the absence of this perspective from the historiography of postwar race relations was historian Gary Gerstle's claim more than a decade ago that "we need to revisit the violent clashes between whites and Blacks in the 1960s and treat them not as sudden and inexplicable explosions of rage but as the continuation of a twenty-year-old pattern of racial violence," and his "urgent" call for "new studies of . . . white hostility . . . in politics, in neighborhoods, and on the street."[88] Working-class youth subcultures were fundamental to this pattern of racial violence as well as to the overall atmosphere of white hostility that African Americans encountered in neighborhoods outside the Black Belt. Yet essential to any examination of the subcultures white working-class youths created in the late 1940s and 1950s is the emergence of the predicaments of masculinity that structured them, and which they, in turn, structured, in an era when Chicago's black population more than doubled.[89] Regardless of the shifting racial demographics of the city, the postwar political economy would have posed similar problems to white young men looking to step into adult roles, but the racial dilemma changed how such youths would attempt to resolve—both symbolically and more palpably—the troubling contradictions between social expectations and material experiences.

Racial transition was thus a crucial backdrop for the activities of white working-class youths in Chicago in the 1950s, and it would be very easy to simply view the rituals of racial violence that emerged among them as mirroring the struggles against racial integration waged by larger communities. Yet as Amanda Seligman shows in her study of racial transition on the West Side of Chicago in this period, neighborhood transformation was "a slow and sometimes agonizing process." Part of this agony resulted from the far-from-monolithic response to racial change, and many decisions invariably entailed deep feelings of guilt and betrayal. Neighborhoods underwent dramatic changes not merely because of racial in-migration, but also because of racial out-migration, or "white flight"—a process that heightened the feeling of downward mobility for those who watched friends and neighbors leave them behind. As Seligman reveals, the experience of white flight was so emotionally wrenching that former West Side residents tried to cope with their decision to leave by likening the arrival of blacks to various forms of natural disaster—earthquakes, tidal waves, and even lava flowing out of volcanoes.[90] Such expressions point to the profound emotional conditions surrounding the drama of flight and resistance—the guilt-ridden anger filling those preparing to leave and the feelings of failure possessing those being left behind. The tendency of residents to seize upon images of natural disaster in the stories they told about their flight from changing communities confirms the view, recognized by Friedrich Hayek, that people are much more prone to accept injustices and setbacks when caused by blind, impersonal forces.[91] However, the fact that some residents possessed the means and wherewithal to leave while others did not stripped away such comforting justifications for the segment of the community left behind, inviting instead painful reflections on the personal circumstances and failings that precluded the possibility of flight. For many of those unable to leave, the operative metaphor to describe the story of racial "invasion" was war rather than natural catastrophe.

By the early 1950s the white exodus was well under way, as more and more working-class families were taking advantage of thirty-year, low-interest loans subsidized by the federal government to buy their dream home in the suburbs. Despite such favorable conditions for home-ownership, however, many families preferred to remain in the old neighborhood. Some wanted to continue living near their jobs, their businesses, their relatives and friends, or their parishes; others refused to let go of their property at a loss. Nonetheless, even if by choice, remaining in a community perceived to be in decline was an experience that focused anger and blame on black residents. The 1948 comments of a young man on the Near Northwest Side, recorded by the youth worker who supervised the dances thrown by his group, speak volumes about how racial fears and class anxieties intermingled powerfully in the minds of working-class young men feeling themselves left behind: "He then launched in to his feeling about the neighborhood, which showed the general insecurity of the neighborhood, and the terrible hurt that the coming of the Negroes had made for them, how they had a pretty nice neighborhood until they had come. . . . He said that he hadn't come from a nice family, but that his wife had. . . . He continued with the usual prejudices about Negroes, body odor, that a Negro would knife you in the back—his cousin had been knifed he said."[92] It was in this way that class problems slipped so easily into crises of masculinity and then so often ended up on the menacing, deracinated bodies of African Americans.

Such circumstances explain why, in the late 1940s and early 1950s, the wartime pattern of hit-and-run strikes on black property gave way to more directly confrontational tactics against people of color. The collection of incidents documented by the black press and the CCHR no doubt represents but a small sample of racially motivated attacks, but most of those on record indicate the influence of distinctly male youth group dynamics in their provocation. Several, in fact, materialized within well-defined male homosocial contexts. In August 1947, for example, fifty white youths wielding baseball bats—about fifteen of them wearing uniforms with the words "Kimbark Theater" stretched across their chests—set upon a group of black adolescents in Jackson Park, around the Sixty-third Street Beach. That same week, at around midnight on Friday, always a prime hour for bar brawls, twenty "white youths armed with beer glasses" poured out of an Englewood bar on 55th and Shields and brutally assaulted a twenty-three-year-old black mail carrier.[93] A similar incident occurred the following summer in nearby Bridgeport, when eight to ten "young white men" filed out of a poolroom on 31st and Union to savagely assault with cue sticks and bricks three older black plasterers leaving their job.[94] These attacks occurred in the area of Englewood, which, like the nearby neighborhoods of Bridgeport and Greater Grand Crossing, had for several decades bordered the swelling Black Belt. These more spontaneous incidents preceded the larger flare-ups at 7153 St. Lawrence and 5643 South Peoria, and they offer a glimpse into why young men behaved so boldly when thousands in the community showed up to witness their exploits. Since before the days of the Shielders around the 1919 race riot, youth gangs had made a tradition out of racial violence in both of these communities, but the level of hostility had risen and fallen in relation to the apparent pressure exerted on the color line. Now, as housing needs pushed African Americans into blocks that whites considered off-limits, male youth gangs once again stepped up their patrolling of racial boundaries, a responsibility that bestowed on its bearers a sense of masculine honor. Unlike in Englewood and Greater Grand Crossing, youth rituals of racial violence in the Bridgeport area never took the stage in quite the same way as they did in the street theaters on St. Lawrence and South Peoria. But that was only because the culture of racial hatred was so intense that things were never permitted to reach that point.

About a month after sending the postal worker to the hospital with a skull fracture, another "gang of youths" from around Bridgeport performed the same deed on a railroad worker from Gary who had lost his way en route to the home of a friend. That same night, vandals smashed the windows of a black barbershop and recreation parlor around the local color line of Wentworth Avenue, a coincidence of events that strongly suggests a correlation between local youth gangs and a wave of vandalism that struck eighteen black-owned businesses in this area in 1948. When, in February 1952, an interracial civil rights group mounted a campaign against such intimidation in this neighborhood by seeking admission to a movie at the Metropole Theater on 31st and Wells, it was a local "strong-arm club" called the Jugheads that was first to the scene. Rallying a crowd of some three hundred people, described as "mostly young men" in one report and "teenage and young adult white residents" in another, the Jugheads and their supporters hurled rocks at cars and beat up several people in the racially mixed group, including a white woman.[95]

This bolder style of racial violence reflected a shared need for peer and community recognition. Unlike during the war years, when hit-and-run strikes so effectively befuddled police, the youthful perpetrators of racial attacks after the war appeared much more eager to be identified, even to the extent of inviting arrest. For example, in February 1948, some thirty youths between the ages of eighteen and twenty, flaming torches in hands, marched up to a black home in the Greater Grand Crossing area and attempted to set it afire right in front of two police officers.[96] Although such brash actions stemmed in part from perceptions of police sympathy for the cause of racial exclusion, the idea that these youths were so cocksure of their immunity as to feel invulnerable is not a credible one. First, as we will explore further, mistrust of city officials and the police was a pervasive sentiment in communities undergoing racial change. Second, the soft treatment afforded the Fernwood rioters received mention only in the black press; to be sure, a clear pattern of police leniency was developing, but it would not have been common knowledge among youths at this time.

In the end, these youths did not pay for their crimes, a state of affairs police justified by claiming they were tied up extinguishing the fires the arsonists had set. Yet the risks they were willing to take suggest that youths carried out such actions not merely to police neighborhood boundaries but also to valorize themselves in the eyes of their peers and their community. The anonymous strike appeared increasingly inadequate in this period, as more gangs felt the need to leave distinguishing marks— threatening notes and graffiti—on the sites of their crimes.[97] It was probably partly because of such behavior, in fact, that police began to make more and more arrests by the early 1950s. Mounting pressure within the black community played a role in such developments, but the fact that youths were even being nabbed for hit-and-run vandalism also had to do with their tendency to make no secret of their activities. This is perhaps why police were able to apprehend seven youths in the Lawndale community for repeatedly breaking windows and setting off explosives at three different black-occupied apartments in the spring of 1953.[98]

It did not take expert police work to make the link between these incidents and the gang of youths seen so often in their vicinity. Such acts were fundamentally communicative; they were meant to be seen, and their authors to be known. That such expressive forms of racial violence were effective in promoting a range of terrorist acts by groups of white working-class youths, even in areas apart from the traditional Black Belt boundaries, is revealed by the wave of violence that swept through the Near Northwest Side in the late 1940s. In this neighborhood threatened

*recreation and movement
and cnatural group' Fs)*

neither by incorporation into the Black Belt nor by the potential presence of a massive integrated housing project, gangs commonly assaulted black students on their way to and from Wells High School beginning in 1947. In September of that year, teenage gangs beat up six black youths and incited hundreds of Wells students to strike over the transfer of sixty blacks to their school, despite these additional students bringing the total number of African Americans at Wells to a mere 130 out of a student body of 2,200. These events culminated in a series of arson fires in black-occupied buildings in the same area, one of which occurred after the discovery of a threatening noted signed by a local youth gang called the Black Widows.[99]

With the migration of southern blacks to Chicago proceeding at a brisk pace throughout the 1950s, similar patterns of racial violence spread throughout racially transitional parts of the city. In addition to traditional areas of racial conflict, like Englewood, Bridgeport, Greater Grand Crossing, as well as the Near West, Near North, and Near Northwest Sides, new patterns of racial violence emerged in many neighborhoods on the West Side of the city. By the summer of 1953, black residents in the West Chicago neighborhoods of East Garfield Park, North Lawndale, and South Lawndale were reporting numerous racial incidents of the kind seen in earlier years—broken windows, amateurish arson strikes, and physical attacks in streets, parks, and schools carried out largely by groups of young men. In August, for example, two brothers, aged eighteen and nineteen, summoned fifteen "boys" from a neighborhood in East Garfield Park to help them smash the windows of a black residence at 3335 West Van Buren with crowbars. The brothers lived just across the street and were taken into custody for the deed the next day.[100] These kinds of activities continued on through the following spring and summer, when a persistent campaign of vandalism targeted several black-occupied buildings in the 3300 and 3400 blocks of West Monroe Avenue in the Garfield Park area.[101] South of there, around Douglas Park, police arrested an eighteen-year-old, a seventeen-year-old, and five juveniles for setting off a pipe bomb on the porch of a building at 2120 South Spaulding Avenue. The group admitted participating in repeated acts of harassment against this and two other black residences in the vicinity.[102]

On May 25, 1954, the Chicago Commission on Human Relations included eight neighborhoods on its list of the "most critical areas" of racial tension in the city, which, according to its report, "extend[ed] over the South and West Sides of Chicago." These areas represented much of what could be considered interracial Chicago—that is, the districts where blacks and whites lived in relatively close proximity—and these were only the neighborhoods deemed "most critical."[103] Others with proven track records of racial tension—the Near Northwest Side, Hyde Park, and Woodlawn, to name a few—could have easily cracked the top eight on a different day. Most of those on the list were also areas in which male youth groups had been particularly active in agitating racial tensions, and several, such as Bridgeport and the Near West Side, were notorious for the activities of well-established street gangs. That this was more of a broad-based, subcultural phenomenon than merely the work of a delinquent fringe is indicated by the wave of antiblack aggression that swept through Chicago high schools during the 1953–54 school year. Between October and February alone, the CCHR received reports of racial disturbances at Tilden, Harper, Farragut, Lindbloom, and Chicago Vocational.[104] The most serious of these occurred at Farragut, in the Lawndale area, where the stabbing of a white student by a black one nearly precipitated a riot.[105] In October and November of the following year, violence broke out at Hyde Park High School and at Riis High School on the Near West Side. In the incident at Riis, a "gang of white boys" stormed into a classroom and demanded the teacher hand over several black youths, who were allegedly members of a rival gang. Upon investigating the situation, the CCHR concluded: "There is reason to believe that students within the Riis School, both boys and girls, have connections with west side gang clubs which are detrimental to the peace and security of the neighborhood."[106]

This outbreak of racial aggression in Chicago high schools marked one of the earliest moments in which groups of teenage girls initiated acts of racial aggression. In the Harper affair, for instance, at least twenty girls took it upon themselves to terrorize the five African American students, all female, that attended the school in 1954. Repeated assaults and threats against these black students as they walked home through the streets around the lily-white West Englewood school forced authorities to suspend four girls and place another eighteen under surveillance.[107] The appearance of teenage girls at the scenes of racial violence became more frequent in the early 1950s, indicating that young women were by no means insulated from the same class predicaments that challenged the masculinity of their male peers. Never having to face the sting of frustrated masculinity in the liminal stage between childhood and adulthood made the investment of teenage girls in rituals of racial hatred somewhat less profound, but their sense of belonging to a community in decline was no less real, and the anger of fathers and brothers was often ingested at home. Thus, even as early as 1951, teenage girls were uniting, on occasion, to defend their neighborhoods. In August of that year, for example, a representative of the CCHR responded to a report of an impending fight between groups of white and black girls at Fuller Park, which lay right around the Wentworth Avenue color line on the Near South Side. Arriving at the scene, he heard the following story of what had precipitated the affair: "Both groups, Negro and white, were standing at the fence of the swimming pool. . . . The white girls led by a Mexican girl started hurling derogatory racial remarks at the Negro girls."[108]

Such incidents suggest that young women in working-class Chicago were beginning to enter the terrain of youth leisure on a more equal footing in the 1950s. Whereas girls' clubs formed mostly within the confines of settlements and under close adult supervision in the interwar period, a number of autonomous female street gangs had taken shape by the mid-1950s. In 1956, for example, the HTRYP assigned a special "girls' worker" to the Near West Side to monitor the activities of the Noblettes—the female counterpart of the reputed Nobles. In Hyde Park, moreover, a youth worker noted the presence of an "all-girls' group" named the Coquettes, as well as some "co-ed" gangs, among the numerous so-called anti-social groups in the neighborhood.[109]

While the historian Elaine Tyler May has argued that the 1950s was a period that witnessed the ideological "containment" of women within the domestic sphere, the youth cultural market, beginning in the mid-1950s, offered up some radically divergent representations of feminine behavior.[110] In films like *Dragstrip Girl* and *Hot Rod Girl,* teenage girls were far from passive bystanders to the havoc wrought by gangs of wild youths. This genre's female gangs and packs of reform school girls on the loose conveyed striking images of autonomous and empowered young women. While these visions of unrestrained femininity largely sought to attract the male voyeuristic gaze, their advent also reflected the increasing emergence of young women into the spheres of commercial culture and public leisure. Unlike the 1930s, when immigrant and first-generation parents rather effectively curtailed the spending habits and social activities of their daughters, many working-class young women in the 1950s were able to gain far greater access to the unsupervised realm of street life. Thus, while one HTRYP study spoke of mothers being "most watchful and protective" over the sexuality of their daughters, it also referred to the existence of "hangouts that serve as exchange points for male and female contacts."[111] While such trends were somewhat slower to penetrate Mexican communities still receiving a steady flow of immigrants in the postwar decades, even Mexican teenage girls were spending more time outside the home and beyond the supervision of parents by the mid-1950s. In some cases, however, their presence on the streets had more to do with their continued supervision than with their evasion of such forms of control. A youth worker on the Near West Side, for example, noted that the female counterparts of Mexican gangs often contained many of the sisters and other relatives of the male members.[112]

The increasing presence of young women in spaces of youth leisure had an important impact on the behavior of male youth gangs in the 1950s. While the continuing interplay of racial migration and deindustrialization in Chicago no doubt played a major role in making racial aggression a quotidian phenomenon in the street-corner milieus of young men, the growing presence of women tended to alter the codes and raise the stakes of such rituals of racial and ethnic violence. In the mid-1950s, when female groups appeared on the streets mostly in the form of contingents to male gangs or informal cliques, male youth gangs in many communities viewed themselves as their protectors against external threats, particularly those jeopardizing their feminine honor or sexual purity. While this role was more clearly defined when members of the female gangs were actually related to those in their male counterpart groups, feelings of ethnic and community solidarity also shaped the bonds that formed between such affiliated male and female groups. As youth workers in three different neighborhoods reported, such feelings tended to make the girls of the neighborhood off-limits in the game of sexual conquest that played such an important role in the realization of male prowess.[113] This explains, in part, the widespread use by white gangs of mostly black and Mexican prostitutes witnessed by observers in the 1950s, and the particular fixation of all gangs with girls of other racial and ethnic groups. As one youth worker commented about a Near West Side Italian gang's habit of making advances toward Mexican girls in their neighborhood: "Because they are Mexican they are not actually what the boys consider part of their 'community.'" According to this worker, both of the gangs he supervised showed "respect" for girls in the "community," while making frequent trips to black prostitutes around 13th and Clinton.[114]

This attraction to women of other ethnic and racial groups was not, however, merely a function of the tendency to consider neighborhood girls as unsuitable for sexual activities. Working-class male youth groups also viewed relations with the girls of certain outsider groups as "status" markers. In addition to seeking out black and Mexican girls for their sexual escapades, Italians youths on the Near West Side idealized the Polish girls on 18th Street, who, lamented the youths in one gang, you needed a car to "get."[115] Similar attitudes also prevailed among Mexican youths, who viewed relations with an "Anglo girl" as the highest form of success, and among Puerto Rican teens, who plotted ways to "pick up an American girl," an objective, they agreed, that could only be accomplished with the use of a car.[116]

Across a range of ethnic and racial communities, then, protecting and sexually "conquering" girls constituted two of the most important facets of male identity on the streets in this moment. If, as Judith Butler has argued, gender is not fixed or given but rather "an identity tenuously constituted in time . . . through a stylized repetition of acts," the numerous forms and rituals that enacted these roles should be seen as the available means of "performing" masculinity or manhood.[117] However, with the entrance of more and more young women into domains—the street corner and club hangout—that were previously sex-segregated, the more aggressive, often misogynist form of masculinity predicated on sexual conquest became the more readily available variant. The centrality of this modality of masculinity appears strikingly in sources that record the language of male street culture in the 1950s. A 1958 HTRYP report on the subject, for example, detailed a number of terms circulating among young men on the streets that connoted sexual prowess or the lack thereof—*stud, lover,* and *siddy,* the latter signifying "a male who is effeminate." The same report also included on its list of common street argot the term *cherried,* which it defined as "a mark of distinction of males who have broken the hymen of a virgin."[118] In addition to such loaded language, young men fashioned this form of masculinity through a range of verbal games structured around boasting of one's sexual potency while degrading an opponent's relations with women. Reports from several settlement houses about these games, which went by such names as "bum rapping," "ball busting" and "the dozens," mentioned that insults frequently revolved around "references to homosexuality." As for boasts about sexual exploits, youth workers reported, notably, that gang youths excluded family members and "girls they respect" from such competitions.[119] That these games were almost universal throughout working-class Chicago suggests that the problem of youth masculinity transcended racial and ethnic lines.

As mentioned earlier, one of the principal causes of the relative fragility of masculinity during this period was a condition of halted maturation that struck working-class youths negotiating the life stage between school and work, childhood and adulthood. This condition shaped the ways young men performed and styled their masculinity on the streets in the 1950s, but the subcultures that emerged out of these performances also bore a close relationship to traditional forms of masculinity that were becoming more and more difficult to realize. This explains why many of the rituals and styles emerging within working-class subcultures in this period adhered somehow to the intertwined roles of lover and protector, both of which reflected the traditional ideal of the male provider. As gang workers and researchers have generally agreed, gangs and street culture in general have served as kinds of waiting areas or staging grounds before marriage; young men who continued to run regularly with the gang after marriage have been the exceptions, although sporadic participation in or involvement with more casual adult clubs was not infrequent in the 1950s. The stakes of the male provider role for conceptions of masculinity at this time can be glimpsed in this conclusion arrived at by HTRYP workers: "It is okay to remain single until around twenty-eight, but if you have not married and settled down by that time, the male is considered 'queer.'"[120] The reality and gravity of such a failure reveals why several Chicago youth workers reported "a rash of marriages that bore no relation to jobs or pregnancy" in 1958 and speculated that in such actions young men were "seeking answers to their problems." "They had tried everything else, maybe this was it," one counselor commented.[121]

That this crisis of masculinity was bound up with injuries caused by racial transition and community breakdown meant that the role of protecting neighborhood women against menacing and often (but not always) racially other outsiders would be stylized in more violent forms. Indeed, if the HTRYP reported that conflicts over women constituted the most common cause of gang violence by the mid-1950s, those involving a crossing of racial and ethnic lines, whether real or imagined, usually sparked the most extreme responses.[122] Reflecting back on his activities with an Italian gang in the 1940s, a youth worker on the Near West Side claimed that fights at that time were almost always along racial or ethnic lines and "often over a girl."[123] Yet while catcalls or more tactful overtures toward women of another community could spark violent retribution, no situation was more provocative than young women initiating contacts with ethnic or racial outsiders.[124] When a white female employee of the Chicago Commons Association was seen dancing with an African American man at the annual fair on the Near Northwest Side, for example, a group of youths reproached her in the severest of terms. One reminded her of another girl in the area who had been beaten up for a similar transgression, while another was more direct: "If you ever dance with a nigger again, I'll break every bone in your body."[125]

The increasing numbers of young women in spaces of youth leisure in the mid-1950s made such situations, real or imagined, more likely. Indeed, whether as spectators or as objects of performances of masculinity, the presence of girls on the streets pushed young men to fashion their male identities in different ways. Yet it would be misleading to view these young women as mostly innocent bystanders or passive objects to be defended. While at this time a still relatively small percentage of women entered the domain of street culture as members of a well-defined gang per se, those that did were in some ways opting for a feminine identity that diverged greatly from and even consciously opposed the hegemonic ideal of domestic femininity in the 1950s. This oppositional tendency would become much more apparent by the early 1960s, when numerous female gangs sprang up throughout working-class Chicago, but the first traces of it could be observed by the mid-1950s.

In addition to seeing participation in acts of intimidation against racial and ethnic others, some youth workers at this time observed that female gangs were capable of engaging in fights with male groups. According to a worker in the area around Hull House, girls were joining such gangs "in order to travel about"—that is to say, to protect themselves against acts of male aggression.[126] Incidents of rape were not infrequent in working-class Chicago during this period, particularly cases involving attacks against African American and Mexican American girls by white youths, and many youths regarded them as normal and even logical occurrences. During his fieldwork on the Near West Side of Chicago, the sociologist Gerald Suttles recorded a conversation between gang youths on the subject of "rape-prone girls" in the neighborhood.[127] Similar observations were made by a youth worker at Association House on the Near Northwest Side, who reported that youths participating in the Dozens there typically evoked their prowess by describing themselves carrying out "an assault on a girl in a school yard."[128] Moreover, a gang worker on the Near West side reported that several of the teens in his group had beaten up girls, presumably for rejecting their sexual advances.[129]

However, the activities of girl gangs under such conditions revealed a posture that was much more than defensive. While outreach programs were just starting to take more seriously the still somewhat small number of female gangs in Chicago in the 1950s, making evidence of their behavior scarce, some youth observers did note activities by these groups that challenged middle-class ideals of femininity and disrupted (if perhaps only temporarily) the order of gender relations on the streets. If fragile masculinities were primary causes of a range of forms of street violence, conflicts between gangs over women sometimes arose from the machinations of the women being fought over. A researcher noted one such instance while studying the Nobles and the Noblettes in 1956. According to this observer, several of the Noblettes had come to the boys after allegedly being insulted by "the Polacks" on 18th Street. When the Nobles displayed reluctance to avenge the incident, "the girls taunted them until they went to the Polish district and beat the boys up." Afterward, the youths "regretted" doing this and sent apologies through a mutual contact.[130] The circumstances of this affair suggest the girls were as concerned with their ability to manipulate their male peers, the Nobles, as with the need to punish the Polish youths on 18th Street; the reluctance and remorse shown by the Nobles speaks to their power to do so.

While these female groups were somewhat dependent on their male associates for protection out on the streets, they often took advantage of this opportunity to construct their own forum for defining their gender identities and experimenting with their sexuality. Those in contact with girl gangs generally commented first and foremost on their use of obscene language and the frequency with which their conversations touched on sexual matters. Summing up the observations of a team of youth workers, one study claimed: "The girls refer to each other as whores, and spend much of their conversation attacking each other in obscene references to sexual behavior, including references to deviant sex practices of homosexuals." Another report concluded: "In general, it was found that girls' gangs are amorphous; they don't know what they want; they use foul language and do not pair off with males for sex play." Indeed, like their male peers, female youth groups valued the anonymity that came with pursuing romantic encounters in other neighborhoods. It was certainly in this spirit of experimentation that "white girls" attended black dances held at the Henry Horner Boys Clubs in the fall of 1956, where, according to one observer, "they c[a]me early and stay[ed] late."[131]

5

Teenage Terrorism, Fighting Gangs, and Collective Action in the Era of Civil Rights

Norm, I'm too old for this kind of shit. If you ever see me
ready to get into a fight again, you kick my ass for me.

> Member of the Clovers to gang worker Norm
> Feldman, April 15, 1958

Also on the way to the game as we passed North Avenue
Beach, the boys remarked that no Negroes were allowed
in this part of Chicago. . . . This points up my feeling that
their world begins and ends here on the west side. Few
members of the group have any conception of what goes
on outside of the west side, because few members of the
group have ever gone any other place in Chicago except
the west side and probably downtown in the loop.

> Gang worker William C. Watson, August 11, 1958

THE "NEW TEENAGE TERRORISM": NEIGHBORHOOD TRANSITION AND RACIAL ALTERITY

Delinquency was largely a back-burner issue in Chicago until 1955, the
year *The Blackboard Jungle* and *Rebel without a Cause* opened to packed
theaters, the hit single *Rock around the Clock* climbed the pop charts,
and the high-profile proceedings of the Senate Subcommittee to Investigate Juvenile Delinquency informed Americans that juvenile delinquency
was the nation's most pressing domestic problem. Such broader trends
touched Chicago as early as March of that year, when the city council
heard a motion to raise the curfew age from sixteen to eighteen.[1] How-

ever, it was not until July that the issue exploded on the local scene, and it did so within the context of what the local press represented as a burgeoning subculture of gang violence. The defining event occurred when a gang of toughs from Bridgeport gunned down seventeen-year-old Kenneth Sleboda in front of a snack joint at 3208 Morgan Street, an incident which prompted the *Tribune* to run a three-part investigative series on "youth gangs and the juvenile delinquency problem."[2] Several months later, after a fatal teen stabbing and a vicious gang beating hit the papers in the span of three days, the *Daily News* reported that Chicago youth were increasingly falling under the influence of a "wolf-pack complex."[3] In response, the YMCA promptly announced plans to infiltrate gangs with "secret agents," and Mayor Richard Daley, who had expanded the ranks of the police juvenile bureau by nearly 50 percent since his recent election, urged stricter enforcement of the city curfew law despite reassuring Chicagoans that "our young people are good."[4]

The discovery of a juvenile crime epidemic and a gang problem in Chicago thus dovetailed with the emergence of delinquency discourses emanating from both Washington and Hollywood in the mid-1950s. Yet while the Senate subcommittee was scrutinizing the iniquitous effects of crime comics and juvenile exploitation films, Chicago's own rendering of the juvenile crime wave invoked much more palpable forces to explain itself. Those events seized upon by the local press to articulate the youth crisis were the stuff of "grudge killings" and "gang feuds," perpetrated by young men afflicted by "gang complexes," "feelings of inadequacy," and "misguided bravado." Although James Dean's gripping portrayal of a troubled suburban teen in *Rebel without a Cause* had demonstrated that delinquency could just as easily strike the bedroom communities of middle-class America, pointing to family dysfunction as the root cause of juvenile crime, the delinquency issue in Chicago came across as it had in the past—as a manifestation of working-class life. The shooter in the Sleboda murder was fourteen-year-old Clement "Cookie" Macis, a student at a Chicago vocational school who was working as a freight handler for the summer. He lived just blocks away from the intersection of 32nd and Halsted, where teenage gangs, according to the state's attorney's investigation, "roam[ed] the area carrying guns and knives." In this and several other working-class districts of Chicago, a *Tribune* reporter found, "bands of teenagers [were] so numerous that it was almost impossible to make a survey of them."[5] Similarly, in the deadly stabbing that gave rise to pronouncements of a "new teen-age terrorism" months later, the murderer was nineteen-year-old Robert Hoffman, a factory worker living with his parents in a low-income West Side neighborhood. The gang that had beaten three rivals with a metal bar two days later, causing the *Daily News* to declare the existence of a "wolf pack complex," inhabited a nearby low-income area on the Near West Side reputed for gangsterism and fearsome street-corner gangs. Elaborating on the malady that had apparently befallen these young men, a Municipal Court psychiatrist explained: "In the 'wolf pack complex' there is a certain degree of resentment against their environment which is one of deprivation."[6]

Thus, in the second half of the 1950s, street gangs and even the juvenile delinquency problem in general had a predominantly white face in Chicago. The languages that circulated through popular discourse to explain what was wrong with "today's youth," which alternated between family pathology, social psychology, and poverty, were also colorless. Largely absent from the mainstream media account of this youth crime epidemic, both nationally and locally, were the racial anxieties and antagonisms that shaped the context of so much of the youth violence being witnessed in Chicago in the late 1950s. Hence, when a well-known Near West Side gang called the Dukes made the papers for two consecutive days in 1958 after being picked up by police for carrying around baseball bats and a length of tire chain, the news coverage failed to mention that the gang they were coming after was black and that such racial attacks were business as usual for this group.[7]

The black press had a somewhat different perspective. When the *Chicago Defender* printed a front-page editorial entitled "Juvenile Terrorism Must Be Stopped" in the spring of 1957, its editors were referring not to the kind of self-contained aggression practiced by Macis or Hoffman, but rather to another "wave of crimes and violence," which was, they claimed, "paralyzing social relations and hampering normal race relations."[8] Two particular incidents prompted their call to Mayor Daley for a "citywide emergency committee" to handle this crisis of juvenile terrorism. In the last week of April 1957, nineteen-year old David Vandersteeg fired a shotgun from a moving car at a group of twenty black youths standing on the corner of 111th and Ashland Avenue, mortally wounding one of them. Yet the more startling episode had happened six weeks earlier, when twelve teens belonging to an Englewood-area gang known as the Rebels surrounded a seventeen-year-old African American, as one of their members, Joseph Schwartz, landed a fatal blow to his head with a ball-peen hammer. The boy was waiting for a bus near his home at 59th and Kedzie, an area that had seen intense resistance to black settlement in previous years.[9]

While such acts were undoubtedly understood by most at the time as aberrations, they signaled two broader interrelated trends that had begun to reshape the street cultures of working-class areas experiencing racial transition in this period. The first was an escalation in the intensity and stakes of racial aggression—a proliferation of more lethal forms of racial violence—that reflected both the increasing use of firearms and a dogged fixation on the presence of racial others, real or imagined, that among youths in certain neighborhoods could be described as bordering on obsessive. The second was the widespread emergence of fairly large (normally between twenty-five and one-hundred members) ethnically or racially defined street gangs—commonly referred to by youth workers as "fighting gangs"—whose principal function was to engage in potentially deadly combat against other groups.

Chicago was not alone in this second development. Indeed, Eric Schneider has documented similar trends in New York around the same period, arguing that the pursuit of "machismo" in a context of deindustrialization, urban renewal, and racial marginalization lay behind the development of such fighting-gang subcultures. Although gang violence in New York could at times revolve around racial and ethnic divisions, Schneider finds that it was more often characterized by struggles over territory, or "turf."[10] Indeed, the protection of turf was also a driving force in Chicago. Some very bitter rivalries, in fact, involved gangs of similar ethnic or racial composition from different neighborhoods, and ethnically different gangs from the same area did, at times, join forces to fend off encroachments by groups from bordering areas.[11] In Chicago, however, turf was usually a euphemism for community, and community was often defined in racial or ethnic terms during this era of rapid demographic change. While the battles waged between fighting gangs quite often arose ostensibly over territorial disputes or encroachments, these were often pretexts for deeper motivations—such as evocations of manliness or of group solidarity. Indeed, geographers building on the theoretical frameworks introduced by Henri Lefebvre have drawn attention to the ways groups "produce space" through their everyday activities—what Lefebvre refers to as "spatial practices." The collective struggle to use and define space thus constitutes a dynamic process out of which political projects oriented around racial and ethnic identities emerge. We have already viewed the involvement of street gangs and youth groups in such spatial practices in Irish Canaryville, Polish Packingtown and the Bush, Italian Little Sicily and Little Italy, as well as in many of the neighborhoods along the color line—black and white—from the late 1940s through the mid-

1950s. In all of these cases, youth groups were among the most active participants in struggles to establish and maintain the link between neighborhood space and group identity—a role that fighting gangs would continue to champion.[12]

This is not to say, however, that the performance of masculinity was not also fundamental to these fighting-gang cultures. Indeed, the forces of deindustrialization and urban renewal contributed greatly to shaping a context that valorized such performances. Between 1955 and 1963, the Chicago metropolitan area lost some 131,000 jobs (or 22 percent) as the number of job seekers increased by some three hundred thousand.[13] While this period is often considered one of national prosperity, employment figures in the Chicago area indicate a slump-and-boom pattern of economic growth that tended to make the labor market precarious for young workers. Recessions struck the city especially hard in 1958 and 1961, causing sharp rises in unemployment.[14] These conditions, moreover, coincided with massive clearance and renewal projects on the Near West and South Sides of the city to make way for the construction of several public housing complexes, new medical facilities around the Cook County Hospital, and a Chicago campus of the University of Illinois. Such events had a significant impact on the lives of working-class youths within the affected communities.

It is hardly surprising that these circumstances would produce such desperate displays of violent bravado. Yet a close examination of the composition and behavior of Chicago fighting gangs in the late 1950s reveals that racial and ethnic identities more often than not served as key determinants of group membership and primary motivations for violent conflicts. In addition to industrial decline, labor market volatility, and the social dislocations caused by urban renewal, the dynamics of postwar racial migration in working-class Chicago heightened the uncertainties felt by working-class youths and shaped their responses to the dilemmas they faced. Constituting just over 14 percent of the city's total population in 1950, African Americans continued migrating from the South. They made up over a quarter of the population by 1962.[15] Paralleling this steady black migration was the arrival of waves of dark-skinned Mexican and Puerto Rican immigrants in the 1950s and 1960s. According to the official census figures, after increasing some 43 percent between 1940 and 1950, the number of Mexicans in Chicago grew almost fivefold between 1950 and 1970 (from 24,000 to 108,000). In this same period, the city's overall "Spanish-speaking" population increased from 35,000 to 247,000, while the total population of the city dropped from 3.6 million to 3.3 million.[16] If the injuries of class would intensify what some have referred to as the "pursuit of machismo" or "the search for respect" among young men out on the streets, these circumstances of rapid racial flux would ensure that the causes of such injuries would be perceived or felt in racial rather than class terms—that race would be, as Stuart Hall has written about Britain, "the modality through which class [was] lived."[17]

Contrary to narratives that depict the late 1950s and early 1960s as a moment of racial consolidation in Chicago and much of urban America, the end of a long process of black ghettoization that reinforced the idea of a black-white binary racial order, a street-level view of the many Chicago neighborhoods whose racial composition resisted simple categorization as white or black reveals a much different situation. The great racial hostility and uncertainty witnessed in such areas, particularly in the milieu of a vibrant youth gang culture that played an essential role in shaping daily life on the streets, evidenced a process of racial formation that was in full stride rather than one in its final stages. While there is certainly some truth to the contention that the whiteness of working-class European Americans was much more secure by the 1950s, the racial identities of Puerto Ricans and Mexicans within the new racial regime of color were far less certain in this moment.

Because of the dark-skinned complexions of many Puerto Ricans, Chicagoans tended to identify them with African Americans. Reflecting on this situation, one Puerto Rican immigrant in Chicago recounted a story of being refused service at a bar on the grounds that he was black: "We were always considered black. I remember this one time, I went to a tavern with a friend and the owner of the bar refused to serve us. I said to the guy, 'We want two beers,' and he said, 'We don't serve niggers here.' I replied that we were Puerto Ricans and he just said, 'That's the same shit.'"[18] That this was hardly an isolated incident is suggested by the large number of Puerto Ricans settling within or beside black neighborhoods in the late 1940s and 1950s, a trend that both reflected and reinforced their racialization.[19] The forces behind this racialization can be glimpsed in the series of mob actions and arson attacks targeting Puerto Ricans on both the Near West and Near Northwest Sides in the mid-1950s, conditions that forced the Chicago Commission on Human Relations and a range of neighborhood organizations to intervene in order to prevent possible riots. Between 1954 and 1955 three fatal arson fires targeted low-rent buildings housing Puerto Ricans in the neighborhood around the Chicago Commons settlement on the Near Northwest Side. Residents interviewed after one of the blazes stated that neighbors had referred to them as "colored" since their arrival.[20] On the Near West Side, such resistance took the form of physical attacks against Puerto Ricans by brick- and bat-wielding mobs.[21] In both cases, neighborhood street gangs had played active roles in mounting this community resistance—a situation that prompted youth worker Dan Nagle's efforts to organize the Northwest Youth Council, a federation of some fifteen gangs with more than three hundred members, as a means of restoring peace to the area.[22]

While the case of Mexicans is much more ambiguous, in the sense that they were generally allowed freer access to white ethnic neighborhoods, racial attacks against Mexicans were nonetheless not uncommon in the 1950s. In 1951, for example, a group of teenagers repeatedly terrorized the home of a Mexican family in a South Chicago neighborhood, leaving behind a note that read: "Get out of here, you Mexicans, we don't want you here!"[23] Even as late as 1960, a group of youths, mistaking a Native American family for Mexicans, repeatedly stoned their home at 3415 West Huron Avenue on the West Side. Suggestive of the anguished racial feelings behind such actions, a note they pinned to the front door with the words "Ha Mex, get out of here" identified the aggressors as "the Whites."[24]

Such experiences of discrimination informed Mexicans in Chicago that their place under the umbrella of whiteness was far from assured. As the historian George Sanchez has argued, since Mexicans are "never quite white," they are prone to being periodically "re-racialized" during periods of strong immigration. At no time was this re-racializing effect more apparent than when Mexican migration flows coincided with those of African Americans and Puerto Ricans. The identities of both Mexicans and Puerto Ricans in postwar Chicago thus took shape in "racially inflected circumstances," an expression Robert Orsi employs to describe the history of Italian immigration in New York.[25] Yet the development of racial and ethnic consciousness for these "in-between" groups involved not only reactions to African Americans but also responses to each other. Substantial evidence points to Mexicans being perhaps the most deeply invested of all Chicagoans in the idea that Puerto Ricans were an essentially nonwhite racial group. As one gang worker described it: "Their hostility towards Puerto Ricans stems from the idea that they have negro blood in them. . . . This hostility is very open although they both have a common language."[26]

As these circumstances suggest, the parallel migrations of blacks, Puerto Ricans, and Mexicans to Chicago further destabilized what were already unstable racial boundaries in the city's working-class districts. For Mexicans perhaps most of all, the ensuing sense of racial uncertainty was palpable rather than merely felt. In South Chicago, an area of considerable Mexican concentration, for example, residents openly complained of politicians using their community as a "buffer-zone" between whites and blacks.[27] According to the report of a social settlement in this neighborhood, "Non-Mexicans are identified as 'whites' to distinguish them from Mexicans (but the Mexicans are not called 'colored'—only blacks are)."[28] Describing another large Mexican enclave on the Near West Side, a Mexican social worker claimed that Mexican residents "referred to any so-called white person as an Anglo," a term that signified "all people outside the Mexican and Negro ethnic groups." "The idea of being hemmed in or becoming inferior," he further reported, was among the principal elements of this community's political outlook.[29]

For Puerto Ricans, the confusion was no less profound. To begin with, Puerto Rican immigrants displayed a broad spectrum of racial characteristics, a situation reflected in the large number of terms they used to identify different racial types within the community. Conducting fieldwork on Chicago's Puerto Rican community in the late 1940s, a University of Chicago anthropology student found that Puerto Ricans used no fewer than six different expressions to identify racial qualities—"*grifo,*" "*moreno,*" "*de color,*" "*indio,*" "*trigueno,*" and "*negro.*" Although claiming that none of these words had the pejorative connotations of terms in the American racial lexicon, the researcher did conclude that among Puerto Ricans "a social value is attached to a light skin color and to Caucasoid features."[30] By the late 1950s, after several more years of Puerto Rican population growth and intergroup conflict, a CCHR report found quite different modalities of racial consciousness among Puerto Ricans:

> The white Puerto Rican without Negroid or Indian features is apt to pick up some of the prejudice against Negroes, whether they are American or Puerto Rican; the intermediate types will orient themselves in a direction where they feel less antagonized or discriminated against; but the dark-skinned Puerto Rican undergoes a traumatic experience in his attempt to adjust to the American reality of race prejudice toward the colored man. . . . The dark Puerto Rican develops unique defensive attitudes in order not to be taken for an American Negro; thus he will speak only a bare minimum of English, trying to convey the impression that he is a foreigner rather than a Negro.[31]

What the authors of this study detected after more than one hundred visits to Puerto Rican homes was the presence of an impulse that Robert

Orsi has referred to as "alterity."[32] In the face of grassroots racial dis-crimination, Puerto Ricans had, at least by the late 1950s, internalized a need to distinguish themselves from their African American neighbors, an ongoing struggle that presented some serious challenges because of their racial and spatial proximity to blacks. The profound emotional toll this struggle presented to Puerto Rican youths in the 1950s and 1960s constitutes one of the principal themes of Piri Thomas's memoir *Down These Mean Streets,* which recounts his experiences as a young, dark-skinned Puerto Rican man in Spanish Harlem in the postwar decades. In one scene, for example, Thomas is stricken with feelings of guilt and am-bivalence after asserting his distinctive "Porty Rican" identity to counter the claims of his black friend Brew that Thomas was a "Negro" like him. Thomas reflects: "What the hell was I trying to put down? Was I trying to tell Brew that I'm better than he is 'cause he's only black and I'm a Puerto Rican dark-skin? Like his people copped trees on a white man's whim, and who ever heard of Puerto Ricans getting hung like that?" Cor-roborating the findings of CCHR researchers concerning the use of the Spanish language as a strategy of alterity by Puerto Ricans, Brew's re-sponse to Thomas includes the remark: "Jus' 'cause you can rattle off some different kinda language don' change your skin one bit."[33]

Observers of Mexican communities in Chicago noted similar tenden-cies. This is what the Near West Side gang worker referred to earlier was describing in 1956 when he remarked on the "open hostility" expressed by Mexican youths toward Puerto Ricans despite their "common lan-guage," and what a Mexican mother was articulating in 1957 when she told an interviewer for the Chicago Welfare Council, "We don't dislike Negroes, but we can't let our children be identified with them. They suf-fer enough from prejudice."[34] For European American groups, the stakes of racial alterity were somewhat different, but in light of the frequency of attacks against African Americans, Puerto Ricans, and Mexicans dur-ing the 1950s and 1960s, they were no less real. Indeed, although the idea that an Italian or Polish ethnic was not white would have seemed implausible by the early 1960s, white ethnic communities nonetheless perceived the presence of darker-skinned groups to be deeply threatening.

This evidence points to a reflexive need for racial alterity created by the conditions of racial migration and neighborhood transition in Chicago in the late 1950s and early 1960s. This need played itself out most visi-bly and perhaps most powerfully on the streets within the context of working-class youth subcultures, For some youth groups in certain com-munities it approached the condition of a collective compulsion that inspired risky, self-destructive behavior. The quest to meet the need for racial alterity was an integral part of the fighting-gang subcultures that took shape in working-class Chicago during this period. When the recently formed Hard-to-Reach-Youth Project called together nineteen of its youth outreach workers to pool their observations in November 1956, for example, the ensuing discussion revealed that the impulse for racial opposition was at the very core of the youth subcultures that had taken shape in several of the neighborhoods to the west, northwest, and south of the Loop. Indeed, while the HTRYP never directly defined its mission in terms of race relations, nearly all of the neighborhoods it targeted were in the throes of racial transition and conflict. In Hyde Park, where the color line had advanced within blocks of the privileged confines of the University of Chicago, the youth worker there, Ralph Fertig, claimed to have contact with seven "anti-social" teenage groups, each with fifteen to twenty members. Identifying themselves by such names as the Tipsters, the Junior Unknowns, the Diablos, Los Gatas, and Los Chicos, these groups of "white boys" had, according to Fertig, "developed a protective alliance against the Negroes." A similar situation characterized the area around the Chicago Commons settlement house on the Near Northwest Side, where outreach worker Paul Lerman monitored nine "male and white" groups—the Titans, Jesters, Satans, Viscounts, Jokers, Capris, and Gamblers, among others—that together formed what he referred to as a "loose council of street clubs." Years before, Dan Nagle had managed to organize several of these gangs into the Northwest Youth Council after an incident described by Lerman as a "race riot."[35]

Although the HTRYP stayed clear of some of Chicago's more insular and communal neighborhoods, such as the white South Side strongholds of South Deering and Bridgeport, similar kinds of fighting-gang subcultures structured around tactics and rituals of alterity appeared in these areas as well. In Bridgeport, "where teenage gangs roam[ed] the area carrying guns and knives," the existence of such fighting-gang subcultures and their preoccupation with racial exclusion was well established by the mid-1940s. In South Deering, a community hemmed in between Wisconsin and Republic Steel mills and Lake Calumet in the southeast corner of the city, fighting gangs emerged in the mid-1950s when its largely Polish, Italian, and Slavic community waged a concerted struggle to oppose CHA plans to move African American families into the Trumbull Park Homes project.

Although the Trumbull Park situation received the most coverage in 1954 and 1955, when NAACP demonstrations at city hall thrust the problem into the political arena in a mayoral election year, the campaign really began in 1953. On the evening of Sunday, August 9 of that year, an angry crowd of some fifteen hundred assembled in front of a building wherein a single black couple had recently moved, thereby commencing a year of unrelenting harassment.[36] Stubborn resistance to a minimal black presence in the Trumbull Park Homes continued throughout the next two years, during which racial anger and aggression became a vital aspect of daily neighborhood life. Recounted in many of the daily reports of an ACLU spy living in the area are the numerous ways bands of teenagers—Polish, Italian, and Mexican alike—created and maintained a culture of terror in the vicinity of the Trumbull Park Homes. In one report, the ACLU spy spoke of "a gang of kids who do all of the damage and create all of the trouble and who also shoot off the bombs."[37] In another, he warned: "These kids are more dangerous than ever and they do not know any better and if they meet one of the Negroes alone and there is a gang of them it would be too bad for that Negro."[38] In June 1954, the Trumbull Park Tenant Council addressed a letter to the mayor for the sole purpose of calling attention to the "alarming number of young people [that] have been involved in acts of violence such as arson, window-breaking, intimidation of adults, and general vandalism," a situation it was "reluctant" to view as "the result of any deliberate organized adult-group action."[39] Drafted in a moment when gangs of youths had been particularly active in physical assaults against black tenants, the council expressed the concern that "permanent habits of delinquent behavior [were] being formed among youths of the area."[40] As predicted, more than four years later, gangs of white teenagers were still doing their best to make life unbearable for the residents of color in South Deering.[41]

That such habitual behavior had taken hold not just in South Deering but throughout much of the far South Side area was indicated even more compellingly by the weeklong explosion of racist youth violence in Calumet Park, in which almost exclusively teenage and young adult mobs numbering in the thousands used stones, bats, knives, and cars in lethal displays of violence against African Americans.[42] As the arrest lists from this riot demonstrate, the mobs coming together in opposition to blacks were not simply "white." Also present in substantial numbers were Mexican youths from the South Chicago and South Deering neighborhoods around the park, where European ethnics had been harassing Mexicans since the 1920s; even around the Trumbull Park Homes, where Mexicans participated in antiblack aggression alongside Poles,

Italians, and Slavs, Mexicans were not infrequently victims of similar attacks. Some Mexican residents would later claim, in fact, that things got tougher for them in South Deering during this period of resistance to black settlement—circumstances that created fertile ground for the emergence of racial anxieties in the Mexican community.[43] In addition to the warnings of the undercover ACLU observer in South Deering about the dangers posed by gangs of youths, just as striking in his reports are the number of references to the dark skin color of the youths and his confusion about who is Italian and who is Mexican. In one report he identifies two youths as being from "a nation of dark people."[44] In another, in which he describes a "mixed up bunch of kids" he observed in a park one evening, he claims, "Every nationality and some of them even blacker than the Negro's and each and every one of them full of devilment and they would do a lot of damage if something would get started and these black ones who are Mexicans seem to hate the Negro even worse than the whites."[45]

Recorded as they were by an observer who was acutely sensitive to such issues, these testimonies to the atmosphere of profound racial anxiety, confusion, and anger in South Deering may present a somewhat extreme version of the situation. Yet viewed beside the record of more than five years of persistent racial aggression by South Deering youths, they indicate that a kind of collective racial obsession had taken hold of many young men in this community. As the perceptions of the presumably racially sympathetic ACLU observer suggest, Mexican youths in this area appeared to be most afflicted by this form of anxiety, a reflection of their precarious and volatile racial status. While the pattern of violence these circumstances elicited is relatively easy to document, the impact such feelings had on the overall emotional conditions of Mexican adolescents is much more elusive. Evidence suggests that the effects were profound, for both Mexican and European American youths on the far South Side. A case file on one troubled Mexican teen in the area, for example, reported in 1956 that the boy had "attempted suicide, stating he hated Negroes and felt like killing them."[46] Another rather extreme situation is revealed by a case report from the Polish Russell Square area that same year. The youth described here, a Polish teen referred to as "Alex B.," was having significant problems in school because "he [had] developed a hatred for the Negro boys." "He will fight them," the report claimed, "at any opportunity."[47]

While these cases may be only anecdotally emblematic, in the context of what was transpiring in the areas of South Chicago and South Deering they appear not at all out of the ordinary. Put most simply, they attest to a groundswell of racial anxiety, which, while touching whole communities, seemed most manifest within male-oriented youth subcultures, where it often translated into the formation of fighting gangs and their increasing engagement in lethal and nihilistic rituals of racial aggression. Yet before moving toward an explanation of these feelings and their relationship to the conditions of youth in working-class Chicago in the late 1950s and early 1960s, it is necessary to describe in greater detail the fighting-gang culture that emerged in this moment and the dynamics of racial alterity within it.

"I'M BLACK ENOUGH AS IT IS; DO YOU WANT ME TO LOOK LIKE A NIGGER?"

There was no place in Chicago where youth gangs were more visible or better documented in this period than in the district to the southwest of the Loop, where in the course of a relatively short stroll one could pass through Little Italy, the African American neighborhoods of the Near West Side and Lawndale, the Mexican enclaves of the Near West Side and Pilsen, and a Puerto Rican section that constituted a buffer between Little Italy and the black areas to its north. If you were a young man, the likelihood of your journey being interrupted by a street-corner gang demanding to know what you were doing in the neighborhood or worse— not bothering to ask—was high. Moreover, this was not the only such area in Chicago at this time. Similar circumstances prevailed around Garfield Park on the Near Northwest Side, around Calumet Park on the far South Side, and in the area below the Loop where the lily-white community of Bridgeport abutted the heterogeneous Armour Square neighborhood and lay just blocks away from the heart of the black Bronzeville district. Yet since Hull House had opened its doors in 1889, the Near West Side had served as a laboratory for examining the problems of the urban poor, particularly those involving the waywardness of its youths, and it was thus here that most of Chicago's youth outreach and research programs would base their operations. Following the approach initiated by the Chicago Area Project decades before, most of these programs sent counselors into the neighborhoods to gain the confidence of youth gangs, record their behavior, and attempt to steer them toward less destructive paths to adulthood. The thousands of often meticulously detailed reports they submitted provide scholars with rich and surprisingly underutilized sources for understanding not only how youths in this period behaved, but also how they made sense of their world.

The insights and observations in these reports illuminate how the emergence and evolution of a fighting-gang subculture on the Near West Side responded to forces of racial and ethnic succession in the neighborhoods. Indeed, among the first gangs to gain widespread notoriety for their violent ways were the Nobles and their allies the Dukes, both of whom laid claim to defending Little Italy from the invasions of Puerto Ricans and African Americans. Possessing well over one hundred members between them, these predominantly Italian gangs operated in the Near West Side Italian district between the early 1950s and the early 1960s. The Dukes was a somewhat larger gang than the Nobles, consisting of between sixty and seventy members divided into junior and senior divisions. According to gang workers, the appearance of each of these gangs on the streets of Little Italy coincided with a series of outbreaks of group violence against the growing presence of Puerto Ricans in the neighborhood in 1954. At the end of July that year, what one observer referred to as a "wild street fight" in front of the Jane Addams Homes brought out some two thousand people after vandals firebombed a Puerto Rican–owned bar and apartment. The incident followed a week of violence that included several brawls between Puerto Rican and Italian youths, one of which erupted into gunfire.[48]

It was in this context that both the Dukes and the Nobles began their practice of terrorizing Puerto Rican and African American residents in the area. According to one observer, the Nobles increased their membership gradually between 1954 and 1956 as a result of their "notoriety by virtue of hostile acts towards the Housing Project and minority groups." The observer also stated: "Largely these hostile acts towards minority groups consisted of beating up Puerto Rican or Negro boys who came into the community either individually or in small numbers."[49] Describing the formation of the Dukes, the gang worker John Giampa noted that the youths in this group were learning that "these newcomers, the 'niggers,' the 'P.R.'s,' etc., [were] a threat to them. . . . Although these groups were exposed to each other in everyday living, in so far as they attended the same school and used the same neighborhood facilities, . . . distinct national lines were constantly drawn, and one group considered the other as an actual, or potential threat."[50]

The Dukes and the Nobles were the most notorious of the white ethnic fighting gangs to emerge around what social workers referred to as the "Addams area" (the blocks surrounding the Jane Addams Homes), and their activities drew repeated newspaper coverage between 1956 and 1958, as well as the worried attention of community workers.[51] In 1957, a series of brutal attacks they perpetrated against blacks and Puerto Ricans necessitated the intervention of a special police task force from the Chicago Commission on Human Relations. These aggressions did not merely consist of sporting bouts between young men; they often looked more like outbursts of pathological aggression mingled with deep-rooted racial anxiety. In 1956, for example, a group of teenagers assaulted a black amputee near the Jane Addams Homes, just steps from the Nobles' main hangout; the following year, the Nobles allegedly beat an elderly Puerto Rican man to death (he died weeks later in the hospital).[52] The Dukes and Nobles, moreover, were hardly the sole agents of such deeds. In addition to these groups, youth workers on the Near West Side noted similar behavior among dozens of other such predominantly Italian street-corner gangs in the late 1950s, such as the Taylor Bishops, the Challengers, the C & L's, the Royal Lords, and the Jousters. On any given night, hundreds of youths could be found arrayed in groups along Taylor Street and in and around the alleys and streets that fed into it, all potentially on the lookout for people who did not belong in the neighborhood.

While mostly consisting of Italian ethnics, the street-corner groups in this neighborhood also included a significant number of Mexicans. Indeed, about one-third of the membership of the original Dukes was of Mexican origin, and several of the other Italian groups possessed more than token numbers of Mexicans in the mid-1950s. By this time, Mexicans had been living on the Near West Side in substantial numbers for some three decades, and their presence had been grudgingly tolerated and even accepted in neighborhood schools and in community institutions like Hull House. Even if Near West Side Italians always considered Mexicans different in a way that was undeniably racializing, they were certainly a group apart from the blacks and the Puerto Ricans moving into the area. Under these circumstances, the increasing presence of these two racialized groups around the Addams area in the late 1950s may have had the effect of pushing Mexicans and Italians here closer together. In fact, the opposite occurred, a situation that resonated down through the Near West Side's racial hierarchy.

Hence, despite the overall growth in the number of street gangs in this general area, youth workers were counting fewer Italian gangs with anything more than a token Mexican presence by the early 1960s. Of a sample of nine Mexican, Italian, and black gangs observed by the Chicago Youth Development Program (CYDP) at this time, for example, only one fit the description of "mostly Italian, some Mexicans."[53] A change in the modalities of racial perception had occurred in a short span of time, one that can be glimpsed rather strikingly in the run of gang worker reports covering this area. The first sign came in August 1957, when an HTRYP worker with the Nobles described the gang splitting up into different factions because "the Italian boys wanted to kick the Mexican boys out."[54] In January of that same year, four Nobles were arrested and later convicted for beating up a Mexican youth and raping his girlfriend (also Mexican). Around this same time, a profile of the Nobles compiled by a researcher for Chicago's Institute for Juvenile Research revealed that of forty-four regular members, thirty-six were Italian (five of these claimed to have one Italian parent), and only four were Mexican. By 1959, most of the remaining Mexican members of both the Nobles and the Dukes had broken away and formed their own entirely Mexican group with the racially suggestive name the "Clay People."[55]

What was transpiring between Near West Side Mexican and Italian youths was closely related to another event: the settlement of a substantial number of Puerto Ricans in the area just north of the Italian community's main drag along Taylor Street. By the early 1960s, Puerto Ricans dominated strips of Harrison, Ashland, and Van Buren Avenue. Because of its proximity to Little Italy, the Puerto Rican settlement along Harrison came to be the most prominent one in the minds of Near West Side Italians; when residents here were not using more derogatory labels, such as "porkeys" and "PR's," they referred to Puerto Rican youths in this area as the "Harrison Street Boys."[56] The hostile reception of Puerto Ricans in the mid-1950s, articulated by numerous near-riot situations precipitated by Italian street-corner youth groups, presaged the increasing separation of Italian and Mexican youths in this area. This reception was prompted not merely by the dark skin color of some of the Puerto Rican migrants, but also by their neighborhood being located amid the deteriorated buildings around the Eisenhower Expressway, just below the Near West Side black ghetto. Regardless of their capacity to speak in a different tongue, Puerto Ricans were racialized people in the minds of both Italians and Mexicans on the Near West Side. Furthermore, the confusion caused by their linguistic and physical affinities with Mexicans made them dangerous to Mexicans, and more indirectly, to Italians. Hence, as early as 1956, CAP worker Perry Miranda was describing persistent conflicts between Italian and Mexican groups in the Addams area, while also noting that they did on several occasions form alliances against black and Puerto Rican gangs. Along with a considerable hatred for Puerto Ricans, Miranda observed an intense color consciousness among Mexican youths. "Although they show contempt towards Anglos," he reported, "they hold color in highest esteem." This idealization of color was so pervasive that it even mediated the interactions between different members of the gang itself. Miranda claimed: "This group exists by means of hostility, expressing their hostility towards each other with emphasis on skin color."[57]

Such feelings crystallized powerfully in response to the increasing settlement of Puerto Ricans around the Addams area, a trend intimately revealed by the reports of Mexican gang worker Frank Delgado on the activities of the Royal Kings, one of the few Puerto Rican–Mexican gangs on the Near West Side. In a series of entries made in April and July 1958, Delgado describes numerous racial insults against Puerto Ricans and African Americans uttered by members of the gang, often audibly enough for the Puerto Rican youths present to hear. On one occasion, when the youths were considering having a beach party, one of the Kings yelled out, "I'm black enough as it is; do you want me to look like a nigger?"[58] Another time, one of the Kings informed Delgado that because of the Puerto Ricans joining the club, the other clubs were calling them "P.R. lovers."[59] Shortly after the Puerto Rican members were pressured to leave the gang, another youth claimed that other groups in the Addams area had threatened to attack the Kings if they continued to have Puerto Rican members.[60] Attempting to account for this behavior, Delgado explained that several of the Mexican youths in the Kings actually lived in a Puerto Rican neighborhood many blocks north of the Addams area and had formerly belonged to predominantly Puerto Rican gangs in their own neighborhood. For this reason, according to Delgado, "these Mexican boys saw in the Kings an opportunity to get into a Mexican club."[61]

Youth subcultures in working-class Chicago thus served as central forums within which youths negotiated and constructed their racial identities in the midst of accelerated racial migration. As Delgado's observations reveal, Mexican youths expelling Puerto Ricans from their groups and even threatening retribution for groups that did not do the same were acting to reconstruct a boundary line between the Near West Side Mexican community and the expanding Puerto Rican community in the area. Youth gangs possessed a keen awareness of the symbolic importance that such public demonstrations of Mexican–Puerto Rican intermixing represented.

Yet such processes of group identity formation were visible not only in the ways youths shaped and defined their gangs. The much more dynamic aspect of this phenomenon involved the rituals of aggression that occurred between different gangs. By the early 1960s, such forces had created a fighting-gang subculture throughout a large portion of the West

Figure 5. Members of the Puerto Rican Viceroys gang talk with a youth outreach worker in Wicker Park, circa 1960. The Viceroys belonged to a Puerto Rican gang subculture that stretched from the Near North Side, Wicker Park, and Eckhart Park areas down to Harrison Street. Photographer unknown; courtesy of the Chicago History Museum, ICHi-51726.

and South Sides of Chicago. This subculture was most vibrant in areas of great racial and ethnic diversity. In the spring of 1962, CYDP supervisor Frank Carney noted that "the most cohesive, organized, and structured fighting gang sub-culture outside of Fillmore now exist[ed] in the area of 18th Street . . . especially the area roughly between Halsted and Damen, 18th and 24th Streets."[62] Fillmore was a police district several blocks west of the Addams area; it encompassed the Polish, Puerto Rican, and African American neighborhoods surrounding Garfield Park, which one Chicago Welfare Council representative had referred to as a "battleground" as early as 1957 because of "the ethnic composition of the communities on either side."[63] This other area highlighted by Carney lay just to the south of Little Italy within the Maxwell police district, encompassing the burgeoning Mexican community of Pilsen (otherwise known as Little Village). To its west were the solidly black neighborhoods of Lawndale, which gave rise to its own thriving fighting-gang subculture in the late 1950s and early 1960s; to its south, across a closely patrolled border, was the lily-white Bridgeport community. Although Carney had made a distinction, in actuality these two districts were really part of the same fighting-gang subculture, the same urban middle ground that attracted gangs from all over the city—Mexican gangs from South Chicago and Puerto Rican gangs from the Near North Side, among others—to defend their friends and test their mettle in street combat.

This fighting-gang culture had begun to take shape in the early 1950s, but it was not until the late 1950s that it started to produce relatively high numbers of arrests, injuries, and fatalities. Indeed, in the spring of 1959, when the HTRYP held a meeting of its Near West Side workers, the composite picture of the neighborhood that emerged from the discussion was that of a fiercely contested battlefield. Workers highlighted several areas of frequent violence between Italian, Mexican, and black groups, including certain residential streets and schools, as well as the El station at the Congress Expressway and Racine. "Altercations usually start," claimed one worker, "when the Negro boys . . . are jumped by the white boys." Another worker reported that clashes between Puerto Rican and Italian and Mexican groups were common around the corner of Harrison and Ashland. An HTRYP representative from the Maxwell Street YMCA, moreover, discussed the activities of the Egyptian Cobras, a large black gang from the Lawndale area that had "developed a reputation as a tough group." While the Cobras had at that time mostly been fighting with other black gangs around the Maxwell Street area, this worker felt that the gang "would probably welcome the opportunity to catch one of the Taylor Street groups south of Roosevelt."[64] In another HTRYP meeting, a Lawndale youth worker reported that African American youths in his area were "cautious" about entering other neighborhoods for fear of being "ambushed" in a place where they are not "sure of an escape route." Other workers noted that Italians refused to pass through black neighborhoods, Puerto Ricans traveled only "in groups from one Puerto Rican ghetto to another," and "Negro youth under 15" from the Henry Horner Homes area on the Near West Side would not venture "even as little as four or five blocks to a dance in a strange place" while "17 to 19 year old fellows" from this same neighborhood would roam outside their neighborhood "but always in a car."[65]

Such accounts point to the existence of a treacherous gangland subculture covering much of Chicago's Southwest Side. The nucleus of this zone lay around the gang-filled Italian and Mexican neighborhoods of the Addams Area, extending north through the Puerto Rican colony along Harrison to the black enclave surrounding the Henry Horner housing project above the Eisenhower Expressway, south to the Mexican area of West Pilsen, west to Garfield Park and to the black ghetto neighborhoods of Lawndale below it (down to about 21st Street), and east to the start of the Loop business district. This was no doubt the area of highest street gang concentration in the entire city. In 1958, a police Lieutenant from the Maxwell district estimated that there were some sixty gangs "roaming the street" in the part of the district between 18th and 24th Street alone.[66] Flare-ups could easily involve any of the large black fighting gangs of Lawndale, such as the Vice Lords, Imperial Chaplains, Clovers, and Cobras; the predominantly Mexican gangs of the Pilsen area, like the Morgan Deuces, Spartans, Gents, Play Boys, and Latin Counts; as well as the more reputable Puerto Rican gangs from Harrison Avenue up to the Eckhart Park area, such as the Rebels, Latin Angels, Diggers, Viceroys, Untouchables, and Top Boys.[67] Wary of being caught by surprise and outnumbered in such a hostile area, Italian gangs from the Addams area to the north and Irish groups from Bridgeport to the south were less frequent combatants in most of this middle zone, but they were reputedly merciless when able to catch their rivals around the periphery of their turf.[68] (See map 3.)

While most of this fighting-gang subculture lay to the west and southwest of the Loop, youth workers at the Chicago Commons settlement on the Near Northwest Side also described an atmosphere of heightened racial and ethnic tensions and frequent gang violence. "Eckhart Park," claimed one Chicago Commons official in 1960, "happens to be located smack in the middle of tension and conflict among Puerto Ricans, Southern Whites, Mexicans, Poles, and Italians. . . . It was here that we had a riot two summers ago and some of us are getting worried about what could happen at the new pool."[69] In September 1959, the shooting of some Italian youths by a Puerto Rican gang exposed the problem of persistent gang violence between these groups in this part of the city.[70] The following year, the Illinois Youth Commission reported "friction and trouble among the colored and Spanish Speaking pupils especially at Franklin School" in this same area.[71] To the east, just below some of Chicago's most valuable lakefront real estate in the Lincoln Park neighborhood, the codirector of the Depaul Settlement House described numerous gang fights and claimed that "rumbles involve[d] rival groups whose composition [was] based on race or nationality—and [were] usually the result of racial hatred bolstered by alcohol."[72]

Chicago's fighting-gang subculture thus extended well into the North Side, particularly in the large area that stretched from Humboldt Park eastward to the border of the Near North Side's affluent Gold Coast neighborhood, where emerging Puerto Rican communities and pockets of black settlement took shape amid white hostility and resistance. It cohered around an area of the city that was, by most contemporary standards, quite racially integrated, and it grew into its most remarkable form in a moment that, according to most accounts, witnessed the completion of a process of black ghettoization that had begun decades before. Such narratives of white resistance to black integration in the postwar years have worked to obscure dynamics within parts of the city that did not fit within a binary racial scheme. While these accounts reveal a great deal about the forces at work in the European American strongholds around the traditional South Side Black Belt, they tell us little about the large part of the city where Chicago's fighting-gang culture spread—an area where neither *white* nor *black* had any certain meaning. Under such conditions, it was not inevitable that groups of young men would define themselves against each other in racial terms and engage in rituals of racial hatred and violence. At other moments in other contexts, similar circumstances have not produced such behavior; in fact, implicit in many current arguments about the sources of racism is the assumption that racial integration tends to have quite the opposite effect.

Yet nothing could have been much further from the truth for a large part of working-class Chicago in the late 1950s and early 1960s. While this moment may have witnessed a certain reduction in racially motivated violence in some districts as a result of diminishing pressures on the traditional color line, such circumstances had little impact in gangland Chicago. In fact, while no reliable quantitative data were kept on racially motivated, gang-related violent crime during these years, the substantial body of extension worker reports generated by the HTRYP and CYDP contains ample evidence that the intensity and stakes of racial violence were sharply increasing in the years after 1958, when the HTRYP noted a rise in the number of kids carrying guns and discussed developing a policy whereby youth workers could better educate youths on "what carrying a gun may mean to [them]."[73] In the years thereafter, youth workers were frequently reporting handguns and shotguns being used or brandished by gang members, and the friction and rumbles that in previous years had yielded cuts and bruises were resulting in a great many more hospitalizations and fatalities. The somewhat impressionistic evidence for this change presented by the much more frequent reports of gunfire, stabbings, and other forms of high-risk violence in CYDP worker reports in 1961 and 1962 is supported by violent crime figures for the entire city.

Between 1958 and 1962, the number of violent crimes known to police per ten thousand people more than tripled, increasing from about 11 in 1958 to 22 in 1960 and then reaching a historic peak of 38 in 1962. The number of homicide arrests rose from 240 in 1958 to 504 in 1964 as the overall population of the city minimally decreased.[74]

In addition to the upheaval caused by racial migrations, several different factors interacted to produce this change: the alarming flight of jobs out of the city, the disruptions caused by periodic short-term economic downturns, and, perhaps most important, the incalculable social dislocation inflicted by the city's massive urban renewal and public housing programs. The period between 1958 and 1962 witnessed the staggeringly rapid culmination of the first phase of the Daley administration's public housing vision for black Chicago with the opening of the Rockwell Gardens, Stateway Gardens, Green Homes (adding to the preexisting Cabrini Homes), and Robert Taylor Homes projects. During these years, the city also pushed forward on its clearance of a large swath of the Near West Side and the construction of university and medical facilities on the vacated land. Not surprisingly, these circumstances had a profound emotional impact on residents and thus generated optimal conditions for waves of crime and gang violence. Surveying the desolation of one Near West Side neighborhood in 1961, for example, a CYDP worker described the situation in unambiguous terms: "Unemployment is always high and is higher than usual now due to the recession. Many men are in evidence on the streets and street corners when it is warm enough. The emptiness of certain sections resulting from land clearance increases the generally depressing atmosphere. It is impossible to escape the feeling that the area is on its way out."[75]

This was the backdrop for the fighting-gang culture that began to develop in the late 1950s. While it is impossible to determine the contribution this culture made to the citywide jump in violent crime between 1958 and 1962, it is safe to assume that street gang culture accounted for more than its fair share of it. As for the dynamics behind the escalation of violence within this fighting-gang culture, the appearance of more and more firearms on the streets was primary among them. Yet behind this change was another phenomenon involving some decisive shifts in the balance of power prevailing in gangland.

By 1958, the Lawndale neighborhood to the southwest of the Addams area had given rise to Chicago's most vicious gang milieu. The rapid proliferation of fighting gangs in this black ghetto neighborhood had led to the spread of coercive recruitment campaigns and a veritable arms race

Figure 6. Puerto Rican gang members roughhousing in Eckhart Park in the early 1960s. Play-fighting could turn deadly serious in the blink of an eye in Chicago's West Side fighting-gang subculture. Photographer unknown; courtesy of the Chicago History Museum, ICHi-51725.

on the streets. While guns were becoming more frequent in other parts of the city as well, violent recruitment tactics were still somewhat unheard of outside of Lawndale, which was home to dozens of large street-fighting groups, the most reputable being the El Commandoes, Van Dykes, Braves, Cherokees, Morphines, Continental Pimps, Imperial Chaplains, Imperial Knights, Comanches, Vice Lords, Clovers, and Cobras. By 1962, most of these gangs had been absorbed, in most cases forcibly, by either the Vice Lords or the Cobras, both of which had become immense federations of street-corner groups capable of rallying several hundred young men for battle. R. Lincoln Keiser, who spent two years in contact with the Vice Lords while completing his ethnographic study of the gang, described this process of consolidation: "As the Cobras to the west, and the Imperial Chaplains to the east grew in strength, pressure was exerted on unorganized boys living in the Clovers' territory. . . . This pressure consisted of shakedowns, demands that nonaffiliated individuals join on one of the two groups, attempts to monopolize girls in the neighborhood, and fights and threats against the unorganized boys."[76] According to Keiser's account, as well as that of community organizer David Dawley, who began working with the Vice Lords in 1967, the rise of the Vice Lords and the Cobras was not only predicated on amassing large armies; it was also about possessing guns and the will to use them.

The Vice Lords and the Cobras acquired both of these attributes rather quickly after 1958. Indeed, it was in June of that year that a gang worker assigned to the Cobras by the Chicago Youth Centers, Jim Foreman, recorded his efforts to dissuade one of the gang members from bringing his "stuff" (a euphemism for his 22-caliber rifle) to an upcoming rumble. "Is it really worth that big a chance?" he asked the youth. "Well, they might have a gun too, Jim," was the response.[77] By 1961, the innocence of this dialogue would have seemed ridiculous to observers in this area. Indeed, as most accounts reveal quite clearly, by then there was little doubt as to whether adversaries would show up packing guns. If the adversary happened to be the Vice Lords, the only question was how many. When police searched the basement of one Vice Lord's home after he was killed by a shotgun blast in October 1961, they turned up six automatic firearms, twelve pistols, and several rifles.[78] Looking back on this change several years later, another member of the gang claimed: "Zip guns got obsolete because you had a lot of misfirings, but then cats went all the way for the real jive, the real gun. You couldn't buy them so you had to find other ways. There were a lot lying around and everybody knew that a guy in the store kept a gun for protection, so you run into the store and say put your hands up. . . . Another place was the police, and Goat used to jump on their scooters and snatch their guns. . . . Guys that wanted to take over started shooting."[79] Moreover, in addition to bringing guns to rumbles (or "humbugs" as they were commonly referred to in this area), the frantic pace of street violence during these years caused the Vice Lords and other Lawndale gangs to add Molotov cocktails to their arsenal and to seize on the practice of stealing cars for the purpose of carrying out drive-by shootings.[80]

Hence, the Lawndale area, particularly the section of it known as K-Town (because of the many street names beginning with the letter *k*), witnessed the most startling increase in violent crime in the late 1950s and early 1960s as a result of the escalating tactics employed by black fighting gangs competing with each other to control the neighborhood. Viewing the circumstances of gang warfare in K-Town in isolation, one might draw the conclusion that this augmentation in the intensity and stakes of gang violence was a manifestation of ghettoization—that it was basically a post-ghetto phenomenon caused by the conditions of ghetto life and largely contained within the boundaries of the ghetto. Yet this overlooks how K-Town was, at least until the mid-1960s, part of a larger youth gang subculture predicated on the articulation of racial alterity through collective acts of violence. The Vice Lords, the Egyptian Cobras, and other Lawndale-area gangs were engaging somewhat regularly in sometimes lethal battles with European American, Mexican, and, most of all, Puerto Rican fighting gangs through the early 1960s. In 1960, for example, observers identified both the Puerto Rican Rebels and the European American Roman Saints as two of the avowed enemies of the Egyptian Cobras.[81] The Saints, in fact, had also been one of the main rivals of the Clovers, one of Lawndale's preeminent gangs prior to the rise of the Vice Lords and the Cobras. Between April 3 and April 8, 1958, the Saints, with the aid of another European American gang calling themselves the Gents, carried out a series of attacks against black youths around Marshall High School and the Sears YMCA on the 3200 block of West Arthington. One of these was a well-planned ambush involving the firebombing of two carloads of Clovers. Knowing that the Clovers would come to avenge the attacks made against some female black students outside of Marshall earlier in the day, the Saints and Gents were ready with Molotov cocktails. When the cars caught fire and the occupants scattered, they began firing gunshots at the fleeing Clovers.[82]

The circumstances of this exchange, particularly the role played by the Clovers in avenging attacks against black students around Marshall, offer a view into another trend that was developing out of the context of fighting-gang culture. If gangs had served to crystallize sentiments of community solidarity and resistance to ethnic and racial prejudice for European Americans in the interwar period, they were coming to play a similar role for some black communities in the late 1950s. Indeed, most of the Clovers did not even attend high school, and thus their actions in defending the rights of those in their community who did may have involved more than the pursuit of honor or the performance of masculinity. Just months before, in the fall of 1957, African Americans in Chicago saw mobs of whites harassing nine black students attempting to attend Little Rock Central High School. It is not unlikely that the Clovers were entering into a process of cross-regional learning that would pick up momentum in the years to come, as blacks in Chicago used events in the South to understand their own situation and the tactics they needed to use to try to change it.

Hence, even in black ghetto areas where African American gangs were locked in mortal combat within an economy of power on the streets, the experience and spectacle of white racial violence—at the edge of Chicago's black ghetto neighborhoods and in the form of images transmitted via television from southern battlegrounds—played important roles in the escalation of cyclical gang violence. Moreover, the number of guns "lying around" that eventually found their way into the hands of Vice Lords and Cobras must also be seen as a legacy of the violence and harassment perpetrated mainly by white gangs in this same era. Since the war years, when Horace Cayton had declared that blacks were "arming themselves," those engaged in the project of monitoring race relations in the city had been issuing warnings about such trends. Surveying a series of racial attacks on the Southwest Side of Chicago in the summer of 1961, including a vicious interracial gang fight that left a black youth hospitalized after being struck with a two-by-four wooden plank "affixed with a protruding nail," community organizer Nicholas Von Hoffman found once again that several families in the area had purchased guns, telling him they did not trust the police to protect them.[83] Any proliferation of arms and the concomitant escalation of violence in black Chicago during this time should thus be viewed in relation to years of white grassroots intimidation and police intransigence in preventing it.

In the context of gangland, where gang rivalries so often crossed racial lines, this trend—the increasing stakes of gang violence due to the use of guns and more lethal weapons—was bound to cross these lines as well. In the early 1960s, black gangs on the Near West Side found themselves in persistent conflict with neighboring Puerto Rican gangs, and to a lesser but still significant extent, with Mexican and European American ones. By August 1961, Puerto Rican CYDP worker Antonio Irrizary reported that the conflicts between Puerto Rican and "colored" gangs around Harrison and California had gotten so bad that they had been the subject of an article in a local Spanish-language newspaper.[84] The following spring, Irrizary was again describing fights between the Vice Lords and the Cobras and Puerto Rican gangs hanging out at the western edge of the Puerto Rican neighborhood along Harrison Avenue, dangerously close to the color line of California Avenue.[85] Around this same time, moreover, CYDP workers also referred to the area around Jackson and Wolcott to the northeast as a "major trouble spot" for fights between groups of blacks and Puerto Ricans.[86] The situation was not much different between Mexicans and African Americans in this district. In the last week of July 1962, the CYDP was put on alert after a group of Mexicans stabbed and killed a black youth in a street fight, an incident that supervisor Frank

Carney believed would cause black groups between Roosevelt and 15th Street to seek revenge on the predominantly Mexican gangs in the vicinity of 18th Street and Halsted, such as the Spartans, the Marquis, the Latin Counts, and the Morgan Deuces.[87]

Moreover, if Puerto Rican and Mexican gangs were quite often focusing their aggression on black youths, they were seldom allying themselves for this purpose. The rising incidence of brown-black violence around Lawndale and the Near West Side paralleled a similar augmentation of tensions between Puerto Rican and Mexican gangs in the area. The latent hostility that could be seen developing between Mexican and Puerto Rican youths in the Addams area beginning in 1956 was fully aroused by the early 1960s. Antonio Irrizary's reports make frequent mention of brutal conflicts between these groups, one of which left the leader of the Latin Angels, one of the more formidable Puerto Rican gangs, hospitalized for a month, and another of which resulted in a Mexican gang member losing an eye.[88] Furthermore, while conflicts between Latino and European American gangs were becoming less frequent, thanks to the continued flight of white residents out of the gangland area and the diminishing presence of white gangs on the streets, potentially lethal battles between European American and Puerto Rican gangs persisted in areas that had seen considerable tensions between these groups in the past. On the Near Northwest Side, for example, Puerto Rican gangs shot Italian youths on several occasions between 1959 and 1962, and Puerto Rican fighting gangs around the Addams area, like the Diggers and the Top Boys, engaged in regular combat with the Taylor Dukes, a gang that had made its name attacking Puerto Rican residents in the area for years.[89]

Thus, the fighting-gang culture that developed in a large area around Chicago's downtown business district bore a close relationship to processes of racial migration and neighborhood succession that were in full swing by the mid-1950s. As male gang subcultures normally do, Chicago's gangland created a forum within which codes of masculinity could be negotiated and articulated. However, the search for respect or honor on the streets does not account for the overwhelming presence of racial forms of consciousness in this world. Indeed, what the patterns of gang violence documented by youth workers in the field reveals is that race was, in fact, an organizing principle of youth violence during this period. This is an impression obtained not only from a consideration of the kinds of rivalries and alliances that characterized gangland, but also from the manner in which youth workers came to naturalize race in their rendering of this milieu. Such evidence demonstrates that rather than witnessing the solidification of the color line and the establishment of a binary racial order, the 1950s and 1960s was a period of heightened racial consciousness and uncertainty. The picture of cyclical racial violence that emerges from the large body of gang worker reports suggests that historians of race have greatly underestimated both the extent of racial instability as a lived experience and the role this experience played in the political culture of neighborhoods in areas like gangland Chicago.

Situated squarely and unavoidably within the flow of everyday neighborhood life, youth gang subcultures served to magnify racial feelings and anxieties and, as we will soon see in greater detail, to transform them into sensibilities of injustice, empowerment, and community. It was also within the milieu of youth gangs, however, that racial anxiety became most pathological, a collective obsession that pushed youths into destructive and decidedly irrational forms of behavior, such as when Joseph Schwartz, the seventeen-year-old member of a white South Side gang called the Rebels with no prior criminal record, crushed the skull of an innocent black youth with a hammer. While the phenomenon of high-stakes gang violence offers a glimpse into this situation, observations of gang workers concerning the intense investment of gang youths in race and color is equally suggestive. They reveal that even among some of the whitest youths on the streets, like the Italian members of Near West Side gangs or the Irish and other European American youths that composed the notorious gangs of lily-white Bridgeport and Englewood, this fixation was marked through the early 1960s.

Years of contact with the most pathological manifestations of such feelings had consequences for youths on the other side of the color line as well. As the observations of Jim Foreman so strikingly reveal, years of harassment by "white" youths had created a tradition of antiwhite sentiment on the streets by the late 1950s. Thus it was necessary for Foreman, after preventing some Cobras from beating up a white youth who had found himself in the wrong neighborhood one day, to tell the youths involved, "You know it might surprise you fellows to know that every individual in the white race isn't as bad or as evil as you guys believe." "Eye for an eye, tooth for a tooth, that's what's happening," was the view of one of the Cobras. On another occasion, when some members of the gang were discussing the dangers of a "gray" (the term for "white") neighborhood around 12th and California, Foreman again felt the need to challenge the idea voiced by one of the youths that "any" white person would attempt to "jump" them. "Any of those gray studs will do it," argued the youth. "If you ever get caught walking through here, you might as well give it up."[90] Moreover, by this time, the widespread contempt for "grays" on the streets extended to Mexicans and darker-skinned Puerto Ricans as well. Thus, after a member of one of Lawndale's elite gangs, the King Clovers, decided to quit his job, the reason he offered was that he was forced to work with Puerto Ricans. "I grew up fighting them and hate them," he claimed.[91]

"VIOLENCE SOMETIMES SERVES ITS PURPOSE": FIGHTING GANGS AND THE POLITICIZATION OF RACIAL IDENTITY

On July 28, 1957, more than eighty members of the Bodine Social Club made their way into Calumet Park in southeast Chicago for a picnic. The black picnickers were by no means unaware of the potentially dangerous situation they were walking into. African Americans attempting to use the park had encountered fierce resistance from whites in the past. In fact, on the previous Sunday, about seventy members of the Ta-Wa-Si Mothers' Club had been menaced by a mob of some "50 young white men." That the group consisted mainly of women and children did not appease the mob, and police had to hurriedly escort the picnickers out of the park as the mob grew larger and angrier. While the attackers managed to rough up a few of the Ta-Wa-Si members and steal some of their personal belongings, the group managed to escape the scene without sustaining any serious injuries. The Bodine picnickers would not be as fortunate.[92]

In the week preceding the event, word had traveled fast through the neighborhoods around the park. The mob that materialized this time was more like a stadium-sized crowd, numbering "about 6,000 or 7,000 Caucasians," according to the estimate of the police sergeant on hand. In the ensuing chaos, at least forty-seven people were injured and some twenty-seven were taken to area hospitals. After police had managed with great difficulty to make a cordon around the Bodine Club members and pack them into police trucks, the frustrated crowd vented its anger by attacking the cars of the black picnickers in an adjacent parking lot. A deployment of more than five hundred police officers was required to restore order to the area. Inevitably, the crowd's rage flowed into the nearby Trumbull Park Homes project. Late that night, "a mob of white boys and men, estimated to have numbered from 50 to 100," raided the apartment of one of the more outspoken black tenants, throwing his television set and radio into the street and attempting to set the place ablaze by igniting the curtains and opening the gas jets in the kitchen. In the days following the initial incident, groups of teenagers patrolled the area around the park in cars, attacking any African Americans they spotted with stones, fireworks, bottles, and baseball bats.[93]

Unlike in the past, news coverage of the disturbances in southeast Chicago was extensive. The sparks it produced blew into several other areas of the city where continued black migration and years of white resistance had created the perfect conditions for brush fires of racial hatred. On the West Side, around East Garfield Park and North Lawndale, where the dual processes of black migration and white flight were rapidly accelerating, white youths took to stoning black students walking to and from summer classes at Marshall High School. On July 31 and August 1, 1957, the Wednesday and Thursday nights after the Calumet riot, crowds ranging from several hundred to over one thousand—composed of "mostly teen-agers," according to police—demonstrated outside the home of a black family at 3714 West Polk Street. Twelve of the thirteen people arrested on the second night were juveniles. Around the same time, violence broke out in several other South Side neighborhoods. At Tuley Park, a mob of some two hundred teenagers threatened and attacked blacks attempting to use the pool there, and police had to intervene to prevent a prearranged "gang fight" between blacks and whites at nearby Grand Crossing Park.[94]

The events of this long week in the summer of 1957 revealed certain prevailing trends in working-class Chicago and other trends that were just beginning to unfold. First, the Calumet Park riot and the smaller disturbances that flared up in its aftermath once again demonstrated the pervasiveness of racial anxiety and fear in neighborhoods undergoing or threatened by racial transition, as well as the privileged relationship of young men to the production of these feelings. The ferocity of the violence witnessed and the rapidity with which it spread into different neighborhoods throughout the city suggested that racial anxiety was a quotidian facet of life in many Chicago neighborhoods, a sentiment articulated and ritualized most expressively within the world of youth subcultures. Indeed, as Arnold Hirsch's analysis of the crowd involved in the Calumet Park riot reveals, the participants were overwhelmingly teenagers and young men. The average age of arrestees was just twenty-two, and only 15 percent of those arrested had reached the age of thirty.[95] Adults—that is, men and women with families and stable jobs—were among those assembled in Calumet Park and the other sites of mob violence, but none of these incidents would have been possible without the well-trained, ready-made armies of youths that composed the most active core of participants. With the exception of some significant flare-ups around the Trumbull Park Homes and the anti–Puerto Rican outbreak on the Near West Side in 1953 and 1954, the spectacle of antiblack demonstrations numbering in the hundreds or thousands had largely disappeared from public view after the highly publicized situation in Cicero in 1951. As revealed in chapter 4, youth groups kept up the pressure on African Americans throughout the early and mid-1950s, but their actions consisted more of limited group attacks against black persons and property. The Calumet riot signaled a kind of revival of broad-based racial action, but this time in a form that rested even more squarely within the context of youth subcultures.

Indeed, in the years to come, Chicago's parks, beaches, and schools would become the principal arenas of racial conflict. If youths had taken the lead in patrolling neighborhood boundaries and spearheading campaigns against integration in the past, they would be even more at the forefront of efforts to bar African Americans from such leisure spaces in the late 1950s and early 1960s. Between 1958 and 1961, for example, attacks against blacks by groups of white youths occurred regularly at Calumet Park, Bessemer Park, and Rainbow Beach in Southeast Chicago. At both Bessemer Park and Rainbow Beach, crowds of between one and two thousand people gathered to oppose integration.[96] The situation was not much different farther north, in the longtime "Bungalow Belt" strongholds surrounding the South Side Black Belt. In the Chatham and Englewood areas, for example, mobs of white youths carried out numerous attacks against blacks attempting to use Tuley Park and Sherman Park. On one occasion in September 1959, Tuley Park was nearly the site of a riot when a mob of "50 white youngsters" attacked a black family with small children having a picnic.[97] During this same period, high schools situated in racially mixed districts continued to be hot spots for racial aggression on the part of white youths, with Marshall, Harrison, and Crane on the West Side, and Lindblom and Harper in the Englewood area witnessing some of the worst outbreaks.[98]

Moreover, the Calumet riot and its related disturbances were emblematic of other shifts then under way in white Chicago. Perhaps never before in the city had a race riot perpetrated by whites appeared more like the reflex of a broader social movement. This was due not merely to the somewhat unprecedented size of the crowd and its relative uniformity of age, class, and religion. Perhaps even more compelling in this sense was the very clear emergence, within the frenzied swirl of events, of a sense of collective identity, as well as a movement culture geared toward the ritualization of that identity.[99]

As we have seen, this was hardly the first time that a shared investment in whiteness had mobilized Chicagoans to oppose racial integration. Indeed, the anti-integration protests of the 1940s most often witnessed the alliance of different ethnic groups under the umbrella of whiteness. Yet the more "communal" nature of many of these prior demonstrations meant that other forms of identity related to ethnically and territorially based conceptions of community tended to mitigate perceived ties to whiteness. Ethnically defined parishes, for example, often provided an infrastructure for collective resistance to integration in the late 1940s, as in the Englewood area around 56th and Peoria, where youths reportedly circulated through the crowd asking, "What parish are you from?" Moreover, even in hardcore South Deering, Poles and Italians referred to each other contemptuously as "Dagos" and "Polacks" throughout their joint campaign against integration, and Mexicans were never quite sure they would not find themselves on the other side of the fence. In brief, while languages of racial supremacy and whiteness could be found lingering around campaigns against integration in the late 1940s and early 1950s, many whites on the front lines of the race war seemed not entirely comfortable with universalized conceptions of whiteness. In fact, ideologically driven white supremacist groups with tenuous ties to the local context, such as the White Circle League, met with limited success; they fell easily into the category of "outside agitators." Languages of whiteness were somewhat inadequate for constructing communities in the early 1950s, even if they did help to define collective interests and mobilize responses in defense of them.

The Calumet riot, however, presented a new face of whiteness, and with it, new forms of consciousness about its meaning in American society. First, the crowd that gathered to defend racial exclusion here was the most ethnically heterogeneous of all the riot crowds recorded by police in the late 1940s and 1950s. Hirsch's data reveal six ethnic groups with substantial representation (over 7.5 percent), while all of the other riots included only three or four with such a level of representation. In addition, the dominant group at Calumet Park, Anglo Americans, constituted just over 22 percent of the crowd, making it the weakest dominant group of any of the riots. Moreover, the Calumet arrest records confirm that whiteness was no longer only a European American domain. While significant Mexican involvement in racial demonstrations was first glimpsed at Trumbull Park some three years before, strong Mexican participation in Calumet (over 10 percent of those arrested had Spanish surnames) confirmed the increasing Mexican investment in whiteness, and to some extent, the increasing acceptance of Mexicans as white.[100] Indeed, as the observations of the ACLU spy in South Deering so strikingly reveal, the color of whiteness had become a shade darker by the mid-1950s, even if Mexicans would hardly feel secure in their claim to whiteness.

Regardless of the actual instability of whiteness in working-class Chicago in the mid-1950s, the demonstration in Calumet Park reflected both the formation of a more universalized idea of whiteness and the increasing attachment of this ideal to the conception of a movement or project that was understood by many of its participants to be more formally "political." To be sure, territorial conceptions of racial exclusion were still at play in each of the disturbances that spread through Chicago that summer—"our park," "our neighborhood," "our community," "our street." However, the movement culture that took shape during such events was associated less with such "communal" ideas than with a celebration of a more global form of whiteness. In a sense, whiteness had never before seemed so much like an end in itself. In Calumet Park, for example, youths hung white handkerchiefs and flags on the radio antennas of their cars and burned an effigy of a black person. On the West Side, they chanted and sang racially derogatory songs—"cheer-leader style," according to one observer.[101]

As suggested earlier, the articulation of this kind of white identity within the context of youth subcultures was a process charged with ambiguity and anxiety, a situation evidenced both by the formation of Chicago's fighting-gang subculture and by the regularity of collective racial actions carried out by mobs and crowds of youths not directly associated with gangs. Different European American groups had indeed coalesced around similar notions of whiteness in the past, but collective racial actions began to take on new political implications around the time of the Calumet riot.

One of the main reasons for this change involved the emergence of the civil rights movement in the South, the major battles of which found increasing exposure in television and print media in the late 1950s, as well as in the upsurge of black activism it provoked in Chicago and other cities in the North. Indeed, as Michael Omi and Howard Winant have argued, the "politicization of black identity" that resulted from the civil rights movement brought about a "'great transformation' of racial awareness, racial meaning, racial subjectivity." One of the manifestations of this shift was what they refer to as a "minority encounter with the state" in the 1960s—that is, the emergence of other mass-based minority social movements challenging the racial practices of the state; another was the development of a reactionary movement on the right in the early 1970s directed at "rearticulat[ing] racial ideology" and otherwise rolling back the gains made by these minority movements.[102] Fighting-gang subcultures and the larger urban youth culture predicated on racial conflict not only reflected these changes but also played an important part in shaping them.

The politicization of black identity went hand in hand with the politicization of white identity. While recent studies have convincingly demonstrated the origins of the white backlash in the urban North in the rash of protests over public housing and neighborhood integration in the early postwar years, the moment encompassing the Supreme Court's 1954 *Brown v. Board of Education* decision declaring segregated schools unconstitutional and its ruling the following year that local authorities desegregate them "with all deliberate speed" represented a watershed in this process of white radicalization. This was particularly true in Chicago, where the Court's historic decisions coincided roughly with the peak of the anti-integration campaign at Trumbull Park Homes, the well-publicized efforts of the NAACP and the Chicago Urban League to oppose it, and a mayoral election that thrust the whole issue of race and neighborhood integration into mainstream political discourse. Indeed, in the midst of controversy over a public housing program that many whites in the Bungalow Belt perceived as a state-driven integration initiative, the *Brown* decision struck working-class whites as further proof that the government, federal or local, was clearly not looking out for their interests. As the ACLU observer in Trumbull Park noted in the weeks following the Court's momentous ruling, residents there spoke repeatedly about its implications for their own struggle; for them it was less about desegregating schools in the South than it was about integrating their neighborhood.[103]

As the highly publicized firing of the Chicago Housing Authority's prointegration director Elizabeth Wood in the fall of 1954 and the NAACP's mass protest over the Trumbull Park situation in front of City Hall a year later pushed the problems of race and housing toward the center of Chicago's local political stage, working-class whites in the Bungalow Belt thus came to develop a salient view of the politics of race, and above all, of the role of the state in this political domain. Once again, the ACLU spy's observations of conversations overheard in the taverns around the Trumbull Park Homes proves an invaluable source for understanding white working-class perceptions of the politics of race in the mid-1950s. The dominant themes finding attentive audiences in the taverns, street corners, and workplaces around South Deering were disenfranchisement—a clear sense of being excluded or at least poorly positioned in the political game—and conspiracy. In the eyes of working-class whites in neighborhoods opposing what they viewed as a state-sponsored racial integration program, the conspirators included city hall, Jewish real estate manipulators, the media, and more than anything else, powerful black organizations like the NAACP and the Chicago Urban League. After listening to conversations in several different bars about the various coalitions of such conspirators backing the blacks at Trumbull Park Homes, for example, the ACLU observer commented: "These whites are not too sure that they have a chance with the Negroes as they argue that the Negro is right about the backing that they are getting and they also say that the politicians are on the side of the Negro now as there are so many of them and they vote the way that their leaders tell them and the whites do not."[104]

Local struggles against racial integration had thus come to define white working-class conceptions of municipal and national politics well before 1957. Social movement theorists such as Alberto Melucci, Alain Touraine, and Manuel Castells argued more than two decades ago that the postwar period in the history of Western democracies witnessed a shift from class-based political action over the work process to identity-oriented mobilization over the conditions of daily life—an observation that holds particular relevance for the northern industrial centers of the American Midwest.[105] In Detroit—the symbolic capital of the industrial labor movement—Democratic, pro-labor candidates went down in defeat in the mayoral elections of 1945 and 1949.[106] In Chicago, blue-collar whites found themselves frequently at odds with the CIO's support of interracialism; some two years after the start of the anti-integration campaign in Trumbull Park, for example, the president of the South Deering Improvement Association applauded residents for taking on such organizations as the CIO Packinghouse Union.[107] According to Melucci, these changes meant that "the defense of identity, continuity and predictability of personal experience [had now come to] constitute the substance of new conflicts."[108] While in the American context such ideas have been more commonly applied to the "minority movements" that Omi and Winant identify—those defending the rights of racial minorities, women, and homosexuals, among others—these qualities also describe the movements emerging on the right in the postwar period. However, while whites in Chicago's Bungalow Belt undoubtedly viewed their predicament in the terms Melucci describes, such conceptions alone were not enough to produce sustained and collective mobilization. As it did for so nearly all of the social movements taking shape at this time, the black campaign for civil rights provided one of the primary inspirations for its white countermovement.

Indeed, the increase of black grassroots militancy and direct action in the late 1950s and early 1960s—whether in the more casual form displayed by the Bodine picnickers and by numerous black families refusing to vacate their homes in the face of white intimidation, or in the more coordinated manner carried out by civil rights organizations mobilizing for the right of African Americans to use beaches and parks—provided the initial impetus for the development of a broad-based movement against racial integration, and ultimately for the politicization of whiteness. By 1961, these forms of direct action were making their mark on Chicago's political landscape, and they were doing so primarily in the domain of youth culture.

During this period blacks throughout the city stepped up their determination to use Chicago's parks and recreational facilities unmolested. For the most part, such grassroots actions were largely unplanned. Yet as the civil rights movement gained more and more national exposure, militant sensibilities took shape throughout black Chicago, making encounters that previously seemed somewhat insignificant into symbolic struggles for basic rights. As we will explore further, street gangs and other more informal youth peer groups played essential roles in this widespread assertion of rights to public space. However, as the Bodine Social Club revealed, such actions were hardly restricted to youth groups, even if such actors were the most capable at mustering forces for concerted resistance on a daily basis.[109]

Moreover, civil rights organizations began to more actively coordinate such forms of grassroots militancy, at times taking their cues from the informal actions of youth groups. In July 1961, for example, a group of white progressives from the University of Chicago and black youths affiliated with the Congress of Racial Equality organized a series of "wade-ins" at Rainbow Beach on the Southeast Side of Chicago. The choice of location for these demonstrations was strategic. In the years following the Calumet Park riot, African American youths trying to use various public recreational facilities had encountered repeated mob actions by whites at both Rainbow Beach and nearby Bessemer Park. Indeed, such local youths swelled the ranks of black protesters at the wade-ins. However, white youths from neighborhoods throughout the city were equally determined to express their opposition to these actions. According to reports, crowds of between one and two thousand white teenagers and young adults turned out to hurl rocks and jeer at the demonstrators. While several fights broke out around the edges of the protest, large police squadrons were able to prevent things from getting out of hand.[110]

Rainbow Beach thus saw the clash of two racial movements emerging in working-class Chicago during these years. Because of the organized nature of the wade-ins, the Chicago Commission on Human Relations and the Chicago Police Department were able to jointly plan for an adequate response to the situation. For the very same reason, white counterprotesters were also able to rally their troops. Yet unlike the black demonstrators, the white counterdemonstrators did not possess an organizational network to coordinate their actions, a circumstance that raises questions about their ability to rally in such numbers.

An examination of how the CCHR attempted to defuse this potentially riotous situation offers a glimpse into the dynamics that made such effective mobilization possible. More than anything else, CCHR efforts revolved around taking advantage of the influence of youth workers and gang leaders throughout the South Side. The commission, for instance, urged the Illinois Youth Commission to "call a meeting of youth leaders who have contact with white gangs in Englewood and the South Chicago—South East side areas."[111] Observations recorded at the wade-ins, moreover, suggest that this approach was indeed a sound one. The accounts of several observers on hand confirm that youth gangs played a central role in coordinating the counterdemonstrations. In a report on police behavior issued shortly after the wade-ins, for example, the Organization for Southwest Chicago (OSC) criticized police at Rainbow Beach for publicly stating on one occasion that "the toughs from 79th and Halsted Avenue should disperse." "Such statements," the OSC claimed, "give the area and the teen-aged gangs associating themselves with the area public notoriety which can do no good whatsoever. . . . In situations such as Rainbow Beach or any other infused with racial hostility such notoriety acts as a spur for action, a 'living-up to one's reputation,' and accelerates the frequency of such incidents."[112] Moreover, sociologist James Short, who was at this time conducting research on gangs, witnessed similar behavior by the groups he was observing. "When the 'wade-ins' became known to the boys," Short reported, "the conflict group immediately took up the battle cry and proceeded to become involved in the planning activities and in the coordination of groups in opposition to the 'wade-ins.'" Short contrasts this gang, which he claims "was oriented much more toward fighting and, in the past, had been involved in attempts to organize a large white fighting gang, primarily it appeared, to fight against Negro gangs," with another, less conflict-oriented gang that favored hard drug use over fisticuffs. Yet even this more "retreatist" gang "expressed considerable racial hostility" and "talked about getting into the coming battle," according to Short. While several of its members made it to Rainbow Beach to support the cause of racial hatred, they opted to get high on pills and stay out of the fray.[113]

The evidence from Rainbow Beach thus points to some important circumstances underlying the emerging movement against integration in the late 1950s and early 1960s. First, it suggests that racially oriented fighting gangs played significant roles in mobilizing collective responses to integration initiatives. They served as "mobilizing structures," the term Douglas McAdam, John McCarthy, and Mayer Zald use to describe the "collective vehicles, informal as well as formal, through which people mobilize and engage in collective action." In addition to the gangs themselves, though, the larger youth subcultures within which they operated constituted what social movement theorists have referred to as "networks"— that is, spheres of activity that convince individuals to involve themselves in a movement and that provide the opportunities for such involvement on a sustained basis.[114] As the foregoing discussion of youth gang subcultures in Chicago in the late 1940s and 1950s demonstrates, street gangs and the milieu that surrounded them provided individuals with ample opportunities to engage in racial hatred. Such opportunities increased within the context of the racially oriented fighting-gang subculture that emerged during the late 1950s and early 1960s. James Short's findings reveal that not every peer group or youth gang out on the streets took as active a role as the "toughs from 79th and Halsted Avenue," but even the more apathetic felt pulled in to the movement by appeals to racial solidarity.

Moreover, unlike in the late 1940s, this sense of racial solidarity clearly stretched beyond neighborhood boundaries. It appeared as something much broader, if not, in certain moments, universal. The unification of Chicago's white working class against integration revealed itself sporadically in the late 1940s and then in Cicero in 1951, but the presence of the White Circle League and the notion of "outside agitators" it brought into the discursive space opened up by these events worked to complicate this sensibility. The Calumet riot and the wave of racial aggression that followed it reified the idea of a broad-based white movement against integration once again. That the buzz around antiblack demonstrations in the years thereafter often involved the rumor that youth groups from other parts of the city were coming over to lend their support was suggestive of this trend. Such rumors, for example, "flew" around a series of attacks against black students at Lindbloom High School in September 1958, when students and residents in the area around the school circulated the idea that aggressors participating in the marauding mobs were students from Gage Park and other nearby high schools.[115]

Hence, if many older working-class whites in the Bungalow Belt believed they were witnessing the deterioration of their communities as a result of racial migration and white flight, real or imagined, teenagers and young men coming of age under these conditions were starting to feel themselves part of a larger white movement against integration. Street gangs and youth groups, whether formally organized or loosely structured, served as important vehicles through which such feelings developed and spread. They served as networks conveying information about events occurring throughout the city, as forums framing the meaning of such events, and as structures mobilizing youths into collective action. In all of these capacities, the drive for alterity played more of a definitive role beginning in the late 1950s. Moreover, as demonstrated by Rainbow Beach and other large crowd actions of this period, street gangs, both black and white, were capable of rallying hundreds and even thousands of unaffiliated youths from their neighborhoods to participate in racially oriented collective actions. If older elements of their communities loathed them and younger ones at times feared them, they nonetheless captured the sympathies of many youths in times of heightened intergroup conflict, when emotions ran high and possibilities for change appeared promising.

Emblematic of the role fighting gangs—white, black, or brown—could play in mobilizing youths to engage in collective racial actions were the events that occurred after the July 12, 1961, fatal shooting of a black teen as he walked home from summer classes at Harrison High School in a "white" section of South Lawndale. While the victim of this unprovoked attack was apparently not affiliated with any gang, the Egyptian Cobras and the Vice Lords, rivals for years in their battles to become North Lawndale's preeminent fighting gang, rallied some five hundred black youths from their neighborhoods to gather around Harrison High School the day after the shooting and carry out reprisal attacks against white residents. Over the next several days, hundreds of black youths continued to pour into this area, committing forty-two acts of violence and injuring scores of whites. To restore order, Mayor Daley marshaled forces of between 150 and 200 police officers, including the city's new K-9 dog patrols. From July 13 to July 18, police arrested eighty people, the vast majority of whom were juveniles. On July 17, five days after the killing and one day after the first Rainbow Beach wade-in, what the press referred to as a "white" crowd estimated at over two thousand people took to the streets around 18th and Racine in a demonstration of solidarity against these attacks. According to police, the area's most reputable fighting gang, the Latin Counts, who were at the time being questioned in connection with the shooting, were pivotal in rallying the young crowd.[116]

The cycle of violence and collective action set off by the shooting of this black teen reveals a great deal about youth subcultures and their deep involvement in the politics of race in Chicago during this time. To begin with, the role played by the Cobras, the Vice Lords, and the Latin Counts in agitating group demonstrations on both sides of the color line is suggestive of the centrality of street gangs in crystallizing, organizing, and articulating racial sensibilities at the neighborhood level. Indeed, while the initial incident was more the result of "racial tension," as witnesses claimed, than gang warfare per se, gangs took the lead in framing the meaning of the incident and in rallying members of the communities involved to act. Their effectiveness in this capacity confirms Paul Gilroy's observation that "collective identities spoken through race, community and locality are, for all their spontaneity, powerful means to co-ordinate actions and create solidarity."[117] Gangs were the most effective (and arguably the only) grassroots organizations capable of bringing such solidarities into existence. The fact that thousands of nongang youths lined up behind the Latin Counts at the July 17 demonstration reveals not only how gangs provided networks for the development of such racial solidarities but also that such feelings of solidarity were in great demand.

Moreover, young men were not the only youths being swept up in such collective demonstrations of racial unity. By the early 1960s, teenage girls had become much more active on the terrain of fighting-gang subcultures. In fact, most of the major male fighting gangs affiliated themselves with female counterparts: the Vice Lords with the Vice Ladies, the Egyptian Cobras with the Cobraettes, the Viscounts with the Viscountettes, the Monarchs with the Monarchettes, the Taylor Dukes with the Taylor Capris, to name but a handful. While the young women in such gangs did not exhibit nearly the same willingness as their male counterparts to engage in lethal forms of combat, reports of violent battles between female gangs and occasionally between female and male gangs became increasingly common during the 1960s. As in the case of male fighting gangs, moreover, conflicts between female gangs quite often grew out of racial tensions. For example, in the midst of the whirlwind of racial aggression stirred up by the Rainbow Beach wade-ins and the violence around Harrison High School, the Mayor's Committee on Youth Welfare found itself forced to send a representative to the Near West Side in order to head off a "rumble" at the Twelfth Street Beach between two girl groups—the Italian Taylor Capris and the Mexican Spanish Queens. Indeed, young women on the Near West Side, whether formally gang-affiliated or not, grasped similar rituals of racial and ethnic alterity to construct feelings of racial solidarity.[118]

Such processes appear vividly in the work of the Mexican poet Ana Castillo, who grew up the daughter of a Near West Side Mexican gang member in this same period. In her poem "Dirty Mexican," for example, Castillo evokes the intensity and relative banality of racial aggression between Mexicans and Italians in her teenage years:

> "Dirty Mexican, dirty, dirty Mexican!"
> And I said: "i'll kick your ass, Dago bitch!"
> tall for my race, strutted right past
> the black projects,
> leather jacket, something sharp
> in my pocket
> to Pompeii School.[119]

In "The Toltec (c. 1955)," Castillo articulates the feelings of pride aroused in a young girl by her father's prowess as a member of his neighborhood gang, the Toltecs.

> My father was a Toltec.
> Everyone knows he was *bad*.
> Kicked the Irish-boy-from-Bridgeport's ass.[120]

Yet in addition to providing insights into the importance of youth gang subcultures in the production and dissemination of such feelings of racial aggression and unity, Castillo also offers a glimpse into the role African Americans and the black civil rights movement played in crystallizing such sensibilities within Mexican communities. Her reference in "Dirty Mexican" to "my race," the presence of the "black projects" in the background, and her description later in the poem of writing "MEXICAN POWER" all over the sidewalks all reflect the ambiguous position Mexican youths, male and female, occupied in such racially mixed areas of Chicago in this period and the feelings of collective racial solidarity such a position created.[121]

The outbreak of racial conflict around Harrison High School revealed that Mexican youths sometimes dealt with this condition of ambiguity by increasing their participation in antiblack actions. While newspaper reportage referred to this area as "predominantly white," with a black section beginning three blocks north of the school, this Polish neighborhood actually contained a substantial percentage of Mexican residents, many of whom were newcomers to the area. By 1970, the percentage of those claiming to speak Spanish as their mother tongue in the four census tracts closest to the school (3001, 3002, 3011, 3012) would reach 65.3, 62.4, 48.9, and 30.2, respectively.[122] Although these percentages were lower in the summer of 1961, many of those referred to in the newspapers as victims or arrestees in the days following the shooting had Spanish surnames. Moreover, that one of the most feared Mexican gangs in the city, the Latin Counts, helped to inspire the large demonstration at 18th and Racine, several blocks away from Harrison in the heart of the burgeoning Mexican neighborhood of Pilsen, further suggests that the collective identity of the crowds involved in these incidents was as much Mexican as it was "white."

The settlement of Mexicans in the colony referred to as Pilsen, or Little Village, located roughly to the west of Lawndale between 18th and 26th Streets, began to accelerate in the late 1950s. In the span of about three or four years, parts of this area began to take on a visibly Mexican identity. In April 1961, for example, CYDP supervisor Frank Carney noted the rapid appearance of Mexican restaurants and bars around 18th Street, as well as the frequency with which Spanish could be heard on the streets, predicting that the neighborhood would turn into a "Mexican ghetto" within a few years.[123] The year before, officials at Howell House, a social services center that had served the area for decades, had made similar observations, while also pointing out that the black population remained minimal and that there were "no Puerto Ricans to speak of."[124] Many of those settling in Pilsen around this time had been pushed out of the Near West Side by the forces of urban renewal—the construction of the Eisenhower Expressway and the new university and medical facilities. Others no doubt had viewed this Mexican colony as a safe haven from the increasing contentiousness of Near West Side neighborhood life.[125]

For these reasons, this Mexican colony developed in a manner that worked to the exclusion of both blacks and Puerto Ricans—a trend gangs like the Latin Counts played a key role in shaping. Yet some Mexican youths in the western part of the Pilsen enclave nonetheless had to cross the local color line of Western Avenue to get to Harrison High School, which also served part of the solidly black neighborhood that lay just three blocks to its north. A 1957 ACLU report counted 496 black students out of a total of 2,481 at Harrison, making it one of Chicago's most racially mixed high schools. In this setting, Mexican students found themselves somewhere in between European Americans and African Americans, a position that their involvement in strategies of alterity tried to—but never could wholly—resolve. Whiteness, after all, was a difficult proposition in the context of Pilsen, a neighborhood that was clearly on the way to becoming a local monument to a sense of ethnic distinctiveness that was years away from being a source of comfort and pride for many Mexicans in Chicago.[126] The Harrison situation illustrates the centrality that youth subculture as a milieu and youth gangs as actors would have in this unfolding process of constructing a new sense of Mexican ethnicity through the "production of space" in this area of the city.

The events of the summer of 1961 also suggest that local movement cultures were already in the making years before national organizations like the Southern Christian Leadership Conference, the Student Nonviolent Coordinating Committee (SNCC), and the Black Panther Party symbolically aligned Chicago's racial struggles with nationwide movements for civil rights and Black Power. In addition to the structures that make collective identity and action possible—what some have referred to as "networks" and "mobilizing structures"—scholars have identified two other elements that shape the development and course of social movements: (1) the political opportunities available to the movements, and (2) the organizations capable of framing their meaning. To be sure, the activities of mass-based civil rights organizations in and outside of Chicago were essential in creating new political opportunities for Chicago's black communities, as well as shaping the meaning of their actions. However, what these organizations encountered upon setting up operations in black Chicago and commencing their efforts to recruit an army of black youths into their ranks was far from a malleable corps waiting for leaders to guide them. Youth gang subcultures in Chicago had already served to frame the meaning of both the conditions and events of ghetto life, and by 1961, they had begun to take advantage of the narrow political opportunities that were available to them.

In the area of recruitment, moreover, gangs had already beaten these organizations to the punch. Between the late 1950s and mid-1960s, gang culture in black Chicago absorbed a larger and larger percentage of young men and women. A great many of these, particularly in neighborhoods like Lawndale, had little choice in the matter. With the escalation of violence came an intensification of recruitment methods. Yet there is also evidence indicating that the fearsome fighting gangs like the Vice Lords and the Cobras expanded as rapidly as they did because of the awe and respect they inspired in local youths. In November 1961, for example, CYDP worker John Ray reported that "the Vice-lords cause a decrease in the agencies attendance when they are engaged in an activity in the area; not because they were afraid to come to the agency, but because they want to be where the Vice-lords are."[127] Three months later, a CHA officer in the Cabrini-Green housing project on the Near North Side reported seeing signs in hallways "inviting people to join the Vice Lords," an activity that suggests that coercion was not the only form of recruitment used by the Vice Lords.[128]

Moreover, the Vice Lords operating in Cabrini-Green, it is important to consider, posted these recruitment notices just six months after the Lords and the Cobras had carried out their retaliatory raids around Harrison. Undoubtedly, the recruitment drive they advanced was part of a larger campaign to grab a greater share of the economy of power and respect that fighting gangs had constructed on the streets. But this does not change the fact that such drives had begun taking on broader political implications. Indeed, while the truce between the Vice Lords and the Cobras following the Harrison incident may have been brief and all too fragile, the sensibilities of racial solidarity underlying it were not. Looking back on this moment, for example, a Vice Lord claimed:

> What happened, this guy was coming from school and he was shot and killed. . . . There was mostly Polish living over there. . . . He wasn't doing nothing, just walking down the street coming from school. . . . And when this happened . . . everybody just thought the same way. The Lords decided to go on over there, and some kind of way we ended up with the Cobras too. It was just that everybody was out there, all the groups on the West Side. You know, before that, any time we went over there—in South Lawndale—we almost always would get dusted, or maybe even killed. But now they think twice. . . . And that's why I say like Malcolm X, "Violence sometimes serves its purpose."[129]

It is not hard to imagine why the members of fighting gangs in Chicago's West Side ghetto would find such ideas attractive. One might argue that this kind of explanation represents a justification after the fact, a grafting of political meaning on to acts produced from a state of sense-less rage. Indeed, the summer of 1961 predates by a few years the adoption of the word *nation* after the names of the larger Chicago fighting gangs. However, there were other signs that the Vice Lords, which would go on to become arguably the most politicized black street gang in Chicago four years later, were somewhat precocious in their turn toward Black Power ideology to make sense of their world. Not long after the Harrison violence, around the time recruitment signs started appearing on the walls of housing projects and a truce with the Egyptian Cobras held precariously, the gang added the word *conservative* in front of its name, a gesture meant to connote that its role and image reached beyond its ability to murder and intimidate its rivals. Moreover, even if one wishes to place the collective violence carried out by hundreds of black West Side youths over the course of several days solely within the context of a cycle of racially motivated gang violence that was more about demonstrating masculinity than articulating solidarity and resistance to racial injustice, it is important not to overlook the transformative potential of such situations.[130] Hearing the talk circulating on the streets and reading the coverage in the Chicago dailies, youths on the West Side, whether gang-affiliated or not, witnessed in such events their own insertion into the flow of history; the image reflected back at them was often one of collective resistance against racial discrimination. The Vice Lords' invocation of the notion that "everybody thought the same way" and "everybody was out there" speaks to the movement culture that was being developed from such experiences—a culture that, in the eyes of this and other Vice Lords, began to make sense in the context of a broader movement for civil rights.

An even more striking example of the emergence of such forms of racial solidarity and political militancy on the youth subcultural terrain was revealed early in the following summer, once again in the context of a school in a racially mixed area of the Near West Side, and once again in response to acts of aggression perpetrated by "white" gangs against black students. The story unfolded in the second week of June 1962, when city officials and youth workers braced themselves for a race riot after two brutal attacks by Mexican and Italian students against black students at predominantly black Crane High School on successive days. In the first of the assaults, a "white" youth slashed a black student just above his eye; the following day, a black girl was struck in the head with a brick on her way home from school. By Friday morning, the day after the sec-

Figure 7. A group of Junior Vice Lords makes it down Roosevelt Road in the North Lawndale area in the early 1960s. Photo reproduced courtesy of James F. Short Jr. and Lorine A. Hughes.

ond attack, youth workers had informed the city's youth bureau of rumors about what one CYDP worker referred to as "a general movement of Crane students." That same afternoon, representatives of the youth bureau came to Crane to question the leaders of several black gangs in the area about the situation, when they learned of the intention of the Crane student body to "march" to the corner of Polk and Leavitt, the site of the attacks against black students, and then on to predominantly white Cregier High School. The eyewitness account of the CYDP director, Frank Carney, poignantly captures the scene ensuing the close of school that day and is worth quoting at length:

> As we passed the corner of Polk and Leavitt we noticed that all the people who live on the block who are mostly Italians were out on the streets looking down Leavitt. We looked down Leavitt street and noticed a huge swarm of kids coming over the bridge. . . . There were a large number of girls, but boys predominated in the crowd. . . . At least 1000 kids came out of Crane, over the bridge, and down Leavitt. No one said anything and no one did anything. They just marched along as if they were on some kind of parade. The police squad cars strung themselves out and just shepherded the group along. The kids went straight down Leavitt Street until they reached Taylor.

They turned left on Taylor and went across the entrance of the Municipal Tuberculosis Sanitarium. They turned south again and cut across the big field surrounding Cregier. The Cregier kids did not get out when the kids from Crane were arriving so the kids from Crane just kept right on going. . . . When the mob was going by the corner of Taylor and Leavitt a number of Negro car wash attendants were standing outside and Supervisor heard one Negro attendant say to another, "They're really bogarting them, ain't they?" It seems to Supervisor that this whole thing was a big "bogart" in effect. The kids did not even look as though they had come prepared to fight. Most of them had their books with them and did not display any aggression or antagonism. The police were never more than a few feet away but it could have been a very ugly situation.[131]

Unlike the violence around Harrison, this striking event did not manage to find its way into the local papers, yet it nevertheless formed an integral part of what was an unfolding local history for West Side African Americans. The behavior of the demonstrators, their conscious emulation of the kinds of nonviolent protest tactics used by civil rights organizations in the South at the time, and their remarkable discipline in carrying them off revealed a more developed awareness of their place in a broader movement for racial justice. The spectacle of more than one thousand black teens marching silently down Taylor Street, the symbolic center of the Near West Side Italian community, would not soon be forgotten in the area, especially not by those actually involved in the demonstration. While fighting gangs were not implicated in this event to the extent that they were in the previous summer's events in Lawndale, the youth bureau's attempts to reach gang leaders so as to head off trouble speaks to their presence at the forefront of such activities. Yet regardless of the direct involvement of gangs in the event, this episode of collective mobilization rested on spatial practices of identity formation and collective resistance that street gangs in black Chicago had been engaging in for years.

6

Youth and Power

When you get into a conversation on racism and discrimination and segregation, you will find young people more
incensed over it—they feel more filled with an urge to
eliminate it.

Malcolm X

The moment the people come together and look at the problem, what you're going to discover is that the boys who live
across the freeway ain't your problem. They aren't your problem because you're raggedy . . . and they raggedy.

Al Raby (speaking to the Blackstone Rangers)

WILLIS WAGONS AND BEAT COPS: YOUTH, MILITANCY, AND COMMUNITY CONTROL

In late July 1963, the *Chicago Daily News* referred to the growing black
mobilization for civil rights in Chicago as "a social revolution in our midst"
and "a story without parallel in the history of our city."[1] Such pronouncements reflected, in part, events transpiring in the southern civil rights struggle. In particular, "Birmingham" was the word on the lips of blacks in
Chicago and elsewhere that spring as the news media brought startling
images of police turning attack dogs and high-pressure hoses on peace-
fully protesting men, women, and children and Governor George Wallace declared he would "stand in the schoolhouse door" to prevent federally ordered integration at the University of Alabama. But Chicago's
civil rights leaders were quick to bring their own fight into the discursive
space opened up by the situation in Birmingham, challenging the notion
long held by the Daley Machine and some middle-class blacks that such
problems were endemic to the South and did not apply to Chicago's black
community.

One could witness such processes in motion in early July, when Mayor Daley addressed NAACP delegates gathered in Chicago for their annual national convention. In classic fashion, Daley had arrived with a speech devoid of any real political substance, but when he proudly declared that there were "no ghettos in Chicago"—meaning that his administration did not view black neighborhoods in such negative terms—the head of the Illinois NAACP, Lucien Holman, blurted out, "We've had enough of this sort of foolishness." "Everybody knows there are ghettos here," he told a dumbfounded Daley, "and we've got more segregated schools than you've got in Alabama, Mississippi and Louisiana combined." Nor was this an isolated incident. A few days later, as Daley again addressed convention delegates and other black Chicagoans at the end of the July 4 "Emancipation Day" parade, his attempt to extend a friendly hand was once more met with derision. This time it was a crowd of about 150 protesters who approached the platform shouting things like "Daley must go!" and "Down with ghettos!" Unable to complete his speech, Daley hurried off the stage, but his replacement, Reverend Joseph H. Jackson, minister of the South Side's fifteen-thousand-member Olivet Baptist Church, fared no better. Jackson, a political ally of Daley's and an outspoken critic of the civil rights movement, was met with a chorus of jeers and boos before he even uttered a word. The situation deteriorated so much that police had to escort him out of the area amid shouts of "Kill him!" and "Uncle Tom must go!" While Daley later dismissed the whole affair with his quip that the protest must have been set up by Republicans, it was clear that something very real was afoot in black Chicago.[2]

By the fall of 1963 the many hundreds of miles stretching between Birmingham and Chicago could no longer keep the cities apart in the minds of many black Chicagoans. Reporters for the *Chicago Defender* missed few opportunities to highlight the link, especially in their coverage of the unraveling struggle being waged by local civil rights groups and ordinary parents to address the deplorable conditions of black schools throughout the city. As Superintendent Benjamin Willis continued to stubbornly cling to ideals of colorblindness in resisting demands for student transfers to alleviate the problem of overcrowding, the *Defender* referred to him as Chicago's own "Gov. Wallace standing in the doorway of an equal education for all Negro kids in the city."[3] Yet if the southern movement for civil rights lent African Americans in Chicago a sense of what theorist Alain Touraine refers to as "historicity"—a feeling of belonging to a larger historic movement that challenged the very foundations of the social order—as they organized to take on the status quo, such ideas were clearly secondary to the more immediate and local dramas within which black militancy was taking shape.[4] The more structured forms of civil rights activism that spread through Chicago neighborhoods in the early 1960s responded to circumstances that African Americans faced in the context of everyday life—namely, the indignities and inequalities encountered by their children in Chicago schools. This was hardly a new development. Since the mid-1940s schools had been hot spots for racial and ethnic conflict in Chicago and, as a consequence, vital sites for the crystallization of group identities and the forms of consciousness and collective action that accompany them. If, for African Americans, the school issue in neighborhoods in the path of the expanding color line had evolved from one about white student violence to one more about institutional discrimination and government neglect between the early 1950s and the early 1960s—a crucial development in that it placed the state much more squarely within the black political imaginary—school had nonetheless remained a key site of racial and political consciousness throughout.

The central role played by school and, more generally, youth issues in black contentious politics during the postwar era is both remarkable and somewhat undertheorized by historians of the African American experience.[5] Moving toward an understanding of the overdetermined meaning of school to African American communities involves first appreciating its very tight relationship with the state. Unlike other sites of political mobilization, such as the housing and labor markets, where the state has a much less visible and less accountable presence, school is much more easily understood as a domain of the state. Along with the police and criminal justice system, the public school system represents the most pervasive interface between ordinary citizens and the state, a quality that explains, in part, why the sociologist Nikolas Rose has argued that "childhood is the most intensively governed sector of personal existence" and why Alberto Melucci has attributed to youth culture the somewhat uncanny ability to render power "visible and confrontable."[6] Yet there is something else about school—as a central element of youth culture—that places it at the heart of contentious politics. If, as Melucci suggests, "youth becomes a mirror held up for the whole of society, a paradigm for the crucial problems of the complex systems," then the conditions of schooling would certainly be among the most compelling indicators of injustice, precariousness, and marginality.[7]

Such perspectives evoke the unique capacity of the youth question to produce the kinds of emotions and feelings of palpable outrage that move individuals to action.[8] Indeed, the mobilizing power of school injustices seems even more impressive when one considers that many older African Americans engaging in such struggles were well aware that the rights and recognition they were fighting for would have little effect on their own future life chances. While one should not underestimate the mobilizing power of feelings of racial pride and solidarity, the importance of school injustices to local civil rights activism across the country suggests that, in some sense, many black adults who participated in the movement politics of the 1950s and 1960s, South and North, did so via their children or the children of their communities. Even the most cursory of glances at the major hot-button images, issues, and events that punctuated the long decade of civil rights struggle from the mid-1950s to the mid-1960s reveals the extent to which notions of racial injustice and racial empowerment were articulated around youths. The examples are numerous: Emmett Till's mutilated body; the "Little Rock Nine" barred from Central High School; the North Carolina A&T lunch-counter sit-ins; the powerful rise of the Student Nonviolent Coordinating Committee on black college campuses; James Meredith's fight to enroll at the University of Mississippi; Governor Wallace "stand[ing] in the schoolhouse door"; the outrage surrounding the rough treatment of children by Birmingham police in 1963; the "Four Little Girls" killed in the Birmingham church bombing; the beatings of college student "Freedom Riders"; the murders of student activists James Chaney, Andrew Goodman, and Michael Schwerner in Mississippi; and the controversy surrounding the image of ghetto youths who sparked race riots across the nation from 1965 to 1968.

These circumstances help to explain why it was black parents protesting against the conditions of their children's schooling that brought civil rights militancy to a new level in Chicago by the early 1960s. Yet the deep psychic investment made by African Americans in defending the young of the community tells only part of the story of how the school issue came to so completely overshadow others like housing and labor market discrimination. On a more direct level, the school problem was most compelling because black schools were in a truly profound state of crisis, the accountability for which lay squarely in the hands of clearly identifiable sources of power—the Board of Education and the mayor's office.

Since school districts are seldom coterminous with neighborhood boundaries, they are more sensitive to shifts in the social geography, and when these shifts occur rapidly, they can far outpace the city's ability to redraw district lines and provide adequate infrastructure to manage the

situation. This was certainly the case in the 1950s when Chicago's overall population declined by almost 2 percent, but the number of African
Americans living there increased by some 300,000, bringing the total to
812,637—nearly a quarter of the city's 3.5 million inhabitants.[9] As the
color line moved quickly across white neighborhoods on the South and
West Sides of the city, the resulting shifts in Chicago's social geography
were nothing less than seismic. The increasing densification of black neighborhoods and the fact that newly arriving black families during these years
tended to be quite a bit younger than the white families they were replacing
further strained existing school facilities in black Chicago. At the Gregory
School in the Garfield Park area of the West Side, for example, the student body rose from 1,590 in 1954 to 1,864 in 1956 to 2,115 in 1959
and then to 4,194 in 1961.[10] Throughout the city, the number of pupils
in the school system shot up from 375,000 to 520,000 between 1953 and
1963. Citing the sanctity of the "neighborhood school" and the need to
separate school policy decisions from city politics, Superintendent Willis
responded to the problem of overcrowded black schools by implement-
ing an extensive double-shift program and then with the use of trailerlike
temporary classrooms—referred to by protesters as "Willis Wagons."[11]

While Willis had dictated that the school district not keep any "record
of race, color or creed of any student or employee," several independent
studies revealed the deep-rooted racial disparities that Willis's colorblind
ideals and Band-Aid policies were attempting to cover up.[12] According
to an NAACP study conducted in 1957, predominantly black elementary schools had, on average, nearly twice the enrollment of white ones,
and black schools in general constituted more than 80 percent of those
on double-shift schedules.[13] A 1962 Chicago Urban League study, moreover, found that class sizes were 25 percent larger in black schools and
expenditures per pupil were 33 percent lower.[14] Most African Americans,
however, did not need such studies to confirm the injustices they confronted on a daily basis. Widespread disgust with the situation led first
to the Chicago NAACP's "Operation Transfer" campaign to have black
parents register their children in white schools, and after that failed, to
a series of parent-led sit-ins in mostly middle-class black areas. One of
the first was in January 1962 at the Burnside School on the far South
Side, where the enrollment had risen dramatically from 1,138 in 1958
to 1,773 in 1960.[15] Speaking in plain terms about their dissatisfaction
with the Board of Education's neglect of their children and managing to
get themselves arrested in the process, the Burnside parents helped spark
a number of other school protests. Months later, in working-class Wood-

lawn, where famed activist Saul Alinsky had organized residents into the Temporary Woodlawn Organization (TWO), parents and members of TWO organized school boycotts and demonstrations against the use of mobile classrooms at a local elementary school. Capitalizing on these uprisings from below, the Chicago Urban League, TWO, the Chicago NAACP, and a number of other newly formed community groups forged a new umbrella civil rights organization, the Coordinating Council of Community Organizations (CCCO), to carry on the fight.[16]

By the summer of 1963, school protests had spread into several black communities on the South and West Sides, including the Englewood area, where CORE, on the heels of a controversial one-week sit-in at the Chicago Board of Education that featured scuffles between protesters and police, rallied its members to join an aggressive parent-led campaign against the installation of mobile classrooms. Laying their bodies down at the construction site at 73rd and Lowe, the Englewood demonstrators provoked police into hauling them off, a spectacle that offered a first glimpse of the Chicago movement that was beginning to come together that summer. Renowned comedian and activist Dick Gregory was among the more than one hundred protesters arrested, some of whom broke with CORE's nonviolent philosophy by kicking and stoning police.[17] A range of grassroots civil rights organizations developed out of this moment of school activism, including the Parents Council for Integrated Schools and the Chicago Area Friends of SNCC (CAFSNCC), and several national organizations—the SNCC, the SCLC, and CORE—began to set their sights on Chicago's increasingly militant school reform campaign as a wellspring of inspiration.

As the end of summer neared, with increasingly militant protests against mobile classrooms springing up in several black neighborhoods, Chicagoans and the rest of the nation beheld what seemed like nonviolence's finest hour when more than two hundred thousand gathered in Washington to hear Martin Luther King evoke his "dream" of racial integration. Yet if the local press generally applauded the peaceful approach manifested during the March on Washington, the coverage also revealed that the school protests that had been transpiring that summer colored the way many were viewing what lay ahead for the city. The *Sun-Times*, for example, highlighted organizer Bayard Rustin's comment that the march marked the beginning of a campaign of "intensified non-violence," and the paper expressed its hope that the event would bring an end to local demonstrations.[18] Rustin's prediction would very soon prevail over such unrealistic hopes.

Just one day after the March on Washington, a chain of events was set in motion that would transform the terrain of black protest politics in Chicago. The initial spark occurred not out on the streets, however, but behind closed doors, when the Board of Education agreed to an out-of-court settlement of the nearly two-year-old lawsuit, *Webb vs. the Board of Education of the City of Chicago,* filed by TWO charging racial segregation in the Chicago school system. In addition to agreeing to name a study group to come up with a racial head count and devise a plan to address racial inequalities, the board also adopted a rather symbolic transfer plan to permit a limited number of top students to switch to schools with honors programs when their own schools did not offer them. This plan provoked virulent reactions in white neighborhoods around several of the schools on the transfer list, particularly the Bogan High School area on the Southwest Side, where thousands gathered to picket and vent their rage at their alderman. Willis quickly caved in to this pressure, removing Bogan and fourteen other schools from the original transfer list of twenty-four. When the board ordered him to reinstate the schools, Willis refused, and then when faced with a court order to do so, he resigned. In a surprising turn of events, however, the board responded by voting not to accept his resignation, a move that received broad support among white residents on the city's Southwest Side.[19]

This outrage—not just the board's decision but also the emergence of Willis as a hero in the Bungalow Belt—provided the spark activists were looking for to consolidate the movement and take it to the citywide level. Two days later, Lawrence Landry, a University of Chicago graduate student and leader of the Chicago Friends of SNCC, called for a mass boycott of Chicago schools on October 22. On the day before the boycott, the CCCO published a list of thirteen demands in the *Chicago Daily News,* which included, among others, the removal of Willis as superintendent, the publication of a racial head count and inventory of classrooms, a "basic policy of integration of staff and students," the replacement of certain pro-Willis members of the study group recently named by the board with researchers Kenneth Clark and Dan Dodson, the recomposition of the Board of Education, the publication of pupil achievement levels on standardized tests, and the request by Mayor Daley of federal emergency funds for remedial programs in all of the schools where test scores were revealed to be subpar.[20] Prior to the boycott, organizers were counting on the participation of between thirty and seventy-five thousand students. When the day arrived, a stunning 225,000 stayed home from school.

To counter charges that students had merely taken the opportunity to skip school, boycott leaders set up "Freedom Schools" in churches and other neighborhood associations, where students sang freedom songs like "We Shall Overcome" and discussed civil rights issues. The organization Teachers for Integrated Schools published and distributed a pamphlet entitled "A Guide for Freedom School Leaders," which contained lesson plans on black history for grades 1 through 12. All students who attended Freedom Schools that day left with a Freedom Diploma. The lessons emphasized the contributions African Americans had made to the country's history, compared the boycott to the Boston Tea Party, and encouraged students to think of themselves as "writing another chapter in the freedom story."[21] Moreover, Landry had taken steps to make sure these classes were well attended, setting up a student movement in the schools through a tutoring program called the Student Woodlawn Project. Through this initiative students found themselves in the thick of things as they distributed thousands of leaflets in schools and churches throughout the city. Such efforts spread through the community, with churches offering their facilities to be used as freedom schools, parents making chain phone calls to urge boycott participation, and the *Chicago Defender* publishing a list of the freedom schools students could attend.[22] The psychological impact of this event for civil rights activism nationwide was enormous. Chicago civil rights leaders had, in some sense, mobilized more people than had the March on Washington, and the majority of those who chose freedom school over public school were not enlightened, middle-class activist types but ordinary young Chicagoans. Chicago's success led to a series of similar boycotts in a number of other major cities, such as Boston, New York, Kansas City, Cleveland, and Milwaukee. After several rounds of fruitless negotiations with school officials, the CCCO called for a second Chicago boycott on February 25, 1964, which, in comparison with the first boycott, was somewhat disappointing, but nonetheless garnered the impressive participation of 175,000 students.[23]

While generally appreciating the magnitude of what had been accomplished during these boycotts, most accounts of this moment view these events largely as failures. As in the case of all the citywide boycotts carried out in 1963 and 1964, the negotiations that followed failed to yield any substantial policy changes. Moreover, the coalitions of civil rights groups that staged these demonstrations were rife with tensions over strategy, and in the course of bringing them to fruition and then engaging in the frustrating negotiations that followed, the rifts between moderates and militants widened even further. This was particularly the

Figure 8. Chicago Area Friends of SNCC militants march in a demonstration against Superintendent Willis during the school boycott on February 25, 1964. One holds a sign criticizing black Second Ward alderman Kenneth Campbell, evidence of the increasing anger against black politicians aligned with the Daley Machine. Photographer unknown; courtesy of the Chicago History Museum, ICHi-19624.

case in Chicago, where as early as December 1963, not even two months after its triumphant first boycott, the CCCO was in disarray. At the end of November it voted not to support a boycott of Loop stores called by SNCC and moved to reign in the increasingly militant Lawrence Landry as its spokesman. At a December 19 rally called by the Chicago Friends of SNCC and attended by some five hundred people, Chicago CORE revealed that it would split into two chapters—a West Side unit headed by Sam Riley and a more militant South Side group led by Milton Davis. Yet despite such divisions and despite the lack of tangible gains won by such anti-Willis demonstrations, a new style of organizing was in the making. Taking the stage at the "Don't Shop Downtown" rally that evening was an emerging class of militants on the Chicago civil rights scene: Lawrence Landry, soon-to-be leader of the Chicago chapter of the ACT organization; Nahaz Rogers, fellow traveler in ACT and leader of the Negro American Labor Council; and Rose Simpson, head of the Parents Council for Integrated Schools. Defined as "militants" or "extremists" because of their lower threshold of anger over the intransigence of school and city officials and their belief in the need to counter it with more aggressive direct-action tactics, these new civil rights leaders also distinguished themselves by their vision of where to tap the potential lifeblood of the movement—in the streets of the poorest black neighborhoods in the city, where youths had been practicing their own forms of direct-action tactics for years.

In fact, the discovery of ghetto youths as the potential vanguard of black protest politics was something of a happening around this time. In an interview published in the *Monthly Review* and *Revolution* in May 1964, Malcolm X, whose *Autobiography* would soon show how a young small-time crook could grow into a heroic activist, declared that the "accent" in the struggle for black community control will be placed on "youth." "The accent is on youth," he explained, "because the youth have less at stake in this corrupt system and therefore can look at it more objectively, whereas the adults usually have a stake in this corrupt system and they lose their ability to look at it objectively because of their stake in it." In the same interview he revealed that he had recently met with a group of local civil rights leaders, including Lawrence Landry.[24] Several months later, Max Stanford, one of the founders of the radical group Revolutionary Action Movement (RAM), published an article in which he argued that as opposed to bourgeois black youth, working-class gang youths offered a potential rich source of oppositional energy. "Gangs are the most dynamic force in the black community," he wrote.

"Instead of fighting their bothers and sisters, they can be trained to fight 'Charlie.' They can be developed into a blood brotherhood (black youth army) that will serve as a liberation force in the black revolution."[25]

Such ideas seemed confirmed during Chicago's second school boycott, when lower-class black youths proved more willing to stay out of school than their middle-class counterparts, who appeared more responsive to the Chicago press campaign to paint boycott leaders as "reckless," as well as the public stand taken against the second boycott by two black aldermen.[26] If not focusing on gangs per se at this time, Landry and the Chicago Friends of SNCC were rallying youths against these black reactionary forces the day before the second boycott, when a group of some thirty-four students picketed the ward offices of South Side aldermen Kenneth Campbell and Claude Holman, the leaders of an organization formed by black machine politicians to oppose the CCCO and the school movement—the Assembly to End Prejudice, Injustice, and Poverty. While somewhat small in numbers, this group of demonstrators, led by Dunbar High School student Steve Jackson and Englewood student James Harvey, exhibited unwavering devotion to the cause in braving twenty-five-degree blustery weather to collect donations, pass out thousands of flyers, and carry signs reading "No Room for Traitors in the Black Community" and "Go Home Uncle Tom—You Don't Represent Us!"[27] Some three weeks later, Jackson and Harvey served as picket captains in another youthful demonstration against the black machine. This time the target was Congressman and longtime South Side Boss William Dawson, and this time the action was much less peaceful. Organized by the recently formed group ACT, under the guidance of CAFSNCC defectors Landry, Dick Gregory, and Nahaz Rogers, the demonstration became tense when Dawson workers attending a political rally at Dunbar Vocational High School faced off with the some seventy-five picketers, several of whom carried signs reading "22 Years of Uncle Tomism Is Too Long, Dawson Must Go!"[28] A few days later, three black students at Hyde Park High School were suspended for passing out pamphlets criticizing the school's privileging of honors students at the expense of students in need of remedial education. The initiative for this action had apparently come not from ACT this time, but from the Chicago Area Friends of SNCC, which quickly came to the defense of the students by denouncing the suspension as a violation of the right to free speech.[29]

By early summer, civil rights organizing among youths was beginning to gain some momentum on the streets. On June 30, for example, nine days after some seventy-five thousand had assembled in Chicago for the

Illinois Rally for Civil Rights, which ended up being a celebration of the passage of the 1964 Civil Rights Act two days earlier, activists marshaled a crowd of over one hundred young protesters for a march on the police headquarters at 1121 South State Street. The demonstration had been called to draw attention to recent incidents of police brutality, but after police arrested several protesters for unlawful assembly and conducting a meeting without a permit, a crowd of over 150 persons—"the majority of whom were in their early teens," according to police observers— marched instead to the Second District Station at 48th and Wabash to demand their release. Singing, chanting, and dancing in a line around the building, the protesters refused to disperse, even when police threatened to arrest the many juveniles present for curfew violations. Police ended up booking over forty more demonstrators that night.[30] In planning this rally several days after the Illinois Rally for Civil Rights, organizers clearly intended to express their opposition to the idea voiced by the *Chicago Sun-Times* and some moderate blacks in Chicago that the Rally for Civil Rights symbolized the end of direct-action mobilization. Indeed, just days before this demonstration, three civil rights activists were reported missing in Mississippi, circumstances that cast a dark shadow on the celebrations surrounding the Civil Rights Act. In Chicago, however, skepticism about the relevance of this legislation for blacks there was already on the rise when, at the end of May, the Board of Education announced its intention to substitute a woefully inadequate transfer plan for the one proposed by the sociologist Philip M. Hauser in the study conducted as part of the *Webb* settlement.

Yet legislation in Washington and school board maneuverings downtown were not the stuff that was pushing young activists into confrontations with the police. ACT's shift to a focus on police brutality, for example, was in line with its strategy of transforming ghetto youths into militant activists. Nor was ACT alone in seeking to capitalize on this issue to crystallize grassroots militancy. Between the fall of 1963 and the spring of 1964, around the time of the high school boycotts, CORE organized demonstrations against police misconduct in San Francisco, Syracuse, Cleveland, and Brooklyn.[31] By the summer of 1964, police brutality had come to serve as a perfect focal point for the more aggressive program ACT was pursuing in Chicago for a number of reasons. As groups like ACT and CORE sought to straddle the fence between a philosophy of nonviolence and increasingly popular calls for armed self-defense from charismatic leaders like Malcolm X and Robert Williams, direct-action protests against police brutality seemed to offer a way to strike back at the police without the use of violence. If being manhandled and hauled off by police did not exactly provide a triumphant sense of turning the tables on police power, at least it showed that demonstrators were not afraid to be subjected to such treatment.

In addition, even more than the school issue, police brutality turned the attention of youths toward the state—toward what activists and youths alike were then referring to as "Mister Charlie," "the man," or the "white power structure." This process of directing the attention of youths toward the state—of, in effect, rendering state power visible in the context of everyday life—constituted perhaps the greatest challenge for anyone seeking to tap the oppositional potential of black working-class youth culture. To do this, one had to first get black young men to stop fighting each other. As African Americans on the South and Southwest Sides of Chicago became increasingly ghettoized, a situation that accelerated with the construction in the late 1950s and early 1960s of the high-rise housing projects Stateway Gardens, Henry Horner Homes, Robert Taylor Homes, and the Robert Brooks Homes extension, the search for respect in rituals of gang violence became much more territorial than racial. Indeed, from June through December 1964, in spite of the buzz of civil rights mobilization that was sweeping through the city, CYDP gang worker Richard Booze reported chronic street fighting pitting youths from the Henry Horner Homes against their peers from the Robert Brooks Homes. This situation had been causing problems for youth workers since at least early April 1963.[32]

On February 11, precisely two weeks before the second school boycott, Booze showed a group of sixteen- to nineteen-year-olds from Horner a film about the sit-in movement in the South, to which, he reported, they responded with great interest. According to Booze, the youths were astonished by this form of nonviolent protest—by the ability of the protesters to stoically withstand the heavy abuse being directed at them. He recorded in his notes that these youths felt themselves incapable of resisting the temptation to strike back in the face of such humiliation.[33] While Booze did not hypothesize about the larger significance of what he had witnessed, it could be argued that he had unwittingly set up an experiment that identified one of the key obstacles organizers faced in incorporating ghetto youths into a nonviolent movement. The more abstract and collective goals of civil rights activism, it seemed, were a tough sell to young men coming of age in the projects. Hence, four months later, as the city geared up for the Illinois Civil Rights Rally in late June, persistent violence between these youths and their rivals from the nearby housing project suggested that, for many lower-income black youths, being swept up into the racial solidarity of civil rights activism was no substitute for the individualistic rewards of street combat. Historians have long emphasized that civil rights organizations, especially the SCLC, greatly underestimated the power of the Daley Machine as they carried out their northern campaign in Chicago. Yet just as devastating to their hopes was the dearth of resources provided by the political culture of the Chicago ghetto; if intergroup violence had offered a politically usable sense of group identification infused, at times, with sensibilities of shared racial injustices, territorial struggles waged for symbolic capital served to depoliticize the experience of social marginality. The trick, as Landry well understood, was to turn youths away from street violence against their brothers and toward visible targets of state injustice in their neighborhoods—namely, shabby schools and hostile cops.

Even more than school, though, police brutality touched in a very immediate way the everyday experiences of youths, because it impinged on the strategies of empowerment they pursued out on the streets. While the street was where a good many young men in working-class Chicago sought to prove their manhood, youths hanging out on the streets during the late 1950s and early 1960s found themselves increasingly running up against antagonistic police officers. The situation was particularly severe in black neighborhoods on the South and West Sides of the city. Two officers in Lawndale, for example, were investigated by the U.S. Attorney's Office and later indicted for tying Clover gang member James Halsell to a post and whipping him on the back with a belt in 1958.[34] This incident reflected a campaign of gratuitous harassment waged by police against youths hanging out on the streets. According to one West Side youth worker, police repeatedly roughed up youths, forced them to remove scarves they wore on their heads, tore up their cigarettes, confiscated their money, and subjected them to verbal abuse.[35] Such tactics clearly went beyond law enforcement; they indicate that the police had entered into the logic of a struggle for dominance predicated on emasculating their young rivals.

Two years later, with the arrival of new police chief O. W. Wilson, an expert criminologist who more than doubled the annual police budget in his first year on the job, the streets got even hotter for black youths. Describing one night he spent with gang workers in Lawndale, for example, an official from the Illinois Youth Commission referred to the "unconscionable police behavior" he witnessed in the manhandling of two young boys and the lining up and searching of another group.[36] Wilson's "stop-and-frisk" policy and his need to show the mayor and the city some tangible statistical results to justify his ballooning budget had the logical effect of dramatically increasing confrontations between police and youths out on the streets in the early 1960s.[37] Moreover, in 1961, following a summer of high-profile gang violence in 1960, Wilson issued the order that "gangs must be crushed" and established the Gang Intelligence Unit (GIU) to get the job done.[38] Yet perhaps the most important of Wilson's policy changes was his effort to recruit black police officers. After just two years of his tenure, the Chicago police department had increased its number of black officers from five hundred to twelve hundred, a change in personnel that was, on the surface, intended to improve relations between the department and black communities, but which actually may have helped facilitate the more aggressive policing tactics being employed by beat cops in black neighborhoods.[39] Under Wilson's rule, notorious black officers like James "Gloves" Davis were given free reign on the streets in the early 1960s. Davis, who years later would participate in the raid that resulted in the death of Black Panther leader Fred Hampton, earned his nickname from his habit of wearing a black glove on his right hand when he administered beatings. After several incidents, including a pistol-whipping of a youth who was awarded $4,800 in damages, youth workers for the Chicago Youth Centers managed to have Davis transferred out of Lawndale.[40] Yet as "Uncle Tom" discourses circulated through the black South and West Sides of Chicago, the idea that black officers would be able to amp up police activities without stirring up too much local opposition turned out to be flawed. Police harassment, as we will see, was on the verge of becoming a highly explosive issue in lower-income black communities in Chicago and elsewhere—an issue that would soon push some areas to the brink of violent rebellion.

Why police interventions would become flashpoints for collective action around this time has a great deal to do with ideological shifts that were transpiring within the milieu of black working-class youth culture. Police stops serve as a kind of canary in the coal mine for gauging oppositional consciousness because of the obvious correlation between the police and the state. Teens and young adults, because of their strong presence on the streets and in other neighborhood spaces, play an integral role in this situation. They represent, to a great extent, the interface between the neighborhood and the police. Hence, the vast majority of the incidents between police and black residents that sparked minor and major uprisings in the years of urban rebellions between 1965 and 1968 logically involved young men in their teens and early twenties. This was due in part to the psychological investment in youth issues being made by black communities at the time and in part to the simple fact that youths were generally more exposed to police tactics. Yet this exposure was not mere happenstance. The aggressive style of policing ushered in by Wilson made challenging beat cops a primary means of demonstrating manhood, as well as a way to claim the role of defending the community. Resistance to police, then, offered the same forms of valorization that gang violence had in earlier years, but with much greater potential for oppositional politics. The interface between the police and youths was, in the early 1960s, a radicalizing space—all the more so because of the languages of Black Power that were increasingly accessible to youths through the popularization of Malcolm X.

Youths, however, were hardly alone in this interface. The case of "Gloves" Davis reveals not only why police brutality was an issue that rallied youths to join more structured forms of protest action, but it also identifies one of the agents in this conversion—youth workers. As direct-action groups like ACT began to penetrate the milieu of black working-class youth culture, they quickly formed relationships with the scores of CYDP and YMCA youth workers who were, in a sense, already after the same thing. As intimate as they were with the realities of ghetto life and the false promises of civil rights legislation, many youth workers fell quickly under the influence of Black Power ideas. Moreover, by the early 1960s the number of full-time youth workers in Chicago's lower-income neighborhoods had risen from around thirty to over one hundred. Over two-thirds of these were indigenous to their communities, making them especially adept at winning the confidence of the youths under their charge.[41] One of the ways they kept this loyalty was by defending the youths against injustices dealt them by certain old-guard police officers and by shepherding them through the court system when necessary. They also worked hard to place their youths in summer jobs, remedial classes, and eventually job-training programs. Yet as more militant forms of rights consciousness and mobilization began spreading through black Chicago in the early 1960s, their role took on new dimensions. Arguing that youth work "shifted its focus from delinquency reduction to social change" around this time, a University of Chicago researcher studying youth workers in Chicago cited two memos that circulated among them in 1964 and 1965. The first posed the question, "Who among us can state with certainty that a lower arrest rate is a good thing?" The second, which was addressed to employees of the federally funded STREETS delinquency-prevention program, asked, "Because Mister Charlie pays your salary the same as he pays me, ask yourself, if the real shit breaks out here, what will be my role."[42]

Such memos reveal the disillusionment felt by many youth workers in the face of a deficient educational system, a depressed labor market, and an unforgiving criminal justice system. Yet they also indicate how much the role of extension worker had changed by the early 1960s. Mandated by the juvenile delinquency panic of the mid-1950s, CYC, HTRYP, and YMCA workers out on the streets at that time defined their jobs around the central goal of delinquency prevention. Far from an object of opposition, the state was generally viewed as a partner in this task. The local state was an important cosponsor of detached worker programs through the Welfare Council and Chicago Area Project. Even the Chicago police department, through the operations of its juvenile bureau, maintained a spirit of cooperation with these youth programs. The bureau's director, Michael Delaney, consciously looked to cultivate a working relationship with youth workers, seeking to recruit officers with a background in the social sciences and a sincere interest in working with youths. That his policy was effective is suggested by the fact that regular officers typically referred to their colleagues in the youth division as "diaper dicks" and "kiddie cops."[43] While youth workers, for their part, certainly had ample opportunities to voice complaints about the harsh treatment of youths by certain police officers, this was a truly different era in police–youth worker relations. By the early 1960s, however, with the spread of more radical forms of racial consciousness around the struggles against school injustices, police brutality, and "Uncle Tomism," youth workers were increasingly viewing themselves as at odds with the state—especially in the form of the educational and criminal justice systems. Moreover, in the context of the broadening rebellion against segregated schools and hostile cops in lower-income neighborhoods, these feelings of opposition could not help but interact with the ideas being voiced by youths about what they were witnessing going on around them.

Richard Booze showing a group of teenagers a film about the southern sit-in movement just weeks before the second school boycott is a striking example of the role youth workers could play, but on several other occasions it was the youths themselves who seemed to take the initiative of turning the group into a discussion forum under the guidance of the extension worker. Booze, for example, recorded youths under his charge commenting one day on the problems caused by young men hanging out on street corners. On another occasion, the discussion involved the detrimental effects of the newly built Robert Taylor Homes project. "With that many people crowded together," one youth told him, "it would be a worse slum in a few years than the ones it was designed to replace."[44] Even more regular were conversations regarding the difficult experiences the youths were having in the various dead-end jobs they worked. "The boys," Booze noted, "talked about the great incentive the jobs gave them to finish school because they realized that without at least a high school education manual labor jobs similar to those they have now would be the only ones they could get."[45] In light of such discussions, it is hardly surprising that during a high point of civil rights consciousness in Chicago, when Martin Luther King's SCLC began planning its northern campaign in the fall of 1965, some of Booze's youths were "speaking eagerly" among themselves about civil rights issues at Crane High School—in particular, the decision of the school principal to fire an African American teacher for his participation in the civil rights movement.[46] Booze's meticulous reports thus reveal the beginnings of a radical critique of race and power within the everyday spaces of working-class black youth culture. While Booze was perhaps exceptional in the level of detail he provided in his reports, his experience was not at all out of the ordinary. In the context of street gangs and peer groups across black Chicago in the early 1960s, youths, with the help of detached workers and local activists, were engaged in a process of piecing together a form of "hidden transcript" that helped them make sense of their precarious position in and between school, the labor market, and the world of the streets. While this transcript incorporated elements of Malcolm X's rhetoric, particularly its emphasis on the constitutive power of racism and the role of the state in maintaining racial inequalities, the indignities young black men confronted in schools and out on the streets were the raw materials out of which they began to fashion their own form of Black Power ideology.

Indeed, while youth workers like Richard Booze were, despite their disillusionment, generally encouraging youths to join nonviolent forms of protest, the mix of Black Power ideology and brutal police tactics out on the streets was by the summer of 1964 creating volatile conditions in many black ghetto neighborhoods in the urban North and Midwest. The first explosion occurred in Harlem in mid-July, when the shooting of a black teenager by a white cop triggered a riot that resulted in hundreds of injuries, hundreds of arrests, and one death. The spark actually came two nights after the shooting, when scuffles broke out between police and protesters during a rally led by some two hundred of the slain youth's classmates at the local precinct station.[47] New York up to that point had witnessed some of the same circumstances as had Chicago. A school boycott in early February that same year had garnered the participation of over 460,000 students, making important inroads into the consciousness of black youths throughout the city. Moreover, youths in black areas like Harlem and Bedford-Stuyvesant were even more exposed to the currents of Black Power ideology. The riot in Harlem reverberated through civil rights organizations nationwide, informing those with an ear to the ground of the impending dangers associated with the spirit of militancy they were trying to foment and channel. On July 29, the leaders of the major national civil rights organizations announced their support for a "broad curtailment, if not total moratorium" on all forms of direct action until the presidential election on November 3. Chicago's fledgling direct-action organizations followed suit. At a rally at the Packinghouse Workers Union Hall in Chicago about one month after the Harlem uprising, leaders told a crowd of more than twelve hundred persons of the need to organize teenage gangs throughout the city to persuade them not to participate in any racial disorders.[48]

What the events in Harlem revealed for all to see was the ability of youths out on the streets to effectively, if only momentarily, seize control of the civil rights struggle. For the mainstream nonviolent organizations, the lesson was that several hundred youths in Harlem had managed to cause a moratorium on civil rights demonstrations across the country; for members of some of the more radical groups, like ACT and RAM, it was that several hundred youths could draw national attention and awaken young brothers nationwide to the cause. Just two months prior to the Harlem riot, Malcolm X had made his famous speech, "The Ballot or the Bullet," in which he claimed that the sit-in style of activism "castrates you," comparing such protesters to old people, cowards, and chumps. "Well you and I been sitting long enough," he declared, "and it's time today for us to start doing some standing, and some fighting to back that up." Events in Harlem seemed to confirm that such thinking was taking hold, and that, if organizers had been pushing the police brutality issue for some time, youths were now mobilizing in impressive numbers on their own. Landry, who had met with Malcolm around that time, was clearly drifting further and further toward the thinking advocated in "The Ballot or the Bullet"—not only his ideas about violent self-defense but also his emphasis on black community control. Indeed, by the summer of 1965, Chicago's direct-action civil rights organizations were turning up the heat out on the streets. With the CCCO's anti-Willis campaign flagging and the local movement running out of steam, local civil rights leaders sought to spark some grassroots activism in the South Side Kenwood area by appealing to youths fed up with police harassment. On July 14, they called what police officers referred to as "a large group of teenagers" at the Second District Police Station to protest police brutality and the lack of black police officers in the area. After hearing a speech that decried "the white power structure," the police, white businesses in the area, and the mobile classrooms currently being constructed at nearby DuSable High School, the youths proceeded to the schoolyard and began filling in the holes that had been dug for the mobile classrooms. In his surveillance report on the demonstration, an undercover officer claimed that if Willis did not step down by July 16, organizers were threatening to "turn to more violent methods of protest."[49] While such rumors in the hands of undercover "Red Squad" operatives must be scrutinized with care, what happened next in West Garfield Park seemed to confirm the move toward aggressive forms of protest. On July 18, ACT called another antipolice demonstration—this time at the Fillmore District Police Station. This time things quickly got out of hand when a crowd of over one hundred teenagers stoned police and beat three white bystanders. Initially outraged by the rumor that police had taken Nahaz Rogers, the crowd became even more aggressive after a police officer applied a chokehold to a nineteen-year-old marcher and sprayed his face with mace. Attesting to the links between youths at the core of this demonstration and the many more potential sympathizers in the surrounding community, the angry crowd outside the police station soon grew to some two thousand people, with many among them throwing rocks, bricks, and bottles. By the time it was over, the watch commander at the station reported that two police officers had been hospitalized and nineteen police cars had been damaged.[50]

Once again police brutality against a young man was the spark that could ignite the kind of outrage that moved people to act with their feet. That same day, CCCO convener Albert Raby had led an anti-Willis march of one hundred demonstrators from Grant Park into the South Side. Three marchers were arrested for blocking traffic at 64th Street and Cottage Grove Avenue, but even with news of an upcoming meeting between the CCCO and Martin Luther King in the air, this march failed to muster much energy. What had happened in Garfield Park, on the other hand, had planted seeds of rebellion. Framing the meaning of why two thousand people found themselves gathered outside the Second District Police Station that night were ACT banners that read "Black People Must Control the Black Community." Protesters, as many in the crowd learned, had begun their demonstration that afternoon by picketing the local firehouse for its failure to recruit black firefighters. Police brutality, especially when it involved a white officer and a black youth, was the ideal expression of the lack of control black residents possessed over their community and their everyday lives, but the turn to police power also opened the way to a broader critique of race and state power at the grass roots— one that fit bogus mobile classrooms, white beat cops, and lily-white firehouses into the same framework. On August 13, as the fires of the Watts rebellion blazed for a third day, this West Side neighborhood showed the fruit that such direct-action tactics and consciousness-raising could yield.

In an uncanny and tragically poetic twist of fate, a speeding fire truck from this same neighborhood firehouse swerved out of control and knocked over a stop sign, which struck and killed a twenty-three-year-old African American woman. The next night a youthful crowd of over three hundred battled with police, sparking two days of rioting that resulted in some sixty injuries and over a hundred arrests. Occurring in the context of the devastating Watts riot, which began with a routine traffic stop gone awry and then continued with clashes between youth gangs and police, the struggle for community control between gangs and police took center stage in black Chicago. For leaders of the nonviolent movement, gangs would need to be reined in so as to allow direct-action protests to continue without the risk of urban disorders; for those who saw the need for more militant tactics, street gang members seemed like the perfect soldiers—if not leaders—in the battle for community control. Relegated to the role of community problems for many years, gangs appeared suddenly in the guises of social bandits and tragic victims of white oppression. Speaking to a crowd gathered in front of Crane High School on the second day of the Watts riot, an activist captured what an increasing number of people were coming to feel about the youth gangs in their neighborhoods:

> "O.k., they tell me they writin' up in the paper big, 'Two Gangs Was Fightin'.' Ain't that awful. But did you ever notice they got 'em where you see four guys standing on a corner, you see the police come and break it up because they know the time has come when you got 18 or 19 or 20 gonna start goin' out and fight for what they want. Not just fightin' each other no more; going over there and taking stuff from the white people that they have took from us. And it's not a gang you understand."[51]

"WE'S ALL PRINCES": NATION GANGS, CIVIL RIGHTS, AND BLACK POWER

It was only a matter of time before gangs themselves began to recognize their part in the drama unfolding around them. Beginning with Chief Wilson's mandate to crush gangs in 1961, the early 1960s was a period in which gangs would have had great difficulties envisioning themselves as anything other than criminals. The script began to change, however, during the rush of civil rights activism that hit Chicago in 1963 and 1964. Explaining their political turn to their biographer years later, members of the Vice Lords, the West Side's most powerful gang during the mid-1960s, dated their awakening to the summer of 1964. Interestingly, the leaders of the Lords at that time—men in their twenties who had met in 1958 while serving sentences at the St. Charles reformatory—appeared as invested in the youth cause as anyone else in their West Side community of Lawndale. What they claimed motivated their decision to "do something constructive" that year was a conversation that transpired on the sixteen hundred block of Lawndale between some of these older members and the "younger dudes" in the gang. As the story was told, after listening to the youngsters complain, "We can't get jobs, we're too old to go back to school, and we're too big to play games," a revelation took hold of the chiefs: "The fellas looked around and saw how many had been killed, hurt, or sent to jail and decided they didn't want the younger fellas coming up to go through the things they did and get bruises and wounds from gangfighting." To be sure, "doing something constructive" was by no means a purely political idea in its inception; no doubt influenced by increasingly fashionable Black Power notions about developing African American communities through black entrepreneurialism, the Lords initially conceived of their turn from gangbanging as an opportunity to "try to open some businesses."[52] Yet Watts had a dramatic effect on their thinking. "When the riots started in Watts in 1965," some Lords later claimed, "most people felt kind of proud because somebody could do something like that."[53]

With a territory that extended into neighborhoods in which ACT was operating in the summer of 1965, it is hardly surprising that the Vice Lords began to see their role in the community in somewhat different terms around this time. However, if the influence of ACT made the Vice Lords a somewhat precocious case in the process of gang politicization, even for them this story had hardly begun. Black Power consciousness was increasingly taking hold among Chicago's African American gangs, especially in the aftermath of Watts, but notions of racial solidarity and empowerment were by no means trumping the often brutal struggle for supremacy and respect on the streets. In fact, between the spring of 1965 and the summer of 1966, Chicago's largest and most fearsome fighting gangs—the Vice Lords and their West Side rivals the Egyptian Cobras, as well as the South Side's Blackstone Rangers and their rivals the Disciples— could think of little more than multiplying their numbers; their very survival depended on it. By the end of 1966, the Blackstone Rangers were believed to represent some two thousand members and the Conservative Vice Lords between fifteen hundred and three thousand; other black gangs like the Disciples, the Roman Saints, and the Cobras likely possessed memberships of at least several hundred—large enough to resist incorporation and maintain their territories.[54]

The way these gangs came to hold the allegiance of thousands of youths across wide swaths of city space by the late 1960s, thus becoming *super gangs* (the term adopted by sociologists in the early 1970s), or *nations* (the term these gangs used beginning in the mid-1960s), was a matter of some debate among those invested in the situation—the gangs themselves, activists and youth workers, the Chicago police department and the mayor's office. As the politics of police brutality became enmeshed with the politics of community control, it is not surprising that Mayor Daley would find himself in a public relations war over the propriety of his police department's aggressive law enforcement tactics in black neighborhoods. Street gangs were naturally positioned squarely in the crossfire. They were, according to their critics, guilty of vicious crimes and therefore deserved rough treatment. But to an increasing number of residents in certain black South and West Side neighborhoods, even those who were not yet quite willing to go so far as casting gangs in the role of social bandits, gang members were nonetheless sons, nephews, cousins, and sometimes daughters and nieces. Nation gangs around this time were overwhelmingly male, to be sure, but they usually encompassed female branches—the Vice Ladies, the Cobraettes, and the Rangerettes, for example. And they always incorporated junior and sometimes midget divisions, a situation that was often disquieting for parents but which also indicated just how broadly representative of the surrounding community these organizations were.[55] Moreover, the school protests and boycotts of previous years had revealed to many black Chicagoans that a great deal of these gang youths had dropped out of school as a result of systemic discrimination. More and more residents thus began viewing the punishment they received from cops on the streets as evidence of such problems.

Still, even with such forms of consciousness gaining ground, the case the police were making against gangs still had plenty of support in black communities. The GIU claimed that street gangs had used "organized terror and violence" to advance their enormously successful recruitment campaigns between 1965 and 1967. A 1969 report issued to the media by the mayor's office entitled "Organized Youth Crime in Chicago" described a pattern of intimidation employed to coerce teens into joining gangs. In one 1965 incident that the mayor's office represented as typifying the "deadly recruitment drives," a leader of the Del Vikings gang, an affiliate of the Disciples, gave the order to "burn" (shoot to kill) two teenagers who had refused to join. The report also highlighted how recruitment methods had terrorized black schools on the South Side: "On a single day at the beginning of the last school year, gang members carried their street battle to the halls of three high schools. Police responded to calls of shootings and possession of guns in the schools. At one high school the principal resorted to negotiations with top gang leaders hoping they would stop recruitment of students on their way to school."[56]

It is not hard to discern the political maneuverings behind such declarations. In the hands of Daley's public relations team, lawless gang behavior now seemed to explain two of the main problems for which the mayor had been criticized by African American residents for most of the decade—defective black schools and brutal cops. Moving even further with this logic and echoing a growing idea among policy makers that black ghetto neighborhoods were culturally dysfunctional or "pathological," the report concluded that gangs were responsible for nothing short of the "destruction of social values in the neighborhoods they terrorize." "Deadly recruitment drives and murderous conflicts over gang territory," the mayor's office pointedly declared, "cannot be justified by self-serving statements of community support."[57] Yet despite so obviously being put to the service of Mayor Daley's political agenda, the GIU's account of recruitment tactics by Chicago's most powerful black gangs held some undeniable truth. In September 1966, for example, the Blackstone Rangers moved to make Woodlawn's Hyde Park High School off-limits to Disciples. The result was a 25 percent enrollment drop; numerous students applied for transfers, and when their requests were turned down, many parents kept their children home from school. After the killing of a local boy scout, a group called Concerned Parents of Woodlawn demanded that police control the Rangers. At a September 26 meeting with police on Disciple turf, enraged residents called for a clampdown, applauding when one person stood up and shouted, "To heck with getting accused of police brutality, let's use some force on these punks!"[58]

Violence was thus an important means of expanding ranks and maintaining discipline. In areas like Woodlawn on the South Side and Lawndale on the West Side, where gangs were engaged in deadly fights to the finish, there were a good many youths who, whether through their own calculation or through pressure exerted by their parents, wanted little to do with this very dangerous world. Faced with such resistance, gangs used violent forms of intimidation to persuade quickly and effectively. It must be remembered, moreover, that in neighborhoods like these, youths were no strangers to gunshots and bloodstains on the streets. To many of them, the risks of staying out of this world might have seemed lower than the risks of entering it. On the other hand, the gangs could not afford to lose unaffiliated youths to their rivals, and they could never be certain a group of teens refusing to join them would not at some point run with their enemies. Violence thrived in such circumstances. Even the former gang leaders and sympathetic community activists who have sought to play down the use of coercive recruitment methods by gangs like the Rangers and the Vice Lords seem mostly to be employing a different notion of violence rather than denying its presence. Several Vice Lords, for example, claimed in 1973 that the gang stopped fighting wars and gangbanging during its period of expansion after 1964.[59] Yet when former leader Bennie Lee spoke of his own incorporation into the Lords in 1967, he described being forced to fight an older and bigger kid in the Vice Lords. A few days later, some forty Vice Lords surrounded his gang in an effort to recruit them. "Now we 12, 13 and they 17, 18," Lee recounted, "and they said who y'all's Chief? And everybody looked right at me and that scared me to death."[60] Once again, Lee's fear at that moment reflected a sense that the danger he was facing was quite real. Yet what happened next in Lee's account reveals that the threat of physical pain was not the only element pushing youths into the ranks of nation gangs: "So they said well you guys gotta come to this meeting at . . . Church, it's a church over here on . . . A business meeting, a Vice Lord meeting, be there." Lee's crew went and soon their gang, the Apache Vice Lords, belonged to the Nation of Lords.[61]

Some obvious reasons explain why this particular confrontation led to confederation rather than violence. The Vice Lords were older and stronger than Lee's group, and they were more numerous. As nation gangs like the Vice Lords, the Rangers, the Disciples, and the Cobras began to expand, their ability to accomplish their recruitment objectives without resorting to violence naturally increased. Yet other significant factors accounted for why these gangs gained adherents so rapidly in these years—

circumstances that lie at the heart of the debate over the nature of the recruitment process and, in a larger sense, over the story of gang politicization. One of these was the emergence of an enlightened and charismatic set of leaders who recognized larger goals than the mere accumulation of muscle on the streets and who viewed themselves as "organizing" or "building something" rather than just recruiting. Another was the realization among more and more youths that joining these gangs was the most promising avenue to empowerment—an idea that in itself was moving somewhat away from traditional conceptions of manhood and street respect and toward a mix of Black Power ideas involving racial unity, the struggle for civil rights, community control, and black entrepreneurialism. Both of these factors appeared to be at play when Bennie Lee and his friends joined up with the Conservative Vice Lords. The Lords who surrounded them were certainly flexing their muscles for effect, but the leadership of the gang at this time was pursuing a different path from previous years—one more inclined to organizing than coercing.

John Fry, a Presbyterian pastor who was working closely with the Blackstone Rangers, attributed a similar "organizing style" to the Rangers: "In dealing with new fellas or new clubs, the Rangers did not force the issue . . . so that after being forced, the new fellas would hate their conquerors.[62] And during 1966 and 1967 gangs like the Rangers and the Vice Lords were in the process of gaining the kind of credibility in their communities that made them effective organizers. The church that the Lords referred to that day, for example, was most likely the Stone Temple Baptist Church at 3622 West Douglas Boulevard, the site of recent meetings between top representatives of the SCLC and the Vice Lords. Such events were frequent between June and August 1966, when virtually every major civil rights organization in Chicago sought an audience with the Conservative Vice Lords and the Blackstone Rangers. Already admired by teens and kids in the community for their swagger, the attention given to these young men by Martin Luther King and other civil rights leaders made them local heroes in the eyes of the younger generation. In Woodlawn, boys as young as eight and nine formed "Pee Wee Ranger" groups, and kids throughout the area could be heard shouting "Mighty, Mighty Blackstone!" in the playgrounds and schoolyards.[63] In Lawndale, young boys crowded around the Vice Lords as they stood on street corners and donned oversized berets like the ones worn by some of the Vice Lord chiefs.[64]

A key turning point in the story of Chicago's super gangs occurred in the spring and summer of 1966, when Martin Luther King and his team

Figure 9. A Blackstone Ranger spars playfully with a neighborhood youngster. The Rangers were idolized by many children in the community. Photo by Declan Haun, courtesy of the Chicago History Museum, ICHi-51722.

of Chicago activists set up meetings with leaders from a number of black gangs—the Rangers, the Vice Lords, the Disciples, the Cobras, the Roman Saints, and the Del Vikings the most notable among them. King's SCLC had responded affirmatively to calls from the CCCO to join its movement, announcing in September 1965 that Chicago would be its first northern campaign. In early January 1966, the new SCLC-CCCO coalition released its Chicago Plan, which included first mobilizing and educating a nonviolent army of protesters and then, beginning in the spring, carrying out a series of demonstrations in an effort to eliminate the city's massive black slums. As the SCLC-CCCO geared up to take its battle to the streets in early May, the focus turned to Chicago's street gangs. Summer was approaching, and after the events of the previous summer, leaders of the Chicago Freedom Movement (CFM) feared that the outbreak of rioting might jeopardize their nonviolent campaign. Some believed that gangs could not only be persuaded to refrain from rioting but might also be convinced to help keep the cool on their respective turfs. Moreover, the sheer numbers of youths loyal to these organizations made them useful to King and Al Raby's objective of amassing an army of nonviolent protesters—even if including them came with the additional challenge of keeping them nonviolent.

On May 9 James Bevel and Jesse Jackson held what they referred to as a leadership conference for a group of over 250 Blackstone Rangers at the Holy Cross School at 65th and Maryland. Wanting to make an imposing first impression, the Rangers gathered beforehand at 64th and Blackstone and marched to the meeting together. Once there, SCLC representatives showed them a film of Watts rioting and engaged them in a discussion on nonviolence. Over the next several days, the SCLC set up additional meetings with both the Disciples and the Rangers, a few of which Martin Luther King attended personally.[65] In the first week in June, the Chicago Freedom Movement's gang point men took their show to the West Side, where they organized meetings with some of the area's most powerful gangs.[66] A relationship was clearly developing between the SCLC, in particular, and gang leaders. In late June, one of the SCLC's key gang organizers, the Reverend James Orange, took several members of the Vice Lords and Rangers on a Freedom Ride to Mississippi. Then, on July 9, the SCLC hosted over fifty gang leaders for a First Annual Gangs Convention at the Sheraton Hotel downtown.[67] Highlighting the great importance with which SCLC-CCCO organizers held the participation of street gangs in their campaign, they had scheduled this event the day before their first big civil rights rally.

The next day, however, when the Chicago Freedom Movement gathered its army at Soldier Field for a show of unity and strength, serious tensions in the relationship between Chicago's black gangs and the movement revealed themselves for all to see. A group of some two hundred Vice Lords, Blackstone Rangers, and Disciples occupied the center of the field, several waving a large white banner with the words "Black Power" written in bold letters. King had on several occasions discouraged the use of this term, and those holding the sign were perfectly aware of the effect it would have on many in the crowd of some thirty thousand. Then a scuffle ensued between some of the gang members and a few journalists snapping photos, and several minutes later, without warning, the whole group abruptly marched out of the stadium. Afterward it was learned that a gang member had apparently heard one of King's top men insult the gangs, remarking something to the effect that they were not needed because they would only cause trouble. Upon hearing about the affront, several gang leaders gathered and decided their groups would all depart in unison on signal.[68]

With CFM officials predicting a crowd of one hundred thousand, the turnout was already being spoken of as a disappointment; the gaping hole in the center of the crowd where the gangs used to be seemed to speak volumes about why. For those close to the gang-organizing effort, however, this incident came as no surprise. The nonviolent style of struggle met with skepticism and outright criticism on the part of gang members from the beginning. On one occasion the Rangers ridiculed the idea of singing freedom songs, causing the physically imposing James Orange to shout back, "You think you're too bad to sing? Well I'm badder than all of you, so we're going to sing."[69] The display of bravado worked at the time, but deeper problems lingered. Perhaps most important, gang members could not stomach the idea of putting their necks on the line for nonviolent demonstrations whose impact was dubious at best. From the start, mainstream civil rights leaders asked them to be prepared to go to jail and take beatings for the cause, an affair that in the minds of many gang members offered little payback.[70] After a meeting with South Side gang members in early May, a detached worker close to the gang told a GIU undercover observer that "the boys would never go for this arrangement, because they were more anxious to get jobs than to be locked up in a sit-down demonstration."[71] Longtime Vice Lord Cupid, one of those who marched out of the Soldier Field rally, later described it this way: "I don't believe in nonviolent marches where those honkies be throwin' at me and I can't throw back. I can't sing no brick off my motherfuckin' head. I just can't overcome. If a motherfucker hit you, knock that motherfucker down."[72]

The prevalence of such thinking among Chicago's black gang members was revealed in a more striking display just two days after the rally, when a massive rebellion shook Chicago's West Side. Once again, community perceptions of overly aggressive police tactics against youths provided the spark. This came after police responding to the theft of some ice creams from a broken-down truck at Throop and Roosevelt on the Near West Side manhandled a group of kids seeking refuge from a heat wave in the cool water of an open fire hydrant. As the officers used their nightsticks to subdue six teenagers, a rapidly growing mob began throwing bricks and bottles. Despite the efforts of community leaders from the local West Side Organization (WSO) to calm the crowd, things got out of control. That same night, Martin Luther King addressed a mass meeting at the nearby Shiloh Baptist Church, issuing a strong plea for nonviolence, but many youthful members of the audience abruptly stormed back out onto the streets amid shouts of "Black Power!" The next evening, a meeting between gang members, police officials, and civil rights leaders yielded similar results. When Andrew Young took the podium to make an appeal for nonviolence, a teenager in the audience immediately interrupted him, inviting his "black brothers . . . out on the street."[73] For the next few days, groups of teenagers, many of whom were allegedly members of the Vice Lords and the Cobras, marauded through parts of the West Side, looting, setting fire to buildings, and battling police. By the time a battalion of National Guardsmen had managed to restore order, the West Side riot had caused two deaths, over eighty injuries, and over 2 million dollars in property damage. Mayor Daley exploited the situation by accusing CFM leaders of inciting violence among gangs, pointing to the SCLC's screening of films about Watts as proof. Such ludicrous charges placed the CFM on the defensive, but what was perhaps even more disconcerting about the riot for civil rights leaders was that it had broken out in a spontaneous manner among youths unaffiliated with any of the city's notorious gangs. It seemed to reveal a general mood, not a plan. While rioting soon spread to the outer edges of Vice Lord territory, at the edge of Garfield Park, the first stages of this rebellion had little to do with the city's rising super gangs. What had transpired related more to a general upsurge of Black Power sensibilities; King and the SCLC, it appeared, were not reaching the younger generation of black Chicago.

Nonetheless, despite this falling out between the CFM and Chicago's black super gangs, and in spite of a general suspicion of nonviolence among many gang members, when the time came to march into some of Chicago's most racist white neighborhoods, at least some of the super gangs were still willing to answer the call. After a mob of angry white residents stoned hundreds of marchers in the lily-white Southwest Side community of Chicago Lawn on July 31, the SCLC-CCCO mustered up a larger group for the next march into Gage Park. Among the group of some fourteen hundred gathered at the New Friendship Baptist Church before the march, a GIU operative counted more than two hundred members from a range of South and West Side gangs; having sworn to observe the rules of nonviolent protest, they were there to serve as marshals for the march.[74] A number of Blackstone Rangers participating in the demonstration wore baseball gloves to catch bottles, bricks, and stones hurled at the marchers.[75] Despite their best efforts, however, they were no match for the thousands of whites who showered them with hate and debris, even fiercely battling with police to get at the demonstrators. A brick struck Martin Luther King in the head, opening a bloody gash, and he was not nearly the only casualty. Faced with such violence, much of it perpetrated by kids and young men of about their same age, the gang members kept their word. As King recalled after the march, "I remember walking with the Blackstone Rangers while bottles were flying from the sidelines, and I saw their noses being broken and blood flowing from their wounds; and I saw them continue and not retaliate, not one of them, with violence."[76]

In spite of this symbolic triumph, that bloody day in Gage Park destroyed what little was left of the alliance between Chicago's nation gangs and the nonviolent movement. South Side gangs like the Rangers and the Disciples had participated in the march because King had personally managed to patch up relations between the gangs and the CFM in the aftermath of the civil rights rally and some West Side riot. On the other hand, relations were still tenuous with some West Side gangs, who were noticeably absent from the event. The gangs who did come no doubt recognized the historic opportunity they had been handed. These gang youths had been marginalized in their own communities, knowing only the glory of a world disparaged by many of those around them. The attention King and other civil rights leaders bestowed on them inserted them into the flow of history itself. Despite losing their loyalty in the end, the SCLC had moved forward a project begun by groups like ACT and SNCC: to develop in gang members and other youths a sense of historicity. Ironically, however, this same consciousness empowered the super gangs to the extent that they no longer needed the SCLC-CCCO, making them wary of being submerged in a movement directed by people they considered outsiders. Although the philosophy of nonviolence was problematic for gang members, especially as frustrating negotiations between the mayor and the CFM leadership revealed the humiliations suffered in Gage Park to have been of little effect, their sense of losing their autonomy was perhaps even more integral to their turn away from the CFM.

Some West Side gangs, for example, had little patience for movement leadership. At one heated June meeting with civil rights organizers, a West Side gang leader stood up and characterized "civil rights leaders as not knowing where they are going themselves," warning that "if the gang was misused the civil rights groups would be blackballed on the Westside."[77] Around this same time, by contrast, members of this very same gang seemed more receptive to organizations focused on their specific neighborhood and on problems that touched them more directly than the idea of being able to purchase a home in a white middle-class area. On June 11, West Side gang leaders were on the podium for a civil rights rally followed by a march to protest the shooting of James Meredith and the murder of Jerome Huey, a black youth beaten to death while job hunting in Cicero.[78] Nine days later, an undercover GIU operative spotted several gang members attending a meeting of a neighborhood tenants' rights group, where nearly a hundred residents discussed strategies for challenging the abuses of their landlords.[79] Such evidence suggests that when the East Garfield Park Community Organization newsletter declared "Vice Lords Join Movement" on July 25, 1966, the "movement" being referred to was not exactly the same one that SCLC-CCCO leaders were trying to incorporate them into. And when Vice Lord leader Duck (James) Harris told the East Garfield Union to End Slums (EGUES) that "the Vice Lords have joined the movement to help organize the people" and that they were "going to stop gang-bangin' and help people get out of the slum," they were mostly talking about the people of their own West Side turf.[80] Martin Luther King had been instrumental in the founding of EGUES, and its members were certainly grateful for his support, but the success of this organization hinged on its local focus. When EGUES brought slumlords to the negotiating table that summer, people were given a direct taste of empowerment that was lacking in the nonviolent movement. They saw immediate and tangible results from their actions.[81]

The SCLC-CCCO was surely somewhat out of touch with the reality of many gang members. However, any citywide movement would have run up against similar problems; these street gangs had developed within a logic that placed a premium on autonomy and the control of turf, and they followed a code by which one never allowed a physical attack to go unchallenged. Black Power ideas of community control and self-defense were thus a much better fit with the consciousness and experience of gang youths. And as the SCLC-CCCO was leading hundreds of marchers into ambushes on the white Southwest Side, others in black Chicago were rallying around Black Power. At a Black Power rally attended by West Side gang members on July 31, 1966, speakers referred to the beatings of civil rights leaders in Gage Park that very day, advocating the use of violence to deal with such acts by "Whitey," and discussed the importance of gangs participating in the defense of the black community.[82] Just four days earlier, Stokely Carmichael, the field secretary of SNCC, had spoken at another Black Power rally in the Chicago area (Evanston), where he had urged blacks in Chicago to regain control of their communities and not be afraid to use violence in doing so. During his speech, Carmichael was flanked by Edward "Fats" Crawford, a leading figure in the Chicago chapter of the Deacons for Defense and Justice, an armed self-defense group that worked with ACT and the Vice Lords on the West Side.

It would be a mistake, however, to attribute the Black Power ideas developing among Chicago's black super gangs to national leaders. Challenging the dominant view held by historians that Black Power was an externally derived ideology that dropped down into urban contexts in the throes of nonviolent civil rights campaigns, Robert Self and Matthew Countryman have recently demonstrated that, in the cases of Oakland and Philadelphia, Black Power consciousness was much more of a homegrown product that reflected the frustrating experiences of activists with integrationist, nonviolent forms of struggle.[83] The story of the Vice Lords and the Rangers suggests this was no less true in Chicago. As the national battleground for the northern civil rights campaign between 1966 and 1968, Chicago represents a somewhat unique case. Stokely Carmichael, H. Rap Brown, and other key figures in Black Power thought were not infrequent visitors to the city, and the links between them and local leaders like Lawrence Landry and Fats Crawford were substantial. The localization of Black Power ideas, however, occurred less through these activists, however important they may have been, than through the words and deeds of a charismatic group of gang elites. The reinterpretation of Black Power by these gang leaders became the gospel of the streets.

While a good many of these leaders were men in their mid- to late

Figure 10. A Blackstone Ranger and Rangerette stroll down the street. The appearance of natural hairstyles and floral African-inspired clothing among some members of the gang reflected the growing influence of black power consciousness in the mid-1960s. Photo by Declan Haun, courtesy of the Chicago History Museum, ICHi-51723.

twenties who were able to use their street experience to garner the respect of teenagers, perhaps the most charismatic of them all was Ranger leader Jeff Fort. At just nineteen in 1966, Fort was already one of the most influential members of the Main 21 governing body that directed the many semiautonomous groups that composed the Blackstone Ranger Nation. Somewhat small in build, Fort's ability to capture the hearts and minds of teens on the South Side, more than his ability to rumble, elevated him through the ranks. Fort articulated a variant of Black Power ideology shaped to the context of black youths on the South Side of Chicago. John Fry, the white pastor of the First Presbyterian Church of Woodlawn, which beginning in 1966 provided the Rangers with a space to organize and meet, captured one of Fort's greatest rhetorical moments in December 1966, during a key moment in the gang's turn to the politics of community control. After invoking images of ancient Africa and describing the advent of the slave trade, according to Fry, Fort whipped the "younger fellas" into a frenzy of excitement when he delivered the following discourse: "We's still dogs—the way they look. They not even let us starve to death. They gotta be messin' over us all the time we's only tryin' to starve to death. Whoeee! No way we gonna run this here govament. All the studyin' we do ain't gonna change one thing. So what we gonna do? We gonna have our own govament, the way our daddies did long time back. And what peoples git messed up by the polices and such is gonna be our peoples. They don't let us in their govament, we git our own."[84]

Then, after speaking about police harassment, Fort brought the house down when he declared, "That ain't right, cause WE'S ALL PRINCES," and then commenced with a description of strong, beautiful princes with rings on their fingers and crowns on their heads. As Fry relates the rest of the story, kids in Woodlawn spent the next several weeks scrawling variations of the word "prince" on walls all over the neighborhood until someone wrote out "Black P. Stone Rangers." The name stuck and Fort thereafter took the nickname of "Black Prince."[85] The sociologist John Ogbu's idea of a "coping mechanism" helps to make sense of why Fort's vision of black princes caught on among youths in Woodlawn. Ogbu has described immigrants as possessing a sort of cultural capital in that when faced with racism they can fall back on their origins in a foreign land, where they occupied positions of status and dignity. Lacking this resource, Ogbu argues, African Americans in the postwar United States have instead created an "oppositional culture" that devalorizes performing well in school and on the job as "acting white."[86] Debatable for its tendency to divert attention from the effects of institutional racism, this idea of a coping mechanism nonetheless seems to explain the fascination with Fort's story, which appeared to answer a need to construct an identity and a history that transcended the ghetto. It is likely this need became more pressing as civil rights consciousness penetrated the South and West Sides and the gap between what was being demanded and the reality of everyday life widened.

The leadership talents of Fort and others—Lamar Bell and Eugene Hairston of the Rangers, David Barksdale and Nick Dorenzo of the Disciples, Bobby Gore and Alfonso Alford of the Vice Lords, among others— were too valuable to be overlooked. Their value derived not only from their ability to mobilize but also from their capacity to demobilize. Watts and then the outbreak of more urban disorders in the summer of 1966 had placed Great Society Democrats on the defensive. Ronald Reagan's use of backlash law-and-order rhetoric had won him the 1966 gubernatorial election in California, and with a presidential election looming in 1968, Johnson administration officials were looking for damage control as the summer of 1967 approached. Moreover, the Great Society project of investing in lower-income urban communities and of allowing them "maximum feasible participation" in the process was put on the line with each outbreak of violence. To successfully incorporate gangs into the legitimate local power structure would have yielded the kind of win-win situation that political strategists dream of. And that gangs were useful to Washington suddenly made them useful to local organizations seeking federal funds for community development programs as well. As it hashed out the details of a youth program with officials from the Office of Economic Opportunity (OEO) in early 1967, the Woodlawn Organization (TWO) found Washington totally unbending on one major point— that the gangs themselves be given a substantial role. The result several months later was a $957,000 OEO grant for a revolutionary youth project that used the Woodlawn area's existing gang structure—the Blackstone Rangers and the Devil's Disciples—as the basis of a program to provide remedial education, recreation, vocational training, and job placement services to youths.[87] Inspired by their South Side rivals, the Vice Lords registered as a corporation in September 1967 with the help of a researcher who met the gang's leaders when conducting a study on gang youths for the President's Council on Youth Opportunity. By early 1968 the gang had obtained a $15,000 grant from the Rockefeller Foundation and a matching grant from a private sector urban renewal campaign called Operation Bootstrap.

The subsequent story of the involvement of the Rangers, the Disci-

Figure 11. Members of the Blackstone Rangers pose in 1967, during the gang's involvement in the Office of Economic Opportunity's Youth Manpower Project. Photo by Declan Haun, courtesy of the Chicago History Museum, ICHi-51724.

ples, and the Vice Lords in youth services and community improvement projects is as complicated as it is controversial. Several scholars and activists, most of them somehow associated firsthand with the organizations involved, have attempted to sort out some of the issues surrounding the scandals and legal proceedings that led to the termination of funding to such programs. For gang sympathizers, the argument is generally that Mayor Daley used the Gang Intelligence Unit to actively harass, infiltrate, and subvert the gangs involved in these programs, because their apparent success compromised his power on the black South and West Sides—areas of the city that had traditionally delivered a strong vote for the Daley Machine.[88] Those who have made this argument have pointed to the reinforcement and reconfiguration of the GIU in 1967 occurring not coincidentally while TWO, the Rangers, and the Disciples awaited notification of funding from the OEO. Gang sympathizers have also referred to the anti-Machine activities of the Rangers and the Vice Lords, including their support of anti-Machine aldermanic candidates and their active promotion of a 1967 mayoral election boycott which dramatically reduced Daley's vote totals in what were formerly known as the "plantation wards."[89] They could have made even stronger cases had they the benefit of seeing the GIU's files, which, as a result of a 1981 court decision in an ACLU lawsuit against the city's political surveillance activities, are now accessible to researchers. Despite the destruction of a large part of the files, what is left provides compelling evidence of the role the GIU played in sabotaging these programs. Readily apparent from a survey of the files is the presence of infiltrators who not only observed proceedings and dug up dirt, but also planted the seeds of destruction in the already fragile alliances of gangs, community organizations, and Black Power groups.

Of particular interest to GIU operatives were any signs of cooperation between the different super gangs, as well as the developing links between the gangs and a range of Black Power groups—ACT, RAM, SNCC, the Afro-American Student Association, the Deacons of Defense, and later the Black Panthers. The intense attention paid to the shifting alliances between these groups suggests a deep concern in the mayor's office about the possible threat posed by the organizing activities under way in black Chicago beginning in the spring of 1967. The surveillance, to be sure, went way beyond sniffing out possible criminal enterprises, and even if the threat of a Black Power plot to foment urban disorders was somewhat credible during these years, the large body of investigators' reports that deal specifically with the political and social activities of the Rangers, the Disciples, and the Vice Lords can hardly be explained away in this manner—as the city attempted to do. As John Hall Fish has argued, most observers, including a team of independent evaluators appointed by the federal government to examine the OEO grant program, tended to agree with TWO's spokesman, the Reverend Arthur Brazier, that "the project was killed because the political establishment could not tolerate an independent community organization such as TWO receiving federal funds that were not controlled by the Establishment itself."[90] According to Fish, there were just too many interests in Chicago—the mayor, the police, and even the social services community—invested in the failure of TWO's program.[91] The team of independent evaluators went so far as to say, "The fact that the program had positive results is remarkable in view of the extraordinary opposition to it."[92]

While the most cynical of detractors would paint these "positive results" as mere attempts to create interference for those suspicious of ongoing criminal activities, the list of achievements that can be credited to the Rangers and the Disciples in a relatively short span of time is impressive: They staged a successful musical production, *Opportunity Please*

Knock, under the direction of jazz pianist Oscar Brown, that played to sold-out audiences for six weekends. They helped to calm near-riot situations in their territories on a number of occasions, including most notably after the assassination of Martin Luther King, when rioting broke out in many other areas of the city. They managed a truce during their involvement in the TWO program, and according to the TWO evaluators, played a key role in significantly reducing the violent crime rate in the Third Police District. Their vocational training efforts led to the placement of between 83 and 107 of 634 trainees in jobs—results that the TWO evaluators qualified as equal to or better than most programs of this kind in the city.[93] Across town, in the Lawndale area, with much less funding but nearly as much police malevolence, the Vice Lords boasted an even more remarkable set of accomplishments, including a highly successful neighborhood cleanup campaign ("Where there was glass there will be grass"), a vocational training program funded by the Coalition for Youth Action and the U.S. Department of Labor, a Tenants' Rights Action Group that blocked forty-three evictions and relocated thirty-two families, the operation of two youth centers and an employment agency, the opening of an African heritage shop and snack restaurant, and the launching of an art gallery ("Art and Soul"). As in Woodlawn, moreover, such activities corresponded with a drop in violent crime.[94]

The memory of these striking accomplishments has been deeply tarnished by the Daley administration, which declared its War on Gangs in 1969, and by the sensationalistic media coverage of the hearings of Senator John McClellan's Permanent Subcommittee on Investigations of the Committee on Government Operations in the spring of 1968. Seeking to expose the shortcomings of the program, McClellan charged, among other things, that the OEO grant was a "payoff" for peace in black neighborhoods, that the Rangers had demanded kickbacks from trainees (who were paid a modest weekly stipend to attend job-training programs), and that the gangs had used the program as a front to continue their criminal activities, which included murder, robbery, rape, and extortion. Such allegations, while substantiated by the subcommittee's very dubious star witness, George "Watusi" Rose, a former Ranger warlord turned police informant, were enough for the OEO to pull the plug on the Youth Manpower Project. For their part, the Vice Lords continued on after 1968, but their image suffered enormously as well from scores of highly publicized legal problems, including the controversial murder conviction of their talented leader Bobby Gore, who to this day maintains his innocence. Typical of how the local press, especially the notoriously pro-Daley *Trib-*

une, exploited the legal problems of the Vice Lords and the Rangers to arouse outrage about their community activities was the June 21, 1969, edition of the *Tribune,* which included a story about Vice Lord murder convictions beside another entitled "U.S. and Private Grants Pay Big Dividends to Street Gangs."[95]

Yet while Gore may have been innocent of the charges against him, he candidly admits that many in his gang were not as able as he was to trade their gangbanging ways for the roles of students, activists, or youth workers. In an interview conducted for a History Channel documentary on the Vice Lords, Gore argues that the GIU's success in sabotaging the efforts of the Vice Lords was made possible by members of his gang continuing to commit murders, robberies, and rapes. Gore claimed: "We screwed ourselves somewhat, because had it not been for guys doing dumb shit—excuse the expression—they wouldn't have had the excuse to pounce on us as they did."[96] Such observations surely apply to the Rangers and the Disciples as well, pointing to a broader interpretation of why the Daley regime was so effective in writing the end to this story. Gore's comments suggest that despite the hopes raised by gang leaders and the political organizations working with them, and in spite of the advent of new notions of respect and pride on the streets, there was still not nearly enough of this emotional capital to go around. The search for manhood and respect continued to push youths affiliated with these gangs into violent acts, and the gang leadership structure was not nearly strong enough to do much about it, especially as the GIU continued to target the most powerful gang leaders in a concerted strategy to cut off the heads of the nation gangs.

Moreover, truces between gangs did not mean that tensions between them disappeared. Sublimated violence resurfaced in new forms—for example, in conflicts between the leaders of different gangs over ideology, strategy, and leadership. The most compelling case of such tendencies occurred in the spring and summer of 1967, when a coalition of Black Power groups and community organizations attempted to bring about an alliance of Chicago's black street gangs. Not surprisingly, this project was an object of intense scrutiny by the GIU. On July 24, GIU operatives spied on a West Side rally of some twenty-five hundred people at the Senate Theater. After hearing rousing speeches on black unity and self-improvement, a representative from a newly formed black youth alliance announced the unification of several black gangs, hailing this step as a way of ending "the senseless killing of black brothers by black brothers."[97] Plans were in place for a meeting of gang leaders from throughout the city on August 1, and hopes were high that such efforts would lead to an accomplishment that would greatly strengthen the power of the loose coalition of Black Power organizations seeking to mobilize residents of the South and West Sides.[98]

Such hopes were in vain. The alliance was finished before it even got started. The challenges such an alliance faced could be observed a few months earlier at a talk given by Stokely Carmichael at the WSO headquarters followed by an SNCC-sponsored dance at the South Side's Grand Ballroom. As a speaker was presenting the cast of *Opportunity Please Knock,* a Vice Lord grabbed the microphone out of his hand and blurted out, "No mother-fucking-body speaks for the Vice Lords—not even the Blackstone Rangers."[99] This was not the only sign of the Vice Lords' jealousy over the new citywide prestige and power enjoyed by the Rangers. Rumors circulated around the streets that the Vice Lords were unhappy about the attention being given to the Rangers and were thinking about assassinating a Ranger to provoke a war between the Rangers and the Disciples.[100] Nor were tensions between the Rangers and Vice Lords the only kind standing in the way of gang unity. The peace between the Disciples and the Rangers was continuously on the verge of breaking down, because of disputes over the gangs' respective roles in the Youth Manpower Project, and the West Side Cobras were frequently hostile to the efforts of the Vice Lords to promote gang unity. Such jealousies and suspicions were quite useful to GIU operatives looking to provoke feuds between gang leaders who were, despite their new political and social vocations, still concerned with keeping up their reputations on the streets.

Even more damaging to the possibilities of gang politicization, however, were tensions developing *within* Chicago's nation gangs in this same moment. What scholars examining the world of black street gangs during these years have overlooked is the degree to which many gangs were divided over questions of ideology and political commitment. By the spring of 1967, Black Power thinking and its most vocal promoters—groups like ACT, RAM, SNCC, the Black Panther Party, the Afro-American Student Association, and the Deacons of Defense—had an increasingly strong influence on local organizations on the South and West Sides, gangs and community organizations alike. As Bobby Gore explained, the Vice Lords were divided between members who were fully engaged in the struggle for community improvement and others who were unable to give up the pursuit of respect on the streets for higher goals. The Rangers present an even more striking case of a gang divided. In the spring and summer of 1967, a number of incidents revealed a deep split in the gang's leadership over its commitment to Black Nationalism and the Black Power movement. In late May, a heated exchanged occurred between the Rangers and the Disciples when four Rangers crashed a Disciple meeting and berated them for not joining the "Black Power movement," as they had. Things got so tense that a Ranger pulled a .38 revolver. By early that summer, some committed Black Nationalist Rangers were beginning to break away from the nation, a trend that prompted a special meeting of the Main 21 to formulate a response to the situation. In a move that indicated how irreconcilable the differences between the faction of Black Nationalists and the rest of the gang had become, those at the meeting decided that allowing the others to split off into their own group was the best idea, even if this new group would remain part of the Ranger Nation. That same day, the Black Nationalist Rangers, many of whom were participants in *Opportunity Please Knock,* held a separate meeting during which they discussed the formation of their own group called the Black Brothers.[101] The members of this faction distinguished themselves from the rest of the gang by wearing African necklaces and their hair in "the natural style." The Disciples as well were rife with such tensions. That same summer, for example, a Disciple leader had "turned Black Nationalist" and was in the process of organizing youths around South State Street between 55th and 63rd.[102]

Such events reveal the importance of Black Power ideology to the consciousness of black youth gangs in the urban North as they became disenchanted with the integrationist struggle and with a political system that continued to exclude them. Even those considered to be outside the influence of Black Nationalism, such as Jeff Fort, drew certain elements from its critique and its mystique as they sought to capture the loyalty of youths out on the streets. "Black Power," as Robert Self has argued, "was an extraordinarily plastic concept."[103] In the hands of people like Jeff Fort it largely represented the continuation of the same logic of turf control that had organized black street gangs since the 1950s. For the Black Nationalist faction within the Ranger Nation, Black Power was part of a larger project that linked the Rangers' own community to some sense of a black diasporic struggle. Dashikis, skull caps, beads, and natural hair styles were all relatively new to black Chicago in the mid-1960s, but the origins of Black Power sensibilities had deep roots in the street gang experience. Street gangs and youths in general had been controlling turf, defending the community (from white attacks and at times from black ones), and challenging police for years. Yet if Black Power ideology turned street gangs toward politicization, it also contained elements that limited how far down this road they could go. In particular, the idea of community control in the minds of street gangs already fixated on the boundaries of their turf made the project of uniting gangs an impossibility. When Jeff Fort electrified his audience of young Rangers by telling them "We gonna have our own govament," few in the room imagined the "we" to include the Disciples or anyone else in the city for that matter. Then there were problems arising from the emphasis that Black Power placed on "power." After being courted by nationally recognized civil rights leaders and then—in the cases of the Rangers, the Vice Lords, and the Disciples—given the chance to earn income and praise by working to improve their communities, the thousands of youths affiliated with these gangs expected a piece of the action. But there was not nearly enough to go around, and affiliation with power is not always the same thing as power.

Yet it would be erroneous to characterize black street gangs in this moment as incapable of imagining communities that stretched beyond their neighborhoods and, as such, largely uncommitted to broader struggles for civil rights and Black Power. Sudhir Venkatesh calls attention to the tendency of scholars to treat the gang "as a monolithic entity, with a single-mindedness of purpose and outlook," reminding us that "within any gang there could be competing and entirely conflicting understandings and expectations of gang activity circulating among the members."[104] This perspective explains a great deal about the political turn of Chicago's nation gangs in the mid-1960s and about the scholars who have sought to make sense of the story of gang politicization. Citing the continuation of gang fights and criminal activities, scholars have tended to view gang politicization as something flawed and disingenuous. Taking up this question with regard to the Rangers and the Disciples, for example, Irving Spergel, who headed the team of evaluators assessing the Youth Manpower Project, argued that these gangs represented "an alternative to politicization" and that they "clearly avoided commitment or systematic engagement in race-related issues and activities. . . . They were primarily concerned with their power, not Black power."[105] This perspective contains some fundamental elements of truth that help us to understand why gangs would encounter great difficulties in working with both civil rights leaders and community organizations—why they would be continuously paranoid of attempts to strip them of their autonomy and power. Yet this view also unfortunately obscures some very important dimensions of the story of gang politicization—in particular, youths' attempts to reconcile their commitment to the struggle for gang empowerment with their engagement in the fight for civil rights and Black Power. Such perspectives tell us very little, for instance, about why a GIU agent would spot two South Side gang members talking with a group of students about Black Power and voting unity outside of Hyde Park High School one afternoon.[106] For such youths and many others in the black gang world, the challenge was to make "their power" and "Black Power" one and the same.

CONTROLLING SCHOOL: RACE, POWER, AND CULTURE IN CHICAGO HIGH SCHOOLS

Important links indeed existed between Chicago's black super gangs and an emerging Black Power student movement in the fall of 1967. Here the motives of gang leaders are often hard to decipher. High school students, particularly dropouts, were the lifeblood of super gangs, and one could argue with good reason that much of the involvement of gangs in the developing student movement in black Chicago had more to do with recruitment goals than with the objective of promoting Black Power. In fact, the two motives are hard to disentangle because the spread of Black Power consciousness among high school students made appeals to racial solidarity, pride, and power essential to any attempt to capture their hearts and minds—even when the ultimate purpose of winning this loyalty was to advance the ends of the gang rather than the community or the race. Gangs, because of their militant style and their ability to mobilize and demobilize thousands, were pushed to the vanguard of the Black Power movement during its early stages, but a wave of youth mobilization soon overtook them.

By the fall of 1967, a range of Black Power student organizations, from informal "Afro-American history clubs" to militant protest groups, had begun to develop in and around Chicago's high schools. Radicalized and mobilized by some of the same forces that had worked to transform black super gangs, student organizations quickly added another key dimension to the politics of community empowerment—the struggle for control of black schools. In pushing school concerns back to the center of black protest politics, where they had been until the SCLC-CCCO turned the CFM toward the segregated real estate market, student groups moved alongside street gangs as networks capable of mobilizing hundreds and even thousands into militant action. In fact, gangs apparently had little to do with the previously mentioned gathering outside Hyde Park High School. According to observers, the meeting grew out of a heated class discussion which, after being cut short by the period-ending bell, students

decided to continue after class.[107] Yet the gang members were likely waiting outside the school, because they were well aware of the new spirit of
militancy that was taking hold of students in South and West Side schools.
As black students revealed their power to organize, agitate, and disrupt
the status quo, they became valuable to both street gangs and political
organizations, both of which needed numbers to advance their objectives.

The subject of intense discussion at Hyde Park High School that day
had something to do with volatile events that were transpiring at a nearby
South Side high school in the Kenwood area. In response to an incident
of police brutality the previous day, a flyer had been circulating around
Forrestville High School on September 14 announcing a school boycott
and "street rally" at a neighborhood spot called "The Wall" at 43rd and
Langley Avenue. "POLICE TOM SQUADS BEAT BLACK BROTHERS AND
SISTERS AT FORRESTVILLE SCHOOL," the flyer declared. "HOW LONG
ARE WE GOING TO TAKE THIS?"[108] The rally brought out an angry crowd
of more than five hundred students and some three hundred police officers.
Speakers described a number of recent incidents of police brutality, including the beating of an eighteen-year-old woman by officers breaking
up a scuffle between youths. As the crowd became more unruly listening
to such outrages, Black Nationalist leader Russ Meek addressed the students, decrying residents in the area for their "apathetic attitude" about
the attack and claiming that right after it had happened "the streets should
have been filled with black people." Later than night, after snipers fired
on police from a rooftop around 43rd and Langley, a mob of youths gathered at Forrestville High School hurled rocks and bricks at police, who
began pushing against the crowd with clubs drawn. A riot seemed im-
minent. Before the situation got out of hand, however, Herbert "Thun-
der" Stephens, leader of the Four Corners Rangers and member of the
Main 21, stood up to talk to the crowd. "The city is going to have to start
listening to people in the neighborhood," he declared. But Stephens was
not there to incite the crowd. He told the angry protesters, "We don't want
this neighborhood to turn into another Newark or Detroit," and then he
ordered them to clear the streets. "All you who are willing to die, step up
now—otherwise, let's go home," Stephens reportedly said. Within five
minutes, the crowd had dispersed. According to police, who as a matter
of policy seldom admitted to the media that gangs were capable of anything redeeming, this intervention helped avert a riot. "If he hadn't stepped
up when he did we'd have had to use force," an officer told the *Tribune*.[109]

The Forrestville High disturbance was the precursor of a broader trend of high school activism that would pull the Black Power movement toward the issue of community control of schools over the next few years, and it reveals a great deal about the circumstances and complexities this trend would bring. While schools had been central to civil rights militancy between 1963 and 1965, the trajectory of mobilization largely began with parents and local civil rights organizations and then moved into the schools themselves, where students became participants by joining the boycott and attending "freedom schools" and meetings. The events around Forrestville revealed very different dynamics of organization and mobilization, with the impetus for action originating within the high school and from there spreading out into the surrounding community. Interestingly, while some of the incidents of police brutality that sparked the Forrestville rally involved students, the demonstration had little to do with school in any direct sense. That school became the focal point for protest action in this case had to do with both the enormous growth of Black Power consciousness among youths and the organizing efforts of a number of Black Power organizations. While high school students constituted most of the participants in the rally, for example, its organizer was Yaree Ameer, the twenty-one-year-old leader of a small Black Nationalist group called the Young Militants and a direct action coordinator for SNCC.[110] And while a crowd of protesters eventually assembled at the high school later in the evening, it is important to point out that the rally itself took place several blocks away from school, in front of the "Wall of Respect"— a huge mural painted earlier that year depicting black cultural figures like Malcolm X, Thelonious Monk, W. E. B. DuBois, Muhammad Ali, and Billie Holiday, which, according to the GIU, was "a regular meeting place for . . . 'Black Nationalist groups'" during this time.[111]

The Wall of Respect and the many rallies that took place in its vicinity thus illuminate the emergence of a full-blown Black Power culture that stretched from classroom to street corner, encompassing average students, young activists, and gang members. Elements of this culture were palpable in the racially charged street battles of the late 1950s and early 1960s, but this new formation represented a dramatic break from the past. Never before had African American youths in Chicago possessed such a keen sense of cultural identity—a consciousness of consciousness itself. This new awareness helps to explain why school once again became vital to black contentious politics. It was not only because of a need for new soldiers in the battle for rights and empowerment, though in the aftermath of the failed campaign in the Bungalow Belt that was certainly an important consideration. School moved to the center of Black Power culture and politics in part because of its centrality to what was becoming to many the movement's greatest challenge—the struggle for control of the black mind. A sign of the times in the fall of 1967 was the appearance of scores of black political groups calling themselves "history clubs" and a number of black student organizations—Students for Freedom, the Afro-American Student Association, the Black Student Alliance, and the Young Militants, among others—defining their objectives in predominantly pedagogical terms. For example, the "purpose" of the Young Militants, according to Ameer, was "to teach Afro-American history, revolutionary politics, and other things to the brother"—not to protest, but to teach.[112] It was not a matter of happenstance, moreover, that the Wall of Respect—a bold metaphor for the project of black psychological liberation and cultural self-determination—served as a meeting place for these groups. Just two weeks after the Forrestville rally, several hundred attended a dedication ceremony for the wall that included poets Don Lee, Larry Neal, and Gwendolyn Brooks, as well as Maulana Karenga and *Ebony* magazine editor Lerone Bennett.[113] Speakers that day returned repeatedly to the theme of cultural liberation, referring to the myriad ways "whitey" had destroyed black people's sense of their own beauty and cultural heritage. The event was, of course, well monitored by the Chicago police, whose reporting officer observed, "A great number of persons present were adorned and dressed in African type clothing and jewelry.[114]

Historians who have sought to make sense of this turn away from political and economic issues toward cultural nationalism have focused on two interrelated sets of causes—one revolving around the contributions of black political leaders, artists, and intellectuals; the other emphasizing the impact of years of frustrated attempts to gain equality and justice in the spheres of school, work, and residential life. Such analyses have pointed to the immense influence among black political leaders of Frantz Fanon's classic book *The Wretched of the Earth*, which was first published in the United States in 1965 and had sold over 750,000 copies by 1970. Heralded by Black Panthers Eldridge Cleaver and Bobby Seale, SNCC's James Foreman and Stokely Carmichael, and CORE's Roy Innis, Fanon's analysis of the consciousness and culture of colonized peoples, as the story goes, elevated the fight for cultural liberation and showed that "Afro-American culture" was potentially the most useful resource in the struggle for empowerment.[115] Such accounts are not inaccurate, but they have done a better job of understanding the thinking and rhetorical postures of political leaders than they have of explaining why ordinary people found such ideas appealing and how they acted on them in the context of their everyday lives.

Black teens in Chicago were no doubt discussing Fanon, cultural liberation, and the politics of history in the organizations and clubs they were forming, but as the Forrestville demonstration reveals, their activism also grew, to a great extent, out of their determination to eliminate the indignities they faced in their daily lives—whether being roughed up by cops, being attacked by white youths (when they attended mixed schools), or being insulted by white teachers. School was where they spent most of their waking hours, and it was thus where they would take up the fight. Moreover, school had also been where many of them had learned powerful lessons about the struggle for rights and justice. Youths in their late teens and early twenties—the predominant members of the student organizations forming in 1967 and 1968—came of age politically during the first push for school integration between 1963 and 1965. Harrison High student Victor Adams, who would emerge the following fall as one of the city's most influential student leaders, had Al Raby as a teacher at Hess Upper Grade Center and was an active participant in the anti-Willis boycotts.[116] Riccardo James, a student activist at Austin High School in 1967 and 1968, was swept into protest politics partly because of his relationship with his older brother Clarence, who as a senior at Marshall High School in 1965–66 helped to organize the Student Union for a Better Education and participated in SCLC-sponsored retreats.[117] And James Harvey, who as a senior at Englewood High School in 1964 served as a picket captain for a protest against black machine politicians opposing the second anti-Willis boycott, was by the fall of 1967 the South Side coordinator of ACT, the chair of the Afro-American History Club at Wilson City College, and an active member of the Afro-American Student Association.[118] These may be exemplary cases, but it is likely that the vast majority of students who participated in Black Power activities in their high schools in the late 1960s had been significantly touched by the anti-Willis boycotts and the integrationist campaign of the Chicago Freedom Movement.

Yet if the anti-Willis boycotts had aroused the passions of youths like Adams, James, and Harvey for political engagement, their experiences as high school students in 1967 and 1968 offered daily reminders of how little progress the past years of nonviolent, integrationist struggle had produced. Classrooms in black schools remained overcrowded, facilities were generally run down, and black students continued to complain of degrading treatment by white teachers, counselors, and principals. James, for example, related being wrongly accused of plagiarizing a poem by one teacher and of being mocked by another when he said he wanted to apply to Harvard—circumstances that would make James's Austin High a hotbed of student revolt in the coming years. In 1968, African Americans constituted 48 percent of the student body at Austin, but out of 134 teachers employed there only one was black.[119] Austin's rapid pace of racial transition (its student body was less than 1 percent black just five years earlier) contributed somewhat to creating these circumstances, but throughout the city's South and West Sides, even in schools that were entirely black, teachers, administrators, and principals of color were relatively few, and allegations of racism were numerous. James was hardly alone in his criticisms. Patricia Smith, another student leader at Marshall High School in the West Side area of Garfield Park, told a *Sun-Times* reporter about a general climate of racial hostility at her school. She described one particularly racist teacher: "If a young man came into class with his hair natural, the teacher would give him a hard time. . . . Right in front of the whole class the teacher would say, 'man, you're a dummy, you can't learn anything.'"[120]

Such stories illuminate why in November 1967 a seventeen-year-old student at Crane Technical High School on the Near West Side had recruited more than thirty teenagers for a Black Power group he referred to as "Afro-Americans," the membership requirements of which, according to one resident, involved wearing a natural hairstyle and "carved idol necklaces."[121] And they help to explain why, of all the causes for protest that black students rallied behind, control over the teaching of black history emerged as perhaps the key hot-button issue of the Black Power student movement. Calls for black principals, administrators, and teachers were of course quite loudly voiced, but such demands almost always went hand in hand with the curriculum question. However, the battle, in the minds of many students, was not metaphysical or postcolonial, but very much grounded in their relationship to the local "white power structure"—the Daley Machine and its people in the educational system. Nor was this battle discovered by Black Power organizations in 1967. As early as September 1965, youth worker Richard Booze was reporting on ten of his teenagers, aged fifteen to eighteen, speaking about "civil rights groups" protesting the refusal of the administration at Crane High School to rehire a teacher because of his participation in civil rights activities that summer.[122] Hence, while new and fashionable ideas about black cultural pride and spiritual renewal framed the wave of black high school student activism that swept through Chicago beginning in the fall of 1967, student militancy sprang less from such ideological currents than from incidents that revealed the arbitrary and unjust power of white administrators over the educational process in black communities. Such experiences served to crystallize the notion that blacks were engaged in a struggle with a local white power structure actively seeking to suppress their attempts to mobilize for their rights. School administrators, moreover, were hardly the only agents of this offensive. Any youth with any connection at all to Chicago's super gangs was fully aware of the GIU's efforts to monitor, manipulate, and sabotage their political projects. Gang leaders and activists alike spoke candidly about the many infiltrators in their midst. It was not hard to put two and two together.

Intimate knowledge of such police tactics perhaps worked to make members of these gangs some of the most militant activists in the fight for control of black schools. When in late November 1967 Englewood High School students boycotted and rallied for a week to protest the firing of Owen Larson, a history teacher and adviser to the school's Afro-American History Club, the Englewood Disciples appeared on the front lines of the protest. According to the white principal of the school, Thomas Van Dam, Lawson had been discharged because of his "administrative incompetence" and his excessive use of class time to teach Afro-American history, but the ousted teacher claimed he had been fired because he was "a black teacher in a black school teaching black children black pride." Englewood High was on Disciple turf, but the gang's enthusiasm for the nonviolent campaign to have Lawson reinstated may also have been related to members' firsthand experiences with the meddling of GIU operatives during their involvement in TWO's Youth Manpower Program. Gang members attended meetings along with parents, teachers, and students concerned about the firing; a spokesperson for the gang told the press that they were "100 percent behind Mr. Lawson" and that they would do "anything necessary" within the bounds of nonviolence to pressure the school to rehire him.[123] Less publicly, however, the gang spoke in more ominous terms, threatening protesters on one occasion that they would have two days to settle the matter and then the gang would take over.[124] Such tensions between gangs and more peaceful participants in the Black Power movement were not uncommon. In the Forrestville demonstration, the Four Corners Rangers somewhat surprisingly played the role of peacemaker, owing to the desire of the Main 21 to avoid riots in its territory for fear of the Daley administration and the media using such disorders to attack their involvement in the Youth Manpower Program. Two months later, with the program under full attack by the

GIU and several Ranger and Disciple leaders under arrest, such concerns seemed less relevant, particularly in the eyes of the disgruntled Disciples, who always saw themselves as secondary participants.

While gangs remained important to the Black Power movement for their capacity to organize and mobilize, by the spring of 1968 students were beginning to take things into their own hands and lead the way. In March, a pulled fire alarm began a demonstration of some three thousand students at South Side DuSable High School against "whites teaching African history."[125] Then, on April 5, a crowd of high school and middle school students gathered in Garfield Park to mourn the killing of Martin Luther King sparked widespread rioting in the city when they began tearing up West Madison Street. While Mayor Daley immediately blamed gangs and Black Power militants for the disorder—a view that would come to justify his order to "shoot to kill" arsonists and "shoot to maim" looters—his own Riot Study Committee found that thousands of ordinary West Side high school students pouring out of schools and meeting up on streets and in parks precipitated the riot.[126] In May, African American students picketed at Gage Park High School to show solidarity against the beating of black students by whites.[127] And in June, students at Farragut High School in the West Side Douglas Park area launched a campaign to raise awareness about inadequate school facilities and overcrowded conditions.[128]

When classes resumed in the fall of 1968, just after the "whole world" watched Chicago cops in riot gear savagely beating demonstrators at the Democratic national convention, rebellion spread through the black student population. During the week beginning on Monday, October 7, black student activists staged wildcat walkouts, sit-ins, and rallies at a number of black high schools, including Waller, Wells, Harrison, Austin, Fenger, Morgan Park, and Lindbloom; at numerous others, school officials reported a sharp increase in scuffles between black and white students, pulled fire alarms, and acts of vandalism.[129] Harrison and Austin, two neighboring West Side schools with roughly half-black student bodies, took center stage in the media coverage. At Austin, a thousand black students walked out of classes and about five hundred of them attended a Black Power rally in the school auditorium voicing demands for more black teachers and administrators. At Harrison, as many as three hundred students attended a three-hour-long sit-in in the school's lunchroom conducted by a student protest group calling itself he "New Breed." After being broken up by police, a crowd of nearly eight hundred marched downtown to the Board of Education. Led by Harrison seniors Victor

Adams and Sharron Matthews, the New Breed had been staging walk-outs and sit-ins since mid-September to pressure the school's white principal to agree to their demands that more black teachers and administrators be hired, that courses in Afro-American history be offered, and that students and parents in the community be granted a role in school decisions and disciplinary procedures.[130]

The following Sunday, Adams, Matthews, and twenty-three other student leaders from thirteen high schools gathered to plan a citywide boycott and hash out a coherent list of demands to put before Superintendent James Redmond and the Chicago Board of Education, forming in the process an umbrella organization called Black Students for Defense. The manifesto they released that day reflected how prominent the politics of cultural recognition had become for student activists in black Chicago. At the top of the list of demands, even before calls for black administrations and more black teachers, were the separate demands for "complete courses in black history" and "inclusion in all courses of the contributions of black persons." A request for school holidays "on the birthdays of such black heroes as Marcus Garvey, Malcolm X, W. E. B. DuBois, and Dr. Martin Luther King Jr." appeared in the seventh spot, complementing the curriculum issue. Rounding out the list was an assortment of more mundane if nonetheless important demands, including more vocational classes, better upkeep of black schools, insurance for athletes, the use of black businesses to supply class photos and school rings, better food, military training "relevant to black people's needs," and more homework. The students told the press they were calling for a citywide boycott every Monday of every week until Superintendent Redmond granted their demands.[131] The next day between twenty-seven thousand and thirty-five thousand students stayed out of school, with many attending numerous rallies going on across the city. The following Monday, October 21, more than twenty thousand students and about six hundred teachers participated in the boycott. However, by the Monday after that, only about nine thousand students boycotted school. The movement had clearly lost its momentum.[132] Throughout the rest of the school year, protests and walkouts occurred periodically at several black high schools, including Harrison, Hyde Park, DuSable, Parker, and Calumet, but the moment had clearly passed.

Despite its somewhat anticlimactic end, the high school student movement could certainly claim some important accomplishments—at least over the short term. At a press conference on October 17 and then again at a Board of Education meeting on October 23, Redmond responded positively to most of the student demands. He pledged to extend the half-year Afro-American history course being offered in thirty-six high schools over the whole year, to purchase new textbooks that "placed greater emphasis upon contributions of minority groups," to pursue "efforts to achieve a racial integration of staff throughout the system," and to strengthen relations with parent-teacher associations and student groups.[133] Yet Redmond's concessions amounted to a Pyrrhic victory. The superintendent's rather prompt and upbeat response took a great deal of energy out of the student uprising, the leaders of which were probably banking on some Willis-style administrative stonewalling to help build movement momentum. And perhaps even more important in causing defections in the student ranks was that Redmond coupled this positive response with his announcement of a stern policy of legally pursuing both students and parents for any further truancy violations. With some face-saving concessions on the table, the threat of legal difficulties in the air, and the grades of student activists in jeopardy, parents began applying pressure on their children to go back to school.

Yet if Redmond was adept at defusing the situation, there were other more important reasons why the student boycotts failed to morph into a broader movement that could effect more enduring changes in the educational system of black Chicago. First, despite receiving words and gestures of support from citywide and community organizations like the Chicago Urban League, TWO, the West Side Federation, and the Hyde Park–Kenwood Community Conference, the movement was never really able to broaden its locus beyond the schools and into the surrounding communities in any meaningful way. Black parents and teachers did rally behind the students, forming organizations like Concerned Parents of Austin and Concerned People of Lawndale, but these efforts remained somewhat limited and isolated. Gangs as well remained largely on the sidelines, a situation that perhaps had as much to do with the reluctance of student leaders to work with them as it did with the debilitating legal troubles they were experiencing at that time. On the first day of the boycott, Victor Adams urged gangs to forget about their names and grudges because they had "a bigger gang now—the black people," but not much was heard about gangs after that.[134] Interviewed the day of the first boycott, TWO's president, Reverend Arthur Brazier, conveyed a sense of frustration about black inaction when he declared, "TWO believes the black adult community must support the youths in their fight for quality education. We cannot stand idly by and let them fight this battle alone."[135] The next day, Chicago Urban League executive director Edwin C. Berry voiced what many older blacks must have been thinking. After commending the students for "focusing on the powerlessness of the black community," Berry told the *Sun-Times* that he did not condone the actions of those who wanted to lead concerned students "into possibly nefarious directions."[136] What exactly Berry was referring to is unclear, but his willingness to utter such vague innuendos suggests that they meant something to a substantial segment of the black community. There was speculation that "outside agitators" or "subversive forces" were possibly behind the boycotts, and the press was reporting on the outbreak of sporadic violence involving black students, including a wild, plate-throwing fracas in the cafeteria at Harrison and several brawls between whites and blacks at Austin.[137] Yet it would have been hard to construe such relatively minor and spontaneous incidents as indicative of concerted attempts to steer what was predominantly a nonviolent movement in "nefarious directions." Moreover, if certain Black Power groups—the Illinois Panther Party, SNCC, ACT, or RAM, for example—could be spotted in the mix, there was little evidence to the effect that they played anything approaching a leading role. The problem was that many student activists looked and talked like the members of such organizations. Perhaps more than anything else, Berry's comment thus reveals a generational gap that was widening in the fall of 1968, as students and youths clad in African robes, skull caps, berets, and Maoist army uniforms put their bodies on the line for issues that to older blacks who had lived through earlier civil rights struggles seemed superficial and symbolic. Bayard Rustin probably spoke for many of these older African Americans remaining outside of Black Power campaigns when he called Black Power "a psychological solution to problems that are profoundly economic."

Yet if the cultural politics of student activism caused divisions within black communities, even more significant were the cleavages it ultimately widened within the political culture of Chicago as a whole. In the two schools that had taken center stage in the movement—Austin and Harrison—the idea of a black fight for control was not nearly as simple as it was in the many entirely black schools on the South and West Sides. At Austin, where the school's student body was split nearly evenly between whites and blacks, white students immediately responded to cries for Black Power with their own calls for White Power. On October 15, some three hundred Austin students protested downtown in front of the Board of Education offices; others demonstrated their opposition to black demands by physically attacking black students and actively avenging black attacks on them.[138] At Harrison, where blacks held a slim majority, white opposition was also in evidence, but further complicating things was the presence of sizable Puerto Rican and Mexican minorities, who used the occasion of the black student movement to organize and press for their own "Latino" curriculum needs. The language, style, and rhetoric of Black Power was therefore not only compelling for African American youths, but also for their Latino and white peers, both of whom began clinging even more tightly to their own racial identities and related notions of community control. While the Black Power student movement managed to accommodate the "Latino," or "Spanish-speaking" student movement, as it was variously referred to, there was no middle ground between Black Power and White Power.

Cooperation between African American and Latino students during the initial stages of the student rebellion was made possible, in part, by the spread of Third World Liberation consciousness. Such thinking found powerful expression on the day of the first boycott at a mass meeting held at the Afro-Arts Theater, where an activist known as Brother Akenti spoke of the common battle "against domination" being fought by blacks, Latin Americans, and Asians.[139] And it was no less present in the last gasp of the mobilization, when Victor Adams, addressing the Board of Education on October 30, declared: "The system is either going to have to be destroyed or rebuilt to include black and Latin American people and Chinese people."[140] But the acceptance of Latinos as fellow travelers was also made possible by more homegrown ideological and cultural shifts on the terrain of Puerto Rican barrio youth culture, which had, in turn, facilitated a street-level rapprochement between blacks and Puerto Ricans in Chicago beginning in the mid-1960s. Hostile feelings between Puerto Ricans and African Americans had largely prevailed since the mid-1950s, conflict rooted in the dynamics of alterity operating in street gang subcultures as well as within a housing market in which Puerto Ricans found themselves relegated to apartment buildings in and around low-rent black neighborhoods. Despite such tensions, the forces of racial segregation kept these groups neighbors and schoolmates in parts of the West and Near North Sides of the city. In addition to Harrison, blacks and Puerto Ricans also shared Near North Side Waller High, the site of one of the more impressive student campaigns in the fall of 1968. While youth workers noted considerable antagonism between black and Puerto Rican youths in these neighborhood areas as late as 1965, some signs of change were visible in June the following year, when Puerto Ricans took to the streets in a violent rebellion in the heart of the Puerto Rican barrio.

The Division Street Barrio riot broke out after a white policeman shot twenty-year-old Arcelis Cruz while attempting to break up a gang fight. Although the officer maintained that Cruz was pulling out a revolver, the rumor that the shooting came without provocation found a more receptive audience in a community in which youths and gang workers had for years been complaining about racially charged police brutality and harassment. Coming in the aftermath of a Puerto Rican carnival in the area, the shooting sparked an immediate explosion of rage that lasted for three days. The thousands that took to the streets vented most of their anger against the police forces that came to quell the disturbance, hurling bricks and bottles at them and setting their cars afire.[141] Many barrio residents had formerly lived in the Near North area, where tensions between Puerto Rican and Italian youths had led to numerous shootings and street brawls. To make matters worse, Puerto Ricans alleged that police regularly took the side of the more established Italian community, a charge that led to a U.S. Attorney's Office investigation after police responded to a street fight between Puerto Ricans and Italians by indiscriminately arresting and roughing up Puerto Rican youths in the vicinity.[142] By the mid-1960s, Puerto Ricans had little patience for such treatment, especially in the heart of the barrio, where they were emboldened by the sense that white police officers were intruders in their community. In the months leading up to the riot, tensions mounted between residents and police, as allegations of police brutality went unanswered and residents complained of police "spying" on and arresting youths without cause.[143]

The Division Street riot rapidly radicalized a large segment of the Puerto Rican community, spawning the formation of a number of community organizations—including the Spanish Action Committee of Chicago and the Latin American Defense Organization—that sought to mobilize Puerto Rican residents against the discriminatory practices of both the police department and welfare agencies.[144] As in black Chicago around this same time, the issue of police brutality moved to the forefront of this developing engagement with the state, a situation that youths out on the streets had played a big role in engineering. That the triggering incident of the Division Street riot involved a police officer and a gang youth was telling, but even more suggestive was the number of youths in the crowds that rose up so swiftly to challenge police in the barrio streets. Reporting on the Puerto Rican uprising, the *Sun-Times* observed that "the crowds were made up largely of teenagers"; the *Tribune* described "bands of young Puerto Ricans and others" at the center of the action. Other observers noted that the Latin American Boys Club in the heart of the barrio was the primary site of crowd gatherings and that local youth workers played essential roles in preventing youths from engaging in violence, at one point even persuading some youth gangs to assist them in pacifying the crowd.[145]

Striking parallels with what was transpiring on the nearby black West Side were readily apparent, and black civil rights leaders quickly took notice. In the days following the Division Street riot, CFM representatives met with some fifty members of three different Puerto Rican gangs on two occasions to discuss marching on city hall and joining ranks.[146] Even more compelling in this regard was the attendance of Vice Lord leaders at a meeting in the barrio of some of the most powerful Puerto Rican gangs, including the Latin Kings and Latin Eagles.[147] While such events directly involved a small contingent within the barrio, news of these cooperative efforts spread fast within the tight-knit barrio gang subculture. Moreover, the idea that Puerto Ricans had much to learn from their black neighbors was not exactly new; Puerto Rican youths in particular had reached across to the black community before in order to make sense of their own situation. If, because of the dangers of racial proximity to blacks, many Puerto Ricans had been ambivalent about considering "Black Power" as something that applied to them, they had been incorporating its ideas about racial solidarity, direct action, and opposition to the "white power structure" into their own context since the early 1960s. As in black Chicago, this spirit of militancy emerged first and foremost within youth subcultural spaces. As early as 1962, Puerto Rican gangs began referring to themselves as "Boricuas" and using the term "Boricua Power." In late July of that year, for example, seventy-five members of a South Chicago gang called the Boricuas came all the way up to an Italian carnival at Our Lady of Pompeii Church to avenge the beating of a Puerto Rican youth from the area.[148]

For some Puerto Ricans, African Americans remained mortal enemies on the streets and people to be avoided in the quest for social mobility; others were no doubt jealous of the attention blacks were receiving while the problems of Puerto Ricans remained invisible. But for an increasing number of young Puerto Ricans, discovering their own historicity and awakening to the struggle for empowerment in the midst of the civil rights and Black Power movements was an experience that brought them spiritually, politically, and culturally closer to their black neighbors and classmates. The most well-known product of this process was the Young Lords street gang, which, under the leadership of José "Cha Cha" Jimenez, had transformed itself into a political organization styled after the Black Panther Party by the fall of 1968. While the Young Lords would eventually form a working relationship with the Illinois Panthers, in early November 1968 they were sharing ideas and socializing with the Disciples and the Blackstone Rangers.

Yet despite such signs of political cooperation between black and Puerto Rican radicals, the relationship between them remained largely trivial throughout this upsurge of student radicalism. At the outset black student leaders took pains to construct the idea of a coalition of nonwhites—generally blacks, Puerto Ricans, and Mexicans—in rebellion against the white power structure, but in practice such assertions rang hollow.[149] Regardless of the lip service paid to such ideas, the black and Latino student movements ran parallel to each other rather than achieving any meaningful collaboration. Emulating their black classmates at Harrison, roughly two hundred Mexican and Puerto Rican students participated in the drafting of their own manifesto, which, much like its black counterpart, called for language and history classes better suited to the cultural and practical needs of Latino students, as well as bilingual teachers and Latino administrators. Somewhat smaller Latino student campaigns making similar demands also crystallized at Waller and at Lakeview High on the North Side. Yet when black student leaders appeared in front of the cameras and reporters, they were seldom seen in the company of their Latino classmates. The same cultural nationalist project that had brought black students together offered few bridges to those groups that lay outside the nation or community they were imagining.

For its part, the Latino student movement fared even worse than its black analog in drawing broader community support, and even among students it remained something of a fringe initiative. To some extent, this was an outgrowth of the identity confusion created by the attempt by student leaders to invent and mobilize youths behind what Felix Padilla refers to as "Latinismo."[150] At Harrison, which drew students from an area that had long witnessed conflictual street-level relations between Puerto Rican and Mexican youths, such a project was ambitious to say the least. Geographer Gerald Ropka has shown that Mexican–Puerto Rican residential association markedly decreased between 1960 and 1970, a trend that contributed to the creation of the Mexican enclave of Pilsen and the Humboldt Park Puerto Rican barrio. And as Padilla discovered when he spoke with residents of the Division Street Barrio, racism, juvenile delinquency, and interethnic gang violence were among the leading reasons cited by those relocating within these ethnic enclaves.[151]

The relatively small number of Mexican students at Harrison High

School was in itself testimony to such dynamics of ethnic separation and segregation; it was not by chance that whites and many Mexicans living around Pilsen attended the Froebel branch of Harrison, whose student body was just 2.7 percent black in 1968 (compared with 55.2 percent at Harrison).[152] Such arrangements demonstrated to young Mexicans on which side of the color line they belonged, a privilege they would take to the streets to aggressively defend in the spring of 1973, when the Board of Education discussed closing the Froebel branch and transferring its students to predominantly black Harrison. On that occasion, a young crowd of more than three hundred—some wearing the uniforms of the recently formed Chicago branch of the Chicano Power group the Brown Berets, others carrying signs reading "Viva La Raza" and "La Raza Unida"—hurled bricks and bottles at police.[153] To be sure, such notions of a Chicano race had yet to develop in Chicago by the fall of 1968, but the Froebel affair nonetheless provides a glimpse into how far many Mexicans were from identifying with a panethnic identity that associated them with a group from whom they had been trying to distance themselves for many years.[154] Such feelings were symptomatic not only of the Latino student movement. In the spring of 1967, Puerto Rican activists working on tenants' rights issues that touched both communities described the reluctance of Mexicans to join their ranks. In the organization's newsletter, an activist with the Latin American Defense Organization wrote, "The biggest thing that impressed me in the office was the presence of not only Puerto Ricans, but Mexicans and Americans also."[155] Despite token representation in some Puerto-Rican-led initiatives, Mexicans in Chicago largely abstained from participation in the contentious politics of this moment. In the context of the high-powered racialist rhetoric of the Black Power movement, Latino identity could not avoid taking on an essentially racial meaning as well. For many Mexicans, embracing this in-between but unequivocally nonwhite racial category meant giving up any claims to a white future.

For some Mexican youths, taking a stance meant not only refraining from political activities that would associate them with African Americans and Puerto Ricans; it also involved the temptation of joining the ranks of the White Power counterreaction gaining momentum during the 1968–69 school year. A GIU investigation of gang activity in the far South Side neighborhood area of South Chicago in early October 1968, for example, uncovered talk of an effort to take on the Disciples and the Blackstone Rangers by uniting several white gangs—the Vandals, the Polish Power, the 95th Street Gents, and the Leather Jackets—with Mexican

Figure 12. An army of white youths bearing swastikas and White Power signs takes to the streets to oppose civil rights marches on Chicago's white Southwest Side in August 1966.

gangs like the Spanish Kings and the Royal Lords. According to the informant, many of the youths in these gangs attended Chicago Vocational School on 87th Street, where whites had recently walked out of school to protest racial attacks on them by their black classmates. The same informant, moreover, described the formation of two other White Power gangs—the Third Reich and the Fourth Reich—that were apparently ready to roam all over the city to challenge blacks.[156] While such talk of White Power gang coalitions going to battle with the city's black nation gangs turned out to be somewhat far-fetched, rumors like these nonetheless reveal the emergence of White Power sensibilities among white students who found themselves at the interface of the Black Power challenge. This was particularly the case at racially mixed schools in which African Americans constituted either a numerically strong minority or a slim majority, such as Austin, Morgan Park, and Chicago Vocational. In schools like these, talk of power and control on both sides of the color line translated frequently into fisticuffs.

This was not, however, the first time white youths had mobilized behind languages of white empowerment and community control. Much like their African American and Puerto Rican peers, white youths in some Chicago neighborhoods, especially those living in the Southwest Side Bungalow Belt targeted by the CFM's Open Housing campaign, discovered their historicity and their political agency in the tumultuous summer of 1966. Mirroring the rhetorical strategies of Black Power advocates, white working-class youths on the South Side seized upon languages that infused local anti-integration efforts with the notion that they belonged to a larger historical movement. Several of the counterdemonstrations, for example, witnessed armies of young men marching behind signs emblazoned with swastikas and a range of White Power slogans. Indeed, it came as a surprise to many of the older eastern and southern European immigrants residing on the Southwest Side was that the teenagers and young men of their neighborhoods proved eagerly receptive to the messages of the American Nazi Party's chief, George Lincoln Rockwell. On August 21, for instance, Rockwell addressed a predominantly young male crowd of some fifteen hundred in one of the Chicago Freedom Movement's key battleground areas, Marquette Park, rousing the youths with his call for the mobilization of a "white guard" to battle integration. After police had broken up the anti-integration rally and arrested organizers from the Ku Klux Klan and the National States Rights Party sharing the podium with Rockwell, a mob of some three to four hundred youths marched to the nearby police station to demand their release.[157] This was only the start of a growing relationship between white youth subcultures and extreme-right politics on the South Side. The following year, Chicago police intelligence would report on connections between two "radical" youth gangs on the South Sides and an "extreme right" militia organization.[158] While youthful sympathizers with neo-Nazi and militia causes no doubt represented the far-right edge of the Bungalow Belt, it would be a mistake to view them as fringe elements of the political culture; their anti-government message, symbolized in numerous battles with police, and their articulation of a Manichean struggle between white and black made them the vanguard soldiers of the Silent Majority backlash that Richard Nixon anointed in November 1968.

Epilogue
Somewhere over the Rainbow

The upsurge in grassroots political mobilization that transpired in Chicago's black, white, and Latino neighborhoods in the 1960s was of historically unprecedented proportions. In its breadth and intensity, one can find nothing even comparable in the decades since. In this book I have shown that the languages, actions, and forms of consciousness that worked to expand the political terrain to incorporate formerly excluded actors and issues grew out of the milieu of youth subcultures. This was not just a question of youths increasingly engaging in politically meaningful activities or of politics itself beginning to take shape around the spaces and institutions where the livelihood of youths was at stake, though both of these developments were critical to the political culture of Chicago in the 1960s. Even more important was the dramatic shift in modes of political organization and confrontation, which by the mid-1950s were becoming inextricably bound with racial identities and racial meanings. This was certainly not the first moment that processes of racial and ethnic formation that were most visible on the terrain of youth subcultures played important roles in the politics of everyday life; in this study I have demonstrated that such processes were a pervasive feature of youth subcultural spaces throughout most of the twentieth century.

Yet what began to change in the 1960s was the role of the state in this story, or rather, the presence of the state in the minds of Chicago youths. For white Chicagoans, we can see early glimpses of antistatist sensibilities in the collective actions against racial integration in South Deering and Calumet Park between 1954 and 1957, but it was not until August 1966, with the spectacle of white youth armies marching behind swastikas and "White Power" signs and clashing violently with police to get at civil rights marchers in the neighborhoods of Belmont-Cragin, Gage Park, and Marquette Park that this cognitive turn toward the state manifested itself openly and actively in the streets. After the open housing march in Gage Park on August 5, when between four and eight thousand counterprotesters doggedly battled twelve hundred policemen trying to shield several hundred marchers, a longtime Chicago police officer remarked, "The outrageous cop-fighting we experienced here was about the most vicious I've seen in nearly thirty years of service."[1] About three weeks later, when some fifteen hundred mostly young men gathered for a lively American Nazi Party rally in Marquette Park, Chicago got a glimpse of what white working-class subcultures oriented around racial exclusion had produced. This should not be dismissed as a marginal or fleeting phenomenon. As Tom Palazzolo's two fine documentaries *Marquette Park* and *Chicago Nazis* so vividly show, the American Nazi Party and white supremacist ideology had an enduring influence on white working-class youth culture on the Southwest Side of Chicago into the mid-1970s. The actions of these youths must of course be understood both in the context of community-wide mobilizations as well as in the broader context of the anti-integrationist movement that took shape in the urban North around an ideology referred to by historians as "reactionary populism" in the 1950s.[2] But the role such youths played should not be reduced to that of a footnote of these larger stories; the active and immediate participation youths contributed was critical to bringing white neighborhood resistance out into the streets, as it had been in many Chicago neighborhoods since the 1940s. The rituals of racial exclusion they maintained in their neighborhoods were critical to the sensibilities of community, racial solidarity, and state-inflicted injustice that mobilized broad support for the cause of racial exclusion across working-class Chicago. Indeed, that the idea of Black Power preceded the rhetorical construct of White Power in the white mind should not mislead us to the conclusion that black activists were the first to, in the words of Manuel Castells, "shrink the world to the size of their community" by fusing the notions of community, race, and locality.[3] While scholars have been accustomed to viewing the minority empowerment movements of the 1960s as the events that brought identity politics into the public sphere, such perspectives overlook the long history of white mobilization around the defense of community and identity—a phenomenon spearheaded by young men.[4]

For African Americans in Chicago, the turn toward the local state as an object of political engagement thus came somewhat later than it did for whites, though, once again, precursors can be detected in the late 1950s in communities like Lawndale, where aggressive policing became an emotional issue. Indeed, the Vice Lords who took to the streets in 1961 to protest the beating of a black student around Harrison, and the Crane students who marched in so orderly a manner through the heart of Little Italy the following year to protest violence against black students demonstrated a will and a capacity to mobilize collectively behind a sense of shared identity—a harbinger of the style of mobilization that would prevail in black Chicago by the mid-1960s. As in the white neighborhoods across the color line, youths led the way in articulating the link between racial identity, community, and locality throughout much of black Chicago, establishing very early the cognitive framework within which Black Power sensibilities would develop and take hold. But these precocious instances of collective action responded to injustices that issued from the white communities around them; they emerged out of a pattern of racial and ethnic conflict that had marked youth subcultures on the West Side of Chicago for years. The Crane demonstration, in particular, by replacing violent revenge with nonviolent protest, constituted a response indicative of a highly developed sense of racial solidarity and shared political purpose. By the mid-1960s, after years of watching the battles of the civil rights movement in the South and being around a local movement targeting problems that touched them directly—the conditions of their schools—black youths began to make a more potent turn toward the state as well. The advent of police brutality as a hot-button issue around 1965 completed the process. Not just gangbangers, but all youths out on the streets responded to the appeal of this problem. Chicago civil rights activists very cleverly managed to politicize the two key areas in the lives of youths, but that they were able to do so was due to the youths themselves having already begun to actively and collectively question and challenge the injustices they faced in their everyday lives. Even if the timely interventions of activists were vital in advancing the politicization of gangs like the Blackstone Rangers and the Vice Lords, it would be difficult to argue that these gangs were not already moving in this direction.

For Chicago Latinos, the story was somewhat more complex. Puerto Ricans, for their part, tended to follow the trajectory of the African Americans with whom they had been so often grouped in the informal racial order of the streets. The existence of a large gang referring to itself as the Boricuas as early as 1962 suggests that in the Puerto Rican community as well, youth subcultures constituted sites wherein solidarities spoken through languages of race and community developed, even if such solidarities did not manifest themselves in the same kind of political actions witnessed in the black community around this same time. The impulse for alterity, directed both at the African Americans and the Mexicans around them, played a key role in the crystallization of racial solidarities in Puerto Rican communities, and youths were certainly among those who deployed the most visible and the most powerful strategies of boundary making. By the early 1960s, Puerto Rican youths were also running up against an increasingly hostile police force, and as the Division Street rebellion surely revealed, a sense of engagement with the state had come to coexist with the impulse for alterity in the milieu of Puerto Rican youths. Here again one cannot overstate the role of youths in providing the catalyst for a much broader wave of community activism that challenged the place of Puerto Ricans in the city's racial system. The Division Street riot began with police breaking up a gang fight; the overwhelming majority of participants in the fight were teens and young adults; and youth workers took the leading role in restoring peace and articulating the grievances of the rioters.

For Chicago's Mexican community, a group that often found itself at odds with Puerto Ricans and somewhere in between white and black throughout the 1950s and 1960s, a sense of engagement with the state came later, and when it did, it also emerged, to a great extent, out of the context of youth subcultures. While Mexicans appeared in the ranks of whiteness in both South Deering and Calumet Park, it is likely that, as not infrequent victims of racial aggression themselves in these very same areas, they did not possess the same sense of white solidarity or the same sense of animosity toward the state that their white peers did. Yet like their Puerto Rican neighbors in areas of the West Side, Mexican youths having a propensity to engage in frequently violent strategies of alterity led to the formation of solidarities spoken through languages of race, ethnicity, and community that set the stage for future forms of political mobilization. A case in point is the friction that developed between African Americans and Mexicans around Harrison High School in 1961, when the Latin Counts rallied thousands of Mexican youths to take to the streets in a show of power and solidarity against the black gangs that had been harassing Mexicans as payback for a recent attack on a black student. It was not until 1968, however, when Mexican youths at Harrison helped to build a movement to address the inadequacies of the school for "Latino" students, that anything approaching a broad-based spirit of opposition to the state became visible among Mexican youths in Chicago. By 1973, these sensibilities had been intermingling long enough in the Mexican cultural enclave of Pilsen to create a movement oriented around the defense of community, a shared racial identity, and a sense of state-inflicted injustice. Yet again youths and youth subcultures played critical roles in these events, as the spectacle of young Brown Berets fighting the police and shouting "¡Viva la Raza!" in the streets so strikingly suggested.

The chaotic events around the Democratic National Convention in Chicago and Richard Nixon's "Silent Majority" election in 1968 have come to mark that year as the death knell for the radical political challenges of the decade, thus obscuring our vision of the enormous potential for grassroots mobilization that remained in urban minority communities as the white backlash was gaining traction. By 1968, a palpable spirit of opposition to the Daley Machine circulated though black, Puerto Rican, and Mexican Chicago, creating fertile ground for the growth of new coalitions and new forms of political opposition. To be sure, things did not look good late in 1968, when Senator McClellan's Permanent Subcommittee scandalized the Office of Economic Opportunity grant given to the Blackstone Rangers and the Woodlawn Organization as a "payoff" for peace on the streets, tensions between the Rangers and the Black Panther Party on the South Side reached a crisis point, and an assertive student movement in Chicago high schools failed to muster the kind of momentum that could force the city into anything more than superficial promises. Yet by the spring of 1969, some major developments revealed that the politicized terrain of Chicago youth subcultures still had some fight left.

The first was the official announcement by Illinois Black Panther chair Fred Hampton of the formation of the "Rainbow Coalition," which included the Panthers, the Young Lords, the Students for a Democratic Society, and a radical organization of working-class white youths from the North Side Uptown neighborhood called the Young Patriots. In the months leading up to this announcement, the Panthers had amassed a sizable and devoted following through aggressive recruiting drives targeting the city's housing projects, high schools, and community colleges. The Young Lords had followed their example, leading campaigns against police brutality, gentrification, and inadequate social services that made a strong name for the organization in Puerto Rican Chicago. The merger of these two groups, and the meaning attributed to that merger by the addition of a white working-class group, was of no minor political significance for city politics. The Panthers were already the objects of continuous harassment and infiltration by FBI agents and Chicago Police Red Squad operatives, and the Red Squad did not wait long to extend such tactics to the Panthers' new allies.

A second momentous event that same spring was the attainment of the long-awaited collaboration between Chicago's most powerful black super gangs—the Conservative Vice Lords, the Blackstone Rangers (now known as the Black P. Stone Nation), and the Black Disciples. LSD, an acronym for Lords, Stones, Disciples, was the name given to the coalition that joined the campaign led by a civil rights umbrella organization, the Coalition for United Community Action (CUCA), against discriminatory hiring practices in Chicago's building trades. Although CUCA consisted of some sixty organizations citywide, the muscle LSD provided to the campaign enabled CUCA to effectively shut down eleven construction sites between July 28 and July 30.[5] Even if the *Defender*'s estimate that LSD possessed the loyalties of some fifty thousand members was a bit far-fetched, the specter of thousands of gang members picketing the city's construction sites brought the Chicago Building Trade Council and the Builders Association to the negotiating table.[6] After negotiations broke down in the beginning of September, LSD's leaders—Leonard Sengali of Black P. Stone, Frank Weathers of the Black Disciples, and Lawrence Patterson of the Conservative Vice Lords—rallied several hundred of its members to join Jesse Jackson and his organization Operation Breadbasket in a picket of a new construction site at the Circle Campus of the University of Illinois on the Near West Side.[7] Such pressure forced the Daley administration to broker an agreement between CUCA and the unions, referred to as the Chicago Plan of 1970, which, while failing to adequately address the problem of racial discrimination in the building trades, nonetheless suggested the great potential of such coordinated actions between civil rights leaders like Jackson and Chicago's super gangs.

Contrary to perceptions that the civil rights movement rolled over and died in the wake of the King assassination and the rise of Black Power consciousness across black urban America, some of Chicago's most potent challenges to the city's political status quo were just getting under way in 1969. So what happened? Why, in retrospect, does this moment appear to be a missed opportunity? Why did such coalitions fade away "not with a bang, but with a whimper," and why did it take a heart at-

Figure 13. Young Lords march in the streets by the Cabrini-Green housing projects after the funeral of Manuel Ramos, who was shot and killed by an off-duty police officer in May 1969. The Young Lords were at that time building an alliance with the Illinois Black Panthers, a situation that aroused suspicion about the circumstances surrounding the shooting. Photographer unknown; courtesy of Chicago History Museum, ICHi-51721.

tack in 1976 to finally remove Richard Daley from the mayor's office? Any answer to such questions must first involve a careful consideration of the massive campaign of infiltration, sabotage, and assassination that the Chicago Police Red Squad, in collaboration with the FBI, brought to bear on those who made such coalitions possible. It was not by chance that the GIU threw its blanket of surveillance over the Rangers and the Disciples after they had partnered with TWO and the Office of Economic Opportunity, and it was hardly a matter of happenstance that Mayor Daley and his state's attorney, Edward Hanrahan, launched their "War on Gangs" as the Rainbow Coalition and LSD were gaining momentum in 1969. The now-declassified files on the FBI's counterintelligence program (COINTELPRO) and the partially declassified files of the Chicago Police Red Squad provide clear documentation of the great lengths to which these organizations went to divide and conquer these two coalitions.

One need go no further than the story of Black Panther Party infiltrator William O'Neal, who as director of security for the Illinois chapter of the party played an integral role in instigating conflicts between the Panthers and the Blackstone Rangers, as well as between the Panthers and Students for a Democratic Society. It was O'Neal who furnished authorities with a map of Fred Hampton's apartment—a map used by the Chicago police to conduct a predawn raid on December 4, 1069, that resulted in the deaths of Hampton and fellow Illinois Panther Mark Clark. While a federal grand jury exonerated the assault team, ballistics evidence points to the conclusion that Hampton's death should be viewed as an assassination. Moreover, the operation targeting Hampton, albeit of high priority, represents but one of a multitude of subterfuges, frame-ups, and bogus arrests orchestrated by the Chicago Police Red Squad to effectively quarantine some of Chicago's most talented, charismatic, and politically committed gang leaders and young activists—people like Bobby Gore of the Vice Lords and José "Cha Cha" Jimenez of the Young Lords. In short, the forces of political repression brought to bear on Chicago's nascent reform movements in the late 1960s and early 1970s were devastating in their effects.[8]

Yet as important as an honest accounting of this political repression is to a clearer understanding of the precipitous decline of movement structures like the Rainbow Coalition and LSD, historians should be wary of overemphasizing such forces to the exclusion of other key dimensions of the story. In addition to documenting the tactics the FBI used to undermine alliances between various grassroots organizations in Chicago, the COINTELPRO files also provide a privileged glimpse into why such tactics seemed to succeed so well. They tell, for example, of recurrent tensions between the Black Panther Party and the Blackstone Rangers—of mistrust, swaggering, and meetings breaking down with guns drawn. At a time when few had doubts as to the sincerity of the Black Panther Party's goals in Chicago, Ranger leadership nonetheless moved to prevent the Panthers from recruiting in a huge swath of the territory the Rangers controlled on the city's South Side.[9] To attribute such dissension merely to anonymous letters penned by FBI agents and the cunning deceptions of infiltrators is to overlook vital elements of the cultural and ideological context that ultimately imposed significant constraints on the project of coalition building in Chicago. Both the Panthers and the Rangers were, on some level, manifestations of the same logic of local control that swept through black communities in the urban North in the mid-1960s. The language of Black Power put such thinking to work in a more focused, formally political manner, but similar ideas had been integral to gang subcultures for decades. As much as these sensibilities represented powerful means of mobilizing collective struggles for empowerment at the neighborhood level—whether in the form of protecting gang turf, defending the neighborhood from racial attacks, or building a political movement—these very same sensibilities hindered gangs like the Rangers from imagining political arrangements beyond their turf boundaries. Moreover, the bonds of racial and cultural solidarity, as strong as they could be in black Chicago in this era, were not quite strong enough to get this job done.

This is, of course, not to say that racial solidarities—whether inflected by everyday street-level experiences or by the cultural nationalism of activists or both—were not effective means of mobilizing collective actions, especially when such solidarities fused with struggles for local control. Yet as I have shown in this study, the processes of forging such solidarities were too often intertwined with strategies of alterity, an aspect that reduced them to limited utility in the labor of developing alliances across racial and ethnic lines. Moreover, even when movements managed to submerge the bitter historical legacies of such divisions though languages of postcolonialism and Third World nationalism, as the Chicago high school student movement of 1968 did, the result was the creation of parallel movements in ideological sympathy but with few meaningful touch points of interracial cooperation. The exception here was the Rainbow Coalition that came together in the spring of 1969, which managed to overcome some deeply rooted forms of alterity in its making. The Young Patriots had often used Confederate flags to define the gang's identity in its earlier days, and many of its members allegedly had family members with ties to the Ku Klux Klan; the Young Lords were embedded in a tradition of Puerto Rican cultural nationalism that resisted forms of Latino identification and dreamed of the project of liberating the Puerto Rican homeland from U.S. control; and the Black Panthers were the very icons of a black cultural identity which, despite their best efforts, was difficult to dissociate from separatist and nationalist notions. Although the Rainbow Coalition's very short life in the Chicago political scene makes it difficult to know how it was able to bring together such elements, its exceptional leadership provides at least a partial answer. As reluctant as I am to invoke the "great man theory" of history, Fred Hampton, Jose "Cha Cha" Jimenez, and William "Preacherman" Fesperman (of the Young Patriots) were, by almost all accounts, rather exceptional leaders; the surest evidence of their definitive role in the making of this coalition was the speed with which the project fell apart after the police had neutralized them.

And yet it would be inaccurate to give the impression that all was somehow lost by 1970. A generation of activists came of age amid the rebellions and protests of the 1960s—people well attuned to the new style of politics in Chicago. When Chicago finally elected a reform mayor who stood for transforming the city's racial order and redistributing its patronage resources, it was in part because of the efforts of community organizers who had been radicalized on the terrain of youth culture in the 1960s. While many of the most talented black super gang leaders of this era were dead or in prison in the years leading up to Harold Washington's triumph in 1983, one should not overlook the key role played by the leadership of the Blackstone Rangers back in 1967, when they helped to engineer an effective boycott of a mayoral election that pitted Daley against an uninspiring Republican candidate who had no chance of winning. This election was a turning point in black Chicago. Whereas 86 percent of Chicago's black wards ranked in the top ten vote producers for the Daley Machine in the 1963 election, only 30 percent did so in 1967; the percentage would sink much further, to 14 percent, in 1971, and then to zero in 1975.[10] Indeed, some of Chicago's most effective black leaders throughout the 1970s and 1980s—people like Jesse Jackson and former Black Panther Bobby Rush—earned their legitimacy and their respect fighting alongside Rangers, Vice Lords, Disciples, and Panthers. Yet Washington needed more than the black vote to win, and it took some talented organizers to overcome the historical legacies of racial alterity in Puerto Rican and Mexican Chicago. Pilsen's Rudy Lozano, a Mexican community activist whose political sensibilities were shaped in 1968 when he helped lead the Latino student movement at Harrison High School, was one among a cohort of activists able to convince Mexican residents that voting for a black candidate was in their interest. And in the Puerto Rican barrio, Cha Cha Jimenez was one among a number of activists involved or otherwise touched by the campaigns of groups like the Young Lords and the Latin American Defense Organization, which, by infusing a class-oriented rainbow coalition vision into their community-organizing efforts, were able to help tip the scales for Washington in 1983.

In retrospect, however, Washington's four years in the mayor's office seem like the exception to a long-standing rule. His great victory represented, in some sense, an echo of the Rainbow Coalition spirit that Hampton had helped to inaugurate some fourteen years earlier and which Jesse Jackson attempted to take to the national level in his presidential run of 1984. The groundwork put in place by longtime community activists like Lozano, Jimenez, Marion Nzinga Stamps, and Bobby Rush had opened the door for such a black reform challenge, and the stars had aligned. Yet ultimately Washington's term would constitute another missed opportunity—not just because of the city council that fought the mayor's every move, but also because the political landscape that had made his election possible began to crumble under the mayor's feet. Losing a focal point of opposition as compelling as the Chicago political machine certainly played a part in dampening the spirit of opposition on the South and West Sides, but there was more to it than that. In fact, a strain of black militancy lived on, but it was not the kind Fred Hampton had championed; it was, rather, a form that continued to cling to languages of cultural nationalism and black control. While militant black nationalists like radio commentator Lu Palmer and the Reverend Al Sharpton, who accused Washington of selling out to white "lakefront liberals," gave public voice to such sensibilities, broader shifts could be detected on the terrain of black youth subcultures. For example, by the late 1970s, Jeff Fort had transformed the Black P. Stone Nation into a new organization oriented around Islamic symbols and beliefs called El Rukns. Indicative of how far this shift took black youths away from the problems that had pulled them into political life in the previous decade was Fort's 1987 conviction for plotting a terrorist attack against the United States with the Libyan government of Mu'ammar Kadhafi.

Somewhat comparable circumstances were developing in Puerto Rican Chicago in the 1970s and 1980s, when a number of activists turned away from organizing working-class Puerto Ricans to fight against the injustices they faced in their everyday lives and toward the project of an independent Puerto Rican homeland. The Young Lords had already begun mobilizing behind Puerto Rican independence in the wake of the Rainbow Coalition's dispersion, but by the early 1980s a radical organization called the Fuerzas Armadas para la Liberación Nacional was leading this struggle. When, in the mid-1980s, thirteen residents of the Humboldt Park Barrio were sentenced to long prison terms for conspiracy to overthrow the U.S. government, it was clear that the independence movement was opening up cleavages in Puerto Rican Chicago between those invested in such nationalist dreams and those looking to carve out a living in the barrio.[11] This nationalist project, moreover, reinforced cultural nationalist tendencies that drove a wedge into potential alliances between Puerto Ricans and Mexicans, who themselves began to imbue their communities with a strong sense of Mexican cultural identity beginning in the early 1970s. Despite some significant signs of cooperation between Mexicans and Puerto Ricans based on appeals to "Latinismo"—the mixed-Latino majority Fourth Congressional District, for example, elected the first Latino congressman from the Midwest in 1992—alterity has generally been a stronger force than association for these groups since the 1970s. By 1995, both Puerto Rican and Mexican activists were calling for the breakup of the shared congressional district that their predecessors had struggled to create on the grounds that they were racially distinct groups with only a language in common.[12]

As divisive a force as cultural nationalism was in post–civil rights era Chicago, however, it was no match for the rise of the crack economy in the 1980s, which made Chicago's super gangs into multimillion-dollar business enterprises and offered financial rewards far greater than what many of the youths involved could hope for in the legitimate economy. One result of this economy was that gangs like the Latin Kings, who had once made some gestures toward political activities in the Puerto Rican barrio, now devoted their energies to controlling their territories so as to protect their points of sale. In black Chicago, moreover, the race to control the crack trade created two enormous gang networks—the People and the Folks—that created the conditions of perpetual warfare on the streets with increasingly deadly weaponry. Ironically, the ever adaptable languages of local control and racial empowerment translated very easily into this new environment, but youth subcultures now offered few resources for political mobilization. More than anything else, they embodied the neoliberal spirit of the new times.

Notes

INTRODUCTION

1. Chicago Commission on Human Relations, Documentary Memorandum: Interracial Disturbances at 7407–7409 South Parkway and 5643 South Peoria Street, American Civil Liberties Union, Illinois Division, Papers (hereafter cited as ACLU Papers), Box 7, Folder 5, University of Chicago Special Collections Research Center (hereafter cited as UC-SCRC).

2. Ibid. Arnold Hirsch, the first historian to analyze these events, has referred to them as the Peoria Street riot. For his account, see Arnold R. Hirsch, *Making the Second Ghetto: Race and Housing in Chicago, 1940–1960* (Cambridge: Cambridge University Press, 1983), 71–76, 80–85, 89–93. For another perspective on the riot, see Eileen M. McMahon, *What Parish Are You From?* (Lexington: University of Kentucky Press, 1995), 123–125.

3. Douglas Massey and Nancy Denton, *American Apartheid: Segregation and the Making of the Underclass* (Cambridge, MA: Harvard University Press, 1998). Some of the key works in this "second ghetto" school are Hirsch, *Making the Second Ghetto;* Hirsch, "Massive Resistance in the Urban North: Trumbull Park, Chicago, 1953–1966," *Journal of American History* 82 (September 1995): 522–550; Hirsch, "Race and Housing: Violence and Communal Protest in Chicago, 1940–1960," in *The Ethnic Frontier: Essays in the History of Group Survival in Chicago and the Midwest,* ed. Melvin G. Holli and Peter D'A. Jones (Grand Rapids, MI.: William B. Eerdmans, 1977); Thomas J. Sugrue, *The Origins of the Urban Crisis: Race and Inequality in Postwar Detroit* (Princeton, NJ: Princeton University Press, 1996); Sugrue, "Crabgrass-Roots Politics: Race,

Rights, and the Reaction against Liberalism in the Urban North, 1940–1964," *Journal of American History* 82 (September 1995): 551–578; Charles F. Casey-Leininger, "Making the Second Ghetto in Cincinnati: Avondale, 1925–1970," in *Race and the City: Work, Community, and Protest in Cincinnati, 1820–1970*, ed. Henry Louis Taylor Jr. (Urbana: University of Illinois Press, 1993); Raymond A. Mohl, "Making the Second Ghetto in Metropolitan Miami, 1940–1960," *Journal of Urban History* 21 (March 1995): 395–427; John F. Bauman, *Public Housing, Race, and Renewal: Urban Planning in Philadelphia, 1920–1974* (Philadelphia: Temple University Press, 1987).

4. All the works cited in the previous note have implications for this interpretation. The most explicit challenges to the durability of the New Deal order between the 1940s and 1960s, however, are Hirsch, "Massive Resistance in the Urban North"; Sugrue, "Crabgrass-Roots Politics"; and Gary Gerstle, "Race and the Myth of the Liberal Consensus," *Journal of American History* 82 (September 1995): 579–586.

For examples of studies that view the New Deal coalition shattering in the 1960s as a result of black nationalist ideology, student radicalism, and Great Society liberals outrunning their white working-class base, see Jonathan Rieder, "The Rise of the 'Silent Majority,'" in *The Rise and Fall of the New Deal Order, 1930–1980*, ed. Steve Fraser and Gary Gerstle (Princeton, NJ: Princeton University Press, 1989), 243–268; Thomas Byrne Edsall and Mary D. Edsall, *Chain Reaction: The Impact of Race, Rights, and Taxes on American Politics* (New York: Norton, 1991); and Jim Sleeper, *The Closest of Strangers: Liberalism and the Politics of Race in New York City* (New York: Norton, 1990).

5. The seminal works in the field of "whiteness studies" examine the question of how European immigrants and their progeny "became white" from the 1830s to the 1910s. See, for example, David Roediger, *The Wages of Whiteness: Race and the Making of the American Working Class* (London: Verso, 1991); James Barrett and David Roediger, "Inbetween Peoples: Race, Nationality, and the 'New' Immigrant Working Class," *Journal of American Ethnic History* 16 (Spring 1997): 3–44; Roediger, *Towards the Abolition of Whiteness: Essays on Race, Politics, and Working Class History* (London: Verso, 1994); Theodore W. Allen, *The Invention of the White Race*, vol. 1, *Racial Oppression and Social Control* (London and New York: Verso, 1994); and Alexander Saxton, *The Rise and Fall of the White Republic: Class, Politics, and Mass Culture in Nineteenth-Century America* (London: Verso, 1991).

For a recent study that attempts to periodize the shifting contours of twentieth-century white identity on a national scale, see Matthew Frye Jacobson, *Whiteness of a Different Color: European Immigrants and the Alchemy of Race* (Cambridge, MA: Harvard University Press, 1998). Jacobson views the shift to a more unified form of whiteness that encompassed European Americans as occurring during the interwar period. Other scholars have used local case studies in ways that suggest that this transformation of the racial order occurred somewhat later—in the 1940s and even 1950s. See Hirsch, *Making the Second Ghetto* and "Massive Resistance in the Urban North"; Sugrue, *Origins of the Urban Crisis*, 234, 241; and Gerstle, "Race and the Myth of the Liberal Consensus." For a recent study that complements this research by arguing for the role of the World

War II mobilization abroad in this process of making white Americans out of European ethnics, see Gary Gerstle, *American Crucible: Race and Nation in the Twentieth Century* (Princeton, NJ: Princeton University Press, 2000), 187–237. Much of the work on white identity cited here does not adequately handle the racial predicament of Latin and Asian groups. Scholars of the Mexican immigrant experience have recently begun to emphasize the relationship between Mexican identity and whiteness, particularly from the 1930s to the 1950s. See, for example, Neil Foley, "Becoming Hispanic: Mexican Americans and the Faustian Pact with Whiteness," in *Reflexiones 1997: New Directions in Mexican American Studies,* ed. Neil Foley (Austin, TX: CMAS Books, 1998), 53–70; and Gabriela F. Arredondo, "Navigating Ethno-Racial Currents: Mexicans in Chicago, 1919–1939," *Journal of Urban History* 30 (March 2004): 399–427.

6. On the new social movements, social theory, and identity politics, see Craig Calhoun, "Social Theory and the Politics of Identity," in *Social Theory and the Politics of Identity,* ed. Craig Calhoun (Cambridge, UK: Blackwell, 1994), 9–36.

7. Michel de Certeau, *The Practice of Everyday Life,* trans. Steven F. Rendall (Berkeley and Los Angeles: University of California Press, 1984).

8. Hirsch, *Making the Second Ghetto,* 71–76, 80–85, 89–93; McMahon, *What Parish Are You From?*

9. Chicago Commission on Human Relations, Documentary Memorandum: Interracial Disturbances at 7407–7409 South Parkway and 5643 South Peoria Street.

10. John M. Hartigan Jr., *Racial Situations: Class Predicaments of Whiteness in Detroit* (Princeton, NJ: Princeton University Press, 1999), 4. Hartigan's approach has drawn praise from scholars critical of the imprecision of much of the research on white identity and racial formation. See, for example, Eric Arnesen, "Whiteness and the Historians' Imagination," *International Labor and Working-Class History* 60 (Fall 2001): 25–27; and Thomas J. Sugrue, "Revisiting the Second Ghetto," *Journal of Urban History* 29 (March 2003): 285. For another useful model for understanding the historically contingent and locally determined nature of racial identities, see Tomás Almaguer, *Racial Fault Lines: The Historical Origins of White Supremacy in California* (Berkeley and Los Angeles: University of California Press, 1994).

11. My use of the term *racial system* borrows from Eduardo Bonilla-Silva's notion of a "racialized social system," a term he employs to convey the idea of a society wherein "the placement of people in racial categories involves some form of hierarchy that produces definite social relations between the races." Eduardo Bonilla-Silva, "Rethinking Racism: Toward a Structural Interpretation," *American Sociological Review* 62 (January 1997): 469. I derive the expression *racial and ethnic formation* from Michael Omi and Howard Winant, who define *racial formation* as the "sociohistorical process by which racial categories are created, inhabited, transformed, and destroyed." Michael Omi and Howard Winant, *Racial Formation in the United States: From the 1960s to the 1990s* (New York: Routledge, 1994), 55. These authors view such processes as occurring on both macro and micro social levels. My project here emphasizes how racial and ethnic formation proceeded within spaces of everyday life. Moreover, unlike Omi and Winant, I have chosen to specify that such processes often in-

volved the forging of group identities that were simultaneously racial and ethnic (as well as national and religious) in nature. For simplicity's sake, my notion of "ethnicity" carries with it national and religious elements as well; "race" refers more to color.

12. My idea of *youth subcultures* derives a great deal from the groundwork laid out in the 1970s by members of the Centre for Contemporary Cultural Studies (CCCS). The major characteristics that defined youth subcultures and made them visible and viable structures in working-class Chicago neighborhoods between the 1910s and the 1970s were their organization around rituals, activities, concerns, styles, and territorial spaces; their separation—spatially and intellectually—from both their parents' culture (working-class, ethnic) and the dominant culture (middle-class, white, American); and their possession of some semblance of a generational consciousness. Unlike the CCCS scholars, however, I conceive the function and meaning of youth subcultures to have much less to do with their role within a Gramscian notion of counterhegemonic class struggle and much more to do with the part they played in racial and ethnic formation and intergroup relations on the neighborhood level. The essential CCCS works on youth subcultures are Stuart Hall and Tony Jefferson, eds., *Resistance through Rituals: Youth Subcultures in Postwar Britain* (London: Harper Collins Academic, 1976); Paul Willis, *Learning to Labor: How Working Class Kids Get Working Class Jobs* (New York: Columbia University Press, 1977); and Dick Hebdige, *Subculture: The Meaning of Style* (London: Routledge, 1979).

13. In line with Bonilla-Silva's notion of a "racialized social system," we can describe the major rungs of interwar Chicago's racial hierarchy—from top to bottom—as consisting of more assimilated, "old" ethnics from northern and western Europe; "new" ethnics from eastern and southern Europe; Latinos; and African Americans. Racial ideologies, varying levels of local political representation, as well as respective positions in the labor and housing markets, among other things, interacted to produce this hierarchy. As we will later see in much greater detail, moreover, my data confirm the view that from the mid-1940s onward a common bond of whiteness developed between the two basic European categories by revealing that national differences between European groups ceased to generate significant intergroup hostilities in the postwar decades.

14. As will be discussed further in the chapter 2, gender norms in ethnic communities meant that parents would sharply restrict the access young women had to such spaces until the mid-1950s. By the early 1960s, however, female participation in the youth subcultures I will describe was significant. While several studies have explored female delinquency and leisure in the late nineteenth and early twentieth centuries, historians have dealt much too little with how working-class girls negotiated urban youth subcultures in the postwar era. For studies of female delinquency and leisure during the Progressive Era and interwar years, see Mary E. Odem, *Delinquent Daughters: Protecting and Policing Adolescent Female Sexuality in the United States, 1885–1920* (Chapel Hill: University of North Carolina Press, 1995); Ruth Alexander, *The Girl Problem: Female Sexual Delinquency in New York, 1900–1930* (Ithaca, N.Y.: Cornell University Press, 1995); Kathy Peiss, *Cheap Amusements: Working Women and Leisure in Turn-of-the-*

Century New York (Philadelphia: Temple University Press, 1986); Victoria W. Wolcott, *Remaking Respectability: African American Women in Interwar Detroit* (Chapel Hill: University of North Carolina Press, 2001). Unfortunately, this study does not provide an adequate corrective to this problem. While I have attempted to understand the different ways working-class women dealt with predicaments of race, class, and gender on the streets, young men will constitute the main subjects of this analysis. They were the central actors in the phenomena of racial and ethnic aggression at the center of this story.

15. For an essay that gets at some of the basic issues behind this historic relationship between white youths and black cultural forms, see David Roediger, "What to Make of Wiggers: A Work in Progress," in *Generations of Youth: Youth Culture and History in Twentieth-Century America,* ed. Joe Austin and Michael Nevin Willard (New York: New York University Press, 1998), 358–366.

16. Kevin Mumford, *Interzones: Black/White Sex Districts in Chicago and New York in the Early Twentieth Century* (New York: Columbia University Press, 1997). The experience of transgressing racial boundaries did not always involve African Americans. In part because of the enforcement of segregation in dance venues by private owners and public officials, other racial others often stood in for blacks in the realization of such experiences. For example, sociologist Paul Cressey found that Filipinos tended to serve such roles in taxi-dance halls during the interwar years. See Paul G. Cressey, *The Taxi-Dance Hall: A Sociological Study in Commercialized Recreation and City Life* (New York: Greenwood Press, 1968), esp. 13–14, 218–221.

17. Thomas C. Holt, "Marking: Race, Race-Making, and the Writing of History," *American Historical Review* 100 (February 1995), 15. For a similar argument, see also Holt, "Explaining Racism in American History," in *Imagined Histories: American Historians Interpret the Past,* ed. Anthony Mohlo and Gordon S. Wood (Princeton, NJ: Princeton University Press, 1998). For these seminal works referred to by Holt on the role and meaning of everyday life in the organization or racial consciousness, see W. E. B. DuBois, *The Souls of Black Folk* (New York: Vintage, 1990); Frantz Fanon, *Black Skins, White Masks: The Experience of a Black Man in a White World,* trans. Charles Lam Markmann (London: MacGibbon & Kee, 1968). For broader theories on the politics of everyday life, see De Certeau, *Practice of Everyday Life;* Henri Lefevre, *Critique of Everyday Life,* trans. John Moore (London and New York: Verso, 1991); Alf Ludtke, "Polymorphous Synchrony: German Industrial Workers and the Politics of Everyday Life," *International Review of Social History* 38 (1993): S39–S84.

18. Scholars have tended to examine the issue of gang politicization in the 1960s in rather narrow terms, using the relative lack of hard evidence of formal political activism and the continuation of delinquent behavior as justifications for the conclusion that the radicalization of the street gang milieu was superficial. See, for example, Eric C. Schneider, *Vampires, Dragons, and Egyptian Kings: Youth Gangs in Postwar New York* (Princeton, NJ: Princeton University Press, 1999), 217–228. For a discussion of why this is a limited way to view such issues, see Andrew Diamond, "Rethinking Culture on the Streets: Agency, Masculinity, and Style in the American City," *Journal of Urban History* 27 (July 2001):

669–685; Timothy J. Gilfoyle, Eric Schneider, and Andrew Diamond, "Gangs in the Post–World War II North American City: A Forum," *Journal of Urban History* 28 (July 2002): 658–663.

19. See, for example, Mauricio Mazon, *The Zoot-Suit Riots: The Psychology of Symbolic Annihilation* (Austin: University of Texas Press, 1984); Domenic J. Capeci Jr. and Martha Wilkerson, *Layered Violence: The Detroit Rioters of 1943* (Jackson and London: University Press of Mississippi, 1991; Domenic J. Capeci Jr., *The Harlem Riot of 1943* (Philadelphia: Temple University Press, 1977).

20. As Karen Miller has pointed out, historians have been somewhat inattentive to the forms of black resistance that grew out of the pattern of white aggression in schools and at the boundaries of neighborhoods in the 1940s and 1950s, thus neglecting a vital source of early civil rights activism. See Karen Miller, "We Cannot Wait for Understanding to Come to Us": Community Activists Respond to Violence at Detroit's Northwestern High School, 1940–1941," in *Groundwork: Local Black Freedom Movements in America*, ed. Jeanne Theoharis and Komozi Woodward (New York: New York University Press, 2005), 236–237.

21. Matthew J. Countryman, *Up South: Civil Rights and Black Power in Philadelphia* (Philadelphia: University of Pennsylvania Press, 2006), 7; Robert O. Self, *American Babylon: Race and the Struggle for Postwar Oakland* (Princeton, NJ: Princeton University Press, 2003), 217–220.

22. For an excellent analysis of why much of the sociological literature on youth gangs does not adequately theorize the relationship between gangs and their communities, see Sudhir A. Venkatesh, "The Social Organization of Street Gang Activity in an Urban Ghetto," *American Journal of Sociology* 103 (July 1997): 82–91. For similar critiques, see Venkatesh, "The Gang in the Community," in *Gangs in America*, ed. Ronald E. Huff (Newbury Park, CA.: Sage Publications, 1996), 241–243; and Daniel J. Monti, "Origins and Problems of Gang Research in the United States," in *Gangs: The Origins and Impact of Contemporary Youth Gangs in the United States*, ed. Scott Cummings and Daniel J. Monti (Albany: State University of New York Press, 1993), 12–14.

Venkatesh's innovative work on the relationship between residents and street gangs in a Chicago housing project in the mid-1990s provides a useful corrective to such problems, but even here the subjects of his research—a marginalized housing project community and a "corporatized" street gang engaged in profitable drug trafficking activities—invoke a categorically different set of concerns from those of the gangs and communities I examine here. See Venkatesh, *American Project: The Rise and Fall of a Modern Ghetto* (Cambridge, MA: Harvard University Press, 2000).

23. For an explanation of this concept, see Don Mitchell, "The End of Public Space? People's Park, Definitions of Public, and Democracy," *Annals of the Association of American Geographers* 85 (1995): 108–133.

24. On the "invention" or "imagination" of racial and ethnic identities, see Herbert J. Gans, "Symbolic Ethnicity: The Future of Ethnic Groups and Cultures in America," *Ethnic and Racial Studies* 2 (January 1979): 1–20; Eric Hobsbawm and Terrence Ranger, *The Invention of Tradition* (Cambridge: Cambridge Uni-

versity Press, 1983); Mary C. Waters, *Ethnic Options: Choosing Identities in America* (Berkeley and Los Angeles: University of California Press, 1990); Benedict Anderson, *Imagined Communities: Reflections on the Origin and Spread of Nationalism* (London: Verso, 1991); Kathleen Neils Conzen, David A. Gerber, Ewa Morawska, Georg E. Pozzetta, and Rudolph J. Vecoli, "The Invention of Ethnicity: A Perspective from the U.S.A." *Journal of American Ethnic History* 12 (Fall 1992): 3–41.

25. Henri Lefebvre, *The Production of Space* (Cambridge, UK: Blackwell, 1991). For a study that brings Lefebvre's theories to the American context, see Mark Gottdeiner, *The Social Construction of Urban Space* (Austin: University of Texas Press, 1985). It is important to note that Lefebvre did not deal explicitly with the relationship between spatial processes and racial and ethnic identities. Much of the work by U.S. scholars that attempts to apply Lefebvre's thinking to the racialized urban geographies of the United States adheres largely to a Marxist framework, illuminating the struggle over space between racially marginalized groups and the state.

26. Alberto Melucci, *Challenging Codes: Collective Action in the Information Age* (Cambridge: Cambridge University Press, 1989), 120.

27. See, for example, Stanley Cohen, *Folk Devils and Moral Panics: The Creation of the Mods and Rockers* (Oxford, UK: Martin Robertson, 1980); Stuart Hall, Charles Critcher, Tony Jefferson, John Clarke, and Brian Robert, *Policing the Crisis: Mugging, the State, the Law, and Order* (New York: Holmes and Meier, 1978); Charles Acland, *Youth, Murder, Spectacle: The Cultural Politics of "Youth in Crisis"* (Boulder: University of Colorado Press, 1995); James Gilbert, *A Cycle of Outrage: America's Reaction to the Juvenile Delinquent in the 1950s* (New York: Oxford University Press, 1986).

28. William A. Gamson, *Talking Politics* (New York: Cambridge University Press, 1992); Gamson, "The Social Psychology of Collective Action," in *Frontiers in Social Movement Theory*, ed. Aldon D. Morris and Carol McClurg Mueller (New Haven, CT: Yale University Press, 1992).

29. On "networks," see Mario Diani and Doug McAdam, *Social Movements and Networks: Regional Approaches to Collective Action* (Oxford: Oxford University Press, 2003). For an explanation of the concept of "mobilizing structures," see Doug McAdam, John D. McCarthy, and Mayer N. Zald, *Comparative Perspectives on Social Movements: Political Opportunities, Mobilizing Structures, and Cultural Framings* (Cambridge: Cambridge University Press, 1996).

30. My conception of youth is similar to the "formational" approach outlined in Joe Austin and Michael Nevin Willard, "Introduction: Angels of History, Demons of Culture," in *Generations of Youth* (see note 15), 1–20.

31. Sixteen was the legal dropout age throughout this period, which made it a natural divider between childhood and young adulthood, although sixteen- and seventeen-year-olds were still considered juveniles before the law.

32. The Asian population in Chicago was relatively small until the late 1960s, when Chinese immigration increased rapidly and a Chinatown community began to expand north of Bridgeport. References to Asian Americans in the documentation covering intergroup conflict, juvenile delinquency, and gang activities are rare. Therefore, in this study I focus only fleetingly on Asian Americans.

33. An exception is the book whose title I borrow here: Herbert Shapiro, *White Violence and Black Response: From Reconstruction to Montgomery* (Amherst: University of Massachusetts Press, 1988).

34. My thinking on this impulse shares a great deal with the conception of "alterity" developed in Robert Orsi, "The Religious Boundaries of an Inbetween People: Street Feste and the Problem of the Dark-Skinned Other in Italian Harlem, 1920–1990," *American Quarterly* 44 (September 1992): 313–347.

1. THE GENERATION OF 1919

Epigraphs: The Chicago Commission on Race Relations (CCRR), *The Negro in Chicago: A Study of Race Relations and a Race Riot* (Chicago: University of Chicago Press, 1922), 451. Robert E. Park, Ernest W. Burgess, and Roderick D. McKenzie, *The City: Suggestions for Investigation of Human Behavior in the Urban Environment* (Chicago: University of Chicago Press, 1967), 112.

1. CCRR, *The Negro in Chicago*, 11, 3.

2. Ibid., 3.

3. *Chicago Defender,* June 28, 1919.

4. William M. Tuttle, *Race Riot: Chicago in the Red Summer of 1919* (New York: Atheneum, 1970), 54–55; Thomas Lee Philpott, *The Slum and the Ghetto: Immigrants, Blacks, and Reformers in Chicago, 1880–1930* (New York: Oxford University Press, 1978), 174–175.

5. Philpott, *The Slum and the Ghetto*, 175.

6. *Chicago Defender,* June 21, 1919; *Chicago Herald Examiner,* June 23, 1919.

7. *Chicago Herald Examiner,* June 23, 1919.

8. *Chicago Defender,* June 28, 1919; Allan H. Spear, *Black Chicago: The Making of a Negro Ghetto, 1890–1920* (Chicago: University of Chicago Press, 1967), 213.

9. Frederic Thrasher, *The Gang: A Study of 1,313 Gangs in Chicago* (Chicago: University of Chicago Press, 1927), 316.

10. John Landesco, "Organized Crime in Chicago," in *Contributions to Urban Sociology,* ed. Ernest W. Burgess and Donald J. Bogue (Chicago: University of Chicago Press, 1964), 569.

11. Tuttle, *Race Riot*, 32.

12. *Chicago Daily Journal,* April 1, 1919.

13. CCRR, *The Negro in Chicago*, 14–16.

14. Ibid., 13.

15. Ibid., 17.

16. Charles Tilly, *The Politics of Collective Violence* (New York: Cambridge University Press, 2003), 34–41.

17. The CCRR spent considerable time investigating this incident, in the end confirming the view of the coroner's jury that the fires were most likely set by whites attempting to incite racial hatred. See CCRR, *The Negro in Chicago,* 20–21.

18. See, for example, Tuttle, *Race Riot.* For a discussion of the riot literature, Tuttle's brilliant methodology, and the timelessness of his contribution to

our understanding of the riot and collective racial violence in general, see Domenic Capeci, "Race Riot Redux: William M. Tuttle, Jr., and the Study of Racial Violence," *Reviews in American History* 29 (March 2001): 165–181.

19. See Matthew Pratt Guterl, "The New Race Consciousness: Race, Nation, and Empire in American Culture, 1910–1925," *Journal of World History* 10 (Fall 1999): 307–352; and Tuttle, *Race Riot,* 208–241.

20. John Landesco, "The Gangster and the Politician," 10, Ernest Burgess Papers (hereafter cited as EB), Box 132, Folder 7, UC-SCRC.

21. For some recent discussions along these lines, see Arnold R. Hirsch, "E Pluribus Duo? Thoughts on 'Whiteness' and Chicago's 'New' Immigration as a Transient Third Tier," *Journal of American Ethnic History* (Summer 2004): 7–44; David Roediger, *Working toward Whiteness: How America's Immigrants Became White: The Strange Journey from Ellis Island to the Suburbs* (New York: Basic Books, 2005), 127–128.

22. See James R. Barrett and David R. Roediger, "The Irish and the 'Americanization' of the 'New Immigrants' in the Streets and in the Churches of the Urban United States, 1900–1930," *Journal of American Ethnic History* (Summer 2005): 3–33; David Roediger and James Barrett, "Making New Immigrants 'Inbetween': Irish Hosts and White Pan-Ethnicity, 1890–1930," in *Not Just Black and White: Historical and Contemporary Perspectives on Immigration, Race, and Ethnicity in the United States,* ed. Nancy Foner and George Fredrickson (New York: Russell Sage, 2004), 167–196; James R. Barrett, "Americanization from the Bottom Up: Immigration and the Remaking of the Working Class in the United States," *Journal of American History* 79 (December 1992): 996–1020.

23. U.S. Bureau of the Census, *Thirteenth Census of the United States,* vol. 1, chap. 2; U.S. Bureau of the Census, *Fourteenth Census of the United States,* vol. 1, chap. 1.

24. Thomas Jablonsky, *Pride in the Jungle: Community and Everyday Life in Back of the Yards Chicago* (Baltimore: Johns Hopkins University Press, 1993), 37.

25. Mike Royko, *Boss: Richard J. Daley of Chicago* (New York: E. P. Dutton and Co., 1971), 25.

26. Tuttle, *Race Riot,* 233–235. Tuttle's observation that the disproportionately high number of black males in Chicago between the ages of twenty and twenty-four was crucial to the spread of New Negro sensibilities accords with Guterl's view that the New Negro movement "was part of a broader reconstruction of masculinity in postwar America." Guterl, "The New Race Consciousness," 330. These circumstances point to the importance of black male youth subcultures as a vital site for the articulation of racial militancy.

27. Thrasher, *The Gang,* 16, 201.

28. James R. Grossman, *Land of Hope: Chicago, Black Southerners, and the Great Migration* (Chicago and London: University of Chicago Press, 1989), 178.

29. John Landesco, "The Gangster and the Politician," 10, EB, Box 132, Folder 7, UC-SCRC.

30. Thrasher, *The Gang,* 16.

31. Adam Cohen and Elizabeth Taylor, *American Pharaoh: Mayor Richard J. Daley: His Battle for Chicago and the Nation* (Boston: Little, Brown and Co., 2000), 25–27.

32. Royko, *Boss*, 37.

33. CCRR, *The Negro in Chicago*, 8.

34. *Annual Report of the Crime Commission*, *1920*, cited in CCRR, *The Negro in Chicago*, 342.

35. John Landesco, "The Gangster and the Politician," 8, EB, Box 132, Folder 7, UC.

36. James R. Barrett, *Work and Community in the Jungle: Chicago's Packinghouse Workers*, *1894–1922* (Urbana and Chicago: University of Illinois Press, 1987), 13–35; see also Rick Halpern, *Down on the Killing Floor: Black and White Workers in Chicago's Packinghouses*, *1904–1954* (Urbana and Chicago: University of Illinois Press, 1997), 7–43.

37. James R. Barrett, introduction to *The Jungle*, by Upton Sinclair (Urbana: University of Illinois Press, 1988), 37.

38. Thrasher, *The Gang*, 203.

39. Ibid., 174.

40. Ibid., 17, 194.

41. Ibid., 102–103.

42. For a fuller exploration of the circumstances behind the shift from ideals of "manly self-denial" to more physical modes of masculinity in this period, see Gail Bederman, *Manliness and Civilization: A Cultural History of Gender and Race in the United States*, *1880–1917* (Chicago: University of Chicago Press, 1995), 1–44.

43. For a fuller treatment of Hart's screen persona and the influence of the social gospel movement on the early silent westerns, see Andrew Brodie Smith, *Shooting Cowboys and Indians: Silent Western Films, American Culture, and the Birth of Hollywood* (Boulder: University of Colorado Press, 2003), 157–185.

44. John Higham, "The Reorientation of American Culture in the 1890s," in *Writing American History: Essays on Modern Scholarship* (Bloomington: Indiana University Press, 1970), 73–102; Bederman, *Manliness and Civilization*, 11.

45. Eileen Bowser, *The Transformation of Cinema*, *1907–1915* (Berkeley and Los Angeles: University of California Press, 1990), 176.

46. Brodie Smith, *Shooting Cowboys and Indians*, 167.

47. Bederman, *Manliness and Civilization*, 219; Thrasher, *The Gang*, 105.

48. Bederman, *Manliness and Civilization*, 226.

49. On the threat Johnson posed to white middle-class masculinity by challenging the link between male power and white supremacy, see Bederman, *Manliness and Civilization*, 1–31. For a comprehensive and compelling biography of Johnson, see Geoffrey C. Ward, *Unforgivable Blackness: The Rise and Fall of Jack Johnson* (London: Pimlico, 2006).

50. *New York Times*, cited in Ward, *Unforgivable Blackness*, 165.

51. Ward, *Unforgivable Blackness*, 309.

52. For a fuller account of the broader social meaning of Johnson's relations with white women, see Kevin J. Mumford, *Interzones: Black/White Sex Districts in Chicago and New York in the Early Twentieth Century* (New York: Columbia University Press, 1997), 3–18.

53. Al-Tony Gilmore, *Bad Nigger! The National Impact of Jack Johnson* (Port Washington, NY: Kennikat Press, 1975), 88.

54. Tuttle, *Race Riot,* 189.

55. *Chicago Tribune,* April 6, 1915.

56. Thrasher, *The Gang,* 100.

57. Howard P. Chudacoff, *The Age of the Bachelor: Creating an American Subculture* (Princeton, NJ: Princeton University Press, 1999), 198–210.

58. The Neighborhood, Albert Ackerman, Druggist, 1500 W. 51st Street, 12/18/24, E. P. Wolcott, Mary McDowell Settlement Records (hereafter cited as MM), Box 2, Folder 10, Chicago History Museum (hereafter cited as CHM).

59. Tuttle, *Race Riot,* 199.

60. Steven A. Riess, *City Games: The Evolution of American Urban Society and the Rise of Sports* (Urbana and Chicago: University of Illinois Press, 1989), 109–113.

61. Michel Foucault, *"Society Must Be Defended": Lectures at the College de France, 1975–1976* (New York: Picador, 2003), 80.

62. For a more detailed discussion of the role of social Darwinist thought in justifying such imperial interventions, see Richard Hofstadter, *Social Darwinism in American Thought* (Boston: Beacon Press, 1992), 170–200. On the uses of such language in debates over immigration policy in the 1910s and early 1920s, see John Higham, *Strangers in the Land: Patterns of American Nativism, 1860–1925* (New York: Atheneum, 1981), 149–157, 264–286, 300–330.

63. Riess, *City Games,* 110.

64. Ibid., 110–111; Thrasher, *The Gang,* 196.

65. Thrasher, *The Gang,* 100, 212; Barrett and Roediger, "The Irish and the 'Americanization' of the 'New Immigrants,'" 7.

66. Foucault, *"Society Must Be Defended,"* 81; Roediger, *Working toward Whiteness,* 139–140.

67. Clifford Geertz, "Deep Play: Notes on the Balinese Cockfight," in *The Interpretation of Cultures* (New York: Basic Books, 1973), 448, 412–453. Thomas C. Holt has also used Geertz's notion of "deep play" to understand the hysteria surrounding Johnson; see Thomas C. Holt, *The Problem of Race in the Twenty-first Century* (Cambridge, MA: Harvard University Press, 2000), 78.

68. Three major Chicago newspapers printed McDonough's famous words: *Chicago Daily Tribune,* July 29, 1919; *Chicago Daily News,* July 30, 1919; *Chicago Herald-Examiner,* July 29, 30, 1919.

69. Stuart Hall and Tony Jefferson, eds., *Resistance through Rituals: Youth Subcultures in Postwar Britain* (London: Harper Collins Academic, 1976), 10.

70. Ibid., 14.

71. Ellen Skerrett, "The Catholic Dimension," in *The Irish in Chicago,* ed. Lawrence J. McCaffrey, Ellen Skerrett, and Charles Fanning (Urbana and Chicago: University of Illinois Press, 1987), 49–50.

72. Meegan (Peter) family, 5242 So. Sangamon Street, December 8, 1924, Nels Anderson, MM, Box 2, Folder 10, CHM. The bracketed words I have added; the parenthetical ones were present in the original document.

73. The Ragen's Colts and the Sherman Park District, Miss Dennis, U. of C. Settlement, 12/17/24, E. P. Wolcott, MM, Box 2, Folder 10, CHM.

74. John Landesco, "The Gangster and the Politician," 11–12, EB, Box 132, Folder 7, UC-SCRC.

75. *Chicago Sunday Tribune,* June 24, 1923; *Chicago Tribune,* June 28, 1923.

76. *Chicago Tribune,* June 29, 1923.

77. Kenneth Jackson, *The Ku Klux Klan in the City, 1915–1930* (New York: Oxford University Press, 1967), 95.

78. John Landesco, "The Gangster and the Politician," 11, EB, Box 132, Folder 7, UC.

79. Ragen Colts and Sherman Park Neighborhood, A. J. Link, Druggist, 1200 W. 51st Street, 12/17/24, E. P. Wolcott, MM, Box 2, Folder 10, CHM; The Neighborhood, Albert Ackerman, Druggist, 1500 W. 51st Street, 12/18/24, E. P. Wolcott, MM, Box 2, Folder 10, CHM.

80. Eileen M. McMahon, *What Parish Are You From? A Chicago Irish Community and Race Relations* (Lexington: University Press of Kentucky, 1995), 29–30.

81. Berman (Nathan) Family, 5150 So. Halsted Street, December 6, 1924, Nels Anderson, MM, Box 2, Folder 10, CHM; Gannes (Benjamin) Family, 1214 Blue Island Avenue, December 6, 1924, Nels Anderson, MM, Box 2, Folder 10, CHM; Commentary on Case Histories of Delinquency of 7 Boys, MM, Box 2, Folder 10, CHM.

82. Berman (Nathan) Family, 5150 So. Halsted Street, December 6, 1924, Nels Anderson, MM, Box 2, Folder 10, CHM

83. McMahon, *What Parish Are You From?* 22; Skerrett, "The Catholic Dimension," 51–52.

84. William Howland Kenney, *Chicago Jazz: A Cultural History, 1904–1930* (New York: Oxford University Press, 1993), 14–15; Hughes, quoted in Grossman, *Land of Hope,* 117.

85. *Chicago Daily News,* July 28, 1919.

86. Kenney, *Chicago Jazz,* 23–24.

87. Quoted in Kenney, *Chicago Jazz,* 72.

88. CCRR, *The Negro in Chicago,* 324.

89. Dick Hebdige, *Subculture: The Meaning of Style* (London: Routledge, 1979), esp. 39–59.

90. In assessing the accuracy of Farrell's rendering of such circumstances, we should consider that he claimed to be striving for "the strictest possible objectivity" in his work. Charles Fanning, introduction to *Studs Lonigan: A Trilogy Comprising "Young Lonigan," "The Young Manhood of Studs Lonigan," and "Judgment Day,"* by James T. Farrell (Urbana: University of Illinois Press, 1993), xi.

91. CCRR, *The Negro in Chicago,* 11, 5.

92. Ibid., 288, 293, 292, 286.

93. Ibid., 287, 289, 293.

94. Ibid., 301–309, 323–325.

95. Farrell, *Studs Lonigan* (see note 90), 645.

96. For studies that examine these dimensions of working-class youth leisure, see Kathy Peiss, *Cheap Amusements: Working Women and Leisure in Turn-of-the-Century New York* (Philadelphia: Temple University Press, 1986); Lizabeth Cohen, *Making a New Deal: Industrial Workers in Chicago, 1919–1939* (New York: Cam-

bridge University Press, 1990), esp. 143–47. For a similar perspective on middle-class youth culture in the 1920s, see Paul Fass, *The Damned and the Beautiful: American Youth in the 1920s* (New York: Oxford University Press, 1977).

97. David Nasaw, *Going Out: The Rise and Fall of Public Amusements* (New York: Basic Books, 1993), 47–61.

98. George Chauncey, *Gay New York: Gender, Urban Culture, and the Making of the Gay Male World* (New York: Basic Books, 1994), 76.

99. For the migration of vice to these areas, see Walter Reckless, *Vice in Chicago* (Chicago: University of Chicago Press, 1933), 194; Herbert Asbury, *Gem of the Prairie: An Informal History of the Chicago Underworld* (DeKalb: Northern Illinois University Press, 1941), 299; Mumford, *Interzones*, 25–28.

100. On the white appropriation of black jazz in the dance hall scene of the 1910s and 1920s, see Kathy Ogren, *The Jazz Revolution: Twenties America and the Meaning of Jazz* (New York: Oxford University Press, 1989); Kenney, *Chicago Jazz*.

101. On the emergence of Black Belt dance halls and black-and-tans as popular destinations for Chicago youths, see Mumford, *Interzones*, 23–35. According to Mumford, this trend coincided with city policies that worked to contain vice within black neighborhoods.

102. Mumford, *Interzones*, 30.

103. CCRR, *The Negro in Chicago*, 324.

104. Farrell, *Studs Lonigan*, 226–227.

105. Ibid., 227.

106. Thrasher, *The Gang*, 166–167.

107. Timothy J. Gilfoyle, *City of Eros: New York City, Prostitution, and the Commercialization of Sex, 1790–1920* (New York: W. W. Norton, 1992), esp. 81–84, 115–116, 119–120, 236–239.

108. Chauncey, *Gay New York*, 77. For a study of the Irish bachelor subculture in this era, see Richard Stivers, *A Hair of the Dog: Irish Drinking and American Stereotype* (University Park: Pennsylvania State University, 1976).

109. David Roediger, *The Wages of Whiteness: Race and the Making of the American Working Class* (London: Verso, 1991).

110. For a historical and psychoanalytic account of minstrelsy, see Eric Lott, *Love and Theft: Blackface Minstrelsy and the American Working Class* (New York: Oxford University Press, 1995).

111. On the relationship between minstrelsy and vaudeville, see Nasaw, *Going Out*, 23–24, 47–61. We should also consider that cinema would soon be popularizing minstrelsy with a series of films oriented around blackface routines.

112. See, for example, Hirsch, "E Pluribus Duo?" This pathbreaking article, which uses evidence from the 1919 race riot to examine how a range of "new" ethnic groups moved "toward a broadly applied and widely accepted 'white' identity" (33) between 1910 and 1930, deals very sensitively with variations between different groups but never considers generational divisions within them.

113. Thrasher, *The Gang*, 316.

114. Ibid., 4.

115. Ibid., 20–22.

116. Ibid., 130–131.

117. Leila Houghteling, *The Income and Standard of Living of Unskilled Laborers in Chicago* (Chicago: University of Chicago Press, 1927), 20–23.

118. Thrasher, *The Gang*, 131.

119. On the Americanization of youths within settlement houses, see Philpott, *The Slum and the Ghetto*, esp. 278–279.

120. Robert Park, "Community Organization and Juvenile Delinquency," in *The City: Suggestions for Investigation of Human Behavior in the Urban Environment*, by Robert Park, Ernest W. Burgess, and Roderick D. McKenzie (Chicago: University of Chicago Press, 1967), 112.

121. Barrett and Roediger, "The Irish and the 'Americanization' of the 'New Immigrants,'" 3–33

122. Barrett, "Americanization from the Bottom Up."

123. Stanley Lieberson, *A Piece of the Pie: Blacks and White Immigrants since 1880* (Berkeley: University of California Press, 1980), 253–267.

124. For a more detailed account of Polish settlement in these neighborhoods, see Dominic Pacyga, *Polish Immigrants and Industrial Chicago: Workers on the South Side, 1880–1922* (Columbus: Ohio State University Press, 1991), 43–110.

125. Farrell, *Studs Lonigan*, 623–624.

126. Harvey Warren Zorbaugh, *The Gold Coast and the Slum: A Sociological Study of Chicago's Near North Side* (Chicago: University of Chicago Press, 1929), 148.

127. Vivien Palmer, "History of the Lower North Side," prepared for the Chicago Historical Society, Document 23, CHM. For similar sentiments, see also Documents 22, 27, 37.

128. William J. Dempsey, "Gangs in the Calumet Park District," unpublished paper for Sociology 270, EB, Box 148, Folder 5, UC-SCRC.

129. Jane Addams, *The Second Twenty Years at Hull House* (New York: Macmillan Co., 1930), 282–283. For an excellent account of such "racializing experiences" in the everyday lives of Mexicans in Chicago in this period, see Gabriela Arredondo, "Navigating Ethno-Racial Currents: Mexicans in Chicago, 1919–1939," *Journal of Urban History* 30 (March 2004): 399–427.

130. In this sense, I view the situation of the Poles and Hungarians alluded to by Farrell's characters as, in some sense, racially "in-between," a condition that had little to do with their color. While these groups may have understood that they were legally "white," such treatment by more assimilated groups informed them that their "wages of whiteness" were by no means assured. On the other hand, because many Mexicans had darker complexions than most (though not all) European Americans, the in-between nature of Mexicans had perhaps as much to do with color as with race. It was partly due to their color that Mexicans were forced to rent apartments within and around black neighborhoods, a situation that further "racialized" (or "colored" them).

131. The Ragen's Colts and the Sherman Park District, Miss Dennis, U. of C. Settlement, 12/17/24, E. P. Wolcott, MM, Box 2, Folder 10, CHM.

132. Thrasher, *The Gang*, 15, 50–51.

133. Jablonsky, *Pride in the Jungle*, 90.

134. Pacyga, *Polish Immigrants and Industrial Chicago*, 219–220.

135. *Dziennik Zjednoczenia,* March 20, 1922, Foreign Language Press Survey (hereafter cited as FLPS), Polish, CHM.

136. The Ragen's Colts and the Sherman Park District, Miss Dennis, U. of C. Settlement, 12/17/24, E. P. Wolcott, MM, Box 2, Folder 10, CHM.

137. Florence Lynn Gaddis, "Conflict Between Mexicans and Poles Living Near Ashland Ave. and 45th St.," unpublished paper submitted for Sociology 270, Prof. Ernest W. Burgess, University of Chicago, 1928, EB, Box 142, Folder 3, UC-SCRC.

138. Arredondo, "Navigating Ethno-Racial Currents," 412–416.

139. Marcia Kijewski, David Brosch, and Robert Bulanda, *The Historical Development of Three Chicago Millgates: South Chicago, East Side, South Deering* (Chicago: Illinois Labor History Society, 1972), 34–35.

140. Louise Año Nuevo Kerr, "The Chicano Experience in Chicago, 1920–1970" (Ph.D. diss., University of Illinois—Chicago, 1976), 29.

2. BETWEEN SCHOOL AND WORK IN THE INTERWAR YEARS

Epigraphs: Nelson Algren, *Somebody in Boots* (New York: Vanguard Press, 1935), 304. "The Nature and Characteristics of Delinquents and Delinquency in the South Chicago Area Project, as Revealed by Three Group Diaries," 6, CAP, Box 110, Folder 1, CHM.

1. "The Nature and Characteristics of Delinquents and Delinquency in the South Chicago Area Project, as Revealed by Three Group Diaries," 5, Chicago Area Project Records (hereafter cited as CAP), Box 110, Folder 1, CHM.

2. Susan Porter Benson, "Gender, Generation, and Consumption in the United States: Working-Class Families in the Interwar Period," in *Getting and Spending: European and American Consumer Societies in the Twentieth Century,* ed. Susan Strasser, Charles McGovern, and Matthias Judt (New York: Cambridge University Press, 1998), 223–240. For another study that draws similar conclusions about restrictions on young working-class women's access to public leisure, see Kathy Peiss, *Cheap Amusements: Working Women and Leisure in Turn-of-the-Century New York* (Philadelphia: Temple University Press, 1986), 56–59.

3. Frederic Thrasher, *The Gang: A Study of 1,313 Gangs in Chicago* (Chicago: University of Chicago Press, 1927). Young women did participate in ethnically bounded social clubs sponsored by settlement houses, churches, and other community organizations in the first two decades of the twentieth century, but these clubs met only once or twice weekly and usually under somewhat supervised conditions. See Peiss, *Cheap Amusements,* 59–62.

4. Lizabeth Cohen makes a similar point about the role of youth groups in mediating mass culture in interwar Chicago. Lizabeth Cohen, *Making a New Deal: Industrial Workers in Chicago, 1919–1939* (New York: Cambridge University Press, 1990), 143–147.

5. Pat Ireland, "Factors in the Americanization of a Second Generation of Immigrant People" (master's thesis, University of Chicago, 1932), 66.

6. Paula Fass, *The Damned and Beautiful: American Youth in the 1920s* (New York: Oxford University Press, 1977). Thrasher indicates that fraternities were

commonplace in the high schools of middle-class areas and that they mainly engaged in extracurricular activities at school. Thrasher, *The Gang*, 57–58.

7. For a detailed account of the conditions of black schools in Chicago during the 1930s, see Michael W. Homel, *Down from Equality: Black Chicagoans
and the Public Schools, 1920–41* (Urbana and Chicago: University of Illinois
Press, 1984), esp. 78–84, 108–127.

8. St. Clair Drake and Horace Cayton, *Black Metropolis: A Study of Negro
Life in a Northern City*, rev. and enlarged ed. (1945; reprint, Chicago: University
of Chicago Press, 1993), 686. For further exploration of the African American
dance scene in this period and its social meaning, see Katrina Hazzard-Gordon,
Jookin': The Rise of Social Dance Formations in African American Culture
(Philadelphia: Temple University Press, 1990); Robin D. G. Kelley, "We Are Not
What We Seem: Rethinking Black Working-Class Opposition in the Jim Crow
South," *Journal of American History* 80 (June 1993): 75–113.

9. For analyses of the representation and segregation of African Americans
in the world of commercial leisure in the interwar period, see David Nasaw, *Going Out: The Rise and Fall of Public Amusements* (New York: Basic Books, 1993),
47–61; Sam Dennison, *Scandalize My Name: Black Imagery in American Popular Music* (New York: Garland Publishing, 1982); Derek Vaillant, "Sounds of
Whiteness: Local Radio, Racial Formation, and Public Culture in Chicago, 1921–
1935," *American Quarterly* 54 (March 2002): 25–66.

10. Kevin J. Mumford, *Interzones: Black/White Sex Districts in Chicago and
New York in the Early Twentieth Century* (New York: Columbia University Press,
1997), 19–49. Mumford's study provides a corrective to the perception that racial
mixing in the interwar years consisted of middle-class whites out slumming.

11. My thinking here benefits from Earl Lewis's notion of "congregation,"
which describes how black communities in the Jim Crow South constructed a
sense of solidarity and "free will" within segregated cultural settings, and from
Robin Kelley's application of this idea to the milieu of black working-class leisure
in the interwar era. Earl Lewis, *In Their Own Interests: Race, Class, and Power
in the Twentieth-Century Norfolk, Virginia* (Berkeley and Los Angeles: University of California Press, 1991), 91–92; Robin D. G. Kelley, *Race Rebels: Culture,
Politics, and the Black Working Class* (New York: Free Press, 1994), 45–53.

12. Joel Perlmann, "Toward a Population History of the Second Generation: Birth Cohorts of Southern-, Central-, and Eastern-European Origins, 1871–
1970" (working paper no. 333, Jerome Levy Institute of Bard College, New York,
2001), 8.

13. "A Study of Behavior Problems of Boys in the Lower North Community,"
24–26, EB, Box 135, Folder 4, UC-SCRC.

14. Ibid., 24.

15. Thrasher, *The Gang*, 5.

16. James Fontana, "A Study of a Community Center in Relation to Its Neighborhood" (Ph.D. diss., University of Chicago, 1942), 53.

17. Anthony Sorrentino, *Organizing against Crime: Redeveloping the Neighborhood* (New York: Human Sciences Press, 1977), 125.

18. Dominic Pacyga, *Polish Immigrants and Industrial Chicago: Workers on
the South Side* (Columbus: Ohio State University Press, 1991), 150.

19. Thrasher, *The Gang,* 9–10.

20. Cohen, *Making a New Deal,* 120.

21. Quoted in William Kenney, *Chicago Jazz: A Cultural History, 1904–1930* (New York: Oxford University Press, 1993), 76.

22. Ireland, "Americanization of a Second Generation," 36–37.

23. Fontana, "Community Center," 37.

24. Edward Jackson Baur, "Delinquency among Mexican Boys in South Chicago" (Ph.D., diss., University of Chicago, 1938), 26.

25. William I. Thomas and Florian Znaniecki, *The Polish Peasant in Europe and America,* vols. 1 and 2 (New York: Dover Publications, 1918–1920). For a discussion of Thomas and Znaniecki's work, see Kathleen Neils Conzen, "Thomas and Znaniecki and the Historiography of American Immigration," *Journal of American Ethnic History* 16 (Fall 1996): 16–25.

26. Ireland, "Americanization of a Second Generation," 4–7, 53.

27. Thomas Lee Philpott, *The Slum and the Ghetto: Immigrants, Blacks, and Reformers in Chicago, 1880–1930* (New York: Oxford University Press, 1978), 280.

28. *Dziennik Zjednoczenia,* vol. 25, no. 58, October 18, 1921, FLPS, CHM.

29. Kenney, *Chicago Jazz,* 74–75.

30. Thomas A. Guglielmo, *White on Arrival: Italians, Race, Color, and Power in Chicago, 1890–1945* (New York: Oxford University Press, 2003). For an earlier work that advances a similar idea of the race/color distinction, see Matthew Pratt Guterl, *The Color of Race in America, 1900–1940* (Cambridge, MA: Harvard University Press, 2001). For some key studies arguing that new immigrants were "inbetween peoples" in the early twentieth century and gradually "became white," see David Roediger, *Working toward Whiteness: How America's Immigrants Became White: The Strange Journey from Ellis Island to the Suburbs* (New York: Basic Books, 2005); Matthew Frye Jacobson, *Whiteness of a Different Color: European Immigrants and the Alchemy of Race* (Cambridge, MA: Harvard University Press, 1998).

31. Leonard Giuliano (GIU-31), Grand Ave., 67, Italians in Chicago Project (hereafter cited as ICP), Box 2, CHM.

32. Victor Turner, *The Ritual Process: Structure and Anti-Structure* (New York: Aldine de Gruyter, 1995), 95–96.

33. McMurray, Reports on Houston Herrings Gang, May 1935, EB, Box 133, Folder 3, UC-SCRC.

34. Ireland, "Americanization of a Second Generation," 34–35.

35. Fontana, "Community Center," 38–39.

36. Ireland, "Americanization of a Second Generation," 89–90.

37. For a discussion of how Mexican men in interwar Chicago used their successes with Polish women as a means of "whitening" themselves, see Gabriela F. Arredondo, "Navigating Ethno-Racial Currents: Mexicans in Chicago, 1919–1939," *Journal of Urban History* 30 (March 2004): 399–427.

38. "Club Dances," CAP, Box 91, Folder 7, CHM.

39. Clifford Shaw, *The Jack-Roller: A Delinquent Boy's Own Story* (Chicago: University of Chicago Press, 1966), 79–80.

40. For Turner's explanation of "liminoid spaces," see Victor Turner, *From*

Ritual to Theater: The Human Seriousness of Play (New York: Performing Arts Journal Publications, 1982), 20–60.

41. Robert Orsi, "The Religious Boundaries of an Inbetween People: Street *Feste* and the Problem of the Dark-Skinned 'Other' in Italian Harlem, 1920–1990," *American Quarterly* 44 (September 1992): 335–336.

42. Paul G. Cressey, *The Taxi-Dance Hall: A Sociological Study in Commercialized Recreation and City Life* (1932; reprint, New York: Greenwood Press, 1968), 9. For more extensive treatment of the interracial experience offered by taxi-dance halls, see Mumford, *Interzones*, 53–71.

43. Ireland, "Americanization of a Second Generation," 85.

44. Cressey, *The Taxi-Dance Hall*, 35–36.

45. Ireland, "Americanization of a Second Generation," 66–67.

46. Orleans Playground Report, Director, Walter Klaus, EB, Box 135, Folder 6, UC-SCRC.

47. The Negro in Little Italy, October 30, 1931, EB, Box 135, Folder 5, UC-SCRC.

48. Annual Report of the West Side Community Committee, 1942, CAP, Box 89, Folder 4, CHM.

49. Gangs—Mackinaws—Reports, February 17, 1936, Stephen Bubacz Papers (hereafter cited as SB), Folder 77, University of Illinois—Chicago Special Collections (hereafter cited as UIC-SC); Gangs—Mackinaws—Reports, February 23, 1936, SB, Folder 77, UIC-SC; Gangs—Mackinaws—Reports, Extract from Leader's Report, Williams Club (Mackinaws)—J. Borberly, SB, Folder 77, UIC-SC; Burley Lions, February 26, 1935, SB, Folder 72, UIC-SC; Gangs—Houston Herrings—Reports, April 25, 1935, SB, Folder 76, UIC-SC.

50. Gangs—Houston Herrings—Reports, April 25, 1935, SB, Folder 76, UIC-SC.

51. Gangs—Mackinaws—Reports, February 17, 1936, SB, Folder 77, UIC-SC.

52. Rachel Shteir, *Striptease: The Untold Story of the Girlie Show* (New York: Oxford University Press, 2004), 203–206.

53. James T. Farrell, *Studs Lonigan: A Trilogy Comprising "Young Lonigan," "The Young Manhood of Studs Lonigan," and "Judgment Day"* (Urbana: University of Illinois Press, 1993).

54. Baur, "Delinquency among Mexican Boys," 164, 74.

55. Algren, *Somebody in Boots*, 197, 285, 287.

56. "The Nature and Characteristics of Delinquents and Delinquency in the South Chicago Area Project, as Revealed by Three Group Diaries," 5, 8, CAP, Box 110, Folder 1, CHM.

57. For a broader discussion of the interracial possibilities of swing in this moment, see Lewis A. Erenberg, *Swingin' the Dream: Big Band and the Rebirth of American Culture* (Chicago: University of Chicago Press, 1998), 35–64.

58. For a more detailed description of this event, see Erenberg, *Swingin' the Dream*, 35–36.

59. "Club Dances," CAP, Box 91, Folder 7, CHM.

60. My Pals, Leader—Dorothy Benson, October 4, 1934, SB, Folder 75, UIC-SC; My Pals, Leader—Dorothy Benson, May 5, 1936, SB, Folder 75, UIC-SC; My Pals, Leader—Dorothy Benson, May 11, 1936, SB, Folder 75, UIC-SC; My

Pals, Leader—Dorothy Benson, May 29, 1936, SB, Folder 75, UIC-SC; My Pals, Leader—Dorothy Benson, September 28, 1936, SB, Folder 75, UIC-SC.

61. Arredondo, "Navigating Ethno-Racial Currents." For further evidence, see also Marcia Kijewski, David Brosch, and Robert Bulanda, *The Historical Development of Three Chicago Millgates: South Chicago, East Side, South Deering* (Chicago: Illinois Labor History Society, 1972), 34–35.

62. Steven Schlossman and Michael Sedlak, *The Chicago Area Project Revisited* (Santa Monica: The Rand Corporation, 1983), 22.

63. Girls' Department Report, 1940–41, Chicago Commons Association Records (hereafter cited as CCA), Box 7, Folder 1, Clubs & Groups, 1940–42, CHM.

64. Burley Lions, February 26, 1935, SB, Folder 72, UIC-SC.

65. My Pals, Leader—Dorothy Benson, May 5, 1936, SB, Folder 75, UIC-SC.

66. Ibid.

67. My Pals, Leader—Dorothy Benson, May 11, 1936, SB, Folder 75, UIC.

68. Ireland, "Americanization of a Second Generation," 46–47.

69. Anna Zaloha, "A Study of the Persistence of Italian Customs among 143 Families of Italian Descent Members of Social Clubs at Chicago Commons" (master's thesis, Department of Sociology and Anthropology, Northwestern University, 1937), 137. On the religious, ethnic, and family barriers faced by working-class women as they sought to enter the world of leisure, see Peiss, *Cheap Amusements*, 67–76.

70. Zaloha, "Persistence of Italian Customs," 137–138.

71. Karl Mannheim, "The Problem of Generations," in *Essays on the Sociology of Knowledge,* ed. Paul Kecskemeti (New York: Routledge and Kegan Paul, 1952), 276–322; Gunter W. Remmling, *The Sociology of Karl Mannheim* (Atlantic Highlands, NJ: Humanities Press, 1975), 42–47. My thinking here borrows somewhat from James Barrett's use of Mannheim. James R. Barrett, "Americanization from the Bottom Up: Immigration and the Remaking of the Working Class in the United States," *Journal of American History* 79 (December 1992): 998–999. However, Barrett's idea of the "historical generation" serves only to highlight the importance of the interaction between the generation of "old" ethnics and that of "new" immigrants between the 1890s and the 1920s. By the 1930s, this latter generation had developed some profound cleavages between immigrant parents and their American-born youths that must also be considered in the story of Americanization.

72. John Bodnar, *The Transplanted: A History of Immigrants in Urban America* (Bloomington: University of Indiana Press, 1985), 212.

73. Illinois was hardly alone in this; thirty-one states had passed such laws by 1900. On the introduction of compulsory education, see David B. Tyack, *The One Best System: A History of American Urban Education* (Cambridge, MA: Harvard University Press, 1974).

74. Chicago Board of Education, *36th Annual Report*, 1890, 126, cited in David J. Hogan, *Class and Reform: School and Society in Chicago, 1880–1930* (Philadelphia: University of Pennsylvania Press, 1985), 58.

75. Chicago Board of Education, *44th Annual Report*, 1898, 170, cited in Hogan, *Class and Reform.*

76. Chicago Board of Education, *Sixtieth Annual Report,* 1914, 405; Department of Education, Chicago, Illinois, *Annual Report of the Superintendent of Schools for the Year Ending June 30, 1924,* MRC, HWLC, 47; *Report of the Superintendent of Schools of the City of Chicago, 1936,* Municipal Reference Collection (hereafter cited as MRC), Harold Washington Library Center (hereafter cited as HWLC), 264.

77. On the "child saver" movement and the creation of a juvenile court system, see Eric C. Schneider, *In the Web of Class: Delinquents and Reformers in Boston, 1810s–1930s* (New York: New York University Press, 1992); Anthony Platt, *The Child Savers: The Invention of Delinquency* (Chicago: University of Chicago Press, 1969).

78. *Fifty-seventh Annual Report of the Board of Education for the Year Ending June 30, 1911,* MRC, HWLC, 134; *Fifty-ninth Annual Report of the Board of Education for the Year Ending June 30, 1913,* MRC, HWLC, 285; *Sixty-sixth Annual Report of the Board of Education, City of Chicago, Report of the Superintendent of Schools for the Year Ending June 30, 1922,* MRC, HWLC, 54; *Annual Report of the Superintendent of Schools for the Year Ending June 30, 1924,* MRC, HWLC, 47.

79. On the rise in public school enrollment nationwide in the first three decades of the twentieth century, see David Nasaw, *Schooled to Order: A Social History of Public Schooling in the United States* (New York: Oxford University Press, 1979); Tyack, *The One Best System;* John H. Ralph and Richard Rubinson, "Immigration and the Expansion of Schooling in the United States, 1890–1970," *American Sociological Review* 45 (December 1980): 943–954.

80. Hogan, *Class and Reform,* 123. While the case of the younger cohort can be attributed to the new forms of state coercion, the predilection for attending school past the legally required age is harder to explain. Scholars have cited many factors to account for this enrollment growth, including improving rates of homeownership, the decline in the demand for youth labor, and a growing awareness of the need for education. For a discussion of this debate, see Hogan, *Class and Reform,* 120–125.

81. A substantial body of research has demonstrated a strong correlation between enrollment growth and poor labor market conditions. See, for example, Pamela Barnhouse Walters, "Occupational and Labor Market Effects on Secondary and Postsecondary Educational Expansion in the United States, 1922–1979," *American Sociological Review* 49 (October 1984): 659–671; Norton W. Grubb and Marvin Lazerson, "Education and the Labor Market: Recycling the Youth Problem," in *Work, Youth, and Schooling,* ed. Harvey Kantor and David Tyack (Stanford, CA: Stanford University Press, 1982), 110–141.

82. Schlossman and Sedlak, *Chicago Area Project Revisited,* 72.

83. The literature on the relationship between child labor and the family economy is extensive. For the theoretical foundations of such scholarship, see Louise Tilly and Joan Scott, *Women, Work, and Family* (New York: Holt, Rinehart & Winston, 1978). For a study demonstrating how child labor laws and compulsory education transformed this relationship in the early twentieth century, see Viviana A. Zelizer, *Pricing the Priceless Child: The Changing Social Value of Children* (New York: Basic Books, 1985). For studies demonstrating the contribu-

tions of child labor to the family economy in the 1920s and 1930s, see Porter Benson, "Gender, Generation, and Consumption"; John Bodnar, Roger Simon, and Michael P. Weber, *Lives of Their Own: Blacks, Italians, and Poles in Pittsburgh, 1900–1960* (Urbana: University of Illinois Press, 1982); Virginia Yans-McLaughlin, *Family and Community: Italian Immigrants in Buffalo, 1880–1930* (Ithaca, NY: Cornell University Press, 1977); David Nasaw, *Children of the City: At Work and at Play* (New York: Basic Books, 1985). While Zelizer has argued that by the 1930s working-class youths had joined their middle-class peers in a "nonproductive world of childhood," (6) the above-mentioned works demonstrate that many working-class families still required the wages of their children to get by during the 1920s and 1930s.

84. Bodnar, *The Transplanted*, 193.

85. For the story of the Chicago Area Project in the Russell Square area, see Schlossman and Sedlak, *Chicago Area Project Revisited*; Sanford Horwitt, *Let Them Call Me Rebel: Saul Alinsky—His Life and Legacy* (New York: Alfred A. Knopf, 1989), 47–55; Dominic Pacyga, "The Russell Square Community Committee: An Ethnic Response to Urban Problems," *Journal of Urban History* 15 (February, 1989): 159–184.

86. Chicago Recreation Commission, *Local Community Fact Book: Chicago Metropolitan Area* (Chicago: Chicago Review Press, 1938).

87. For a detailed study of Polish resistance to Mexican settlement in South Chicago in this period, see Arredondo, "Navigating Ethno-Racial Currents." On Mexican-Polish tensions in South Chicago, see Louise Año Nuevo Kerr, "The Chicano Experience in Chicago, 1920–1970" (PhD diss., University of Illinois—Chicago, 1976); Kijewski, Brosch, and Bulanda, *Three Chicago Millgates*, 46. Baur, "Delinquency among Mexican Boys," 121, 170.

88. Kijewski, Brosch, and Bulanda, *Three Chicago Millgates*, 53.

89. Ibid., 57; Chicago Recreation Commission, *Local Community Fact Book.* On Mexican industrial workers in Chicago and the urban Midwest in the 1920s and 1930s, see Zaragosa Vargas, *Proletarians of the North: A History of Mexican Industrial Workers in Detroit and the Midwest* (Berkeley and Los Angeles: University of California Press, 1993); Paul S. Taylor, *Mexican Labor in the United States: Chicago and the Calumet Region* (Berkeley: University of California Press, 1931); Kerr, "Chicano Experience."

90. "The Nature and Characteristics of Delinquents and Delinquency in the South Chicago Area Project, as Revealed by Three Group Diaries," 4–5, 8, CAP, Box 110, Folder 1, CHM; "Burley Lions, February 26, 1935," SB, Folder 72, UIC-SC.

91. John McGreevy, *Parish Boundaries: The Catholic Encounter with Race in the Twentieth-Century Urban North* (Chicago: University of Chicago Press, 1996), 26; Joseph Chalasinski, "Parish and Parochial School among Polish Immigrants in America: A Study of a Polish Neighborhood in South Chicago," CAP, Box 33, Folder 2, CHM; Pacyga, "Russell Square Community Committee," 159–184; Schlossman and Sedlak, *Chicago Area Project Revisited*, 6.

92. Schlossman and Sedlak, *Chicago Area Project Revisited*, 6.

93. Chalasinski, "Parish and Parochial School," 40.

94. Baur, "Delinquency among Mexican Boys," 24–25.

95. Ibid., 227; "The Nature and Characteristics of Delinquents and Delinquency in the South Chicago Area Project, as Revealed by Three Group Diaries," 4, CAP, Box 110, Folder 1, CHM.

96. Schlossman and Sedlak, *Chicago Area Project Revisited,* 72.

97. Historians have observed that a comparatively high number of Mexican immigrants in this era viewed themselves as "birds of passage." Such an outlook no doubt made them reluctant to make the investment in American life entailed in school attendance. This unwillingness to make such investments was further compounded by the threat of repatriation and the generally tenuous place of Mexicans in the industrial labor market. For an overview of how such issues shaped the Mexican views on citizenship in the Midwest, see Vargas, *Proletarians of the North,* 201–209; Arredondo, "Navigating Ethno-Racial Currents," 418–420. Historians of Mexicans in the Southwest have described similar conditions: George J. Sanchez, *Becoming Mexican American: Ethnicity, Culture and Identity in Chicano Los Angeles, 1900–1945* (New York: Oxford University Press, 1993).

98. Baur, "Delinquency among Mexican Boys," 208.

99. Ibid., 81.

100. Zaloha, "Persistence of Italian Customs," 42.

101. Leila Houghteling, *The Income and Standard of Living of Unskilled Laborers in Chicago* (Chicago: University of Chicago Press, 1927). For a discussion of the economic position of Chicago industrial workers in the 1920s, see Cohen, *Making A New Deal,* 101–103.

102. "The Employment Attitudes of the Delinquent Boy," EB, Box 132, Folder 8, UC-SCRC.

103. Cohen, Making *A New Deal,* 241. Susan Porter Benson's research on the consumption habits of working-class families in the interwar period describes the Depression not as a break but as a continuation of patterns of economic insecurity, albeit in more intensified forms. Porter Benson, "Gender, Generation, and Consumption."

104. Anita Edgar Jones, "Conditions Surrounding Mexicans in Chicago" (master's thesis, University of Chicago, 1928), 61–62. For a detailed discussion of the employment discrimination faced by Mexicans in interwar Chicago, see Arredondo, "Navigating Ethno-Racial Currents," 406–410.

105. Giovanni Schiavo, *The Italians in Chicago: A Study in Americanization* (Chicago: Italian American Publishing, 1928), 45.

106. Zaloha, "Persistence of Italian Customs," 28.

107. For a detailed account of the formation of national ethnic parishes and the tensions between them in Chicago, see McGreevy, *Parish Boundaries;* James Sanders, *The Education of an Urban Minority: Catholics in Chicago, 1833–1965* (New York: Oxford University Press, 1977), 40–71.

108. *Dziennik Zjednoczenia,* vol. 27, no. 137, June 12, 1923, FLPS, CHM; *Dziennik Chicagoski,* January 3, 1928, FLPS, CHM; *Przebudzenie,* vol. 2, no. 6, February 5, 1928, FLPS, CHM; *The Weekly Zgoda,* February 19, 1931, FLPS, CHM.

109. On this Italian reluctance, see McGreevy, *Parish Boundaries,* 12; Sanders, *Education of an Urban Minority,* 69–71.

110. Steven Joseph Shaw, "Chicago's Germans and Italians, 1903–1939: The

Catholic Parish as a Way-Station of Ethnicity and Americanization" (PhD diss., University of Chicago, 1981), 242.

111. Ibid.

112. Ibid.

113. Quite often the ethnic prejudices of the media were most overt in the coverage of youth-oriented issues. Throughout the early 1930s, the Italian-language press railed against movie producers and newspaper editors for propagating images of the Italian gangsters—young men themselves and heroes to youths of all types.

114. "A Study of Behavior Problems of Boys in the Lower North Community," 19, EB, Box 135, Folder 4, UC-SCRC.

115. For a discussion of this struggle, see Humbert S. Nelli, *Italians in Chicago, 1880–1930: A Study in Ethnic Mobility* (New York: Oxford University Press, 1983), 235–39.

116. For further discussion of the role of church leaders and Italian-language newspapers in negotiating Italian ethnic identity in Chicago during the 1920s and 1930s, see Guglielmo, *White on Arrival*, esp. chaps. 1–2.

117. Chalasinski, "Parish and Parochial School," 40–41.

118. Ibid., 43.

119. Thomas and Znaniecki, *Polish Peasant*, 1:252–253. For a discussion of this generational struggle over foreign-language instruction, which uses Poles in Chicago as one of its main case studies, see Jonathan Zimmerman, "Ethnics against Ethnicity: European Immigrants and Foreign-Language Instruction, 1890–1940," *Journal of American History* 88 (March 2002): 1383–1404.

120. Like the literature on public education, studies of Catholic education have largely dealt with how administrators, teachers, and religious leaders conceived of and organized the institutions; largely unexamined is how students responded to such conditions. See, for example, McGreevy, *Parish Boundaries;* and Sanders, *Education of an Urban Minority.*

121. McGreevy, *Parish Boundaries,* 5.

122. Shaw, "Chicago's Germans and Italians," 207.

123. Vivien Palmer, History of the Lower North Side, Prepared for the Chicago Historical Society, Document 27, CHM.

124. Ibid., Document 15.

125. James T. Farrell, *Studs Lonigan: A Trilogy Comprising "Young Lonigan," "The Young Manhood of Studs Lonigan," and "Judgment Day"* (Urbana: University of Illinois Press, 1993), 560.

126. McGreevy, *Parish Boundaries,* 94–97.

127. Sanders, *Education of an Urban Minority,* 4–13.

128. Ibid., 207–210. For more background on Mundelein's racial segregation policy, see Edward R. Kantowicz, *Corporation Sole: Cardinal Mundelein and Chicago Catholicism* (Notre Dame, IN: University of Notre Dame Press, 1983), 212–213.

129. Kantowicz, *Corporation Sole,* 91–104.

130. "The Nature and Characteristics of Delinquents and Delinquency in the South Chicago Area Project, as Revealed by Three Group Diaries," 6, CAP, Box 110, Folder 1, CHM.

131. Ibid., 2.
132. Paul Willis, *Learning to Labor: How Working-Class Kids Get Working-Class Jobs* (New York: Columbia University Press, 1977), 22.
133. Schlossman and Sedlak, *Chicago Area Project Revisited*, 7.
134. "A Study of Behavior Problems of Boys in the Lower North Community," 23, EB, Box 135, Folder 4, UC-SCRC.
135. Ibid., 21.
136. "The Nature and Characteristics of Delinquents and Delinquency in the South Chicago Area Project, as Revealed by Three Group Diaries," 3, CAP, Box 110, Folder 1, CHM.
137. Ibid.; Schlossman and Sedlak, *Chicago Area Project Revisited*, 71.
138. Schlossman and Sedlak, *Chicago Area Project Revisited*, 73.
139. Baur, "Delinquency among Mexican Boys," 208.
140. Ibid., 193.
141. Ibid.
142. Ibid., 221.
143. George Sanchez's research on Mexicans in Los Angeles reveals very similar conditions of racial discrimination marking the educational experience of Mexican adolescents in the 1930s. Sanchez, *Becoming Mexican American*, 255–259.
144. Kijewski, Brosch, and Bulanda, *Three Chicago Millgates*, 45; Arredondo, "Navigating Ethno-Racial Currents," 405.
145. This later emergence of the Mexican second generation in Chicago concurs with George Sanchez's account of the rise of the second generation of Mexican Americans in Los Angeles, which, he argues, did not occur until the 1930s. Sanchez, *Becoming Mexican American*, 254.
146. Baur, "Delinquency among Mexican Boys," 163.
147. Willis, *Learning to Labor*, 26.
148. "The Nature and Characteristics of Delinquents and Delinquency in the South Chicago Area Project, as Revealed by Three Group Diaries," 34, CAP, Box 110, Folder 1, CHM.
149. Ibid., 33.
150. Cressey, *The Taxi-Dance Hall*, 11–12.
151. Clifford R. Shaw and Henry D. McKay, *Juvenile Delinquency and Urban Areas: A Study of Rates of Delinquents in Relation to Differential Characteristics of Local Communities in American Cities* (Chicago: University of Chicago Press, 1942), 60.
152. Historians have described the 1920s as a crucial moment in the emergence of consumer-oriented forms of masculinity. Yet most of this research focuses on middle-class society and confines its analysis mainly to discursive forms. See, for example, Howard Chudacoff, *The Age of the Bachelor: Creating an American Subculture* (Princeton, NJ: Princeton University Press, 2000).
153. Cressey, *The Taxi-Dance Hall*, 13–14, 218–221. For another account of male group violence at taxi-dance halls, see Ireland, "Americanization of a Second Generation," 66–67.
154. "The Nature and Characteristics of Delinquents and Delinquency in the South Chicago Area Project, as Revealed by Three Group Diaries," 34, CAP, Box 110, Folder 1, CHM.

155. Baur, "Delinquency among Mexican Boys," 172.

156. Ruth Horowitz, *Honor and the American Dream: Culture and Identity in a Chicano Community* (New Brunswick, NJ: Rutgers University Press, 1983); Philippe Bourgois, *In Search of Respect: Selling Crack in El Barrio* (Cambridge: Cambridge University Press, 1995). For a historical study that places the construction of "honor and masculinity" at the center of street gang culture and views this process in relation to declining labor market opportunities in the postwar era, see Eric Schneider, *Vampires, Dragons, and Egyptian Kings: Youth Gangs in Postwar New York* (Princeton, NJ: Princeton University Press, 1999).

157. Bodnar, Simon, and Weber, *Lives of Their Own,* 89–97.

158. See John Bodnar, "Immigration, Kinship, and the Rise of Working-Class Realism, *Journal of Social History* 14 (Fall 1980): 45–65; Victor Greene, *The Slavic Community on Strike* (Notre Dame, IN: Notre Dame University Press, 1968); Yans-McLaughlin, *Family and Community.*

159. Porter Benson, "Gender, Generation, and Consumption," 230.

160. Zelizer, *Pricing the Priceless Child,* 6.

161. Ireland, "Americanization of a Second Generation," 9.

162. Schlossman and Sedlak, *Chicago Area Project Revisited,* 77–78.

163. "The Nature and Characteristics of Delinquents and Delinquency in the South Chicago Area Project, as Revealed by Three Group Diaries," 5, CAP, Box 110, Folder 1, CHM.

164. Ibid.

165. "A Study of Behavior Problems of Boys in the Lower North Community," 23, EB, Box 135, Folder 4, UC-SCRC.

166. "The Nature and Characteristics of Delinquents and Delinquency in the South Chicago Area Project, as Revealed by Three Group Diaries," 33, CAP, Box 110, Folder 1, CHM.

167. Baur, "Delinquency among Mexican Boys," 228.

168. Ibid., 193.

169. Schlossman and Sedlak, *Chicago Area Project Revisited,* 71.

170. "The Nature and Characteristics of Delinquents and Delinquency in the South Chicago Area Project, as Revealed by Three Group Diaries," 5, CAP, Box 110, Folder 1, CHM.

171. Baur, "Delinquency among Mexican Boys," 220.

172. For a recent study of Dillinger's role as a "social bandit," and his political meaning for the New Deal's War on Crime, see Claire Bond Potter, *War on Crime: Bandits, G-Men, and the Politics of Mass Culture* (New Brunswick, NJ: Rutgers University Press, 1998), 1–9, 138–168.

173. Baur, "Delinquency among Mexican Boys," 220.

174. The literature on gangster films is vast. Two studies that examine the social meaning of the gangster image in relation to Americanization, ethnicity, and consumption are Jonathan Munby, *Public Enemies, Public Heroes: Screening the Gangster from Little Caesar to Touch of Evil* (Chicago: University of Chicago Press, 1999); David Ruth, *Inventing the Public Enemy: The Gangster in American Culture, 1918–1934* (Chicago: University of Chicago Press, 1996).

175. On the gangster's subversion of the Protestant work ethic and the censorship movement, see Munby, *Public Enemies, Public Heroes,* 1–17.

176. Baur, "Delinquency among Mexican Boys, 218.

177. For further discussion see Munby's insightful analysis of the blockbuster films *Little Caesar, Public Enemy, and Scarface*. Munby, *Public Enemies, Public Heroes*, 39–65.

178. My thinking on how working-class youths took their own messages from these films, despite the efforts of producers to show that "crime does not pay," benefits from the work of "reception theorists." See, for example, Janice Radway, *Reading the Romance: Women, Patriarchy, and Popular Literature* (Chapel Hill: University of North Carolina Press, 1984).

179. "The Nature and Characteristics of Delinquents and Delinquency in the South Chicago Area Project, as Revealed by Three Group Diaries," 35, CAP, Box 110, Folder 1, CHM.

180. Ibid., 34.

181. Shaw, *The Jack-Roller*, 40.

182. "The Nature and Characteristics of Delinquents and Delinquency in the South Chicago Area Project, as Revealed by Three Group Diaries," 4, CAP, Box 110, Folder 1, CHM.

183. *Bulletin Italo-American National Union*, June 1925, FLPS, CHM; *Bulletin Italo-American National Union*, October 1928, FLPS, CHM; see also, *Bulletin Order Sons of Italy in America*, November-December 1933, FLPS, CHM.

184. *Bulletin Italo-American National Union*, c. 1930, FLPS, CHM. For a detailed account of the stigmatization of Italians as criminals in Chicago, see Guglielmo, *White on Arrival*, chap. 4.

185. *Mens Italica*, October 1928, FLPS, CHM.

186. *Dziennik Zjedonoczenia*, December 19, 1921, FLPS, CHM.

187. Ruth, *Inventing the Public Enemy*, 63–86.

3. HOODLUMS AND ZOOT-SUITERS

Epigraphs: Frank DeLiberto (DEL-55), ICP, Box 4, CHM, 44. James Baldwin, *Notes of a Native Son* (Boston: Beacon Press, 1955), 111.

1. Conference of the Committee on Minority Groups with agencies in the neighborhood of Chicago Commons, Re: Recent Incidents following the moving of Negroes into the community, April 3, 1944, Welfare Council of Metropolitan Chicago Collection (hereafter cited as WC), Box 145, Folder 3, CHM.

2. U.S. Bureau of the Census, *Sixteenth Census of the United States, Characteristics of the Nonwhite Population by Race;* U.S. Bureau of the Census, *Seventeenth Census of the United States*, vol. 2, *Characteristics of the Population*.

3. St. Clair Drake and Horace Cayton, *Black Metropolis: A Study of Negro Life in a Northern City* (Chicago: University of Chicago Press, 1993), 90–91.

4. Arnold R. Hirsch, *Making the Second Ghetto: Race and Housing in Chicago, 1940–1960* (Cambridge: Cambridge University Press, 1983), 23.

5. *Chicago Defender*, July 31, 1943. For a richly documented account of the wartime housing problem, see Drake and Cayton, *Black Metropolis*, 99–213.

6. Conference of the Committee on Minority Groups with agencies in the neighborhood of Chicago Commons, Re: Recent Incidents following the moving of Negroes into the community, April 3, 1944, WC, Box 145, Folder 3, CHM.

7. These figures are cited in Hirsch, *Making the Second Ghetto*, 5.

8. Figures derived from Philip M. Hauser and Evelyn Kitagawa, eds., *Local Community Fact Book* [1950] (Chicago: University of Chicago, Chicago Community Inventory, 1953).

9. Otis Dudley Duncan and Beverly Duncan, *The Negro Population of Chicago: A Study of Residential Succession* (Chicago: University of Chicago Press, 1957), 98. According to the authors, 215,000 of the 227,193 were "Negro."

10. Hirsch, *Making the Second Ghetto*, 4.

11. *Chicago Defender*, May 22, 1943.

12. *Chicago Defender*, February 20, 1943, and March 6, 1943.

13. Council of Social Agencies, Chicago, Informal Meeting, Friday, June 25, 1943, WC, Box 145, Folder 4, CHM.

14. *Chicago Tribune*, June 22, 1943.

15. Meeting on Inter-Racial Situation, Friday, June 25, 1943, WC, Box 145, Folder 2, CHM; Council of Social Agencies, Chicago, Informal Meeting, Friday, June 25, 1943, WC, Box 145, Folder 4, CHM. For a study that demonstrates that such tensions escalated into violence in cities across the country during this time, see Harvard Sitkoff, "Racial Militancy and Interracial Violence in the Second World War," *Journal of American History* 58 (December 1971): 661–681.

16. Quoted in Herbert Shapiro, *White Violence and Black Response: From Reconstruction to Montgomery* (Amherst: University of Massachusetts Press, 1988), 311.

17. *Chicago Tribune*, June 22, 1943.

18. Rumors of Communist Party involvement circulated during the first days of the riot, but the Chicago coverage did not mention this possibility in explaining the mayor's explicit rejection of the idea of organized agitation.

19. City Planning in Race Relations, Proceedings of the Mayor's Conference on Race Relations, February 1944, 52, Chicago Urban League (hereafter cited as CUL), Folder 229, UIC-SC.

20. On the wartime delinquency scare, see James Gilbert, *A Cycle of Outrage: America's Reaction to the Juvenile Delinquent in the 1950s* (New York: Oxford University Press, 1986), 24–41; Walter C. Reckless, "The Impact of War on Crime and Delinquency and Prostitution," *American Journal of Sociology* 48 (November 1942): 378–386.

21. *Chicago Tribune*, June 5, 1943.

22. *Chicago Tribune*, June 13, 1943.

23. For further discussion of the circumstances of the Zoot Suit Riots and their meaning in wartime America, see Mauricio Mazon, *The Zoot-Suit Riots: The Psychology of Symbolic Annihilation* (Austin: University of Texas Press, 1984); Robin D. G. Kelley, "The Riddle of the Zoot: Malcolm Little and Black Cultural Politics during World War II," in *Race Rebels: Culture, Politics, and the Black Working Class* (New York: Free Press, 1994): 161–181; Fritz Redl, "Zoot Suits: An Interpretation," in *America at War: The Home Front, 1941–1945*, ed. Richard Polenberg (Englewood Cliffs, NJ: Prentice-Hall, 1968), 148–151; Richard Lingeman, *Don't You Know There's a War On? The American Home Front, 1941–1945* (New York: Putnam, 1970), 333–334; Stuart Cosgrove, "The Zoot-Suit and Style Warfare," *History Workshop Journal* 18 (Autumn 1984): 77–91.

24. City Planning in Race Relations, Proceedings of the Mayor's Conference on Race Relations, February 1944, 52, CUL, Folder 229, UIC-SC.

25. *Chicago Daily News,* June 11, 1943.

26. Domenic J. Capeci Jr. and Martha Wilkerson, *Layered Violence: The Detroit Rioters of 1943* (Jackson and London: University Press of Mississippi, 1991), 5, 9–10.

27. For the story of the Savoy closing, see Dominic Capeci Jr., *The Harlem Riot of 1943* (Philadelphia: Temple University Press, 1977), 138–140.

28. *Chicago Defender,* May 20, 1944.

29. *Chicago Defender,* June 3, 1944.

30. *Chicago Defender,* October 20, 1945.

31. *Chicago Defender,* September 29, 1945; *Chicago Defender,* October 6, 1945.

32. *Chicago Defender,* October 20, 1945.

33. Stanley Cohen, *Folk Devils and Moral Panics: The Creation of the Mods and Rockers* (Oxford: Martin Robertson, 1980); Stuart Hall, Charles Critcher, Tony Jefferson, John Clarke, and Brian Roberts, *Policing the Crisis: Mugging, the State, the Law, and Order* (New York: Holmes and Meier, 1978); Charles R. Acland, *Youth, Murder, Spectacle: The Cultural Politics of "Youth in Crisis"* (Boulder: University of Colorado Press, 1995).

34. Alberto Melucci, *Challenging Codes: Collective Action in the Information Age* (Cambridge: Cambridge University Press, 1996), 118.

35. Jack Lait and Lee Mortimer, *Chicago Confidential* (New York: Dell Publishing, 1950), 288.

36. See examples of these ads in *North Loop News,* May 10, 1945, and May 24, 1945.

37. Council of Social Agencies, Chicago, Informal Meeting, Friday, June 25, 1943, WC, Box 145, Folder 4, CHM; Meeting on Inter-Racial Situation, Friday, June 25, 1943, WC, Box 145, Folder 2, CHM.

38. Minutes of the Board of Directors, May 26, 1944, CAP, Box 18, Folder 2, CHM. While minstrel shows were perhaps not common around this time, this was not the only such event recorded in the mid-1940s. In November 1947, another minstrel show was put on at Harrison High School on the Near West Side (see *West Side News,* November 21, 1947).

39. My thinking here owes to Eric Lott's idea that minstrelsy has more to do with "the vagaries of racial desire" than "racial aversion." See Eric Lott, *Love and Theft: Blackface Minstrelsy and the American Working Class* (New York: Oxford University Press, 1995), 6.

40. Conference of the Committee on Minority Groups with agencies in the neighborhood of Chicago Commons, Re: Recent Incidents following the moving of Negroes into the community, April 3, 1944, WC, Box 145, Folder 3, CHM.

41. Orleans Playground Report, Director, Walter Klaus, EB, Box 135, Folder 6, UC-SC; The Negro in Little Italy, October 30, 1931, EB, Box 135, Folder 5, UC-SC.

42. Thomas A. Guglielmo, "Encountering the Color Line in the Everyday: Italians in Interwar Chicago," *Journal of American Ethnic History* (Summer 2004): 49–50.

43. Eagles, January 20, 1942, L. Stanton, CCA, Box 7, Folder—Clubs and Groups, 1940–42, CHM.
44. Philia Rafaelli (RAF-84), ICP, Box 6, CHM, 29.
45. *Chicago Defender,* August 23 and September 6, 1941.
46. Analysis of Chicago School Strikes, American Council on Race Relations, WC, Box 145, Folder 3, CHM. A number of scholars have examined the role played by interracial rape rumors in triggering white mob violence against racial others between 1917 and 1943. See, for example, Marilynn S. Johnson, "Gender, Race, and Rumours: Re-examining the 1943 Race Riots," *Gender and History* 10 (August 1998): 252–277. For a related interpretation of the role of rape narratives in sparking lynch mobs in the South, see Jacquelyn Dowd Hall, "The Mind That Burns in Each Body: Women, Rape, and Racial Violence," in *The Powers of Desire: The Politics of Sexuality,* by Ann Snitow, Christine Stansell, and Sharon Thompson (New York: Monthly Review Press, 1983), 328–349.
47. For two important studies that make this argument about race relations on the home front, see Michael Denning, *The Cultural Front: The Laboring of American Culture in the Twentieth Century* (London and New York: Verso, 1996), 33–35; Matthew Frye Jacobson, *Whiteness of a Different Color: European Immigrants and the Alchemy of Race* (Cambridge, MA: Harvard University Press, 1998), 113–117. On European Americans developing a common sense of whiteness in the armed forces, see Gary Gerstle, *American Crucible: Race and Nation in the Twentieth Century* (Princeton, NJ: Princeton University Press, 2001), 187–237.
48. For another study that complements my own in emphasizing spheres of everyday experience as critical in racial learning, see Guglielmo, "Encountering the Color Line."
49. Slavoj Žižek, "Eastern Europe's Republics of Gilead," *New Left Review* 183 (September/October 1990): 50–62. I owe my use of Žižek here to Eric Lott's application of Žižek's thinking to his analysis of the allure of minstrelsy in nineteenth-century America. See Lott, *Love and Theft,* 97, 148.
50. Council of Social Agencies, Chicago, Informal Meeting, Friday, June 25, 1943, WC, Box 145, Folder 4, CHM; Meeting on Inter-Racial Situation, Friday, June 25, 1943, WC, Box 145, Folder 2, CHM.
51. Baldwin, *Notes of a Native Son,* 92–94.
52. For two mentions of the existence of such rumors, see *The Chicago Sun,* June 7, 1945; Analysis of Chicago School Strikes, American Council on Race Relations, WC, Box 145, Folder 3, CHM. In each case, such rumors were investigated and found to be groundless.
53. Baldwin, *Notes of a Native Son,* 86.
54. John Ogbu, "Minority Status and Literacy in Comparative Perspective," *Daedelus* 119, no. 2 (Spring 1990): 141–168.
55. *Chicago Defender,* June 12, 1943.
56. Robin D. G. Kelley, *Race Rebels: Culture, Politics, and the Black Working Class* (New York: Free Press, 1994), 166.
57. Ibid., 161–181. For other studies focusing specifically on the significance of the zoot suit in African American culture, see Cosgrove, "Zoot-Suit," 77–91; Bruce M. Tyler, "Black Jive and White Repression," *Journal of Ethnic Studies* 16, no. 4 (1989): 32–38.

58. *Negro Digest* 1, no. 4 (Winter-Spring 1943): 301.

59. Council of Social Agencies, Chicago, Informal Meeting, Friday, June 25, 1943, WC, Box 145, Folder 4, CHM.

60. Kelley, *Race Rebels*, 8-9.

61. Lait and Mortimer, *Chicago Confidential*, 43.

62. Ibid., 46.

63. Memorandum for the Operating Director, April 27, 1945, Re: 5th Police District, Virgil W. Peterson Papers (hereafter cited as VP), Series 3, Box 58, Folder 4, CHM.

64. Memorandum for the Operating Director, June 20, 1945, Re: 5th Police District, VP, Series 3, Box 58, Folder 4, CHM.

65. Memorandum for the Files, May 24, 1945, Re: Crime Conditions in Fifth Police District and Fourth Police District, Ida B. Wells Project, VP, Series 3, Box 58, Folder 4, CHM; Memorandum for the Operating Director, June 20, 1945, Re: 5th Police District, VP, Series 3, Box 58, Folder 4, CHM; Chicago Crime Commission, Woodlawn District (7th Police District), Survey of Conditions, November 13th to and including January 22, 1946, VP, Series 3, Box 58, Folder 4, CHM.

66. Capeci, *Harlem Riot of 1943*, 127. The term was coined in Kenneth B. Clark and James Barker, "The Zoot Effect in Personality: A Race Riot Participant," *Journal of Abnormal Psychology* 40, no. 2 (1945): 143-148.

67. *Chicago Defender*, October 2, 1943.

68. For an account of the sense of racial militancy pervading the zoot suit milieu during the war, and a provocative analysis of the link between this militancy and the rise of bebop, see Eric Lott, "Double V, Double-Time: Bebop's Politics of Style," *Callaloo* 11, no. 3 (1988): 587-605.

69. *Chicago Defender*, July 7, 1945.

70. Chicago Crime Commission, Woodlawn District (7th Police District), Survey of Conditions, November 13th to and including January 22, 1946, VP, Series 3, Box 58, Folder 4, CHM.

71. Ibid.

72. Human Relations in Chicago: Report for the Year 1946 of the Mayor's Commission on Human Relations, 72, CUL, Folder 229, UIC-SC; White City Roller Skating Rink Demonstration, Events/Demonstrations/Illinois—Chicago, Folder 2, ICHi—19601, ICHi—22745, CHM Photographic Files.

73. *Chicago Defender*, April 13, 1946; Human Relations in Chicago: Report for the Year 1946 of the Mayor's Commission on Human Relations, 72, CUL, Folder 229, UIC-SC.

74. *Chicago Defender*, December 26, 1942.

75. Progress Report to Co-ordinator of Inter-American Affairs on Latin-American Community Program, Conducted by the Chicago Area Project, June 1, 1943, CAP, Box 89, Folder 2, CHM.

76. *Chicago Defender*, August 23, 1941.

77. *Chicago Defender*, May 27, 1944.

78. Human Relations in Chicago: Report for the Year 1946 of the Mayor's Commission on Human Relations, 72, CUL, Folder 229, UIC-SC.

79. Useni Eugene Perkins, *The Explosion of Chicago's Black Street Gangs: 1900 to the Present* (Chicago: Third World Press, 1987), 27.

80. *Chicago Defender,* April 22, 1944.

81. *Chicago Defender,* May 27, 1944; Memorandum for the Operating Director, June 20, 1945, Re: 5th Police District, VP, Series 3, Box 58, Folder 4, CHM.

82. *Chicago Defender,* August 2, 1947.

83. For some useful discussions of the role of violence in the construction of gang youth masculinity, see Eric Schneider, *Vampires, Dragons, and Egyptian Kings: Youth Gangs in Postwar New York* (Princeton, NJ: Princeton University Press, 1999), 123–129; Fox Butterfield, *All God's Children: The Bosket Family and the American Tradition of Violence* (New York: Avon Books, 1996), 61–64; Ruth Horowitz, *Honor and the American Dream: Culture and Identity in a Chicano Community* (New Brunswick, NJ: Rutgers University Press, 1983), chap. 5.

84. Perkins, *Chicago's Black Street Gangs,* 74.

85. Memorandum for the Files, May 24, 1945, Re: Crime Conditions in Fifth Police District and Fourth Police District, Ida B. Wells Project, VP, Series 3, Box 58, Folder 4, CHM.

86. Memorandum for the Operating Director, June 20, 1945, Re: 5th Police District, VP, Series 3, Box 58, Folder 4, CHM.

87. Perkins, *Chicago's Black Street Gangs,* 27–28; Memorandum for the Files, May 24, 1945, Re: Crime Conditions in Fifth Police District and Fourth Police District, Ida B. Wells Project, VP, Series 3, Box 58, Folder 4, CHM; Lait and Mortimer, *Chicago Confidential,* 43; *Chicago Defender,* August 2, 1947.

88. Memorandum Brief of Facts Regarding Survey of Conditions in Woodlawn District, Chicago Crime Commission, January 22, 1946, VP, Series 3, Box 58, Folder 4, CHM.

89. Woodlawn District (7th Police District), Survey of Conditions, November 13th to and including January 22, 1946, Chicago Crime Commission, VP, Series 3, Box 58, Folder 4, CHM.

90. Memorandum for the Files, May 24, 1945, Re: Crime Conditions in Fifth Police District and Fourth Police District, Ida B. Wells Project, VP, Series 3, Box 58, Folder 4, CHM; Memorandum for the Operating Director, April 27, 1945, Re: 5th Police District, VP, Series 3, Box 58, Folder 4, CHM.

91. Drake and Cayton, *Black Metropolis,* 589.

92. Perkins, *Chicago's Black Street Gangs,* 28.

93. *Chicago Defender,* May 27, 1944; Memorandum for the Files, May 24, 1945, Re: Crime Conditions in Fifth Police District and Fourth Police District, Ida B. Wells Project, VP, Series 3, Box 58, Folder 4, CHM; Memorandum for the Operating Director, June 20, 1945, Re: 5th Police District, VP, Series 3, Box 58, Folder 4, CHM.

94. *Chicago Defender,* April 13, 1946.

95. *Chicago Defender,* June 12, 1943.

96. Area Project in the Negro District, Box 145, Folder 1, WC, CHM.

97. Minutes of the Board of Directors, Chicago Area Project, May 7, 1946, CAP, Box 18, Folder 2, CHM.

98. Drake and Cayton, *Black Metropolis,* 684.

99. Letter to James B. McCahey from Resolutions Committee, Parents' Club of Abraham Lincoln Centre, March 29, 1944, WC, Box 145, Folder 6, CHM.

4. ANGRY YOUNG MEN

Epigraph: Confidential Report, Case no. E-77, June 9, 1954, ACLU, Illinois Division, Box 11, Folder 9, UC-SCRC.

1. *Chicago Defender,* July 13, 1946.
2. Ibid.
3. *Chicago Defender,* July 6, 1946.
4. *Chicago Defender,* July 20, 1946.
5. Mayor's Commission on Human Relations, Progress Report, July 1946, CAP, Box 32, Folder 1, CHM.
6. Human Relations in Chicago: Report for the Year 1946 of the Mayor's Commission on Human Relations, CUL, Folder 229, UIC-SC.
7. Mayor's Commission on Human Relations, Progress Report, July 1946, CAP, Box 32, Folder 1, CHM.
8. Minutes of the Meeting of the Committee on Minority Groups, October 3, 1947, WC, Box 145, Folder 2, CHM.
9. For further discussion of police behavior in mob actions over housing, see Arnold R. Hirsch, *Making the Second Ghetto: Race and Housing in Chicago, 1940–1960* (Cambridge: Cambridge University Press, 1983), 97–98; Lawrence Rieser, "An Analysis of the Reporting of Racial Incidents in Chicago, 1945 to 1950," (master's thesis, University of Chicago, 1951), 60–68.
10. Mayor's Commission on Human Relations, Progress Report, July 1946, CAP, Box 32, Folder 1, CHM.
11. Human Relations in Chicago: Report for the Year 1946 of the Mayor's Commission on Human Relations, 72, CUL, Folder 229, UIC-SC.
12. Ibid.
13. *Chicago Defender,* September 14, 1946.
14. Mayor's Commission on Human Relations, Progress Report, July 1946, CAP, Box 32, Folder 1, CHM.
15. *Chicago Defender,* April 13, 1946.
16. Human Relations in Chicago: Report for the Year 1946 of the Mayor's Commission on Human Relations, 72, CUL, Folder 229, UIC-SC.
17. Ibid.
18. Ibid.; *Chicago Defender,* October 12, 1946.
19. *Chicago Defender,* October 5, 1946.
20. Anthony Sorrentino, *Organizing against Crime: Redeveloping the Neighborhood* (New York: Human Sciences Press, 1977), 138.
21. Ibid., 122.
22. James Gilbert, *A Cycle of Outrage: America's Reaction to the Juvenile Delinquent in the 1950s* (New York: Oxford University Press, 1986), 19–20.
23. Wesley G. Skogan, *Chicago since 1840: A Time-Series Handbook* (Urbana: University of Illinois Press, 1976), 25.
24. William Tuttle, *"Daddy's Gone to War": The Second World War in the Lives of America's Children* (New York: Oxford University Press, 1993), 220.
25. Skogan, *Chicago since 1840,* 91. The increase in the number of police employees does not explain away these increases in crime. Gambling and prostitution arrests, for example, both fell between 1945 and 1946. Moreover, while

the number of police employees dropped in 1947, nontraffic arrests and arrests for public intoxication, disorderly conduct, and vagrancy rose once again, although at a somewhat more modest rate.

26. Tuttle, *"Daddy's Gone to War,"* 218–219.

27. *Chicago Sun-Times,* July 25, 1949.

28. Chicago Police Department, *Report of Work Performed by the Officers Assigned to Juvenile Work at the Various Districts, Year Ending December 31, 1944,* MRC, HWLC; Chicago Police Department, *Report of Work Performed by the Officers Assigned to Juvenile Work at the Various Districts, Year Ending December 31, 1946,* MRC, HWLC.

29. Tuttle, *"Daddy's Gone to War,"* 217. While such observations are indeed compelling, our knowledge of how the return of white veterans changed life at home is largely anecdotal. Whereas the mobilizing effect of black veterans is a theme the literature on the civil rights movement has visited frequently in its search for origins, a similar inquiry into the political effects of the war experience has not yet been taken on by scholars tracing the emergence of the postwar white backlash.

30. Eric C. Schneider, *Vampires, Dragons, and Egyptian Kings: Youth Gangs in Postwar New York* (Princeton, NJ: Princeton University Press, 1999), 71–77.

31. Chicago Police Department Annual Reports for 1944 and 1946, MRC, HWLC.

32. Ibid.

33. In his research on the languages home owners in Detroit used to justify racial exclusion, Thomas Sugrue finds strong appeals to wartime sacrifices. See Thomas Sugrue, "Crabgrass-Roots Politics: Race, Rights and the Reaction against Liberalism in the Urban North, 1940–1964," *Journal of American History* 82 (September 1995): 551–578.

34. For studies that point to the years between 1946 and 1949 as pivotal ones in the development of white grassroots resistance to racial integration in other U.S. cities, see Thomas Sugrue, *The Origins of the Urban Crisis: Race and Inequality in Postwar Detroit* (Princeton, NJ: Princeton University Press, 1996), 32–88; Sugrue, "Crabgrass-Roots Politics"; Mike Davis, *City of Quartz: Excavating the Future in Los Angeles* (New York: Vintage Books, 1992), 293; Matthew Frye Jacobson, *Whiteness of a Different Color: European Immigrants and the Alchemy of Race* (Cambridge, MA: Harvard University Press, 1998), 113–117. We should also remember that 1948 was the year the Supreme Court ruled restrictive covenants (contracts between home-owners barring the sale or rental of real estate to African Americans) unenforceable (*Shelley v. Kraemer*).

35. Quoted in Hirsch, *Making the Second Ghetto,* 55.

36. Ibid., 56; *Chicago Defender,* July 5, 1947.

37. Two works that make this point quite clearly are Gary Gerstle, "Race and the Myth of the Liberal Consensus," *Journal of American History* 82 (September 1995): 579–586; Sugrue, "Crabgrass-Roots Politics." For examples of the literature they are arguing against, see Allen J. Matusow, *The Unraveling of America: A History of Liberalism in the 1960s* (New York: Harper and Row, 1984); Jonathan Rieder, "The Rise of the 'Silent Majority,'" in *The Rise and Fall of the New Deal Order, 1930–1980,* ed. Steve Fraser and Gary Gerstle (Prince-

ton, NJ: Princeton University Press, 1989), 243–268; Thomas Byrne Edsall and Mary D. Edsall, *Chain Reaction: The Impact of Race, Rights, and Taxes on American Politics* (New York: Norton, 1991); Jim Sleeper, *The Closest of Strangers: Liberalism and the Politics of Race in New York City* (New York: Norton, 1990).

38. *Chicago Defender,* August 30, 1947.

39. Chicago Park District, "The Police and Minority Groups: A Manual Prepared for Use in the Chicago Park District Training School," 37, CHM.

40. Mayor's Commission on Human Relations, Memorandum on Fernwood Park Homes, CUL, Folder 709, UIC-SC; *Chicago Defender,* August 30, 1947. Significantly, the Fernwood riot, along with the one in Park Manor in 1949, brought out the oldest crowds of any such demonstrations in these years. For the average ages of participants in the major housing riots, see Hirsch, *Making the Second Ghetto,* 74–75. Hirsch largely dismisses the significance of the youthfulness of the crowd at Fernwood and other housing protests for several reasons. First, he does not consider the distortion the unrepresentative handful of older arrestees (in their fifties and sixties) creates in the average age figures he generates, while the ages of adolescents are not included in arrest figures and therefore do not weigh in the averages. Second, there is reason to believe that the police in these situations—especially in view of what we know about their lack of enthusiasm for their role in protecting the rights of blacks—would have been averse to the physical challenges involved in arresting the stronger and more agile young men in the crowds, which in many cases would have involved taking on whole groups. Last, there is simply the matter of perspective. Even with these distortions, more than half and perhaps as much as two-thirds of the members of even the older of Hirsch's crowds were still aged somewhere between their early teens and mid-twenties. These were thus predominantly young crowds.

41. A Report on the Mob Violence at the Fernwood Veterans' Housing Project on the Evening of August 13, 1947, in Mayor's Commission on Human Relations, Memorandum on Fernwood Park Homes, CUL, Folder 709, UIC-SC.

42. Monthly Report of the Executive Director, Chicago Commission on Human Relations, March 1948, CAP, Box 32, Folder 1, CHM.

43. Minutes of the Meeting of the Committee on Minority Group Relationships, October 1, 1948, WC, Box 145, Folder 2, CHM.

44. *Chicago Defender,* July 30, 1949; *Chicago Defender,* September 17, 1949.

45. Chicago Commission on Human Relations, Documentary Memorandum: Interracial Disturbances at 7407–7409 South Parkway and 5643 South Peoria Street, ACLU, Box 7, Folder 5, UC-SCRC.

46. Ibid.

47. Douglas McAdam, *Political Process and the Development of Black Insurgency, 1930–1970* (Chicago: University of Chicago Press, 1999), 51.

48. William Gamson, *Talking Politics* (New York: Cambridge University Press, 1992).

49. My thinking on the role of emotions in collective action and community identification is informed by two works: Ron Aminzade and Doug McAdam, "Emotions and Contentious Politics," in *Silence and Voice in the Study of Contentious Politics,* by Ronald R. Aminzade, Jack A. Goldstone, Doug McAdam,

Elizabeth J. Perry, William H. Sewell Jr., Sidney Tarrow, and Charles Tilly (Cambridge: Cambridge University Press, 2001), 14–50; Thomas J. Scheff, "Emotions and Identity: A Theory of Ethnic Nationalism," in *Social Theory and the Politics of Identity*, ed. Craig Calhoun (Cambridge, U.K.: Blackwell Publishers, 1994).

50. Photographs taken of the scene in Cicero before the story hit the dailies also indicate that young men of these ages were overwhelmingly the core actors at the outset. See, DN-N-7949, Events/Riots Folder, CHM.

51. *Chicago Tribune*, July 13, 1951.

52. *Chicago Tribune*, July 17, 1951.

53. *Chicago Tribune*, July 14, 1951.

54. On the 1946 General Motors strike and the retreat of organized labor in the first several years after the end of the war, see David Brody, *Workers in Industrial America: Essays on the Twentieth Century Struggle* (New York: Oxford University Press, 1980), 174, 183; Nelson Lichtenstein, "From Corporatism to Collective Bargaining: Organized Labor and the Eclipse of Social Democracy in the Postwar Era," in *New Deal Order* (see note 37), 122–152.

55. Sorrentino, *Organizing against Crime*, 138.

56. Minutes of the Board of Directors, Chicago Area Project, April 12, 1950, CAP, Box 18, Folder 2, CHM.

57. Stuart Hall and Tony Jefferson, eds., *Resistance through Rituals: Youth Subcultures in Postwar Britain* (London: Harper Collins Academic, 1976), 13–14.

58. Raymond Williams, "Base and Superstructure in Marxist Cultural Theory," *New Left Review* 82 (November–December, 1973): 3–16.

59. Thomas Doherty, *Teenagers and Teenpics: The Juvenilization of American Movies in the 1950s* (Philadelphia: Temple University Press, 2002); W. T. Lhamon, *Deliberate Speed: The Origins of a Cultural Style in the American 1950s* (Washington, DC: Smithsonian Institute Press, 1990), 8; See also Bill Osgerby, *Playboys in Paradise: Masculinity, Youth, and Leisure-Style in Modern America* (Oxford: Berg, 2001), which argues that the mythology of "vibrant youth" born in this era would serve as a primary signifier for masculinity and postwar prosperity through the 1960s.

60. Gilbert, *A Cycle of Outrage.*

61. *Chicago Tribune*, July 14, 1951.

62. A Preliminary Report on Racial Disturbances in Chicago for the Period July 21 to August 4, 1957, ACLU, Box 9, Folder 8, UC-SCRC.

63. *Chicago Daily News*, July 29, 1957.

64. On the emergence of a teenage market in the 1950s and the concomitant advent of the various genres of teen films, see Doherty, *Teenagers and Teenpics*, 32–114.

65. Don T. Blackiston, "A Survey of Community Committees in the Near West Side, the Southside, and Russell Square," paper submitted for Sociology 404, CAP, Box 104, Folder 10, CHM.

66. *Chicago Daily News*, January 27, 1956.

67. The Barons—A Street Gang, 16–17, CAP, Box 105, Folder 13, CHM.

68. For an interesting study of the centrality of the automobile in the con-

struction of class, gender, and national identities in the 1950s, see David Gart-
man, *Auto Opium: A Social History of American Automobile Design* (London:
Routledge, 1994), 136–181.

69. For an excellent description of the problems Chicago renters faced as they
attempted to make ends meet in the demobilization years, see Laura McEnaney,
"Nightmares on Elm Street: Demobilizing in Chicago, 1945–1953," *Journal of
American History* 92 (March 2006): 1265–1291.

70. A Report on the Mob Violence at the Fernwood Veterans' Housing Project
on the Evening of August 13, 1947, in Mayor's Commission on Human Relations, Memorandum on Fernwood Park Homes, CUL, Folder 709, UIC-SC.

71. Skogan, *Chicago since 1840*, 25.

72. Ibid., 20; Proceedings of the Second Annual Counseling Institute, Committee on Employment and Guidance and Division on Family and Child Welfare, 3, WC, Box 77, Folder 2, CHM.

73. John F. McDonald, *Employment Location and Industrial Land Use in
Metropolitan Chicago* (Urbana: University of Illinois Press, 1984), 10–18. While
1958 witnessed a marked economic downturn, McDonald's figures for 1954 show
that the declines in every job category were well under way prior to that.

74. *Chicago Tribune,* July 14, 1951; *Chicago Daily News,* July 29, 1957. On
the effects of automation on the industrial labor market in the late 1940s and
1950s, see Sugrue, *Origins of the Urban Crisis,* 130–135.

75. Perhaps the most nuanced example of this argument can be found in
Philippe Bourgois, *In Search of Respect: Selling Crack in El Barrio* (Cambridge:
Cambridge University Press, 1995), 114–173. For a more recent study that places
the development of such forms of masculinity in the context of postwar deindustrialization, see Schneider, *Vampires, Dragons,* 106–136.

76. Blackiston, "Survey of Community Committees."

77. Chicago Commons Association, Annual Report, January 1952, CCA, Box
5a, Folder 2, CHM.

78. Welfare Council of Metropolitan Chicago, Division on Education and
Recreation, Youth Services Committee, CAP, Box 56, Folder 2, CHM.

79. Ibid.

80. Alberto Melucci, *Challenging Codes: Collective Action in the Information Age* (Cambridge: Cambridge University Press, 1996), 119–120.

81. "Breaking through Barriers: Report on the Hard-to-Reach-Youth Project,"
Welfare Council of Metropolitan Chicago, Institute for Juvenile Research Records
(hereafter cited as IJR), Box 25, Folder 2, CHM.

82. "On Breaking Through the Drop-Out Problem (A Limited Examination
and Proposals)," Chicago Federation of Settlements and Neighborhood Centers,
WC, Box 337, Folder 3, CHM.

83. For further discussion on how structural conditions affected the labor
market opportunities of the urban white working class, see Thomas J. Sugrue,
"The Structures of Urban Poverty: The Reorganization of Space and Work in
Three Periods of American History," in *The "Underclass" Debate: Views from
History,* ed. Michael B. Katz (Princeton, NJ: Princeton University Press, 1993),
85–117.

84. "Youth and Culture," Operating Bulletin no. 7, Welfare Council of Met-

ropolitan Chicago, Div. 3—Education and Recreation, Hard-to-Reach-Youth Project, CAP, Box 56, Folder 3, CHM.

85. Minutes of Hard-to-Reach-Youth Project Workers' Meeting, Friday, November 16, 1956, WC, Box 696, Folder 1, CHM.

86. "Youth and Culture," Operating Bulletin no. 7, Welfare Council of Metropolitan Chicago, Div. 3—Education and Recreation, Hard-to-Reach-Youth Project, CAP, Box 56, Folder 3, CHM.

87. Two key works of the second generation of gang studies (Frederic Thrasher, *The Gang: A Study of 1,313 Gangs in Chicago* [Chicago: University of Chicago Press, 1927]; and Herbert Asbury, *Gem of the Prairie: An Informal History of the Chicago Underworld* [DeKalb: Northern Illinois University Press, 1941] representing the first), all of which, in one way or another, view delinquent subcultures as attempts to resolve "status" problems associated with the limited opportunity structures of lower-class society, are Albert Cohen, *Delinquent Boys* (Glencoe: Free Press, 1955); and Richard A. Cloward and Lloyd B. Ohlin, *Delinquency and Opportunity: A Theory of Delinquent Gangs* (New York: Free Press, 1960). A third generation of "underclass" gang studies focusing on the relationship between pervasive and structural poverty and the codes and behavioral forms of gangs emerged in the late 1970s and 1980s. See, for example, Joan W. Moore, *Homeboys: Gangs, Drugs, and Prisons in the Barrios of Los Angeles* (Philadelphia: Temple University Press, 1978); John M. Hagedorn, *People and Folks: Gangs, Crime, and the Underclass in a Rustbelt City* (Chicago: Lakeview Press, 1988); James Diego Vigil, *Barrio Gangs: Street Life and Identity in Southern California* (Austin: University of Texas Press, 1988). While these studies are of course about the effects of racism and social marginalization, they deal primarily with the post-1970s city, a context in which racial boundaries—both in a spatial and in a cognitive sense—were far more stable and conflicts across racial and ethnic lines far less frequent. They therefore tell us little about the role of gangs and youth subcultures in processes of ethnic and racial identification.

88. Gerstle, "Myth of the Liberal Consensus," 583.

89. Skogan, *Chicago since 1840*, 20.

90. Amanda Seligman, *Block by Block: Neighborhoods and Public Policy on Chicago's West Side* (Chicago: University of Chicago Press, 2005), 3, 6, 165.

91. Friedrich Hayek, *The Road to Serfdom* (Chicago: University of Chicago Press, 1994).

92. Thursday Night Dancing Club, February 12, 1948, CAP, Box 31, Folder 3, CHM.

93. *Chicago Defender,* August 16, 1947.

94. Monthly Report of the Executive Director, Chicago Commission on Human Relations, August 1948, CUL, Folder 624, UIC-SC.

95. Commission on Human Relations, February 1952, Metropole Theater Incident Number 1 and Number 2, MRC, HWLC; Chicago Council against Racial and Religious Discrimination, Report of February 20, 1952, Metropole Theater Incident Number 1 and Number 2, MRC, HWLC; Chicago Council against Racial and Religious Discrimination, Report of March 1952, Metropole Theater Incident Number 1 and Number 2, MRC, HWLC.

96. *Chicago Defender,* February 28, 1948.

97. *Chicago Defender,* October 18, 1947; Monthly Report of the Executive Director, Chicago Commission on Human Relations, January–June 1954, CUL, Folder 211, UIC-SC; Preliminary Memorandum on the West Ohio Street Fire, Chicago Council against Racial and Religious Discrimination, CCA, Box 31, CHM.

98. Commission on Human Relations, Current Racial Tension Areas in Chicago—May 1954, CUL, Folder 709, UIC-SC.

99. *Chicago Defender,* September 13, 1947; Documented Memorandum 11: 1947 School Race Strike at Wells High School in Chicago, Council against Racial and Religious Discrimination, CCA, Box 31, Folder 1, CHM; Preliminary Memorandum on the West Ohio Street Fire, Chicago Council against Racial and Religious Discrimination, CCA, Box 31, Folder 1, CHM; *Chicago Defender,* October 18, 1947; *Chicago Defender,* April 30, 1949.

100. Monthly Report of the Executive Director, Chicago Commission on Human Relations, July–August 1953, CUL, Folder 210, UIC-SC.

101. Monthly Report of the Executive Director, Chicago Commission on Human Relations, January–June 1954, CUL, Folder 211, UIC-SC.

102. Current Racial Tension Areas in Chicago—May 1954, Commission on Human Relations, CUL, Folder 709, UIC-SC.

103. Ibid.

104. Monthly Report of the Executive Director, Chicago Commission on Human Relations, September–October 1953, CUL, Folder 210, UIC-SC.

105. Monthly Report of the Executive Director, Chicago Commission on Human Relations, January–June 1954, CUL, Folder 211, UIC-SC.

106. Monthly Report of the Executive Director, Chicago Commission on Human Relations, October–November-December, CUL, Folder 211, UIC-SC.

107. Monthly Report of the Executive Director, Chicago Commission on Human Relations, September–October 1953, CUL, Folder 210, UIC-SC.

108. Monthly Report of the Executive Director, Chicago Commission on Human Relations, July–August 1951, CUL, Folder 210, UIC-SC.

109. Minutes of the Hard-to-Reach-Youth Project Workers' Meeting, Friday, November 16, 1956, WC, Box 696, Folder 1, CHM.

110. Elaine Tyler May, *Homeward Bound: American Families in the Cold War Era* (New York: Basic Books, 1988). The historiography of young women in postwar America focuses largely on the suburban middle class and revolves primarily around the relationship between sexuality, femininity, and domesticity in the Cold War context. In addition to May's work, see, for example, Wini Breines, *Young, White, and Miserable: Growing Up Female in the Fifties* (Chicago: University of Chicago Press, 1992); Joanne Myerowitz, ed., *Not June Cleaver: Women and Gender in Postwar America* (Philadelphia: Temple University Press, 1994).

111. "Youth and Culture," Operating Bulletin no. 7, Welfare Council of Metropolitan Chicago, Div. 3—Education and Recreation, Hard-to-Reach-Youth Project, CAP, Box 56, Folder 3, CHM.

112. Record of Meeting of the Hard-to-Reach-Youth Project Workers, January 3, 1958, 10:30 A.M., Hull House, WC, Box 696, Folder 1, CHM.

113. Ibid.

114. Hard-to-Reach-Youth Project, West Side Community Committee (WSCC), December 6, 1957, CAP, Box 111, Folder 9, CHM.

115. Ricci, Group B, October 28, 1957, CAP, Box 111, Folder 9, CHM.

116. Report by Perry Miranda to Chicago Area Project, CAP, Box 88, Folder 10, CHM; Hard-to-Reach-Youth Project, Cavalliers, WSCC, December 27, 1957, CAP, Box 111, Folder 6, CHM.

117. Judith Butler, *Gender Trouble: Feminism and the Subversion of Identity* (New York: Routledge, 1990), 128–149.

118. "Youth and Culture," Operating Bulletin no. 7, Welfare Council of Metropolitan Chicago, Div. 3—Education and Recreation, Hard-to-Reach Youth Project, CAP, Box 56, Folder 3, CHM.

119. Minutes of the Workers' Meeting of the Hard-to-Reach-Youth Project, June 6, 1958, Northwest Side Community Committee (NWSCC), Folder 391, UIC-SC.

120. "Youth and Culture," Operating Bulletin no. 7, Welfare Council of Metropolitan Chicago, Div. 3—Education and Recreation, Hard-to-Reach-Youth Project, CAP, Box 56, Folder 3, CHM.

121. Record of Meeting of the Hard-to-Reach-Youth Project Workers, January 3, 1958, 10:30 A.M., Hull House, WC, Box 696, Folder 1, CHM.

122. "Youth and Culture," Operating Bulletin no. 7, Welfare Council of Metropolitan Chicago, Div. 3—Education and Recreation, Hard-to-Reach-Youth Project, CAP, Box 56, Folder 3, CHM.

123. Hard-to-Reach-Youth Project, May 16, 1958, WSCC, Conference: Ricci, Re: Gang fights, CAP, Box 111, Folder 8, CHM.

124. Outsiders were not always different racial or ethnic groups. A transgression involving a neighborhood girl perpetrated by the member of a gang representing the same ethnic group but from a different neighborhood could also spark a particularly violent response. As Gerald Suttles points out in his study of the Near West Side in the early 1960s, youths were more prone to travel to other neighborhoods to chase women, because doing so in their own area was sure to provoke a reaction from a group or individual they would continue to see in the course of everyday life. Gerald Suttles, *The Social Order of the Slum: Ethnicity and Territory in the Inner City* (Chicago: University of Chicago Press, 1968).

125. Thursday Night Dancing Club, February 12, 1948, CC, Box 31, Folder 3, CHM.

126. Record of Meeting of the Hard-to-Reach-Youth Project Workers, January 3, 1958, 10:30 A.M., Hull House, WC, Box 696, Folder 1, CHM.

127. Suttles, *Social Order of the Slum*, 87.

128. Minutes of the Workers' Meeting of the Hard-to-Reach-Youth Project, June 6, 1958, NWSCC, Folder 391, UIC-SC.

129. Report by Perry Miranda to Chicago Area Project, CAP, Box 88, Folder 10, CHM.

130. George Klumpner, , "The Nobles: A Preliminary Consideration of Methods of Integrating Psychiatric Consultation with Sociological Research on Street Corner Delinquent Gangs," submitted to the Department of Sociology, Institute for Juvenile Research, October 1960, IJR, Box 23, Folder 6, CHM.

131. "Breaking Through Barriers: Report on the Hard-to-Reach-Youth Project," IJR, Box 25, Folder 2, CHM; Record of Meeting of the Hard-to-Reach-Youth Project Workers, January 3, 1958, 10:30 A.M., Hull House, WC, Box 696, Folder 1, CHM.

5. TEENAGE TERRORISM, FIGHTING GANGS, AND COLLECTIVE ACTION IN THE ERA OF CIVIL RIGHTS

Epigraphs: Clovers, Norman Feldman, Tuesday, April 15, 1958, WC, Box 227, Folder 2, CHM. William C. Watson, Jr., Group—King Clovers, 8/11/58, WC, Box 227, Folder 2, CHM.

1. *Chicago Daily News,* March 2, 1955.
2. *Chicago Tribune,* July 3–4, 16, 1955.
3. *Chicago Daily News,* January 25–26, 30, 1956.
4. *Chicago Daily News,* January 25, 27, 1956.
5. *Chicago Tribune,* July 16, 1955.
6. *Chicago Daily News,* January 25, 1956.
7. *Chicago Daily News,* March 4–5, 1958.
8. *Chicago Defender,* April 27, 1957.
9. *Chicago Defender,* June 22, 1957; *Chicago Daily News,* March 12, 1957; *Chicago Tribune,* March 13–14, 1957.
10. Eric Schneider, *Vampires, Dragons, and Egyptian Kings: Youth Gangs in Postwar New York* (Princeton, NJ: Princeton University Press, 1999).
11. For accounts of such intraethnic conflicts on the Near West Side of Chicago in the early 1960s, see Gerald Suttles, *The Social Order of the Slum: Ethnicity and Territory in the Inner City* (Chicago: University of Chicago Press, 1968).
12. For two fine introductions to Lefebvre's thinking on the "production of space," see Rob Shields, *Lefebvre, Love, and Struggle: Spatial Dialectics* (London and New York: Routledge, 1998), 141–185; Edward W. Soja, *Postmodern Geographies: The Reassertion of Space in Critical Social Theory* (London: Verso, 1989), 76–93. For some of the more influential works by geographers who have built on Lefebvre's theories of the relationship between social and spatial structures, see David Harvey, *Social Justice and the City* (Baltimore: Johns Hopkins University Press, 1973); Manuel Castells, *The City and the Grassroots* (Berkeley and Los Angeles: University of California Press, 1983).
13. John F. McDonald, *Employment Location and Industrial Land Use in Metropolitan Chicago* (Urbana: University of Illinois Press, 1984), 71–73.
14. Total Work Force Employment and Unemployment in the Chicago SMSA, 1952–1963, Chicago Labor Market Analysis Unit, Illinois State Employment Service, CHM.
15. Wesley G. Skogan, *Chicago since 1840: A Time-Series Handbook* (Urbana: University of Illinois Press, 1976), 20.
16. Louise Año Nuevo Kerr, "The Chicano Experience in Chicago, 1920–1970" (PhD diss., University of Illinois—Chicago, 1976), 166.
17. Schneider, *Vampires, Dragons;* Phillipe Bourgois, *In Search of Respect: Selling Crack in El Barrio* (Cambridge: Cambridge University Press, 1995); Stu-

art Hall, "New Ethnicities," in *Stuart Hall: Critical Dialogues in Cultural Studies*, ed. David Morley and Kuan-Hsing Chen (London and New York: Routledge, 1996), 441–449.

18. Felix Padilla, *Puerto Rican Chicago* (Notre Dame: University of Notre Dame Press, 1987), 59.

19. Gerald W. Ropka, "The Evolving Residential Patterns of the Mexican, Puerto Rican, and Cuban Population in the City of Chicago" (PhD diss., Michigan State University, 1973).

20. Report by Rafael Martinez, Chicago Commons Association, January 5, 1954, CCA, Box 37, Folder 1, CHM; Letter from William Brueckner, executive director, Chicago Commons Association, to Mr. Turner, Mayor's Commission on Human Relations, June 29, 1955, CCA, Box 39, Folder 3.

21. Memorandum from Edward M. Kralovec, president, Catholic Interracial Council, July 30, 1954, NWSCC, Folder 675, UIC-SC; Outline Memorandum, Catholic Interracial Council Meeting, Tuesday, August 3, 1954, Subject: Disturbances at Jane Addams Housing Project, NWSCC, Folder 675, UIC-SC; Outline Memorandum no. 2, Catholic Interracial Council Meeting, Wednesday, August 11, 1954, Subject: Disturbances at Jane Addams Housing Project, NWSCC, Folder 675, UIC-SC.

22. *Chicago Sun-Times*, May 14, 1957.

23. Report on investigation of vandalism and other property damage reported by Mr. Pedro Romero and family at 10633 S. Buffalo to police and Commission on Human Relations, CAP, Box 88, Folder 11, CHM; Monthly Report of the Executive Director, Mexican American Council of Chicago Incorporated, August 1951, CAP, Box 108, Folder 7, CHM.

24. *Chicago Daily Defender*, May 26, 1960.

25. Robert Orsi, "The Religious Boundaries of an Inbetween People: Street *Feste* and the Problem of the Dark-Skinned 'Other' in Italian Harlem, 1920–1990," *American Quarterly* 44 (September 1992): 314.

26. Report by P. J. Miranda to Chicago Area Project, CAP, Box 88, Folder 10, CHM.

27. Marcia Kijewski, David Brosch, and Robert Bulanda, *The Historical Development of Three Chicago Millgates: South Chicago, East Side, South Deering* (Chicago: Illinois Labor History Society, 1972), 54.

28. "South Chicago Neighborhood House: A Report on Its Neighborhood Services and Affiliations," January 11, 1965, quoted in Kijewski, Brosch, and Bulanda, *Three Chicago Millgates,* 37.

29. Report by P. J. Miranda to Chicago Area Project, CAP, Box 88, Folder 10, CHM.

30. Elena Padilla, "Puerto Rican Immigrants in New York and Chicago: A Study in Comparative Assimilation" (master's thesis, University of Chicago, 1947), 47. On such distinctions of color in Puerto Rican society, see Sidney W. Mintz, "Groups, Group Boundaries, and the Perception of Race," *Comparative Studies in Society and History* 13 (October 1971): 437–444; Clara E. Rodriguez, *Changing Race: Latinos, the Census, and the History of Ethnicity in the United States* (New York: New York University Press, 2000).

31. Mayor's Committee on New Residents—CCHR, "Puerto Ricans in

Chicago: A Study of a Representative Group of 103 Households of Puerto Rican Migrants on Chicago's Northwest Side—and Their Adjustment to Big-City Living," June 1960, CHM. These findings have been confirmed by a number of studies that demonstrate that Puerto Ricans opt for a Latino or Puerto Rican identity to distance themselves from African Americans. See, for example, Rodriguez, *Changing Race;* Clara E. Rodriguez, *Puerto Ricans: Born in the USA* (Boulder, CO: Westview Press, 1991); Alejandro Portes and Rubén Rumbaut, *Legacies: The Story of the Immigrant Second Generation* (Berkeley: University of California Press, 2001).

32. Orsi, "Religious Boundaries," 321.

33. Piri Thomas, *Down These Mean Streets* (New York: Vintage Books, 1967), 122–124.

34. Report by P. J. Miranda to Chicago Area Project, CAP, Box 88, Folder 10, CHM; Study by Welfare Council Research Group on Mexicans in Chicago, WC, Box 147, Folder 5, CHM.

35. Minutes of Hard-to-Reach-Youth Project Workers' Meeting, Friday, November 16, 1956, WC, Box 696, Folder 1, CHM; *Chicago Sun-Times,* May 14, 1957.

36. For a full account of this campaign of harassment and its significance for local and national politics, see Arnold R. Hirsch, "Massive Resistance in the Urban North: Trumbull Park, Chicago, 1953–1966," *Journal of American History* 82 (September 1995): 522–550. This article expands on research laid out earlier in Hirsch, *Making the Second Ghetto: Race and Housing in Chicago, 1940–1960* (Cambridge: Cambridge University Press, 1983), 80–89, 97–99, 232–241.

37. Confidential Report, Case no. E-77, May 8, 1954, ACLU, Illinois Division, Box 11, Folder 9, UC-SCRC.

38. Report, Case no. E-77, June 9, 1954, ACLU, Illinois Division, Box 11, Folder 9, UC-SCRC.

39. Letter from Trumbull Park Tenant Council to Mayor Martin H. Kennelly et al., June 3, 1954, CUL, Folder 649, UIC-SC.

40. The Trumbull Park Homes Disturbances: A Chronological Report, August 4, 1953, to June 30, 1955, Chicago Commission on Human Relations, 1955, CHM.

41. *Chicago Defender,* October 11, 1958.

42. A Preliminary Report on Racial Disturbances in Chicago for the Period July 21 to August 4, 1957, ACLU, Box 9, Folder 8, UC-SCRC.

43. Kijewski, Brosch, and Bulanda, *Three Chicago Millgates,* 35.

44. Confidential Report, Case no. E-77, Operative L. G., May 1, 1954, ACLU, Illinois Division, Box 11, Folder 9, UC-SCRC.

45. Confidential Report, Case no. E-77, Operative L. G., June 10, 1954, ACLU, Illinois Division, Box 11, Folder 9, UC-SCRC.

46. Letter from Bill Meeks to Clifford Shaw, administrative director, Chicago Area Project, October 8, 1956, CAP, Box 105, Folder 3, CHM.

47. State of Illinois Department of Public Welfare, Subsequent Community Worker Report, Re: Alex B. of Brandon Avenue, SB, Folder 90, UIC-SC.

48. Memorandum from Edward M. Kralovec, president, Catholic Interra-

cial Council, July 30, 1954, NWSCC, Folder 675, UIC-SC; Outline Memorandum, Catholic Interracial Council Meeting, Tuesday, August 3, 1954, Subject: Disturbances at Jane Addams Housing Project, NWSCC, Folder 675, UIC-SC; Outline Memorandum no. 2, Catholic Interracial Council Meeting, Wednesday, August 11, 1954, Subject: Disturbances at Jane Addams Housing Project, NWSCC, Folder 675, UIC-SC; The Dukes: A Street Gang, CAP, Box 102, Folder 5, CHM; George H. Klumpner, "The Nobles: A Preliminary Consideration of Methods of Integrating Psychiatric Consultation with Sociological Research on Street Corner Delinquent Gangs, Submitted to Department of Sociology, Institute for Juvenile Research, IJR, Box 23, Folder 6, CHM.

49. Klumpner, "The Nobles."

50. The Dukes: A Street Gang, CAP, Box 102, Folder 5, CHM.

51. Klumpner, "The Nobles"; *Chicago Daily News,* March 4–5, 1958; *Chicago Sunday Tribune,* October 5, 1958.

52. Inter-Agency Committee, Near West Side Community Council, June 23, 1959, NWSCC, Folder 582, UIC-SC; Klumpner, "The Nobles." The author of this study claims that because the police never bothered to open up a thorough investigation of this crime, none of the gang members were ever brought to justice.

53. Daily Journal Appendix: April 18, 1961, From Frank F. Carney, Addams Area, Hans Mattick Papers (hereafter cited as HM), Box 3, Folder 4, CHM.

54. Summary Highlight Report, HTRYP, WSCC, August 27, 1957, CAP, Box 110, Folder 13, CHM.

55. Klumpner, "The Nobles"; Leon Jansyn, "Solidarity and Delinquency in a Street Corner Group," *American Sociological Review* 31 (October, 1966): 600–614.

56. Suttles, *Social Order of the Slum,* 148–152.

57. Report by Perry Miranda to Chicago Area Project, CAP, Box 88, Folder 10, CHM.

58. Frank Delgado report on the Royal Kings, April 3, 1958, CAP, Box 111, Folder 1, CHM.

59. Frank Delgado report on the Royal Kings, April 17, 1958, CAP, Box 111, Folder 1, CHM.

60. Hard-to-Reach-Youth Project, WSCC, April 28, 1958, Frank Delgado, Royal Kings, CAP, Box 11, Folder 1, CHM.

61. Frank Delgado report on the Royal Kings, July 9, 1958, CAP, Box 111, Folder 1, CHM.

62. Supervisory Report, May 14, 1962, with Addams Club Staff, Horner Staff, and Lincoln Club Staff, from Francis J. Carney, associate director of extension work, HM, Box 3, Folder 5, CHM.

63. Report by William Friedlander of the Welfare Council, August 1, 1957, WC, Box 267, Folder 3, CHM.

64. Minutes of the Meeting of Near West Side Area Hard-to-Reach-Youth Project Workers, May 25, 1959, CAP, Box 103, Folder 3, CHM.

65. Record of the Workers' Meeting of the Hard-to-Reach-Youth Project, September 5, 1958, WC, Box 696, Folder 1, CHM.

66. Minutes of Planning for Services Committee, March 11, 1958, police dis-

trict no. 22, Project for Combating Delinquency of Juvenile and Young Adults, WC, Box 381, Folder 7, CHM.

67. Young Men's Christian Association, Detached Workers Program, Lists of Street Gangs, 1959–60, WC, Box 424, Folder 6, CHM.

68. David Dawley, *A Nation of Lords: The Autobiography of the Vice Lords* (Prospect Heights, IL: Waveland Press, 1992), 34.

69. Letter from Murray Frank, Chicago Commons Association, to Tony Irrizary, 5/3/60, CAP, Box 90, Folder 7, CHM.

70. *Saturday Evening Post,* November 5, 1960.

71. Illinois Youth Commission, Division of Community Services, Community Project Report, Near Northwest Spanish Speaking Area, September 1960, CAP, Box 93, Folder 12, CHM.

72. *Chicago Sun-Times,* May 24, 1962.

73. Welfare Council of Metropolitan Chicago, Division 3, Hard-to-Reach Youth Project, Record of Meeting, March 7, 1958, WC, Box 696, Folder 1, CHM.

74. James A. Mercy, "Social Control and Criminal Behavior in Chicago: 1940–1973" (PhD diss., Emory University, 1982), 79; Skogan, *Chicago since 1840,* 92.

75. Report on Activities, February 1, 1961, to February 17, 1961, to Hans W. Mattick, from: Frank Carney, HM, Box 3, Folder 4, CHM.

76. R. Lincoln Keiser, *The Vice Lords: Warriors of the Streets* (New York: Holt, Rinehart and Winston, 1969), 3. A similar account can be found in Dawley, *A Nation of Lords,* 3–23.

77. Worker Report—Jim Foreman, Egyptian Cobras, Tuesday, June 10, 1958, WC, Box 227, Folder 3, CHM.

78. Dawley, *A Nation of Lords,* 30; *Chicago Daily News,* October 3, 1961.

79. Dawley, *A Nation of Lords,* 43–44. For an account of such methods of taking guns from the police, see *Chicago Daily News,* November 10, 1961.

80. Dawley, *A Nation of Lords,* 44.

81. Mayor's Committee on New Residents, "Puerto Ricans in Chicago," 54; Young Men's Christian Association, Detached Workers Program, Lists of Street Gangs, 1959–60, WC, Box 424, Folder 6, CHM.

82. Record of Meeting of the Hard-to-Reach-Youth Project Workers, April 11, 1958, WC, Box 696, Folder 1, CHM; CYC Report, Worker—Norm Feldman, Conference with Captain Enright, Fillmore Police Station, April 4, 1958, WC, Box 217, Folder 2, CHM.

83. Memorandum to Msgr. John J. Egan from Edward Chambers and Nick Von Hoffman concerning police activity in connection with race violence on the South West Side, August 7, 1961, AC, Folder 334, UIC-SC.

84. Extension Worker Reports—Antonio Irrizary, August 14, 1961, and August 18, 1961, HM, Box 13, Folder 1, CHM.

85. Extension Worker Report—Antonio Irrizary, May 11, 1962, HM, Box 13, Folder 4, CHM.

86. Extension Worker Reports– Antonio Irrizary, October 1, 1962, HM, Box 13, Folder 5, CHM.

87. Chicago Youth Development Project, CYDP—Activity Report, Francis J. Carney, July 27, 1962, HM, Box 3, Folder 5, CHM.

88. Extension Worker Reports—Antonio Irrizary, July 13, 1962, and July 20, 1962, HM, Box 13, Folder 5, CHM.

89. Illinois Youth Commission, Division of Community Services, Community Project Report, Near Northwest Spanish Speaking Area, September 1960, CAP, Box 93, Folder 12, CHM; Chicago Youth Development Project Daily Activity Report, Antonio Irrizary, August 29, 1961, HM, Box 13, Folder 1, CHM; Extension Worker Report—Antonio Irrizary, May 22, 1962, HM, Box 13, Folder 4, CHM.

90. Reports of Jim Foreman on the Egyptian Cobras, June 19 and October 17, 1958, WC, Box 227, Folder 3, CHM.

91. Report of William C. Watson Jr. on the King Clovers, September 9, 1958, WC, Box 227, Folder 2, CHM.

92. A Preliminary Report on Racial Disturbances in Chicago for the Period July 21 to August 4, 1957, ACLU, Box 9, Folder 8, UC-SCRC.

93. Ibid.; *Chicago Daily News,* July 29–30, 1957; Hirsch, *Making the Second Ghetto,* 65–66.

94. A Preliminary Report on Racial Disturbances in Chicago for the Period July 21 to August 4, 1957, ACLU, Box 9, Folder 8, UC-SCRC; *Chicago Defender,* August 3, 1957.

95. Hirsch, *Making the Second Ghetto,* 74; A Preliminary Report on Racial Disturbances in Chicago for the Period July 21 to August 4, 1957, ACLU, Box 9, Folder 8, UC-SCRC.

96. Hirsch, *Making the Second Ghetto,* 65; A Preliminary Report on Racial Disturbances in Chicago for the Period July 21 to August 4, 1957, ACLU, Box 9, Folder 8, UC-SCRC.

97. *Chicago Defender,* September 27, 1958; *Chicago Defender,* February 28, 1959.

98. *Chicago Defender,* September 5, 1959; *Chicago American,* July 13, 1961; *Chicago Tribune,* July 15, 1961.

99. My idea of a "social movement" is based on the groundwork laid out by Alberto Melucci, Alain Touraine, Douglas McAdam, and Ron Eyerman and Andrew Jamison, all of whom emphasize the cognitive and cultural aspects of social action. For discussions of this school of social movement theory, see Ron Eyerman and Andrew Jamison, *Social Movements: A Cognitive Approach* (University Park: Pennsylvania State University Press, 1991); Douglas McAdam, "Culture and Social Movements," in *New Social Movements: From Ideology to Identity,* ed. Enrique Larana, Hank Johnston, and Joseph R. Gusfield (Philadelphia: Temple University Press, 1994), 36–57.

100. Hirsch, *Making the Second Ghetto,* 82–83.

101. A Preliminary Report on Racial Disturbances in Chicago for the Period July 21 to August 4, 1957, ACLU, Box 9, Folder 8, UC-SCRC.

102. Michael Omi and Howard Winant, *Racial Formation in the United States: From the 1960s the 1980s* (New York and London: Routledge, 1986), 89–108.

103. Confidential Report, Case no. E-77, Operative L. G., July 28, 1954, ACLU, Illinois Division, Box 11, Folder 9, UC-SCRC. I am indebted to Arnold Hirsch for this idea. Hirsch, *Making the Second Ghetto,* 196.

104. Confidential Report, Case no. E-77, Operative L. G., July 28, 1954, ACLU, Illinois Division, Box 11, Folder 9, UC-SCRC.

105. Alain Touraine, *The Voice and the Eye: An Analysis of Social Movements* (Cambridge: Cambridge University Press, 1981); Alberto Melucci, "The New Social Movements: A Theoretical Approach," *Social Science Information* 19, No. 2 (1980): 199–226; Castells, *City and the Grassroots.*

106. For a discussion of the roles of race and the public housing issue in these elections, see Thomas Sugrue, *The Origins of the Urban Crisis: Race and Inequality in Postwar Detroit* (Princeton, NJ: Princeton University Press, 1996), 77–88.

107. Hirsch, *Making the Second Ghetto,* 199.

108. Melucci, "The New Social Movements."

109. Recent research on New York City and Buffalo has revealed the growth of civil rights militancy—of both coordinated and spontaneous forms—at beaches, amusement parks, and other leisure accommodations in the postwar period. See Martha Biondi, *To Stand and Fight: The Struggle for Civil Rights in Postwar New York City* (Cambridge, MA: Harvard University Press, 2003), 79–84; Victoria W. Wolcott, "Recreation and Race in the Postwar City: Buffalo's 1956 Crystal Beach Riot," *Journal of American History* 93 (June 2006): 63–90; Lizabeth Cohen, *A Consumer's Republic: The Politics of Mass Consumption in Postwar America* (New York: Vintage Books, 2003), 183–191. For a collection of some of the latest work on the civil rights movement in the North, see Jeanne F. Theoharis and Komozi Woodard, eds., *Freedom North: Black Freedom Struggles Outside the South, 1940–1980* (New York: Palgrave Macmillan, 2003).

110. Report on Rainbow Beach, August 1961, CIC, Box 46, Folder 1, CHM; Hirsch, *Making the Second Ghetto,* 65; James R. Ralph Jr., *Northern Protest: Martin Luther King, Jr., Chicago, and the Civil Rights Movement* (Cambridge, MA: Harvard University Press, 1993), 13.

111. Revised Report on Commission Activities Regarding Rainbow Beach, Commission of Human Relations, July 24, 1961, CAP, Box 151, Folder 2, CHM; Letter from Anthony Sorrentino, supervisor, Cook County Unit, Division of Community Services, to Mr. Edward Marciniak, Chicago Commission on Human Relations, July 27, 1961, CAP, Box 151, Folder 2, CHM.

112. OSC Recommendations to Superintendent Wilson, Saul Alinsky Papers,, Folder 334, UIC-SC.

113. James F. Short Jr. and Fred L. Strodtbeck, "The Response of Gang Leaders to Status Threats: An Observation on Group Process and Delinquent Behavior" (draft version), CAP, Box 63, Folder 2, CHM; later published as James F. Short Jr. and Fred L. Strodtbeck, "The Response of Gang Leaders to Status Threats: An Observation on Group Process and Delinquent Behavior," *American Journal of Sociology* 68 (March 1963): 571–579.

114. Doug McAdam, John D. McCarthy, and Mayer N. Zald, *Comparative Perspectives on Social Movements: Political Opportunities, Mobilizing Structures, and Cultural Framings* (Cambridge: Cambridge University Press, 1996), 3. For discussions on "networks," see Mario Diani and Doug McAdam, *Social Move-*

ments and Networks: Regional Approaches to Collective Action (Oxford: Oxford University Press, 2003).

115. *Chicago Defender,* September 27, 1958.

116. *Chicago American,* July 13, 1961; *Chicago Tribune,* July 15, 1961; *Chicago Daily News,* July 17, 1961; *Chicago Daily News,* July 18, 1961; *Chicago Daily News,* July 19, 1961; Confidential memorandum from Edward Marciniak, executive director, to the commissioners, Commission on Human Relations, July 25, 1961, CAP, Box 151, Folder 2, CHM.

117. Paul Gilroy, *"There Ain't No Black in the Union Jack": The Cultural Politics of Race and Nation* (Chicago: University of Chicago Press, 1991), 247.

118. Daily journal: Friday, July 14, 1961, from F. Carney, Addams Area, HM, Box 3, Folder 4, CHM. Victoria Wolcott's research on juvenile delinquency and racial militancy in Buffalo in the late 1950s reveals substantial female involvement in gang activities. Wolcott, "Recreation and Race."

119. Ana Castillo, *My Father Was a Toltec* (Novato, CA.: West End Press, 1988), 8.

120. Ibid., 3.

121. Ibid., 8.

122. Chicago Fact Book Consortium, ed., *Local Community Fact Book: Chicago Metropolitan Area: Based on the 1970 and 1980 Censuses* (Chicago: Chicago Review Press, 1984), 86.

123. Daily journal: April 21, 1961, from F. Carney, Addams Area: re. Pilsen, HM, Box 3, Folder 4, CHM.

124. Report by William Friedlander on conference with Ellsworth Shephard, executive, Howell House, March 28, 1960, WC, Box 330, Folder 1, CHM.

125. Kerr, "Chicano Experience," 192.

126. Estimated Number of Negro Pupils in Chicago Public Schools, by Schools, with Estimated Concentrations of 25% and More Jewish Pupils Noted, Education Committee of the Chicago Branch, 1957, ACLU, Box 14, Folder 8, UC-SCRC.

127. Chicago Youth Development Project Daily Activity Report, November 16, 1961: meeting of reps of social agencies in the Midwest area re. Vice Lords problem, HM, Box 20, Folder 5, CHM.

128. Supervisory Report, February 23, 1962, from Francis J. Carney, associate director of extension work, with Leveret King, Lincoln Club, HM, Box 3, Folder 3, CHM.

129. Keiser, *Vice Lords,* 7–8.

130. As Matthew Countryman has demonstrated in his research on black protest in Philadelphia around this same time, the emergence of discourses of violent resistance to racial injustices made civil rights activism into the "masculine work" of black working-class youths. Countryman argues, furthermore, that such processes pulled many gang members and former gang members into arenas of civil rights protest. Matthew J. Countryman, "'Jingle Bells, Shotgun Shells': Violence Talk, Masculinity, and Black Protest in Philadelphia, 1963–1970," unpublished paper presented at the 1999 Annual Meeting of the Social Science History Association.

131. Supervisory report, June 15, 1962, Crane High School Riot Incident, Frank Carney, associate director of extension work, HM, Box 3, Folder 5, CHM.

6. YOUTH AND POWER

Epigraphs: Steve Clark, ed., *Malcolm X Talks to Young People: Speeches in the U.S., Britain, and Africa* (Pathfinder: New York, 1991), 6. James R. Ralph Jr., *Northern Protest: Martin Luther King, Jr., Chicago, and the Civil Rights Movement* (Cambridge, MA: Harvard University Press, 1993), 94.

1. *Chicago Daily News*, July 29, 1963.

2. Adam Cohen and Elizabeth Taylor, *American Pharaoh: Mayor Richard J. Daley: His Battle for Chicago and the Nation* (Boston: Little, Brown, 2000), 302–304.

3. *Chicago Defender*, October 12, 1963.

4. Alain Touraine, *The Voice and the Eye: An Analysis of Social Movements* (Cambridge: Cambridge University Press, 1981), 81.

5. While numerous studies have analyzed civil rights struggles over school integration in the South, few historians have dealt extensively with the battle over schools in Chicago and the rest of the urban North. A notable exception is Alan B. Anderson and George W. Pickering, *Confronting the Color Line: The Broken Promise of the Civil Rights Movement in Chicago* (Athens: University of Georgia Press, 1986). Chicago was by no means an exceptional case among northern cities. For an excellent account of black grassroots activism in Philadelphia that places schools at the center of struggle for community control, see Matthew J. Countryman, *Up South: Civil Rights and Black Power in Philadelphia* (Philadelphia: University of Pennsylvania Press, 2006), 223–257.

6. Nikolas Rose, *Governing the Soul: The Shaping of the Private Self* (London: Routledge, 1990), 121; Alberto Melucci, *Challenging Codes: Collective Action in the Information Age* (Cambridge: Cambridge University Press, 1996), 121.

7. Melucci, *Challenging Codes,* 120.

8. These ideas also inform an understanding of why school played a similarly key role in the mobilization of white communities against school integration programs. As with the historiography of civil rights activism, a rapidly growing body of literature on postwar white flight and resistance to integration has focused on schools as central sites for the development of ideologies and identities while somewhat taking for granted the question of what this youth orientation has meant for American political culture. It may seem self-evident that schools have played this role, but conservative languages and ideologies having so often been articulated around school issues (busing, affirmative action, and curriculum control) has helped shape the contours of American conservatism.

9. Anderson and Pickering, *Confronting the Color Line,* 73.

10. Anderson and Pickering, *Confronting the Color Line,* 80.

11. For a more detailed discussion of Willis and his conception of the "neighborhood school," see John L. Rury, "Race, Space, and the Politics of Chicago's Public Schools: Benjamin Willis and the Tragedy of Urban Education," *History of Education Quarterly* 39 (Summer 1999): 117–142; Ralph, *Northern Protest,* 14.

12. Rury, "Race, Space," 126.

13. "De Facto Segregation in the Chicago Public Schools," *Crisis* 65 (February 1958): 88–90.

14. Rury, "Race, Space," 130.

15. Anderson and Pickering, *Confronting the Color Line*, 80.

16. Ralph, *Northern Protest*, 17.

17. August Meier and Elliot Rudwick, *CORE: A Study on the Civil Rights Movement, 1942–1968* (New York: Oxford University Press, 1973), 247–248.

18. *Chicago Sun-Times*, August 29, 1963, as cited in Anderson and Pickering, *Confronting the Color Line*, 116.

19. For a more detailed account of this controversy, see Dionne Danns, *Something Better for Our Children: Black Organizing in Chicago Public Schools, 1963–1971* (New York: Routledge, 2003), 27–33; Anderson and Pickering, *Confronting the Color Line*, 116–118.

20. *Chicago Daily News*, October 21, 1963.

21. "A Guide for Freedom School Leaders: Freedom Day—October 22, 1963," Teachers for Integrated Schools, Congress of Racial Equality Chicago Chapter Records, Box 1, Folder 7, CHM.

22. Danns, *Something Better*, 35.

23. In fact, Boston was the first city to stage such a boycott, but it was Chicago that gave the tactic nationwide visibility. After the success in Chicago, organizers in Boston carried out a second boycott. For an account of these boycotts from the standpoint of CORE's involvement, see Meier and Rudwick, *CORE*, 247–251.

24. A. B. Spellman, "Interview with Malcolm X," *Monthly Review* 16, no. 1 (1964): 1–11.

25. Cited in Robin D. G. Kelley, *Freedom Dreams: The Black Radical Imagination* (Boston: Beacon Press, 2002), 85.

26. The editors of the *Chicago Tribune* alleged "recklessness" and "lawlessness" on October 24, 1963.

27. *Chicago Defender*, February 24, 1964.

28. *Chicago Defender*, April 13, 1964.

29. *Chicago Tribune*, April 17, 1964.

30. Investigator's Report, Intelligence Division, Chicago Police Department, July 1, 1964, Chicago Police Department Red Squad Records (hereafter cited as CPRS), Series 2, Box 156, File 973, CHM.

31. Meier and Rudwick, *CORE*, 250–251.

32. Chicago Youth Development Project, CYDP—Activity Report, Francis J. Carney, April 8, 1963, HM, Extension Worker Reports, Box 3, Folder 7; Chicago Youth Development Project, CYDP—Activity Report, Richard Booze, June 25, 1964, HM, Extension Worker Reports, Box 2, Folder 3, CHM; Chicago Youth Development Project, CYDP—Activity Report, Richard Booze, December 17, 1964, HM, Extension Worker Reports, Box 2, Folder 4, CHM.

33. Chicago Youth Development Project, CYDP—Activity Report, Richard Booze, February 11, 1964, HM, Extension Worker Reports, Box 2, Folder 2, CHM.

34. For details of the Halsell affair, see Norman Feldman, Work with the Clovers, Summary of Contacts from Thursday, June 27, 1957, through Thursday,

July 24, 1957, WC, Box 227, Folder 2, CHM; Minutes of the Board of Directors, Chicago Youth Centers, March 20 and May 29, 1958, Chicago Youth Centers Papers (hereafter cited as CYC), Box 1, CHM. Two officers were later convicted.

35. William C. Watson Jr., "Conference with Captain Enright of the Fillmore Police Station," November 14, 1958, WC, Box 227, CHM; Norman Feldman, "Work with the Clovers."

36. Minutes of the Board of Directors of the Chicago Youth Centers, May 18, 1960, CYC, Box 1, Folder 1, CHM.

37. On Wilson's support of a "stop-and-frisk" policy, see William J. Bopp, *O. W. Wilson and the Search for a Police Profession* (Port Washington, NY: National University Publications/Kennikat Press, 1977), 111.

38. L. W. Sherman, "Youth Workers, Police, and Gangs: Chicago, 1956–70" (master's thesis, University of Chicago, 1971), 16; *Chicago American,* September 7, 1961.

39. While many observers viewed Wilson as a progressive police chief, recent scholarship is beginning to challenge this idea by showing how Wilson's reforms contributed to the militarization of the Chicago police department and thus to greater tension between the police and minority youths. For more on Wilson and the politics of policing in Chicago, we eagerly await the completion of Joseph Lipari, "Policing the Color Line: Race, Power, and the Policing of Black Chicago, 1897–1988" (PhD diss., University of Illinois—Chicago, forthcoming). Lipari's research promises to fill a gaping hole in our understanding of the interface between the police and minority communities.

40. Sherman, "Youth Workers, Police, and Gangs," 19.

41. Ibid., 14.

42. Ibid., 25.

43. Ibid., 11.

44. Chicago Youth Development Project, CYDP—Activity Report, Richard Booze, April 5, 1964, HM, Extension Worker Reports, Box 2, Folder 5, CHM; Chicago Youth Development Project, CYDP—Activity Report, Richard Booze, August 27, 1965, HM, Extension Worker Reports, Box 2, Folder 6, CHM.

45. Chicago Youth Development Project, CYDP—Activity Report, Richard Booze, August 11, 1964, HM, Extension Worker Reports, Box 2, Folder 3, CHM.

46. Chicago Youth Development Project, CYDP—Activity Report, Richard Booze, September 9, 1965, HM, Extension Worker Reports, Box 2, Folder 6, CHM.

47. Meier and Rudwick, *CORE,* 301–302.

48. Human Relations Section, August 13, 1964, CPRS, File 973, 1964–65, Box 156, CHM.

49. Human Relations Section, July 14, 1965, CPRS, File 973-A, 1965–67, Box 156, CHM.

50. *Chicago Tribune,* July 19, 1965; *Chicago Sun-Times,* July 19, 1965; *Chicago Defender,* July 23, 1965.

51. Tape no. 21 in front of Crane High School, southwest Corner Oakley and Jackson, August 12, 1965, speaker unknown, CPRS, File 973-A, 1965–67, Box 156, CHM.

52. David Dawley, *A Nation of Lords: The Autobiography of the Vice Lords,* 2nd ed. (Prospect Heights, IL: Waveland Press, 1992; 1st. ed., 1973), 103.

53. Dawley, *A Nation of Lords*, 107.

54. Reliable estimates for the Cobras, the Disciples, and the Saints are hard to find, but their numbers would have to have been this substantial for them to have survived as distinct entities; for a well-informed estimate of the Rangers, see John Hall Fish, *Black Power/White Control: The Struggle of the Woodlawn Organization in Chicago* (Princeton, NJ: Princeton University Press, 1973), 119; for an estimate of the Vice Lord membership, see Edmund J. Rooney, "Dr. King's New Address Just Off 'Bloody 16th St.,'" *Chicago Daily News*, January 25, 1966.

55. Young Men's Christian Association, Detached Worker Program, List of Street Gangs, 1959–60, WC, Box 424, Folder 6, CHM.

56. Office of the Mayor of the City of Chicago, "Organized Youth Crime in Chicago" (August 1969), CHM.

57. Ibid.

58. Noble de Salvi, "Angry Demand for Police Crackdown," *Daily Calumet*, September 28, 1966; on the Rangers' attempt to control Hyde Park High, see Fish, *Black Power/White Control*, 128–130. As Fish points out, even the most sympathetic observers of the Rangers did not deny their attempt to rid Hyde Park High School of Disciples.

59. Dawley, *A Nation of Lords*, 107.

60. "Former Vice Lord Leader Bennie Lee on the Evolution of the Conservative Vice Lords," Chicago Gang History Project: February 28, 2002, http://gangresearch.net/ChicagoGangs/vicelords/Bennielee.html

61. Ibid.

62. John R. Fry, *Locked-Out Americans: A Memoir* (New York: Harper and Row, 1973), 14.

63. "A Statement Regarding the Relationship of the First Presbyterian Church and the Blackstone Rangers," VP, Box 42, Folder 15, CHM.

64. See the many photos of Lawndale street scenes in Dawley, *A Nation of Lords*, 55–96.

65. These events are recounted in Cohen and Taylor, *American Pharaoh*, 362, 378–379; Ralph, *Northern Protest*, 94–95.

66. Investigator's Report, Meeting at Stone Temple Baptist Church, June 6, 1966, CPRS, File 940-B, Box 139, CHM.

67. *Chicago Sun-Times*, July 12, 1966.

68. Investigator's Report, Intelligence Division, CPD, July 11, 1966, CPRS, File 940-B, Box 137, CHM; Ralph, *Northern Protest*, 106; Dawley, *A Nation of Lords*, 110.

69. Ralph, *Northern Protest*, 94.

70. Investigator's Report, Intelligence Division, May 10, 1966, Leadership Conference at Holy Cross School at 65th and Maryland, CPRS, File 940-A, Box 137, CHM.

71. Information Report, Acting District Commander, 007th District, Report Submitted Relative to a Meeting Held at the Englewood Methodist Church on May 11, 1966, CPRS, File 940-A, Box 139, CHM

72. Dawley, *A Nation of Lords*, 110.

73. Anderson and Pickering, *Confronting the Color Line*, 210–16; Ralph, *Northern Protest*, 109–113; Cohen and Taylor, *American Pharaoh*, 387–392.

364 NOTES TO PAGES 270-279

74. Information Report, "The Departure and Return of Demonstrators in the Gage Park Vigil," August 5, 1966, CPRS, File 940-D, Box 139, CHM.

75. Jon Rice, "The World of the Illinois Panthers," in *Freedom North: Black Freedom Struggles Outside the South*, ed. Jeanne Theoharis and Komozi Woodard (New York: Palgrave Macmillan, 2003), 48.

76. Ralph, *Northern Protest*, 137.

77. Investigator's Report, Meeting at Stone Temple Baptist Church, June 6, 1966, CPRS, File 940-B, Box 139, CHM.

78. Investigator's Report, June 13, 1966, CPRS, File 973-A, Box 156, CHM.

79. Investigator's Report, June 21, 1966, File 940-B, Box 139, CHM.

80. East Garfield Park Organization newsletter, July 25, 1966 (in author's possession).

81. For more on the EGUES victory against Condor and Costalis, see Anderson and Pickering, *Confronting the Color Line*, 218.

82. Investigator's Report, August 1, 1966, Washington Park Forum, CPRS, File 973-A, Box 156, CHM.

83. Robert O. Self, *American Babylon: Race and the Struggle for Postwar Oakland* (Princeton, NJ: Princeton University Press, 2003); Countryman, *Up South*.

84. Fry, *Locked-Out Americans*, 19.

85. Ibid., 20.

86. John Ogbu, "Minority Status and Literacy in Comparative Perspective," *Daedelus* 119, no. 2 (Spring 1990): 141–168.

87. For an in-depth and balanced account of TWO's work with the Blackstone Rangers on this youth program, see Fish, *Black Power/White Control*, 115–174.

88. See, for example, Dawley, *A Nation of Lords*, esp. 158–176; Fish, *Black Power/White Control*, esp. 115–174; Fry, *Locked-Out Americans*, esp. chap. 4; James B. Jacobs, *Stateville: The Penitentiary in Mass Society* (Chicago: University of Chicago Press, 1979), 141–143.

89. For an excellent study of Chicago's black political machine and the changes it underwent during these years, see William J. Grimshaw, *Bitter Fruit: Black Politics and the Chicago Machine, 1931–1991* (Chicago: University of Chicago Press, 1992).

90. Arthur M. Brazier, *Black Self-Determination: The Story of the Woodlawn Organization* (Grand Rapids, MI: Eerdman, 1969), 125.

91. Fish, *Black Power/White Control*, 148–174.

92. Irving Spergel, *Evaluation of the Youth Manpower Demonstration of the Woodlawn Organization* (Chicago: University of Chicago, School of Social Service Administration, 1969), 346.

93. Fish, *Black Power/White Control*, 163–164; James McPherson, "Almighty Black P. Stone and What Does That Mean?" *Atlantic Monthly* 223 (May and June, 1969).

94. "Conservative Vice Lords Inc.: A Report to the Public, 1968–69." For a comprehensive array of clippings and documentation on Vice Lord involvement in these projects, see Dawley, *A Nation of Lords*, 122–171.

95. *Chicago Tribune*, June 21, 1969.

96. *Street Gangs: A Secret History*, History Channel.

97. Investigator's Report, Rally: Operation Opportunity, July 25, 1967, CPRS, File 1081, Box 206, CHM.

98. *Chicago Daily Defender,* July 17, 1967.

99. Confidential source.

100. Confidential source.

101. Confidential source.

102. Confidential source.

103. Self, *American Babylon,* 218.

104. Sudhir Venktesh, "A Note on Social Theory and the American Street Gang," in *Gangs and Society: Alternative Perspectives,* ed. Louis Kontos, David Brotherton, and Luis Barrios (New York: Columbia University Press, 2003), 8.

105. Irving Spergel, "Youth Manpower Project: What Happened in Woodlawn" (University of Chicago, School of Social Service Administration, 1969).

106. Information Report, September 15, 1967, Black Power Student Group Meeting, CPRS, Box 68, CHM.

107. Ibid.

108. Copy of flyer in CPRS, Box 205, Forrestville Disturbances, September 14, 1967, CHM.

109. *Chicago Tribune,* September 15, 1967; *Chicago Daily Defender,* September 15, 1967.

110. *Chicago Daily Defender,* September 15, 1967.

111. Investigator's Report, September 19, 1967, CPRS, File No. 939-C, Box 136, CHM.

112. *Chicago Daily Defender,* September 15, 1967.

113. *Chicago Daily Defender,* September 29, 1967.

114. Investigator's Report, Dedication Ceremony, "The Wall" (Black Nationalist Meeting Area), October 4, 1967, CPRS, File 1054, Box 195, CHM.

115. For a more detailed account of the impact of Fanon in the turn toward cultural nationalism, see William L. Van Deburg, *New Day in Babylon: The Black Power Movement and American Culture, 1965–1975* (Chicago: University of Chicago Press, 1992), 29–62.

116. *Chicago Sun-Times,* October 13, 1968.

117. Dionne Danns, "Chicago High School Students' Movement for Quality Public Education, 1966–1971," *Journal of African American History* 88 (Spring 2003): 141.

118. *Chicago Defender,* February 24, 1964; Dionne Danns, "Black Student Empowerment and Chicago: School Reform Efforts in 1968," *Urban Education* 37 (November 2002): 644.

119. Danns, "Black Student Empowerment," 640–641. For more student accounts of such discriminatory treatment on the part of white teachers, see Danns, "Chicago High School Students' Movement," 141–143.

120. *Chicago Sun-Times,* September 8, 1968.

121. Interview Report, Organizing of "Afro-Americans," November 20, 1967, CPRS, File 1077, Box 203, CHM.

122. Chicago Youth Development Project, CYDP—Activity Report, Richard Booze, September 9, 1965, HM, Extension Worker Reports, Box 2, Folder 6, CHM.

123. *Chicago Daily Defender,* November 29, 1967.

124. Confidential source.

125. *Daily News,* March 6, 1968.

126. Report of the Chicago Riot Study Committee to the Honorable Richard J. Daley, August 1, 1968, Municipal Archives, HWLC, 27.

127. *Chicago Daily Defender,* May 25, 1968.

128. *Chicago Daily Defender,* June 8-14, 1968.

129. *Chicago Sun-Times,* October 8, 1968; *Chicago Tribune,* October 8, 10-11, 1968; *Chicago Daily News,* October 9-10, 1968.

130. *Chicago Daily News,* September 18, 1968; *Chicago Tribune,* October 4, 6, 1968.

131. *Chicago Sun-Times,* October 14, 1968.

132. *Chicago Sun-Times,* October 15, 16, 22, 29, 1968; *Chicago Tribune,* October 15, 17, 22, 1968; *Chicago Daily News,* October 15, 22, 1968. For a detailed accounted of the boycotts, see Danns, "Black Student Empowerment," 643-651.

133. *Chicago Tribune,* October 18, 1968.

134. *Chicago Tribune,* October 15, 1968.

135. *Chicago Daily News,* October 15, 1968.

136. *Chicago Sun-Times,* October 17, 1968.

137. *Chicago Sun-Times,* October 8, 1968.

138. *Chicago Tribune,* October 16, 1968.

139. *Chicago Daily Defender,* October 15, 1968.

140. *Chicago Sun-Times,* October 31, 1968.

141. On the circumstances of the Division Street riot, see Felix Padilla, *Puerto Rican Chicago* (Notre Dame, IN: University of Notre Dame Press, 1987), chap. 4; Cohen and Taylor, *American Pharaoh,* 379; Mervin Méndez, "Recollections: The 1966 Division Street Riots," *Diálogo* 2 (1997): 29-35.

142. Letter from Kenneth Douty, executive director, ACLU, to Mr. Edmund A. Brooks, director of the Civil Rights Department, Commission of Human Relations, October 3, 1958, ACLU, Box 7, Folder 4, UC-SCRC; Letter from Ernst Liebman to Robert Tieken, Esq., United States Attorney for the Northern District of Illinois, ACLU, Box 7, Folder 4, UC-SCRC.

143. On police brutality in the Puerto Rican barrio at this time, see Padilla, *Puerto Rican Chicago,* 123-125.

144. Clara Lopéz, "LADO: The Latin American Defense Organization," *Diálogo* 2 (1997): 23-27.

145. *Chicago Sun-Times,* June 13, 1966; *Chicago Tribune,* June 13, 1966; "The West Town STREETS Unit's Role in the Division Street Puerto Rican Incidents," Young Men's Christian Association of Metropolitan Chicago, CAP, Box 93, Folder 12, CHM; Padilla, *Puerto Rican Chicago,* chap. 4.

146. Information Report, to director, Youth Division, from Youth Officer, Youth Group, June 15, 1966, 2030 Hours, File 940-B, CPRS, Box 139, CHM.

147. Confidential source.

148. CYDP Reports, July 30 and August 1, 1962, Tony Irrizary, HM/CYDP, Box 13, Folder 5, CHM.

149. *Chicago Daily Defender,* October 8, 1968.

150. Felix Padilla, "On the Nature of Latino Ethnicity," *Social Science*

Quarterly 65, no. 2 (1984): 651–664; Felix Padilla, *Latino Ethnic Conscious-ness: The Case of Mexican Americans and Puerto Ricans in Chicago* (Notre Dame, IN.: University of Notre Dame Press, 1985).

151. Gerald W. Ropka, "The Evolving Residential Patterns of the Mexican, Puerto Rican, and Cuban Population in the City of Chicago" (PhD diss., Michigan State University, 1973); Padilla, *Puerto Rican Chicago*, 80–91.

152. *Chicago Tribune*, November 13, 1968.

153. *Chicago Tribune*, June 5, 1973; *Chicago Sun-Times*, June 5, 1973.

154. For a theoretical discussion of Latino and Latina panethnicities, see José Itzigsohn, "The Formation of Latino and Latina Panethnic Identities," in *Not Just Black and White: Historical and Contemporary Perspectives on Immigration, Race, and Ethnicity in the United States*, ed. Nancy Foner and George M. Fredrickson (New York: Russell Sage Foundation, 2004), 197–216.

155. Editorial, *LADO* 1 (June 1967), CPRS, Box 106, Folder 15, CHM.

156. Interview Report, October 4, 1968, CPRS, Series 17, Box 105, Folder 7.

157. Ralph, *Northern Protest*, 164; Anderson and Pickering, *Confronting the Color Line*, 223–233, 278; *Chicago Sun-Times*, August 15, 1966.

158. Informational Report, Gang Intelligence, Chicago Police, 16/8/67, File 67–543, CPRS, Series 17, Box 109, Folder 8.

EPILOGUE

1. Alan B. Anderson and George W. Pickering, *Confronting the Color Line: The Broken Promise of the Civil Rights Movement in Chicago* (Athens: University of Georgia Press, 1986), 228.

2. See, for example, Ronald Formisano, *Boston against Busing: Race, Class, and Ethnicity in the 1960s and 1970s* (Chapel Hill: University of North Carolina Press, 1991); Matthew D. Lassiter, "'Socioeconomic Integration' in the Suburbs: From Reactionary Populism to Class Fairness in Metropolitan Charlotte," in *The New Suburban History*, ed. Kevin M. Kruse and Thomas J. Sugrue (Chicago: University of Chicago Press, 2006), 120–143.

3. Manuel Castells, *The City and the Grassroots* (Berkeley: University of California Press, 1983), 331.

4. This is the operating assumption of the highly influential book by Michael Omi and Howard Winant, *Racial Formation in the United States: From the 1960s to the 1990s* (New York: Routledge, 1994).

5. *Chicago Defender*, July 29–31, 1969.

6. *Chicago Defender*, October 9, 1969.

7. *Chicago Defender*, September 9, 1969.

8. For the FBI's war against the Black Panthers and other radical organizations, see Ward Churchill, *Agents of Repression: The FBI's Secret War against the Black Panther Party and the American Indian Movement* (Boston: South End Press, 1996); Ward Churchill, "'To Disrupt, Discredit, and Destroy': The FBI's Secret War against the Black Panther Party," in *Liberation, Imagination, and the Black Panther Party: A New Look at the Panthers and Their Legacy*, ed. Kathleen Cleaver and George Katsiaficas (New York: Routledge, 2001), 78–117.

9. The FBI's Covert Action Program to Destroy the Black Panther Party, Sup-

plementary Detailed Staff Reports on Intelligence Activities and the Rights of Americans, Book 3, Final Report of the Select Committee to Study Governmental Operations with Respect to Intelligence Activities, United States Senate, April 23, 1976.

10. For a fuller account of this defection from the Daley Machine in Black Chicago, see William J. Grimshaw, *Bitter Fruit: Black Politics and the Chicago Machine, 1931–1991* (Chicago: University of Chicago Press, 1992), 124–128.

11. Nicholas De Genova and Ana Y. Ramos-Zayas, *Latino Crossings: Mexicans, Puerto Ricans, and the Politics of Race and Citizenship* (New York: Routledge, 2003), 47–50.

12. Ibid., 50–56. De Genova and Ramos-Zayas provide an excellent account of the troubled relationship between Mexicans and Puerto Ricans in Chicago. For a rich discussion of Mexican identity in Chicago in more recent years, see Nicholas Genova, *Working the Boundaries: Race, Space, and "Illegality" in Mexican Chicago* (Durham, NC: Duke University Press, 2005).

Index

Aberdeens, 62
Acland, Charles, 130
ACLU (American Civil Liberties Union):
on civil rights talk, 226–227; on
color of whiteness, 225; on fighting
gangs, 203, 204; on Harrison High
School students, 235; lawsuit on
surveillance, 277
ACT: alliances of, 272; demonstrations
of, 250–252, 259–260; leadership
of, 249, 287; lessons of Harlem riot
for, 258–259; mentioned, 9; police
surveillance of, 277; Vice Lords and,
261–262; youth workers enlisted
by, 255
Adams, Victor, 287, 290–291, 292, 294
Addams, Jane, 61, 88
African American migration: high crime
rate blamed on, 145–147; in 1910s
and 1920s, 18–19, 33, 56, 71; post-
WWII, 159–160, 197; racial transition prompted by, 122, 123–124;
statistics on 1940s, 121–124; white
response to, 119–120, 134–136;
WWII period, 120–121. *See also*
racial succession (transition)
African Americans: attacks on property
of, 152–153, 154–155, 160–168,

183–185, 346n40; Catholic parish
for, 101; dance and expressive forms
of, 76–78, 80, 83; everyday conditions for, 7–8, 17–18, 179–180;
fighting-gang attacks on, 206–207;
historiography of, 242; ideological
shifts among, 254–255; mid-1960s
styles of, 281; militant sensibilities
emerging among, 131–132, 137–
138, 140–142; number of youths,
321n26; Polish and Irish hostility
toward, 52–53, 61–63; politicization
against state, 303; politicization of
identity, 225–226; population in
1950s, 244; Puerto Ricans and Mexicans distinguished from, 200–201,
353–354n31; racial and sexual
epithets for, 133–134; racial consciousness among, 10, 137–139,
150–151, 328n11; in sex industry,
80–83; sexuality of, 133–136, 188–
189; tensions between northern and
southern, 138–139. *See also* civil
rights activism; schools
African American women and girls: civil
rights activism of, 144, 150–151,
156; Double-V hairstyle of, 143;
gangs of, 149–150; rapes of, 52;

369

threats due to, 190–191; variety of, 6–7, 45–46, 70, 131–133, 328n10; whites' exploring black styles in, 6–7; WWII-era venues of, 131–133. *See also* black-and-tan cabarets; boxing; dances and dance venues; public beaches; public parks and spaces; sex industry
interracial urban spaces ("interzones"): as key sites, 6–7, 11; vice districts as, 47–48, 50–52. *See also* interracial leisure spaces; public parks and spaces
Invaders, 147
involuntary minorities concept, 138
Irish and Irish Americans: Americanization of, 30–31; boxing dominated by, 40; community changes among, 44–45, 47; discrimination against, 31–32; generational differences among, 42–44; hostilities of, 2, 26–28, 52–53, 61–63, 100; idea of whiteness and, 25–26; race war idea among, 25
Irish youth gangs: blacks as threat to identity of, 52–53; boxing and, 38–40; culture of physical combat in, 32–34; dilemmas and solutions of, 47–49; funding for, 21–22; hostility for Eastern Europeans, 60–61; as influence in communities, 54–55; leisure activities of, 45–47, 52–53, 82; older generation's differences with, 42–44; percentage of gangs as, 56; Polish compared with, 57; Polish confrontations of, 44, 45, 61–63; race riot caused by, 4, 8, 17–18, 19–22, 25–26; social geography shaping, 26–32, 59. *See also* athletic clubs
Irrizary, Antonio, 218, 219
Italians and Italian Americans: commercial leisure and generation gap among, 74; cultural nationalist rhetoric of, 97–98, 100; expectations of family support among, 109; girls' activities restrained by, 86; hostilities of, 27–28, 60–61, 119–120; neighborhood dances of, 84; racial uncertainties of, 77–79; stereotypical representations of, 115; work, school, and leisure negotiations among, 95–97
Italian youth gangs: in Harrison High School violence, 232, 233; hostilities of, 61, 207–208, 295; investigation of, 72; leisure activities of, 80, 82;

number and notoriety of, 72–73; percentage of gangs as, 56; sexual activities of, 133–134, 188–189

Jack Diamond's, 81, 93
jackrolling, 108
Jackson, Jesse, 267, 306, 310
Jackson, Joseph H., 241
Jackson, Steve, 250
Jackson Park, 182
Jacobson, Matthew Frye, 314–315n5
James, Clarence, 287
James, Riccardo, 287–288
Jamison, Andrew, 357n99
Jane Addams Homes, 206–209, 211–212
Jefferson, Tony, 42, 169
Jeffries, Jim, 36, 37
Jesters, 202
Jewish immigrants, 27–28, 40, 44–45
Jewish youth gangs, 72–73
Jimenez, José "Cha-Cha," 296–297, 308, 309, 310
jitterbugs, 83, 149–150
John Marshall High School, 156
Johnson, Ethel, 164
Johnson, Jack, 36–38, 39
Johnson, Lyndon B., 275–277. *See also* Great Society
Johnson, Roscoe, 164
Jokers, 202
Jousters, 207
judicial system: active or tacit complicity of, 20–21; compulsory education enforcement and, 89–90; parents of truant students prosecuted in, 90–91; post-WWII demographic changes evidenced in, 158; post-WWII juvenile terrorism and, 153–155. *See also* Boys' Court
Jugheads, 183
Junior Unknowns, 202
Junior Vice Lords, 238*fig. See also* Vice Lords
junking, 107–108
Juvenile Bureau, 155
Juvenile Protective Association (JPA), 46
juveniles: youths as role models of, 13–14. *See also* delinquency; youth and youths
juvenile terrorism: acts of, 152–153; collective action linked to, 165–168; municipal and judicial response to, 153–155; public discourse on, 194–195; in Trumbull Park Homes area, 203; use of term, 4. *See also* delinquency; fighting gangs (1950s)

278; alliances among, 279–280,
305–306; appearance of, 273*fig.*;
Black Power ideas of, 272, 274–275;
black student movement linked to,
283–286; building trades discrimination and, 306; changing focus of,
309–312; crack economy of, 312;
development of, 28–29; divisions
among and within, 280–281, 308–
309; King and SCLC's meetings
with, 267; leadership of, 275, 279,
307–310; legal problems of, 278–
279; nonviolence rejected by, 268–
271; OEO youth program and, 275–
277; politicization of, 261–263, 265,
281–283, 303; recruitment of, 262,
263–265; in school boycotts, 289;
SCLC-CCCO relations after Gage
Park march, 270–272; use of term,
237
Native Americans, 35, 199
Neal, Larry, 286
Near North Side: attempted murder on,
134–135; fighting gang recruitment
on, 236; fighting gangs on, 210*fig.*,
211, 212–213; racial uncertainties
on, 78–79; schools on, 97–98, 102,
110; vice areas on, 131–132, 133.
See also specific communities
Near Northwest Side: black residents
of, 119–120, 121; fighting gangs
on, 212, 219; Italian-Polish tensions
on, 85; Puerto Ricans attacked on,
198–199; racial alterity and fighting
gangs on, 202; racial attacks and
arson in 1940s, 184–185; racial
epithets on, 134; racial fears and
class anxieties on, 182; racial uncertainties on, 78–79; racial violence
around, and student strikes at Wells
High School, 185; rapes on, 191;
school attendance on, 95; vice areas
on, 132, 133; youth gangs on, 73,
173*fig*. *See also specific communities*
Near West Side: clearance and renewal
projects on, 197, 234, 306; Crane
High School demonstration in, 238–
239; crime syndicates on, 114; delinquency prevention efforts on, 151;
fighting gangs on, 206–219; generational conflicts on, 74; juvenile
terrorism on, 195; as laboratory,
205; Puerto Ricans attacked on,
198–199; Puerto Rican settlement
on, 208–209; racial identifications
on, 200; rapes on, 191; response to
police brutality on, 269; roller rink

and racial violence on, 144, 150,
156; school violence on, 186; segregated dances on, 132; urban renewal
on, 214; vice area on, 81; WWII-era
changes on, 157; youths' sexual
banter on, 133–134. *See also specific
communities*
Negro American Labor Council, 249
The Negro in Chicago (report, 1922):
on interracial recreation spaces, 47,
48; on Lithuanian tenement fire,
320n17; map of deaths and injuries
in, 26; on mob profile, 22; on 1919
race riot, 8, 17–18, 21, 22. *See also*
Chicago Commission on Race
Relations (CCRR)
New Breed, 290–291
New City neighborhood, 21
New Deal, 3, 314n4
New Friendship Baptist Church, 270
New Negro movement, 25, 28, 321n26
newspapers. *See* media and newspapers;
specific newspapers
New York City: gay male subcultures in,
50; school boycott in, 258. *See also*
Harlem
New York Times, 37
95th Street Gents, 298–299
Nixon, Richard M., 161, 300, 305
Nobles, 187, 192, 206–207, 208
Noblettes, 187, 192. *See also* Nobles
North Avenue Beach, 193
North Carolina sit-ins, 243
North Side Boys' Club, 133
North Side Improvement Association,
133
Northwest Youth Council, 199, 202

Oak Street Beach, 156
Office of Economic Opportunity (OEO):
Senate investigation of, 278, 305;
Youth Manpower Project of, 275–
278, 280, 289, 307
Ogbu, John, 138, 274
Ogden Park, 22
Old Elite (club), 46
Omi, Michael, 225–226, 227–228, 315–
316n11
O'Neal, William, 307–308
Operation Bootstrap, 275
Operation Breadbasket, 306
Operation Transfer, 244
Opportunity Please Knock (musical),
277–278, 280, 281
Orange, James, 267, 268
Organization for Southwest Chicago
(OSC), 229

Young Patriots, 305, 309
youth and youths: as central to collective action, 5–12, 301; as central to Peoria Street riot, 3–5; community expectations for, 190; as conflictual actors, 130–131; consumerist dilemma of, 65–68, 109–110; coping mechanisms of, 274–275; as jitterbugs, 83, 149–150; middle-class networks of, 68–69, 70; as mirror of society, 242–243; psychological discourse on, 195; as social and historical construction, 12–14; terms used for, 5, 22, 189. *See also* identity; leisure and entertainment; masculinity; race; sexuality; social geography; youth subcultures
youth gangs: approach to, 54; community relationships of, 9–10, 42–45, 54–55, 318n22; dynamics of, 7–8; golden age for, 71–72; historiography of, 349n87; injustice frames constructed by, 12; performances of, 7, 10; politicization in 1960s, 317–318n18; rumors about, 231; terms used for, 5, 22, 55; as violence specialists, 23–24. *See also* African American youth gangs; athletic clubs; female youth gangs; fighting gangs (1950s); ghetto youth gangs; Irish youth gangs; Italian youth gangs; Mexican youth gangs; nation gangs; Polish youth gangs; turf (territory); Polish youth gangs; Puerto Rican youth gangs; rituals of youth gangs; youth gangs, generation of 1919; youth gangs, interwar years; youth gangs, post-WWII; youth gangs, WWII-era
youth gangs, generation of 1919: athletic clubs linked to, 20–21; character formation of members, 17; culture of physical combat in, 32–34; generational and ethnic specificity in, 55–57; interracial leisure spaces for, 47–54; race and Americanness linked for, 61–62, 64; race war idea and, 25–30, 35–36, 39–41; in racial hierarchy context, 58–62; racial segregation enforced by, 19; sexual assaults by, 43, 45, 52; as violence specialists, 23–24. *See also* race riot (1919)
youth gangs, interwar years: attitudes

toward work, 105–106, 111–112, 113–114; belligerence toward women, 110–111; commercial leisure participation of, 68–71, 106–108; compulsory education enforcement and, 88–91; consumerist dilemma of, 65–68, 109–110; "echo boom" group of, 71–72; economic position of, 65–67; everyday visibility of, 69, 72–73; gangsters as models for, 112–118; generational gap evidenced by, 55, 73–77; generational style of, 87–88; girls' activities in context of, 84–87; junking and jackrolling by, 107–108; racial uncertainties of, 77–80; school, work, and family negotiated by, 91–105; sex industry participation of, 80–83
youth gangs, post-WWII: age and occupation in, 172–174, 176; as alternative subculture, 169–170; appearance of, 173*fig.*; attacks on black property by, 152–153, 154–155, 160–168; attacks on blacks in public and leisure spaces, 155–157; automobiles and mobility of, 174–175; as core actors in racial violence, 162–168, 180–181, 182–187; demographic changes and, 157–158; masculine gender identity of, 189–192; masculinity and job issues for, 176–180; as mass culture targets, 170–172; milieu of hatred among, 156–157; municipal and judicial response to, 153–155; recognition desired by, 182–185; revitalization of, 168–169; sexual concerns of, 188–189; veterans as models for, 158–159
youth gangs, WWII-era: blacks targeted by, 134–135; as central to collective racial violence, 129–131, 133, 150; interracial sexual leisure activities of, 131–132; street warfare of, 146–147. *See also* African American youth gangs
Youth Manpower Project (OEO), 275–278, 280, 289, 307
youth subcultures: Americanization via, 58; characteristics of, 42, 54, 316n12; comparisons of, 14; creation of, 41–42; criminal activities and status in, 107; cultural context of, 6–7; discrimination in dynamics of, 7–8; efficacy of networks of, 12; ethnic context of, 5–6; feared after 1943 race riots,

AMERICAN CROSSROADS

Edited by Earl Lewis, George Lipsitz, Peggy Pascoe, George Sánchez, and Dana Takagi

Text:	10/13 Sabon
Display:	Akzidenz Grotesk, Tasse
Compositor:	Integrated Composition Systems
Indexer:	Margie Towery
Cartographer:	Bill Nelson
Printer and binder:	Thomson-Shore, Inc.